W9-BHV-491

SCJP™ Exam for J2SE™ 5 Platform

A Concise and Comprehensive Study Guide for The Sun Certified Java Programmer™ Exam

Paul Sanghera, Ph.D.

Apress®

SCJP™ Exam for J2SE™ 5 Platform: A Concise and Comprehensive Study Guide for The Sun Certified Java Programmer™ Exam

Copyright © 2006 by Paul Sanghera, Ph.D.

ISBN-13 (pbk): 978-1-59059-697-5

ISBN-10 (pbk): 1-59059-697-8

Printed and bound in the United States of America 9 8 7 6 5 4 3 2

Trademarked names may appear in this book. Rather than use a trademark symbol with every occurrence of a trademarked name, we use the names only in an editorial fashion and to the benefit of the trademark owner, with no intention of infringement of the trademark.

Java™ and all Java-based marks are trademarks or registered trademarks of Sun Microsystems, Inc. in the US and other countries. Apress, Inc. is not affiliated with Sun Microsystems, Inc., and this book was written without endorsement from Sun Microsystems, Inc.

Lead Editor: Steve Anglin
Technical Reviewer: Simon Liu
Editorial Board: Steve Anglin, Ewan Buckingham, Gary Cornell, Jason Gilmore, Jonathan Gennick, Jonathan Hassell, James Huddleston, Chris Mills, Matthew Moodie, Dominic Shakeshaft, Jim Sumser, Keir Thomas, Matt Wade
Project Manager: Kylie Johnston
Copy Edit Manager: Nicole LeClerc
Copy Editor: Bill McManus
Assistant Production Director: Kari Brooks-Copony
Production Editor: Laura Cheu
Compositor: Lynn L'Heureux, M&M Composition, LLC
Proofreader: Kim Burton
Indexer: Julie Grady
Artist: April Milne
Cover Designer: Kurt Krames
Manufacturing Director: Tom Debolski

Distributed to the book trade worldwide by Springer-Verlag New York, Inc., 233 Spring Street, 6th Floor, New York, NY 10013. Phone 1-800-SPRINGER, fax 201-348-4505, e-mail orders-ny@springer-sbm.com, or visit http://www.springeronline.com.

For information on translations, please contact Apress directly at 2560 Ninth Street, Suite 219, Berkeley, CA 94710. Phone 510-549-5930, fax 510-549-5939, e-mail info@apress.com, or visit http://www.apress.com.

The information in this book is distributed on an "as is" basis, without warranty. Although every precaution has been taken in the preparation of this work, neither the author(s) nor Apress shall have any liability to any person or entity with respect to any loss or damage caused or alleged to be caused directly or indirectly by the information contained in this work.

The source code for this book is available to readers at http://www.apress.com in the Source Code section.

To all the Java enthusiasts across the oceans
To all the programmers of the Java lang
From Mount Everest to Sierra Mountains
From Madagascar to New York Island

Contents at a Glance

PART 1 ■■■ Scratching the Surface

PART 2 ■■■ Basic Java Programming

PART 3 ■■■ Advanced Java Programming

PART 4 ■■■ Appendixes

v

Contents

PART 1 ■■■ Scratching the Surface

PART 2 ■■■ Basic Java Programming

PART 3 ■ ■ ■ Advanced Java Programming

PART 4 ■■■ Appendixes

About the Author

PAUL SANGHERA, Ph.D., SCJP, SCBCD, who contributed to developing the SCJP exam for Java 5, has been programming in Java for 10 years and has substantial experience teaching Java. As a software engineer, Paul has contributed to the development of world-class technologies such as Netscape Communicator and Novell's NDS. He has been director of software development and director of project management at successful startups such as WebOrder and MP3.com. He has taught Java and other technology courses at several institutes in the San Francisco Bay Area, including San Jose State University, Golden Gate University, California State University, Hayward, and Brooks College. With a master's degree in computer science from Cornell University and a Ph.D. in physics from Carleton University, he has authored and co-authored more than 100 technical papers published in well-reputed European and American research journals. Paul has also presented talks by invitation at several international scientific conferences. He is the best-selling author of several books on technology and project management. Paul lives in Silicon Valley, California, where he works as an independent information consultant.

About the Technical Reviewer

■**SIMON LIU** has worked with Java for six years and mainly has developed Java-based financial applications. He loves to read technical books and has reviewed several certification books.

Simon received bachelor's and master's degrees in Computer Science from the University of Hong Kong, and has acquired several certificates, including SCJP, SCJA, SCWCD, SCBCD, SCDJWS, SCMAD, ICSD, ICED, ICDBA, and OCP.

Acknowledgments

As they say (well, if they don't any more, they should), first things first. Let me begin by thanking Steve Anglin, whose e-mail message triggered this project. With two thumbs up, thanks to Kylie Johnston, the project manager of this book, for her focus, dedication, professionalism, and results-oriented approach.

It takes a team to materialize a book idea into a published book. It is my great pleasure to acknowledge the hard and smart work of the Apress team that made it happen. Here are a few names to mention: Bill McManus for copy editing, Laura Cheu for managing the production process, Lynn L'Heureux for compositing, Kim Burton for proofreading, and Julie Grady for indexing. My special thanks to Stephanie Parker, the marketing manager for this book, for bridging the gap between the author and the reader. The actions of all these folks spoke to me in one voice: Apress means Author's Press. I am thankful to Simon Liu, the technical editor of this book, for doing an excellent job in thoroughly reviewing the manuscript and offering valuable feedback. Thanks are also due to Corey Cotton for reading the manuscript and offering useful comments and suggestions.

In some ways, writing this book is an expression of the technologist and educator inside me. I thank my fellow technologists who guided me at various places during my journey in the computer industry from Novell to Dream Logic: Chuck Castleton at Novell, Delon Dotson at Netscape and MP3.com, Kate Peterson at WebOrder, and Dr. John Serri at Dream Logic. I also thank my colleagues and seniors in the field of education for helping me in so many ways to become a better educator. Here are a few to mention: Dr. Gerald Pauler (Brooks College), Professor David Hayes (San Jose State University), Professor Michael Burke (San Jose State University), and Dr. John Serri (University of Phoenix).

Friends always lend a helping hand, in many visible and invisible ways, in almost anything important we do in our lives. Without them, the world would be a very boring and uncreative place. Here are a few I would like to mention: Stanley Wong, Patrick Smith, Kulwinder, Major Bhupinder Singh Daler, Ruth Gordon, Srilatha Moturi, Baldev Khullar, and the Kandola family (Gurmail and Sukhwinder).

Last, but not least, my appreciation (along with my heart) goes to my wife Renee and my son Adam for not only peacefully coexisting with my book projects but also supporting them.

Introduction

I have made this letter longer than usual, only because I have not had the time to make it shorter.

Blaise Pascal

This book covers the topics determined by the exam objectives for the Sun Certified Java Programmer (SCJP) for Java 5 exam, CX-310-055. Each chapter explores topics in Java programming specified by a set of exam objectives in a manner that makes the presentation cohesive, concise, and yet comprehensive.

Who This Book Is For

This book is primarily targeted at the Java programmers and students who want to prepare for the SCJP certification exam for Java 5, CX-310-055, or the update exam, CX-310-056. Since the book has a laser-sharp focus on the exam objectives, expert Java programmers who want to pass the exam can use this book to ensure that they do not overlook any objective. Yet, it is not an exam-cram book. The chapters and the sections inside each chapter are presented in a logical learning sequence: every new chapter builds upon knowledge acquired in previous chapters, and there is no hopping from topic to topic. The concepts and topics, simple and complex, are explained in a concise yet comprehensive fashion. This facilitates stepwise learning and prevents confusion. Furthermore, Chapter 1 presents a very basic introduction to computer programming and the Java programming language for absolute beginners. Hence, this book is also very useful for beginners to get up to speed quickly even if they are new to Java and computer programming. Even after the exam, you will find yourself returning to this book as a useful reference for basic Java programming.

In a nutshell, this book can be used by the following audiences:

- Beginners with no prior Java experience can use this book to learn basic Java programming, pass the SCJP exam, or both.

- Advanced Java programmers who want to pass the SCJP exam can use this book to ensure they don't miss any exam objectives.

- Instructors teaching a first course in Java can use this book as a text book.

How This Book Is Structured

The structure of this book is determined by the following two requirements:

- The book is equally useful for both beginners and experts who want to pass the SCJP exam for Java 5.

- Although it has a laser-sharp focus on the exam objectives, the book is not an exam cram. It presents the material in a logical learning sequence so that the book can be used for learning (or teaching) basic Java programming.

This book has four parts:

Part	Topic	Chapters/Appendixes
1	Introduction to computer programming and Java	1
2	Basic Java programming	2 through 6
3	Advanced topics in Java programming	7 through 11
4	Appendixes, including a complete practice exam, answers to review questions, and Exam Quick Prep	A, B, C, D, and E

How Each Chapter Is Organized

With the exception of Chapter 1, which covers the basics of computer programming and Java, each chapter begins with a list of exam objectives on which the chapter is focused. I have somewhat rearranged the order of the objectives to keep the topics and the subject matter in line with sequential learning and to avoid hopping from topic to topic.

Each chapter starts with an introduction that establishes the concepts or topics that will be explored in the chapter. As you read through a chapter, you will find the following features:

- *Notes*: Emphasize important concepts or information.

- *Cautions*: Point out information that may be contrary to your expectations depending upon your level of experience with Java programming. Both Notes and Cautions are important from the exam viewpoint.

- *Summary*: This section provides the big picture and reviews the important concepts in the chapter.

- *Exam's-Eye View*: This section highlights the important points in the chapter from the perspective of the exam: the information that you must comprehend, the things that you should look out for because they might seem counterintuitive, and the facts that you should memorize for the exam.

- *Review Questions*: This section has a two-pronged purpose: to help you test your knowledge about the material presented in the chapter, and to help you evaluate your ability to answer the exam questions based on the exam objectives covered in the chapter. The answers to the review questions are presented in Appendix C.

A single feature of the SCJP exam that makes it difficult is that it is very code intensive. In order to succeed in the exam, you must develop stamina for reading and understanding code. To raise your comfort level with the code, this book offers the following three unique features:

- *Complete code examples*: Most of the code examples in the book are complete, tested, and runnable programs that you can download and experiment with.

- *Code for the practice exam*: The code for the practice exam questions is also provided for download so that you can execute and experiment with it.

- *Codewalk Quicklets*: Each chapter offers a "Codewalk Quicklet" section in which you are encouraged to follow a process-based codewalk, which is a way of looking at the code from the perspective of a process. A process, by definition, has an input, operation on the input, and output as a result of the operation. The focus here is not necessarily the complexity of the code, but rather a way of looking at the code. If you develop this way of looking at the code, you will be able to answer most of the code-intensive questions on the exam in an efficient and effective manner.

Other special features of the book are the following:

- A complete practice exam (Appendix D) with questions modeled after the real exam and fully explained answers

- An Exam Quick Prep (Appendix E) that recaps all the important points for the last hour of preparation before taking the exam

- An appendix (Appendix B) that provides useful information and analysis for programmers who are considering updating their J2SE 1.4 certification to J2SE 5

This book and the exam are based on Java 2 Standard Edition (J2SE) 5.0, which you can download from the Sun website, install on your computer, and test the installation as described in Appendix A. You will be using this environment to try the code examples in this book, and in the practice exam.

Conventions

The following are some of the conventions used in this book:

- Conventions used in referring to methods are as follows:

  - When a method name ends with (...), it means the method has one or more arguments.

  - When a method name ends with ( ), it means the method may or may not have one or more arguments.

- In presenting the syntax, a word in angle brackets (< >) represents a variable part of a construct. You must provide its value when actually using it in your program. The generic programming explained in Chapter 10 is an exception to this convention, and has its own meaning for the angle brackets.

Downloading the Code

The SCJP exam is very code intensive. To pass the exam, it's absolutely imperative that you feel comfortable with the code under time pressure. To help you with that, this book offers complete runnable programs corresponding to the examples in the book and the questions in the practice exam. You are recommended to actually execute these programs and experiment with them to find the answers to the questions that may pop up as you are preparing for the exam.

The following downloads are available:

- Source code for the programming examples in the book chapters

- Source code for the programming examples in the practice exam

You can download these items from the Source Code area of the Apress website (www.apress.com).

About the Exam

With the popularity of Java in the enterprise, SCJP certification is an important credential for a Java programmer to earn. It is also a prerequisite to the whole spectrum of specialty certifications in Java available from Sun.

The Java Certification Exams from Sun

The Java platform comes in three flavors: Java 2 Standard Edition (J2SE), Java 2 Enterprise Edition (J2EE), and Java 2 Micro Edition (J2ME). As shown in Figure 1, the certification paths based on these platforms include exams for the following certifications: Sun Certified Java Programmer (SCJP), Sun Certified Java Developer (SCJD), Sun Certified Web Component Developer (SCWCD), Sun Certified Business Component Developer (SCBCD), Sun Certified Developer for Java Web Services (SCDJWS), and Sun Certified Mobile Application Developer (SCMAD). The SCJP is the prerequisite for all other certifications in this list.

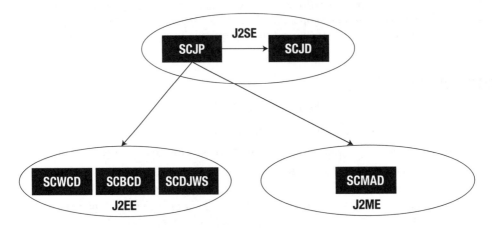

Figure 1. *Certification paths based on the J2SE, J2EE, and J2ME platforms. SCJP certification is a prerequisite for all other certifications shown here.*

The SCJP exam is not a prerequisite only for the following two Java certifications:

- Sun Certified Java Associate (SCJA)
- Sun Certified Enterprise Architect for J2EE Technology (SCEA)

Preparing for the SCJP Exam

The SCJP for Java 5 certification is the first Java certification on the career path in Java. Achieving this certification provides evidence that you understand the basic syntax and structure of the Java programming language and that you can create Java applications using J2SE 5.0 to run on server and desktop systems.

This exam is for programmers who have experience using the Java programming language. If you are a beginner, you will learn Java programming while preparing for the exam because this book is not a mere exam cram. On the other end of the spectrum, even an expert Java programmer may fail this exam if not prepared for it properly. From the exam point of view, pay special attention to the following items while preparing for the exam:

- Carefully read the exam objectives at the beginning of each chapter.
- Make sure you understand the Notes and Cautions in each chapter.
- Study the review questions at the end of each chapter.
- Take the practice exam in Appendix D toward the end your exam preparation.
- Review the "Exam's-Eye View" sections and the Exam Quick Prep in Appendix E during the last hours of your preparation.

The most important point to remember for this exam is this: it is a code-intensive exam. Make sure your comfort level with the code is such that if you encounter a code fragment of up to 30 lines, you can read it and understand it without panic.

Taking the SCJP Exam

The SCJP certification consists of one exam available at authorized Prometric Testing Centers throughout the world. Following are some important details about the exam:

- Exam ID: CX-310-055
- Prerequisite: None
- Cost: $150 (which may vary by country and if you have discount coupons)
- Number of questions: 72
- Pass score: 59 percent; that is, answer at least 43 questions correctly out of 72
- Maximum time allowed: 175 minutes

The question format is multiple choice, including some drag-and-drop questions. In most of the questions, you are asked to select the correct answer or answers from multiple answer choices presented for a question. The number of correct answers is given. Pay attention to the Exhibit button if it appears in a question. You click it to get the required information for the question. Drag and drop is a special kind of multiple-choice question that requires you to choose the right box from multiple boxes and drag it to the right spot.

According to many exam takers, there are hardly any questions with true/false answers, a lot of questions with three (or sometimes two) correct answers, and quite a few questions with radio button answers. A question with radio button answers means that only one answer is correct. The questions vary from very easy to very difficult, but mostly difficult.

If you can't make up your mind about the answer to a question, you can skip it and come back to it later. That way, you avoid running out of time while there are still some easy questions waiting for you. Make sure you understand when a compilation error is generated and when an exception is thrown at runtime. You will encounter both of these choices in the answer options to most of the questions.

Above all, make sure you feel comfortable reading and understanding code. The code in the exam will mostly have the code lines numbered. If the numbering starts from 1, it means the entire code from a source file is there. When the first code line is numbered with a number greater than 1, that means you are looking at only a part of the code from the source file. In this case, you can assume that the code you cannot see is correct.

Like other Sun exams, the SCJP exam starts with a survey that asks you questions regarding your level of knowledge and experience with different topics on Java technology. Please don't get confused or panic; rest assured that this is not part of the actual exam.

Following are the main steps in the process of taking the exam:

1. You should purchase an exam voucher from your local Sun Education Services Office. You can also purchase the voucher online by going to http://suned.sun.com/US/certification/register/index.html.

2. The exams are conducted by Prometric all across the world, and you need to schedule your exam time and location with them. After you have purchased the exam voucher, contact an authorized Prometric Testing Center near you. You can get the information from www.prometric.com.

3. Reach the testing center at least 15 minutes before the test start time, and be prepared to show two forms of identification, one of which should be a photo ID.

4. After you finish the test, the computer screen will display your result (whether you have passed or not). You will also receive a printed copy of the detailed results.

5. Within a month or so, you will receive your certificate from Sun in the mail if you passed the exam.

For current and complete information on the exam, you can visit the Sun exam site: www.sun.com/training/certification/.

Best wishes for the exam. Go for it!

Contacting the Author

More information about Dr. Paul Sanghera can be found at www.paulsanghera.com. He can be reached at: paul_s_sanghera@yahoo.com.

Exam Readiness Checklist: Exam CX-310-055

Exam Objective	Chapter Number
1.1 Develop code that declares classes (including abstract and all forms of nested classes), interfaces, and enums, and includes the appropriate use of package and import statements (including static imports). **1.2** Develop code that declares an interface. Develop code that implements or extends one or more interfaces. Develop code that declares an abstract class. Develop code that extends an abstract class.	3, 4
1.3 Develop code that declares, initializes, and uses primitives, arrays, enums, and objects as static, instance, and local variables. Also, use legal identifiers for variable names.	2
1.4 Develop code that declares both static and non-static methods, and— if appropriate—use method names that adhere to the JavaBeans naming standards. Also develop code that declares and uses a variable-length argument list.	3
1.5 Given a code example, determine if a method is correctly overriding or overloading another method, and identify legal return values (including covariant returns), for the method.	5
1.6 Given a set of classes and superclasses, develop constructors for one or more of the classes. Given a class declaration, determine if a default constructor will be created, and if so, determine the behavior of that constructor. Given a nested or non-nested class listing, write code to instantiate the class.	3
2.1 Develop code that implements an if or switch statement; and identify legal argument types for these statements. **2.2** Develop code that implements all forms of loops and iterators, including the use of for, the enhanced for loop (for-each), do, while, labels, break, and continue; and explain the values taken by loop counter variables during and after loop execution.	6

Exam Objective	Chapter Number
2.3 Develop code that makes use of assertions, and distinguish appropriate from inappropriate uses of assertions.	7
2.4 Develop code that makes use of exceptions and exception handling clauses (try, catch, finally), and declares methods and overriding methods that throw exceptions.	
2.5 Recognize the effect of an exception arising at a specified point in a code fragment. Note that the exception may be a runtime exception, a checked exception, or an error.	
2.6 Recognize situations that will result in any of the following being thrown: ArrayIndexOutOfBoundsException,ClassCastException, IllegalArgumentException, IllegalStateException, NullPointerException, NumberFormatException, AssertionError, ExceptionInInitializerError, StackOverflowError, or NoClassDefFoundError. Understand which of these are thrown by the virtual machine and recognize situations in which others should be thrown programatically.	
3.1 Develop code that uses the primitive wrapper classes (such as Boolean, Character, Double, Integer, etc.), and/or autoboxing & unboxing. Discuss the differences between the String, StringBuilder, and StringBuffer classes.	9
3.2 Given a scenario involving navigating file systems, reading from files, or writing to files, develop the correct solution using the following classes (sometimes in combination), from java.io: BufferedReader,BufferedWriter, File, FileReader, FileWriter, and PrintWriter.	8
3.3 Develop code that serializes and/or de-serializes objects using the following APIs from java.io: DataInputStream, DataOutputStream, FileInputStream, FileOutputStream, ObjectInputStream, ObjectOutputStream, and Serializable.	
3.4 Use standard J2SE APIs in the java.text package to correctly format or parse dates, numbers, and currency values for a specific locale; and, given a scenario, determine the appropriate methods to use if you want to use the default locale or a specific locale. Describe the purpose and use of the java.util.Locale class.	9
3.5 Write code that uses standard J2SE APIs in the java.util and java.util.regex packages to format or parse strings or streams. For strings, write code that uses the Pattern and Matcher classes and the String.split method. Recognize and use regular expression patterns for matching (limited to: . (dot), * (star), + (plus), ?, \d, \s, \w, [], ()). The use of *, +, and ? will be limited to greedy quantifiers, and the parenthesis operator will only be used as a grouping mechanism, not for capturing content during matching. For streams, write code using the Formatter and Scanner classes and the PrintWriter.format/printf methods. Recognize and use formatting parameters (limited to: %b, %c, %d, %f, %s) in format strings.	
4.1 Write code to define, instantiate, and start new threads using both java.lang. Thread and java.lang.Runnable.	11
4.2 Recognize the states in which a thread can exist, and identify ways in which a thread can transition from one state to another.	
4.3 Given a scenario, write code that makes appropriate use of object locking to protect static or instance variables from concurrent access problems.	
4.4 Given a scenario, write code that makes appropriate use of wait, notify, or notifyAll.	
5.1 Develop code that implements tight encapsulation, loose coupling, and high cohesion in classes, and describe the benefits.	5
5.2 Given a scenario, develop code that demonstrates the use of polymorphism. Further, determine when casting will be necessary and recognize compiler vs. runtime errors related to object reference casting.	

continued

Exam Objective	Chapter Number
5.3 Explain the effect of modifiers on inheritance with respect to constructors, instance or static variables, and instance or static methods.	4
5.4 Given a scenario, develop code that declares and/or invokes overridden or overloaded methods and code that declares and/or invokes superclass, overridden, or overloaded constructors.	5
5.5 Develop code that implements "is-a" and/or "has-a" relationships.	
6.1 Given a design scenario, determine which collection classes and/or interfaces should be used to properly implement that design, including the use of the Comparable interface.	10
6.2 Distinguish between correct and incorrect overrides of corresponding hashCode and equals methods, and explain the difference between == and the equals method.	
6.3 Write code that uses the generic versions of the Collections API, in particular, the Set, List, and Map interfaces and implementation classes. Recognize the limitations of the non-generic Collections API and how to refactor code to use the generic versions.	
6.4 Develop code that makes proper use of type parameters in class/interface declarations, instance variables, method arguments, and return types; and write generic methods or methods that make use of wildcard types and understand the similarities and differences between these two approaches.	
6.5 Use capabilities in the java.util package to write code to manipulate a list by sorting, performing a binary search, or converting the list to an array. Use capabilities in the java.util package to write code to manipulate an array by sorting, performing a binary search, or converting the array to a list. Use the java.util.Comparator and java.lang.Comparable interfaces to affect the sorting of lists and arrays. Furthermore, recognize the effect of the "natural ordering" of primitive wrapper classes and java.lang.String on sorting.	
7.1 Given a code example and a scenario, write code that uses the appropriate access modifiers, package declarations, and import statements to interact with (through access or inheritance) the code in the example.	4
7.2 Given an example of a class and a command-line, determine the expected runtime behavior.	
7.3 Determine the effect upon object references and primitive values when they are passed into methods that perform assignments or other modifying operations on the parameters.	
7.4 Given a code example, recognize the point at which an object becomes eligible for garbage collection, and determine what is and is not guaranteed by the garbage collection system. Recognize the behaviors of System.gc and finalization.	
7.5 Given the fully-qualified name of a class that is deployed inside and/or outside a JAR file, construct the appropriate directory structure for that class. Given a code example and a classpath, determine whether the classpath will allow the code to compile successfully.	
7.6 Write code that correctly applies the appropriate operators including assignment operators (limited to: =, +=, -=), arithmetic operators (limited to: +, -, *, /, %, ++, --), relational operators (limited to: <, <=, >, >=, ==, !=), the instanceof operator, logical operators (limited to: &, |, ^, !, &&, ||), and the conditional operator (? :), to produce a desired result. Write code that determines the equality of two objects or two primitives.	2

PART 1

■■■

Scratching the Surface

The primary purpose of this book is to help you pass the Sun Certified Java Programmer (SCJP) exam for Java 5 (CX-310-055), and therefore the book has a laser sharp focus on the SCJP exam objectives. That said, the material is presented in such a fashion that this will also be your book of choice if you just want to learn Java programming, even if you are a beginner. Learning, as opposed to cramming, is the best way to earn certification as well. While preparing for the exam, you will also be learning the fundamentals of Java programming, with the scope and depth determined by the SCJP exam.

Because the book assumes no prior programming experience, Part 1 is meant for readers who are relatively new to programming, Java programming, or both. If you are a beginner, before you can dive into the details of specific topics on Java programming in Part 2, you need to understand a few basics of programming and Java. So, in this part, we take a bird's-eye view of the Java programming landscape, starting with how programs, in general, work on a computer.

If you are already familiar with computer programming and the basics of Java, you can move to Part 2.

CHAPTER 1

■■■

Fundamentals of Java Programming

Learning Objectives

- Understand how computers and computer programs work.
- Understand how a Java program is written, compiled, and executed.
- Understand what makes Java platform independent.
- Identify the object-oriented features of Java.
- Identify different elements of a Java program: primitive variable, reference variable, local variable, instance variable, method, and class.
- Identify where in memory the method invocations, objects, and variables are stored.
- Understand how access modifiers define the accessibility of classes and class members.
- Understand the concepts of early binding and late binding in the context of program errors.

The computer revolution continues after entering its latest phase, the Internet. Computers are not only in your office and home, but are everywhere: serving you from behind walls (e.g. automatic teller machines), sitting ready to protect you in your car by inflating the air bag in an accident, letting you work while enjoying your favorite cup of coffee in Starbucks (the laptop), powering projects such as the human genome project, and so on. The most popular application platform on computers is, of course, the World Wide Web, which is powering countless applications, such as e-commerce and e-mail applications, transforming the whole world in the process.

Obviously, computers are useful because they can run *applications*, which are computer programs that are written in a human-readable format by using a programming language. So, before a computer program can be executed by a computer, it needs to be translated into a format that the computer understands. The Java programming language performs this translation in such a way that makes it a machine-independent language. Another salient feature of the Java programming language is that it adopts the basic philosophy of object-oriented programming (OOP): adapt computing to the problem that it's solving instead of molding the problem to computability.

The focus of this chapter is to help you understand computer programming and the fundamentals of Java programming. In order to accomplish this, we explore three avenues: how the computers and computer programs work, how Java implements platform independence, and how Java implements object-oriented programming. If you are already familiar with computer programming and Java, you can start directly with Chapter 2.

Computers and Computer Programming

You write a computer program in an English-like language, called a *high-level language*, such as Java or C++. Your program is eventually translated into a form that the computer understands, and it runs of course on the computer. So, to be an effective programmer, you must have a basic understanding of how computers work and how a computer executes a program after you write it. Entire books have been written on this topic, but this chapter presents only a very high-level view of this topic, which is sufficient for the subject of this book.

How a Computer Works

Your computer is an electronic machine. Most of the electronics of your computer are placed on the PC board (also called mother board) that contains packages of integrated circuits (also called chips). A chip combines dozens to millions of transistors. These chips form the different components of the computer, such as the processor and memory, to support the basic functions that every computer performs: inputting and outputting data, processing data, and storing data. So, from a computer program's perspective, a computer consists of components to do the following:

- Receive data from a user
- Process the data according to instructions from a program or a user
- Place the results somewhere

Without going into the hardware details, this section presents a functional description of these components of a computer.

Places to Store Data

The program code and the data need to be stored somewhere. A computer has two kinds of storage places: permanent storage and temporary storage. An example of a permanent storage device is your computer's hard drive, which generally stores the programs and the data currently not being used by the computer. It is called *permanent* storage because the data survives even if the computer shuts down.

Temporary storage is the physical memory of the computer, which is used to store the instructions from the currently running programs and their data. The running program can access the memory, also called random access memory (RAM), faster than it can access the hard drive. Therefore, memory improves the performance of the computer programs. It is called *temporary* (or *volatile*) because all data in memory is lost when the computer is shut down or rebooted.

A very important part of any application (program) is processing some kind of data. The data comes to a computer through an input device, it's processed by the computer for the application, and the results, in the form of output data, go to the output device.

Input and Output Devices

You can look at a computer as a processor. It takes some input data from the user, processes it, and produces results in the form of output data. You use some input device to feed the input data to the computer, and the computer uses some output device to place the results or the output data. Examples of input and output (I/O) devices connected to a computer are the monitor, keyboard, disk, and printer.

When an application (or a program) is running, the activities of different hardware components of a computer are coordinated by the central processor unit (CPU).

CPU: The Brain of the Computer

The central processor unit (CPU) is the component that actually executes the instructions of a computer program, which are loaded into the memory when you give a command to run the program. Based on the instructions in the program, the CPU performs the arithmetic operations and tells the memory and the I/O devices what to do. In other words, it coordinates the activities of all the computer components just like your brain coordinates the activities of your body parts.

So, what happens after you issue a command on the monitor to execute a program, but before the CPU actually executes the instructions in the program? In other words, how does a program tell the CPU "please execute me"?

How a Computer Program Works

First, let's straighten out what we mean by *computer program* and *application*. A computer program is a set of instructions that the CPU executes. An application is a program that does something useful for the user, such as a shopping cart program that lets a user order an item from an online store, or a web browser that lets the user browse the Web.

Either the user or an already executing program issues the command to execute a program. This command is eventually received by a software program (or a set of programs) called the *operating system (OS)*. The operating system sees to it that the program is loaded into the computer memory and executed by the CPU. So, an operating system is a software system that controls and manages the computer resources, such as CPU time and file systems, and acts as an agent between the user and the computer hardware. To be specific, an operating system performs the following two roles:

- *Control program*: An operating system controls the I/O devices and execution of the user's programs to ensure correct operation of the computer. For example, if two programs are trying to access the hard disk at the same time, the OS decides in which order they have the access.

- *Resource manager*: An operating system works as a resource manager. For example, it allocates the hardware and software resources needed by a running program such as the CPU, I/O devices, and files.

So, an operating system interfaces between a software application and the computer hardware as shown in Figure 1-1.

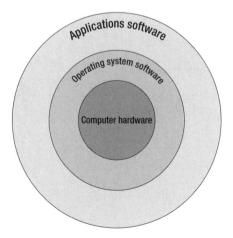

Figure 1-1. *A simplified view of a computer as hardware and software layers, each of which may have its own sublayers*

When you issue a command to execute a program, you are really talking to the operating system, which in turn talks to the computer hardware, such as the CPU, for you.

Generally, you write a human-readable program in a high-level language, such as Java or C++, that looks and sounds pretty much like the English language, but the computer hardware only understands the programs written in the binary bits: 1 and 0. So, a program written by you needs to be translated to a binary format.

Writing and Executing a Java Program

In high-level programming languages such as C and C++, you write a program in a human-readable format, and a program called a *compiler* translates it to a binary format called *executable code* that the computer can understand and execute. The executable code depends upon the computer machine that you use to execute your program; it is machine dependent. In Java, this process from writing to executing a program is very similar but with one important difference that allows you to write Java programs that are machine independent. To understand that difference, pay attention to the term *Java virtual machine (JVM)*.

Writing a Java Program

A Java program that you write contains a set of instructions in text format written according to the rules of the Java programming language. These instructions are called *source code*. The file that contains these instructions is called the *source file* and has the file extension .java. You can use a text editor such as Notepad to create and edit Java source files.

As an exercise, open a new text document (for example, using Notepad on your Windows machine), type the code presented in Listing 1-1 into the document, and save the document as RobotManager.java. Do not type the line numbers; they are not part of the code, and are given here for reference only. This is true about all the code in this book.

Listing 1-1. *RobotManager.java*

```
1. public class RobotManager {
2.   public static void main(String[] args) {
3.     Robot robot;
4.     int nargs=args.length;
5.     if(nargs <= 1){
6.       System.out.println("There must be at least two arguments in the
           command!");
7.           System.out.println("Example: java RobotManager Mary Kaan");
8.           System.exit(0);
9.     }else {
10.      for(int i=1; i<nargs; i++){
11.          robot = new Robot();
12.          robot.setName(args[i]);
13.          robot.sayHelloTo(args[0]);
14.      }
15.    }
16.  }
17. }
18. class Robot {
19.   private String myName = "nobody";
20.   public void setName(String name) {
```

```
21.    myName = name;
22.  }
23.  public void sayHelloTo(String name) {
24.    System.out.println("Hello " + name + "!");
25.    System.out.println("I'm Robo" + myName + ".");
26.  }
27. }
```

You can also use the file RobotManager.java from the code folder that comes with this book (scjp\code\chapters\chap1). However, if you are a beginner, it's a good idea to type this code yourself to get a real feel of the syntax, which is explained in the upcoming section "Elements of a Java Program." Remember two things: when you write a bunch of classes together in a file, only one of those classes can have the attribute public (line 1), and the file name must be exactly the same as the name of the public class, with the file extension .java.

■**Note** The class names are case sensitive; that is, RobotManager and robotManager are not the same.

You will learn more about the content of this file later in this chapter. Once you have a source file in place, the next step is to compile the program in the file.

Compiling a Java Program

As you know by now, computers cannot understand the source code that you write. Before a CPU of a computer can execute the instructions written by you, the instructions need to be translated into a *machine language*—that is, into a binary format. In most of the programming languages, such as C and C++, a compiler compiles the source code into the machine language, and this compiled code is called *executable code*. However, in Java, the compiler compiles the code into *bytecode*, which is not executable code. Bytecode is somewhere in the middle of source code and executable code. For example, to create the bytecode files from the source file RobotManager.java, you run the Java compiler by issuing the following command:

```
javac RobotManager.java
```

The compiler converts the text instructions into bytecode form and places them in files with the .class extension: Robot.class and RobotManager.class. One class file is created corresponding to each class in the source file. You will learn what a class is later in this chapter.

■**Caution** The command to compile a program in the source code file is javac, and you must include the file extension .java when specifying the file name.

The bytecode in the class files is interpreted by the JVM when you execute (or run) the program.

Executing a Java Program

You can execute a Java program by issuing the java command. To execute the program in our running example, issue the following command:

```
java RobotManager Ginny 420
```

This generates the following output:

```
Hello Ginny!
I'm Robo420
```

The first word in the command line, java, is the command name, and the second word, RobotManager, is the class file name corresponding to the class in the source file that contains the main(...) method. We will look at the methods in our program later in this chapter. The last two items are the command arguments, which are optional; that is, whether you are required to give the arguments in the command line depends upon the program.

When you issue the java command, the JVM reads your bytecode file and translates the instructions to the executable format that your computer can understand. The executable form of a program is specific to a particular machine. This is why you need a specific JVM for a specific kind of platform such as Windows, Solaris, or Linux. However, as illustrated in Figure 1-2, you need to write the program only once, but you can execute it on a number of different machines with different operating systems by using different JVMs.

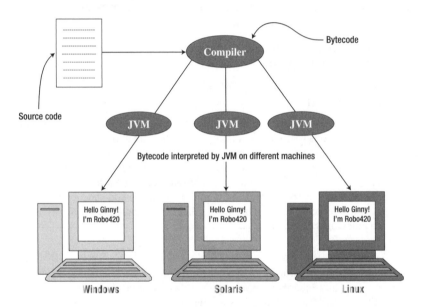

Figure 1-2. *The Java compiler compiles the source code into bytecode that can be interpreted by different JVMs installed on different kinds of machines. This is how the "write once, run anywhere" principle is implemented.*

So, Java implements platform independence by introducing the concept of virtual machines. If you want to run your application on a new platform, all you need is the JVM for that platform.

■**Caution** The command name to execute a Java program is java, and you must not include any file extension when specifying the class file name.

In summary, when you compile your Java program, it does not generate instructions for one specific platform. Instead, it generates what is called Java bytecode, instructions for the JVM. If your platform, such as Windows, Solaris, Linux, Mac OS X, or an Internet browser, has the corresponding JVM, it can understand the bytecode instructions and translate them for that specific machine/platform. This is what is meant by write once, run anywhere.

Now that you know how to compile a given source file and execute it, it's time to take a closer look at the source code to understand some basic elements of a Java program.

Elements of a Java Program

A Java program is composed of classes, and a class consists of methods and variables. This section introduces these elements of a Java program. The underlying philosophy of any object-oriented language is to adapt computing to the problem that it will solve rather than to adapt the problem to the computing, which you end up doing if you are using a procedural language such as C or Pascal. Any real-world problem contains objects (entities), so the first step in designing a Java program is to recognize the objects in the problem that your program will solve. Your running program will contain the Java objects corresponding to the objects in the problem, and the classes in a Java program are the blueprints for those objects.

Classes and Objects

Objects, which represent the entities in the real-world problem that the program is trying to solve, form the building blocks of any Java program. A class is a template (or a blueprint) from which objects are created (yes, you can create more than one objects from the same class). So, in your source code, you do not write an object, you write a class, and the code to create objects from the class. When a program is running, the objects are created and do the job for which you created them.

Writing a class is called *implementing* a class, and the implementation of a class has two components: the class declaration and the class body. The class declaration contains the name of the class and some other attributes. For example, consider the RobotManager class in Listing 1-1. Line 1 declares the class named RobotManager and assigns to it the public attribute, which is called an *access modifier* because it modifies the accessibility of the class. There are other modifiers or keywords that you can use in a class declaration to declare other properties of the class, such as that the class is being derived from another class, that the class cannot be used to derive another class, or that the class cannot be used to create an object.

The class body follows the class declaration and is contained within curly braces: { to begin the body and } to end the body. The class body contains methods, variables, and the program logic.

■**Caution** Java is case sensitive. For example, myClass and MyClass are two different names.

To sum up, a class is a template that you write, and an object is created from the class. In technical terms, you say that an object is *instantiated* from a class, and the process is called *instantiation*. For this reason, the objects of a class are also called the *instances* of that class.

As said earlier, these objects *in a Java program* represent the objects in a real-world problem that the program is trying to solve. The real world (and hence its problems) is full of objects: cars, books, students, courses, donuts, pizzas, beer, and so on. For example, all cars can be represented by a class called Car, and then specific cars (your car, my car, Michael Jackson's car) can be represented by the objects of this class. Each object has a *state*, that is, a set of characteristics, such as my car is black and its price is $20,000, Michael Jackson's car is blue and its price is $200,000, and so on. The characteristics are represented by data that is managed by using variables. For example, price could be a variable that holds the value 20000 corresponding to $20,000. Each object also has a *behavior*, such as my car is parked, or it's running, and so on. While the state is represented by the values of its data items, represented by variables, the behavior is represented by what are called *methods*.

Accordingly, a class consists of methods and variables.

Methods

A computer program, written in any programming language, is basically made of three elements: data, operations on data, and the logic that determines the operations. In Java, the data held by variables determines the state of an object, and the operations on data and the logic for the operation are held inside a method that determines the behavior of an object.

The structure of a method is very similar to that of a class: it has a declaration and a body. The declaration contains some attributes that define the name of the method and some attributes that indicate some properties of the method such as the accessibility, the type of values returned by the method, and so on. You execute a method by specifying the method name (and the name of the class to which the method belongs, if it's not obvious) in a code statement, just as you specify the class name in the java command to execute a Java program. Executing a method is also called *calling* or *invoking* the method. The declaration of a method can also contain a number of variables declared inside the brackets, ( ), immediately following the name of the method. These variables in the declaration are traditionally called *method parameters*, and the values for these parameters, called *arguments*, can be passed as input when the method is invoked (called). These days, both the parameters and the passed-in values are often referred to as *arguments*.

The structure of the RobotManager class and the main(…) method in our example is illustrated in Figure 1-3.

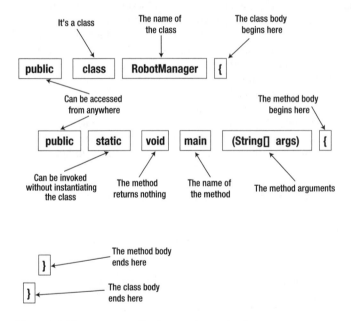

Figure 1-3. *The structure of a class and a method*

The static attribute of the main(…) method indicates that the method can be invoked without referring to a particular object—that is, without instantiating the class. This capability is needed to start a program, because objects are created when a program is running, and when you have just started a program, there is no object. So, the JVM invokes the main(…) method in the class that you named in the run (java) command. This is why the main(…) method has to be static.

A method consists of variables to hold data and the application logic to operate on the data in order to determine the behavior of an object.

Variables and Data Types

As you know by now, the state of an object is represented by a set of data items that are handled by using variables. You can look at a variable as a symbol that represents a value (data item) stored in the computer memory; it is not the value itself. In other words, the value represented by a variable can be changed any time without changing the name of the variable. That is why it is called variable. The value of a variable is the value it's holding (or representing).

Like a class and a method, a variable has a declaration, which must specify a name and a type for the variable. The variable's name must be a *legal identifier* and not one of the reserved names (or *keywords*) of the Java language. The following rules determine a legal name:

- The name must begin with a letter (a–z, A–Z), _, $, or any Unicode character that denotes a letter in a language. Do not begin the name with a digit.

- The first character of the name can be followed by a series of letters or digits, where a digit is 0–9 or any Unicode character that denotes a digit in a language.

- The name must not be a Java language keyword. You can find a list of keywords in Chapter 2.

You use the variable name to refer to the data that the variable contains: to assign the data to the variable and to retrieve the data from the variable. The variable's type determines what kind of values it can hold, which in turn can determine what kind of operations can be performed on it. The declaration of a variable, declaring its name and type, looks like the following:

```
<type> <name>;
```

You can also assign an initial value to a variable while declaring it by using the following syntax:

```
<type> <name> = <value>;
```

For example, consider line 4 in Listing 1-1:

```
int nargs=args.length;
```

Here you declare a variable with name `nargs` that is of type `int`, meaning that its value could be an integer number such as 9. The `args.length` expression calculates the number of arguments given in the command line, and the equal sign (=) assigns this number to the variable `nargs`. The equal sign is an example of what are called *assignment operators*. The `int` type is one of several basic data types called *primitive* data types, which are explored in Chapter 2.

Classes in Java are also considered data types, and you can declare variables of this type as well. For example, consider line 3 in Listing 1-1:

```
Robot robot;
```

In this code line, `Robot` is the name of the class implemented in Listing 1-1 (lines 18 to 27), and `robot` is the name of the variable of type `Robot`. Such a variable is called an *object reference variable* because it is created to refer to an object. However, variable `robot` does not refer to any object until line 11:

```
robot = new Robot();
```

When this line of code is executed, an object of the class `Robot` is created and stored in memory due to the code: `new Robot()`. The = operator assigns the address of the object to the `robot` reference variable. Note the difference here between a variable of primitive type (the primitive variable) and an object reference variable. The value of the primitive variable is the value of the data item that it is holding or representing, while the value of an object reference variable is the reference to the object and not the object itself.

The data is processed according to some application logic, which also controls the flow of execution of program instructions.

Execution Flow of a Program

So, you wrote a program, compiled it with the javac command, and issued the java command to execute it. But in which order will its instructions be executed? Generally speaking, the execution happens from top to bottom. But, will an instruction be skipped, or will an instruction be executed more than once? Before you can understand this kind of order of the execution of instructions in a program, you must understand some basic elements related to the execution: expressions, statements, and blocks.

Expressions

An *expression* is a combination of very basic elements of a program, such as variables, operators, literals, and method calls, that evaluates to a single value. Some examples of expressions used in Listing 1-1 are described in Table 1-1. This table refers to a variable args, which is of type array. An array is a built-in Java object that can hold a number of data items of the same type.

Table 1-1. *Examples of Expressions from Listing 1-1*

Expression	Action	Returned Value
myName = name	Assigns the value of the String variable name to another string variable myName	The value of myName after the assignment
"Hello " + name + "!"	Concatenates the string Hello, the value of the string variable name, and the string !	The combined string
args.length	Determines the number of elements in an elements array represented by the variable args	The number of in the args array
nargs <= 1	Determines whether the value of the int variable nargs is either less than 1 or equal to 1 (that is, not greater than 1)	true if the value of nargs is less than or equal to 1, and false if it is greater than 1

Note that the function of an expression is twofold: to perform the computation indicated by the elements of the expression, and to return the result of the computation, a single value. One or more expressions make a statement, which is a unit of execution for computers.

Statements

Although an expression also involves computation, a complete execution unit of a program is called a *statement*. A statement may contain one or more expressions. For example, the following kinds of expressions can be turned into a statement by terminating them with a semicolon:

- *Assignment expressions*: For example, myName=name is an expression, while myName=name; is a statement.

- *Any use of ++ or -- operators*: For example, ++nargs is an expression, while ++nargs; is a statement.

- *Method calls*: For example, robot.sayHelloTo(args[0]) is an expression, while robot.sayHelloTo(args[0]); is a statement.

- *Object creation expressions*: For example, robot=new Robot() is an expression, while robot=new Robot(); is a statement.

In addition to these kinds of statements, called *expression statements*, there are two other kinds of statements: *declaration statements* and *control flow statements*. A declaration statement is a statement that involves declarations such as the following:

```
private String myName = "nobody";
```

This statement declares a variable myName of type String.

A control flow statement determines whether a set of statements is executed at all or is executed repeatedly; that is, it helps determine the flow of execution control. In Listing 1-1, the for() loop (line 10) and the if() statement (line 5) are examples of control flow statements.

Blocks

A *block* is a group of zero or more statements between an opening brace and a closing brace, and can be used anywhere a single statement is allowed. For example, lines 5 to 9 in Listing 1-1 form one block called the if block. There can be blocks inside a block, called *nested blocks*. For example, lines 10 to 14 form a nested for block inside an else block.

Execution Flow Control

The statements in a program are executed in the order in which they appear in the file from left to right, and top to bottom. However, you can use the control flow statements in your programs to skip a block of statements, to execute a block of statements, or to repeatedly execute a block of statements. The if statement (line 5) and a for statement (line 10) in Listing 1-1 are two examples of control flow statements. For example, in line 5, if the value of nargs is greater than 1, lines 6, 7, and 8 will not be executed. The statements in the for() loop (lines 11 to 13) are executed repeatedly until the value of the variable i becomes equal to or greater than the value of nargs. More control flow statements will be covered in Chapter 6.

Features of Java

The World Wide Web and Java grew up together during the same time, and thus Java implemented most of the Internet programming requirements. As a result, you can develop an enterprise web application end to end (from client to server) in one language: Java. So, the Java language has a multitude of features. However, the scope of the topics covered in this book demands that you understand only the two defining features of the Java language: it is a platform-independent language, and it supports object-oriented programming.

Platform Independence

When people say that Java is platform independent, they usually refer to the well-celebrated Java phrase, "write once, run anywhere." As described earlier in this chapter, this platform independence is made possible by introducing the JVM. The Java compiler compiles the code into *bytecode*, which can be interpreted by a suitable JVM on any platform chosen from a wide variety of platforms.

Because bytecode is executed under the control of the JVM, the JVM can prevent the code from generating side effects outside the system. This helps make a Java program secure. There is a price that you pay for the platform independence in terms of performance. The interpreted programs run slower than the fully compiled programs. However, the JIT (Just-In-Time) compilers (which cache the interpretations) offer the solution to this problem.

You must have heard the phrase "everything in Java is an object." Well, this is just another way of saying that Java supports object-oriented programming.

Object-Oriented Programming

Object-oriented programming (OOP) is a way of solving problems with computers. The OOP philosophy is to adapt the computer to the problem instead of molding the problem into something that is familiar to the computer. In OOP, you identify the entities (objects) in the problem and their relationship with each other independent of the issues of how they will be computed. These entities will be represented by objects in a computer program. The goal is to have one-to-one correspondence between the entities in the problem and the objects in the program.

Some salient features of OOP implemented in Java are described in this section, including encapsulation, inheritance, and polymorphism.

Encapsulation

Two of the three important elements of a computer program are data and operations on data, the third being the logic that determines the operation. Accordingly, a class in Java is made of data variables (that hold data) and methods (that hold the logic for operations and perform operations on the data). This approach of combining an object's data with its methods is called *encapsulation*. The user can retrieve, store, or change the data by invoking methods on the object. Therefore, the user of an object can view the object as a black box that provides services. You, the programmer, can change, add, or delete the instance variables (the variables of the object) and methods in the class, but as long as the services provided by the object remain the same, the client code that uses the services offered by the object can continue to use it without being rewritten. Encapsulation is also called *data abstraction* or *data hiding*.

So, a class in Java can be looked upon as a basic unit of encapsulation. A variable outside of a method is called a *class variable* or an *instance variable*. These variables and the methods of a class are called *members* of the class.

Encapsulation helps make the code more robust and makes tracking bugs easier. Encapsulation in a Java program reflects reality in a typical real-world problem to the extent that an entity in the real world has characteristics and a behavior. Another reality of real-world problems is that the entities in a problem are related to each other in a hierarchical fashion. For example, a cow is an animal, and an animal is a living being.

Inheritance

An object is an instance of a class, which is a blueprint to create objects. You can create multiple objects from the same class. However, instead of programming from scratch, you can derive a class from another class. If you do so, your class, called a *subclass*, inherits the state (variables) and the behavior (methods) of the class from which it is derived. The class from which you derive your class is called the *superclass*. The property of inheriting the state and behavior of the superclass is called *inheritance*.

In your subclass, you can override the inherited methods, and also write new methods and declare new variables. Furthermore, you are not limited to just one layer of inheritance. You can create a whole tree of inheritance, called a *class hierarchy*, as deep as needed. The methods and variables are inherited down through the levels. The rule of thumb for building the class hierarchy is: the farther down in the hierarchy a class appears, the more specialized its behavior is.

There are some built-in classes in the Java language organized into a hierarchy tree, and the Object class is at the top of this class hierarchy. Also, each class that you write automatically becomes a subclass of the Object class even if you do not explicitly derive it from the Object class. The Object class provides some methods representing the behaviors that are common to all the objects created from different classes.

■**Caution** Unlike C++, Java offers only *single inheritance*; that is, a class can be directly derived only from one superclass.

The main advantages of inheritance are described here:

- *Code reusability*: Inheritance automates the process of reusing the code of the superclasses in the subclasses. With inheritance, an object can inherit its more general properties from its parent object, and that saves the redundancy in programming.

- *Code maintenance*: In any discipline, knowledge is made more manageable by hierarchical classification. Organizing code into hierarchical classes makes its maintenance and management easier.

- *Implementing OOP*: Inheritance helps to implement the basic OOP philosophy to adapt computing to the problem and not the other way around, because entities (objects) in the real world are often organized into a hierarchy. For example, in addition to their own specifics, all different specific students in your class share the properties of what is called a student, all the different specific employees at your workplace share the properties of what is called an employee, and so on.

Polymorphism

Polymorphism refers to a feature of Java that allows an object of a superclass to refer to an object of any subclass. This is possible because all objects of a base class are also objects of its superclass. For example, assume that all circles are represented by a class called Circle, which is a subclass of the class Shape (which thus is the superclass of Circle). Further assume that Triangle is another subclass of Shape. Now assume that Shape has a method draw(). You can implement these classes in such a way that when you invoke the draw() method on a Shape variable (referring to an object of Triangle), it draws a triangle, and when you invoke the same method on the same Shape variable (which now is referring to an object of Circle), it draws a circle. It is the same method of the Shape class with different implementations in the subclasses.

So, polymorphism helps to prevent the code from becoming more complex and cumbersome, by allowing you to make different implementations of related functionalities (behaviors) under one name: object or method.

The object-oriented feature encapsulation allows you to control the accessibility to the elements contained by the class: variables and methods. For example, going back to Listing 1-1, line 10 accesses the nargs variable from the same class in which this variable exists. In lines 11 through 13, the Robot class and its methods are being accessed from a class other than the class in which they are defined. Let's briefly explore the access issue.

Accessing the Classes and Class Members

The variables (including reference variables) and methods in a class are called *class members*. A class can also have other classes, called *nested classes*, as members of the class. A class that is not a nested class is called the *top-level class*. In this book, "class" refers to the top-level class unless mentioned otherwise. The access to the class members can be controlled by using *access modifiers* specified in the member definition, for example:

```
public void myMethod();
```

In this example, public is an access modifier. Some access modifiers can also be specified for classes. The following list defines the four access modifiers supported by Java:

- public: A class member declared public can be accessed by any code from any class in your application. An application declares its main(…) method to be public so that it can be invoked from any JVM. This modifier makes a class or a class member most accessible.

- protected: A member declared protected is accessible to all classes in the same package in which the class that declares the member exists. A *package* is a set of classes grouped together. The protected member can also be accessed from a subclass of the class that contains the member even if the subclass is in a different package. You cannot declare a class protected. The protected modifier provides less accessibility than the public modifier.

- *default*: If you do not specify any access modifier while declaring a class or a class member, the default access is assumed. A class or a class member with default access (that is, no access modifier specified) can be accessed by any class in the same package as the class in question. Unlike a protected member, a member with default access cannot be accessed by a subclass that is in a different package from that of the class that contains the member. So, the default modifier provides less accessibility than the protected modifier.

- private: A member declared private is only accessible to objects of the class in which the member is declared. A top-level class cannot be declared private. This modifier makes a member least accessible.

The access and non-access modifiers are discussed in detail in Chapter 4.

When the program is executing, the elements of the program need to be stored in the memory temporarily.

The Memory Usage by a Java Program

The instructions of a running program and the related data are temporarily stored in the computer memory. Java has good news for you here: you don't need to worry about memory management because the JVM and garbage collector will take care of it. However, you can help by being aware of where different things are stored in the memory. This will also help you to understand how objects are created. As shown in Figure 1-4, a program's data is placed in two different areas in memory: the stack and the heap. Stack and heap refers to the different ways (or places) to store the elements of a running program in memory.

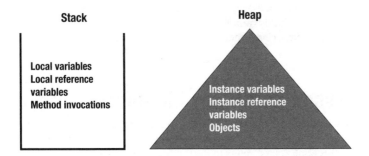

Figure 1-4. *Two different areas of memory: stack and heap*

Living on the Stack

The following elements of a Java program live on the stack:

- *Local variables*: The variables of primitive types defined inside a method or as method parameters.

- *Local reference variables*: The variables that refer to an object and are defined inside a method or as a method parameter. Remember that an object that a local variable refers to lives on the heap and not on the stack.

- *Method invocations*: When you invoke (call) a method, the method is pushed onto the stack (that is, placed on top of the stack).

Local variables live inside a method, and the scope of a local variable is the execution of the method. When the method execution is complete, the local variables inside the method are gone. But the objects, to which some of these local variables may be referring, are still alive and well on the heap.

Living on the Heap

The following elements of a Java program live on the heap:

- *Instance variables*: The variables of primitive types defined inside a class but outside of all its methods.

- *Instance reference variables*: The variables that refer to an object and are defined inside a class but outside of all its methods.

- *Objects*: Represent the entities in the real-world problem that the Java program is trying to solve. All the objects live on the heap, always.

Remembering whether a particular element lives on the stack or on the heap is easy: a local variable (primitive or reference) belongs to a method and lives with it on the stack, while an instance variable belongs to an object and lives with it on a heap. However, also note that a local reference variable on a stack points to an object on the heap, and the object will not die with the local reference variable.

The objects on the heap that are no longer in use are eventually collected by a program called a garbage collector to free up the memory used by them. For this reason, the heaps are also called garbage-collectible heaps.

So far in this chapter, you have learned how to write, compile, and execute a Java program, and where in the memory the different elements of a program are stored. The next issue that you need to consider is that a program that you have written may have problems that will cause errors.

When Will the Error Occur?

You have learned that after you write a Java program, it goes through two stages: compilation and execution. The Java compiler compiles the source code (that you wrote) into the bytecode, which is halfway to becoming the machine code. When you issue a command to run the program, the JVM interprets the bytecode for the machine (computer) and facilitates its execution. The compiler and the JVM also act as two checkpoints for your Java program, by checking the validity of your code.

Some (but not all) problems in your code will be captured by the compiler, and others will make it all the way to the JVM. If a problem with your code is captured by the compiler, the code will not compile, and the compiler will issue an error message. You can fix the problem and compile your code before executing the program. However, if a problem makes it to the JVM, an error condition will happen when the application is executing, and an error message will be issued (technically speaking, an exception will be thrown) at runtime. This is important for you to understand because most of the SCJP exam questions will have these two options among the multiple-choice answers:

- Compilation fails
- An exception is thrown at runtime

Generally speaking, the compiler does not have all the information needed to check the validity of the code. For example, consider the task of associating a method call with the actual method (that is, the method body) that will be executed as a result of the call. This association is called *binding*. An association made by the compiler is called *early binding*, and the association made by the JVM (at runtime) is called *late binding* (or *dynamic binding*). Late binding may happen because the type (class) of the object being used to make the method call may not be known until runtime. For example, consider the following method call:

```
obj.myMethod();
```

The variable obj is only a reference variable that refers to an object. The class of the object to which obj refers and the class of obj itself do not have to be the same (you will learn more about this issue as you go through the book). That means the decision on which myMethod() to call cannot be made based on the type of the obj variable, and the class of the object to which obj actually refers cannot be known until runtime. In this situation, the binding will be delayed until runtime, and therefore the compiler cannot catch the related problem with the code, if any.

The technical terms early binding and late binding are considered by some to be jargon. Each programming language has its own specific bag of jargon or buzzwords.

What's in a Name?

These days, it is not enough to be an expert; you must also sound like an expert, and for that you need to be familiar with the jargon and the buzzwords of your field of expertise. With that in mind, this section introduces you to the names of the Java versions and to the Java buzzwords.

A Brief History of Java Versions

Sun started naming Java versions with JDK (Java Development Kit), and then shifted to J2SE (Java 2 Standard Edition) from version 1.2 onward. Versions 1.2 to 1.4 are also popularly known as Java 2, and 1.5 is also known as Java 5.

Table 1-2 presents a brief history of the release of different Java versions. Versions 1.3 and 1.4 offer only incremental improvements over the initial Java 2 release (J2SE 1.2), which included additions to the standard library, increased performance, and included bug fixes. Java 5 (J2SE 5, also known as J2SE 1.5) is the first release since version 1.1 that significantly updates the Java language by introducing new language features.

Table 1-2. *A Brief History of Java Versions*

Version	Year of Release	New Language Features
JDK 1.0	1996	Introduced the language
JDK 1.1	1997	Inner classes
J2SE 1.2 (Java 2)	1998	None

Version	Year of Release	New Language Features
J2SE 1.3	2000	None
J2SE 1.4	2002	Assertions
J2SE 5.0 (Java 5)	2004	Autoboxing, enumerations, for-each loop, generic classes, metadata, static import, and varargs

As stated earlier in the chapter, Java is an object-oriented and platform-independent language. In addition to these two popular buzzwords, there are several others that you need to know.

Java Buzzwords

You will hear and see quite a few Java buzzwords in the Java world. It's important to know the Java buzzwords because they represent the factors that have played important roles in shaping the Java language. These words are summarized in Table 1-3.

Table 1-3. *Java Buzzwords*

Buzzword	Description
Architecture neutral	The Java compiler compiles the source code into bytecode, which does not depend upon any machine architecture, but can be easily translated into a specific machine by a JVM for that machine.
Distributed	Java offers extensive support for the distributed environment of the Internet.
Dynamic	New code can be added to the libraries without affecting the applications that are using the libraries, runtime type information can be found easily, and so on.
High performance	The Just-In-Time (JIT) compilers improve the performance of interpreting the bytecode by caching the interpretations.
Interpreted	The Java compiler compiles the source code into bytecode, which can be executed on any machine by the Java interpreter of an appropriate JVM.
Multithreaded	Java provides support for multithreaded programming.
Object oriented	Java supports the features and philosophy of object-oriented programming.
Portable	There are no implementation-dependent aspects of the language specifications. For example, the sizes of primitive data types and the behavior of the arithmetic on them are specified. This contributes to making programs portable among different platforms such as Windows, Mac, and Unix.
Robust	Java provides support for error checking at various stages: early checking at compile time, and dynamic checking at runtime. This eliminates some situations that are error prone such as pointers in the C language.
Secure	Because Java supports the distributed environment of the Internet, it also offers multiple security features.
Simple	Java omits many clumsy and confusing features of other programming languages such as C++. Also, Java is designed to be able to run stand-alone on small machines. The size of the basic interpreter and class support is 40 KB.

The most popular buzzwords are architecture neutral (or platform independent), object oriented, and portable.

The three most important takeaways from this chapter are the following:

- You write a computer program in a high-level language and use the compiler to convert it into an executable program that will actually be executed by the computer.

- Following the underlying philosophy of object-oriented programming, Java allows you to adapt computing to the problem that you are trying to solve by directly representing the objects in the problem with objects in the Java program. The objects are created from classes that you write.

- The Java compiler creates bytecode that can be translated by a Java virtual machine (JVM) for a specific platform, such as Windows, Solaris, or Mac, into executable instructions. So, a Java program written once can be run on different platforms by using different JVMs.

Summary

You write a human-readable computer program, called source code, in a high-level language such as Java or C++. The source code is compiled by a compiler into an executable program that can be understood by a computer of a specific kind. However, the Java compiler compiles the source code into bytecode, which can be translated by an appropriate Java virtual machine (JVM) into executable code for a machine with a specific platform. That means in order to run your program on a new kind of machine (platform), all you need is a JVM that can translate the bytecode into executable code for that machine. This is what makes Java architecture neutral (platform independent).

Java supports object-oriented programming (OOP), the basic philosophy of which is to adapt computing to the problem rather than to mold the problem to make it computable. There is one-to-one correspondence between the entities in the problem and the objects in the program that is written to solve the problem. Java implements OOP by implementing its salient features such as encapsulation, inheritance, and polymorphism. Encapsulation is represented by a class that holds both the data and the methods that will operate on the data. Inheritance is enabled by allowing classes to be derived from already existing classes and thereby building a tree of class hierarchy. Polymorphism enables you to represent related behaviors with the same name.

The code of a running program and its data are temporarily stored in the computer memory, which has two areas for such storage: the stack and the heap. The method invocations and local variables (variables declared inside a method) are stored on the stack, while the instance variables (variables declared outside the methods) and objects are stored on the heap.

PART 2

■ ■ ■

Basic Java Programming

Every programming language offers some basic features. The most basic features of a programming language are the data types and the operators to handle and manipulate data in a program. Being an object-oriented programming language, Java, in addition to supporting basic data types called primitives, lets you write your own data types called classes, giving you endless freedom to build your own data types. A class encapsulates data and methods to operate on that data according to the business logic in the problem that's being solved. The business logic is implemented by using execution flow control: the order in which the instructions in a program are executed. Because Java is an object-oriented language, it implements several object-oriented programming features such as encapsulation, polymorphism, and class hierarchy.

So, in this part, we explore the basics of Java programming, including data types and operators, methods, classes, and class hierarchy.

■■■

CHAPTER 2

Data Types and Operators

Exam Objectives

1.3 Develop code that declares, initializes, and uses primitives, arrays, enums, and objects as static, instance, and local variables. Also, use legal identifiers for variable names.

7.6 Write code that correctly applies the appropriate operators including assignment operators (limited to: =, +=, -=), arithmetic operators (limited to: +, -, *, /, %, ++, --), relational operators (limited to: <, <=, >, >=, ==, !=), the instanceof operator, logical operators (limited to: &, |, ^, !, &&, ||), and the conditional operator (? :), to produce a desired result. Write code that determines the equality of two objects or two primitives.

A computer program, written in any programming language, is basically made of three elements: data, operations on data, and the logic that determines the operations. Therefore, manipulating the data (i.e. holding and operating on it) is at the core of a typical computer program. The data is held by variables, and the operations are made by using what are called operators. Data handled by the program may come in different types, such as integer or character. Every language supports certain basic data types, called primitive data types. However, a given variable may hold data of one specific type only. As you know from Chapter 1, Java, in addition to supporting primitive data types, supports an infinite number of data types by letting you write classes. In this chapter, I discuss the primitive data types in detail, and introduce some nonprimitive data types built into the Java language.

The core topic in this chapter is how you hold and operate upon the data in a Java program. To understand that, we explore three avenues: variables, data types, and operators.

Data-Related Concepts

Problems solved by a computer program often involve operations on data. From a program's perspective, data is stored and retrieved by using variables. We refer to the variables by using their names, called identifiers. The data is operated upon by using the operators along with the variables. This section introduces all of these data-related concepts: variables, data types, identifiers, and operators.

Understanding Variables, Data Types, and Operators

Each data item in a computer program has a type such as integer or character. Because there are two kinds of data types, primitive (basic) and nonprimitive (advanced), there are two corresponding kinds of variables: *primitive variables*, which are commonly called just variables, and *reference variables*, which are also called object references.

As shown in Figure 2-1, a primitive variable holds the value for a primitive data type, such as an integer value, while a reference variable holds the reference to an object stored elsewhere in memory. For example, a student ID may be represented by a primitive variable with a primitive type int and an object of the class Student may be represented by a reference variable, say John, that refers to the actual object of the class Student. (You were introduced to classes and objects in Chapter 1.) We explore the primitive data types and variables in this section, and cover the reference variables later in the chapter, in the section "Working with Nonprimitive Data Types."

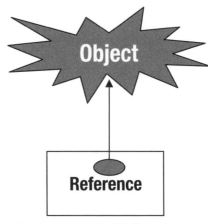

Primitive variable name   **Reference variable name**

Figure 2-1. *A primitive variable holds the value of the data item, while a reference variable holds the memory address where the data item (object) is stored.*

As just mentioned, a primitive data item such as an id of a student of int type is stored in a piece of memory referred to as a variable (the primitive variable). The values stored in a variable (piece of memory) may generally be changed, hence the name variable. A given variable can hold only a specific kind of data, which is called the *data type*. You need to specify the data type when you declare the variable. Declaring a variable includes naming the variable and specifying the data type that the variable will hold; for example:

```
int id;
```

This code statement, by declaring the variable, requests the allocation of memory for storing an integer number, and the memory will be referred to by using the variable named id. For example, we can store the number 9 in this piece of memory by the following code statement:

```
id = 9;
```

Here, the symbol = is an example of one type of operator, called an assignment operator. You learn more about operators later in this chapter. The name of a variable, id in this example, is called an identifier. The following section explores the rules for naming variables.

Naming the Variables: Legal Identifiers

Each variable has a name, given to it by the programmer while declaring the variable. This name is called an *identifier*. For example, id in the example in the previous section is an example of an identifier. Following are the rules to name a variable (or define an identifier):

- The first character of an identifier must be a letter, a dollar sign ($), or an underscore (_).
- A character other than the first character in an identifier may be a letter, a dollar sign, an underscore, or a digit.
- None of the Java language keywords (or reserved words) can be used as identifiers.

So, name your variables according to the first two rules, and do not use a reserved name because it will make an illegal identifier. Following are some examples of legal and illegal identifiers:

- 4us: This is an illegal identifier because the first character of a legal identifier must be a letter, a dollar sign, or an underscore, not a number.
- weigh#110: This is an illegal identifier due to the presence of the # sign. The only allowed characters are a dollar sign, an underscore, a digit, and a letter.
- __420_lotto$: As weird as this may look, it is a legal identifier. Compare it to the rules in the preceding list.

For the exam, you must also remember the reserved names, which are listed in the next section.

Reserved Names: The Keywords

Java keywords are the reserved words in the Java language. Each keyword has a specific meaning within the language. Therefore, a programmer cannot use these words to name the variables, classes, or methods. For example, the word int is a keyword used to declare a variable of type integer. The Java keywords are listed in Table 2-1. You will become familiar with these keywords, if you are already not, as you explore through the book.

Table 2-1. *Java Keywords*

abstract	const	final	int	public	throw
assert	continue	finally	interface	return	throws
boolean	default	float	long	short	transient
break	do	for	native	static	true
byte	double	goto	new	strictfp	try
case	else	if	null	super	void
catch	enum	implements	package	switch	volatile
char	extends	import	private	synchronized	while
class	false	instanceof	protected	this	

Following are a few points to remember when dealing with exam questions about keywords:

- Keywords use letters only; they do not use special characters (such as $, _, etc.) or digits.
- All keywords are in all lowercase letters.
- Watch out for keywords that are from languages other than Java, such as friend, include, and unsigned, which are not keywords in Java.
- The words goto and const are reserved to the extent that programmers cannot use them, but they have no specific meaning in the Java language. The meanings of other keywords will be explained at appropriate places in this book.

In addition to naming a variable, you need to declare its data type, discussed next.

Working with Primitive Data Types

Java, like other programming languages such as C and C++, supports basic built-in data types, which are also called primitive data types. There are eight primitive data types in Java:

- boolean: This data type is used to represent a binary condition: true or false. So, at Java level, its size is 1 bit. The bit turned on represents true, and off represents false.

- byte: This type is an 8-bit, signed, two's complement integer. Therefore, the range of values it can support is -2^7 to $2^7 - 1$ (i.e. -128 to 127).

- short: This type is a 16-bit, signed, two's complement integer. Therefore, the range of values it can support is -2^{15} to $2^{15} - 1$ (-32,768 to 32,767).

- char: This type is a 16-bit, unsigned integer that is used to represent keyboard characters. Remember that a variable of this type never holds a negative value. Therefore, the range of values it can support is 0 to $2^{16} - 1$ (0 to 65,535).

- int: This type is a 32-bit, signed, two's complement integer. Consequently, the range of values it can support is -2^{31} to $2^{31} - 1$ (–2,147,483,648 to 2,147,483,647). This is the default type in the integer arithmetic—that is, the arithmetic manipulations of integers that specifically could be represented by byte, short, or int.

- long: This type is a 64-bit, signed, two's complement integer. Consequently, the range of values it can support is -2^{63} to $2^{63} - 1$ (-9,223,372,036,854,775,808 to 9,223,372,036,854,775,807).

- float: The variable of type float can hold a 32-bit, signed floating-point number. The range of values it can support is +/–3.40282347^{38}.

- double: A variable of type double can hold a 64-bit, signed floating-point number. The range of values it can support is +/–$1.79769313486231570^{308}$.

Note All the numeric types (i.e. all the primitive types except boolean and char) are signed.

The sizes and value ranges for all the primitive data types supported by Java are summarized in Table 2-2.

Table 2-2. *Primitive Data Types, Their Sizes, and the Ranges of Their Values*

Data Type	Size in Bits	Range of Values	Signed/Unsigned
boolean	1	true or false	NA
byte	8	-2^7 to $2^7 - 1$	Signed
short	16	-2^{15} to $2^{15} - 1$	Signed
char	16	0 to $2^{16} - 1$	Unsigned
int	32	-2^{31} to $2^{31} - 1$	Signed
float	32	-2^{31} to $2^{31} - 1$	Signed
double	64	-2^{63} to $2^{63} - 1$	Signed
long	64	-2^{63} to $2^{63} - 1$	Signed

Note that all primitives except `boolean` and `char` are signed. Now you know all the primitive data types supported by Java and the range of values that they can hold. Recall that a given variable can hold only a specific data type. So, how do you actually declare a variable for a specific data type, and then assign it an initial value? We explore the answer to this question in the next section.

Declaring and Initializing Primitive Variables

Before you can use a variable in code, it must hold a value corresponding to a specific data type. This involves a two-step process: declaring the name and data type of a variable, and assigning it a value. Depending upon its scope, a variable may live on a stack or on a heap, two different areas of memory introduced in Chapter 1. The process of assigning an initial value (which may later be changed) to a variable is called *initialization*.

Syntax for Declaring Variables

The general syntax for declaring and initializing a variable is shown here:

```
<modifier> <dataType> <variableName> = <initialValue>
```

For example, the following statement declares a private variable `id` of data type `int` and assigns it an initial value of 10 that can later be changed:

```
private int id = 10;
```

The modifier `private` means the variable `id` can be accessed only from within the class in which it is defined. Modifiers were briefly introduced in Chapter 1, and you will learn more about them in Chapter 4. To use the modifier and to assign an initial value is not always mandatory. If you declare a variable inside a method, you have to initialize it before you can use it, but if you declare it outside of the method, a default initial value will be assigned to it, in case you don't initialize it. For example, the following statement inside a class but outside a method declares a variable named `id` of data type `int` and assigns it a default value:

```
int id;
```

The default value of 0 will be assigned to the variable id. Default initial values are discussed later in this section. Once you have declared a variable, and the variable is holding a data value, you need to access the variable to manipulate the data.

Accessing Variables

You declare a variable so that you can use it to hold and manipulate a data item. For both of these tasks, you need to access the variable. Once you declare a variable, you can access it by referring to it by its name; for example:

```
x = y;
```

In this example, you access the variable y and assign its value to the variable x. Of course, both variables are assumed to be declared already. A variable can be accessed only within its scope, which is the area in the program from which it can be legally referred to. From the viewpoint of scope, variables can be classified into three categories:

- *Local variables*: All the variables declared inside a method (methods are introduced in Chapter 1 and described in Chapter 3). Their scope is the method. In other words, they can be accessed only from inside the method in which they are declared, and they are destroyed when the method completes. Local variables are also called *stack* variables because they live on the stack.

- *Instance variables*: The variables declared inside a class but outside of any method. Their scope is the instance of the class in which they are declared. These variables, for example, can be used to maintain a counter at instance level. Instance variables live on the heap.

- *Static variables*: The instance variables declared with the modifier `static`. Their scope is the class in which they are declared. These variables can be used to maintain a counter at class level, which is a variable shared by all the objects of the class.

You will learn more about these three kinds of variables in Chapters 3 and 4.

As you know by now, the primitive variables hold data values. There are two ways in which the values can be assigned to them: the values are calculated and assigned during the program execution, or the values are assigned by the programmer in the source code. The values assigned to variables in the source code are called literals, discussed next.

Literals

A literal is a value assigned to a variable in the source code as opposed to the value determined at the time of program execution; i.e. a literal is a value and not a variable. Therefore, a literal can appear only on the right side of the assignment operator, such as

```
int id = 10;
```

Literals corresponding to different primitive data types are discussed in this section.

The boolean Literals

A variable of `boolean` type can have only one of two possible values, `true` or `false`. Therefore, these two values are the only available `boolean` literals:

```
boolean  youLoveMe = true;
boolean  iLoveYou = false;
```

Caution Unlike in C/C++, in Java, the following is an invalid line of code:

```
boolean finished = 0;
```

And so is a statement such as

```
if(finished = 0)
```

where `finished` is a `boolean` variable. The key here is that `true` and `false` are the only two valid values for a `boolean` type.

The char Literals

A char literal may be represented by a single character enclosed in single quotes, such as the following:

```
char ohMy = 'L';  // valid
```

However, the following is an invalid statement:

```
char ohMy = 'L!'; // invalid
```

The latter statement would cause a compiler error because it contains more than one character in the single quotes. A char literal may also be represented by Unicode (i.e. four hexadecimal characters preceded by \u), such as

```
char question = '\u4567';
```

In this case, the variable question will hold a character represented by hexadecimal number 0x4567. Note that the char u in the preceding statement is not taken literally as u, but it acquires a special meaning that a Unicode value follows. This is an example of what is called an escape sequence. Java supports the following escape sequences for denoting special characters:

- \n: Used to denote new line
- \r: Used to denote a return
- \t: Used to denote a tab
- \b: Used to denote a backspace
- \f: Used to denote a form feed
- \': Used to denote a single quote
- \": Used to denote a double quote
- \\: Used to denote a backslash

■**Caution** A char literal may be represented only by a single character enclosed in single quotes. However, the Unicode representation of a character may have multiple characters enclosed in the single quotes, preceded by the escape sequence \u.

The Integral Literals

Integral literals may be represented by decimal, octal, or hexadecimal numbers. The octal number is prefixed with 0, and hexadecimal with 0x or 0X. For example, the value 43 may be represented by any of the following:

- 43
- 053
- 0x2b
- 0x2B
- 0X2b
- 0X2B

Note that the hexadecimal characters may be in upper- or lowercase. By default, an integral literal is 32 bits in size. To indicate a 64-bit size (that is long), the literal should be suffixed with the character L.

The Floating-Point Literals

A floating-point literal is represented by a floating-point number, and is used for both float and double data types. The numerical expression expressing the floating-point number must contain one of the following items:

- A decimal point, such as 12.33

- The character e or E representing scientific notation, such as 1.25E+8

- The suffix f or F indicating a floating-point number, such as 1.2534f

- The suffix d or D indicating double number, such as 156d

If the suffix f or d is not used, the literal is interpreted as of type double.

So, you can initialize a variable by assigning a literal value to it. What if you do not specify an initial value when you declare a variable? It may assume a default value, as described next.

Default Initial Values

Depending upon where in the program the variables are declared, the uninitialized variables may acquire initial values by default. These initial values, shown in Table 2-3, essentially correspond to zero.

Table 2-3. *Default Initial Values for Variables of Different Data Types*

Type	Default Initial Value
boolean	false
byte	0
short	0
char	`\u0000`
int	0
float	0.0f
double	0.0d
long	0L

As mentioned previously, only the instance variables acquire the default values if not explicitly initialized. You must initialize the local variables explicitly before you use them in the code, otherwise you will receive a compiler error. Consider Listing 2-1 as an example.

Listing 2-1. *InitialTest.java*

```
1. public class InitialTest {
2.     int x;
3.   public static void main(String[] args) {
4.       new InitialTest().printIt();
5.   }
6.   public void printIt(){
7.       int y;
```

```
8.        int z;
9.        y=2;
10.     System.out.println(x +" "+ y);
11.   // System.out.println(z);
12.   }
13. }
```

As long as line 11 remains commented, you receive the following output:

```
0 2
```

If you uncomment line 11, the code will generate a compiler error because you are using the local variable z without initializing it. Note that lines 7 and 8 did not generate compiler errors. That means you do not have to initialize a local variable in the same statement where you declare it. However, you must initialize it before using it.

The basic data types discussed in this section are offered by both procedural and object-oriented languages such as Java. A salient feature of an object-oriented language such as Java is that it offers classes, which represent another kind of data types, the *nonprimitive* data types. Let's explore the nonprimitive data types supported by Java.

Working with Nonprimitive Data Types

All nonprimitive data types in Java are objects. You create an object by instantiating a class. (Chapter 1 introduced classes and objects.) The objects are of two kinds: one corresponding to built-in classes in Java and the other corresponding to the classes that you write.

When you declare a variable of a nonprimitive data type, you actually declare a variable that is a reference to the memory where an object lives. Therefore, the variable of a nonprimitive data type is called a *reference variable*, or an *object reference*. While a variable of a primitive data type holds the value itself, the reference variable of a nonprimitive data type is only a reference to the memory where the object is actually placed. This reference variable may live on the stack or the heap, depending upon whether it is a local variable or an instance variable, respectively. However, the object to which it refers always lives on the heap. You will often see literature (including this book) that refers to an object reference variable simply as an object, for brevity, but always remember that it is the pointer to (or the memory address of) an object and never holds the object itself.

Objects

As explained in Chapter 1, objects are created by instantiating classes. We use object references to refer to the objects. An object reference (a reference variable) is declared just like a primitive variable is declared:

```
Student studentOne;
```

In this example, Student is the name of an already existing class and studentOne is the name of the reference variable, which you choose. No object has yet been created.

You create an object with the new operator. For example, the following statement creates an object of the class Student and assigns it to the reference variable studentOne:

```
studentOne = new Student();
```

Here, Student() is a constructor of the class Student. Recall from Chapter 1 that a constructor is a special method of a class that is invoked during the process of constructing an object of the class; generally, a constructor is used to initialize the object.

Now, an object of the class Student lives on the heap and the object reference variable studentOne refers to it. The declaration of the object reference variable, object creation, and initialization of the reference variable can also be done in a single code statement:

```
Student studentOne = new Student();
```

Computer programs are written to solve the real-world problems in which the data items are usually related to each other. For example, the data items in a program that tracks the student grades are the names of all the students in a class, the scores that a student earned in different courses, and so on (A score must be related to a specific course and a specific student.) In order to handle the related data items, there is a whole field in computer science called data structures and algorithms that involves dealing with sophisticated data structures such as lists, trees, hashes, and sets. The Java standard library offers implementations of a number of these data structures in order to store data items related to one another. Two of these implementations included in your exam objectives are discussed next: arrays and enums.

Arrays

Arrays in Java are objects that are used to store multiple variables of the same type. These variables may be of primitive types or of nonprimitive types (i.e. object references). Whether an array stores a primitive variable or an object reference, the array itself is always an object.

You declare an array by specifying the data type of the elements that the array will hold, followed by the identifier, plus a pair of square brackets before or after the identifier. The data type may be a primitive or a class. Making an array of data items consists of three logical steps:

1. Declare an array variable.
2. Create an array of a certain size and assign it to the array variable.
3. Assign a value to each array element.

Declaring an Array Variable

Following is an example of declaring an array variable of primitive data type int:

```
int[] scores;
```

The preceding syntax is used in this book, but the following is also legal:

```
int scores [];
```

Similarly, the following is an example of declaring an array variable of a nonprimitive data type, where Student is the name of a class:

```
Student[] students;
```

Again, the following is also a legal declaration:

```
Student students[];
```

It is not legal to include the size of an array in the declaration. For example, the compiler will generate an error on the following statement:

```
int [5] scores;
```

The size is included when you create the array.

Creating an Array

Because an array is an object, you create it with the new operator. An array of primitives is created and assigned to an already declared array variable as shown in this example:

```
scores = new int[3];
```

This statement creates an array of three elements that can hold integer values and assigns it to the array variable scores, which is already declared.

An array of a nonprimitive data type is created and assigned to an already declared array variable as shown in the following example:

```
students = new Student[3];
```

This statement creates an array of three elements that can hold object references (which will reference to the objects of the Student class) and assigns it to the array variable students, which we have already declared.

▓**Caution** The number of elements in an array, that is, the array size, is specified when you create an array, not when you declare it. Once you create an array of a specific size, you cannot change the size later.

Assigning Values to Array Elements

Each element of an array needs to be assigned a value, which may be data of a primitive type or a reference to an object, depending upon the type of the array. The value is assigned by referring to the array element, as shown in the following code fragment:

```
scores[0] = 75;
scores[1] = 80;
scores[2] = 100;
```

So, elements of an int array just act like int variables. Similarly, elements in an object array act like object reference variables:

```
students[0] = new Student();
students[1] = new Student();
students[2] = new Student();
```

This code will create three Student objects on the heap and assign each of them to the corresponding array element. Note that the index value for an array starts from 0; that is, if an array is of size 5, the index for the first element is 0 and the index for the last element is 4. Also, once you have created an array of a specific size, you cannot change the size.

As you just read, an array can be used to hold related items. There is a special kind of related items: a set of constant items. To handle such items, Java offers another built-in nonprimitive data type, enum.

The Data Type enum

Sometimes, in a real-world problem, a set of data can be conveniently represented by a variable that can hold only a restricted set of constant values; for example, a variable dayOfTheWeek can have only one of the seven values ranging from Monday to Sunday, a variable allowedCreditCard can have a value of VISA, MASTER_CARD, or AMERICAN_EXPRESS, and a variable trafficSignal can have a value of green, yellow, or red. In some other languages, such as C and C++, there are data types called enumerations to handle such situations.

In Java, until now, there have been workarounds but no real solutions to this problem.

The Need for a New Type

In Java, before J2SE 5.0, the solution to the problem of handling a restricted set of constant values is left for the programmer, that is, you, to design. For example, to restrict which credit cards an application accepts, you can define constants of type int and let each constant represent a particular value:

```
public static final int VISA = 1;
public static final int MASTER_CARD = 2;
public static final int AMERICAN_EXPRESS = 3;
```

So, you have predetermined the values for the credit card. But problems still exist: there is nothing that binds these three values into a kind of set, and there is nothing to stop you from passing in the wrong values—after all, these are just some variables with type int, and the compiler will allow you to pass in the wrong values for these variables. This situation is called *not type safe*.

You can improve this situation and make is it relatively type safe by defining a class, say AllowedCreditCard, defining these constants inside the class, defining a variable to represent the state of the class object, and defining a private constructor to set the state. As an example, consider Listing 2-2.

Listing 2-2. *CreditCardTest.java*

```
1. public class CreditCardTest {
2.   public static void main(String[] args){
3.    String creditCard = args[0].toUpperCase();
4.    if(creditCard.equals(AllowedCreditCard.VISA.getName())){
5.      System.out.println("Your credit card " + args[0] + " is accepted.");
6.    } else if (creditCard.equals(AllowedCreditCard.MASTER_CARD.getName())){
7.      System.out.println("Your credit card " + args[0] + " is accepted.");
8.     }else if
         (creditCard.equals(AllowedCreditCard.AMERICAN_EXPRESS.getName())){
9.       System.out.println("Your credit card " + args[0] + " is accepted.");
10.    } else {
11.         System.out.println("Sorry, we do not accept the credit card " +
              args[0] + " at this time.");
12.    }
13.  }
14. }

15. class AllowedCreditCard {
16.    protected final String card;
17.    public final static AllowedCreditCard VISA = new
            AllowedCreditCard("VISA");
18.    public final static AllowedCreditCard MASTER_CARD = new
          AllowedCreditCard("MASTER_CARD");
19.    public final static AllowedCreditCard AMERICAN_EXPRESS = new
          AllowedCreditCard("AMERICAN_EXPRESS");
20.    private AllowedCreditCard(String str){
21.       card=str;
22.    }
23.    public String getName(){
24.     return card;
25.    }
26. }
```

Note that line 3 expects that you pass in the name of the credit card as a command argument. As an example, assume that you issue the following command:

```
java CreditCardTest  visa
```

The output of this command will be

```
Your credit card visa is accepted.
```

Now assume that you issue the following command:

```
java CreditCardTest  discover
```

The output of this command will be

```
Sorry, we do not accept the credit card discover at this time.
```

In this approach, the three states of the `AllowedCreditCard` class (lines 15 through 26 of Listing 2-2) are represented by its three instances created with different values of the `card` variable (lines 17 through 19). Because the constructor is `private` (lines 20 through 22), you cannot create any other instance outside the class. So the only unexpected value that is possible is `null`, and therefore this design is considered *type safe* and is called a type-safe enumeration design pattern. However, the fact remains that the solution to the enumeration problem is left to the programmer to do manually. So, all of these approaches to represent an enumeration in Java are Band-Aids and not robust solutions. The good news, however, is that J2SE 5.0 presents a robust solution by introducing a new type called `enum`.

Understanding the enum Type

The data type `enum`, introduced in J2SE 5.0, is useful when you want a variable to hold only a predetermined set of values. You should use enums any time you need a fixed set of constants, including natural enumerated types such as days of the week. You define an `enum` variable in two steps:

1. Define the `enum` type with a set of named values.
2. Define a variable to hold one of those values.

Following is an example:

```
enum AllowedCreditCard {VISA, MASTER_CARD, AMERICAN_EXPRESS};

AllowedCreditCard visa = AllowedCreditCard.VISA;
```

You can think of `enum` as an alternative to defining a regular class, or you can think of it as a special kind of class. In other words, it differs from yet has similarities with the regular Java class. The preceding code defines a class named `AllowedCreditCard` with the restriction that you can create only three instances (a regular class does not have such a restriction) of this class, corresponding to each value defined in the curly braces. However, just like a normal class, a public enum must be in a file named after the `enum` name. A value stored in an instance of an `enum` is retrieved by referring to it just like a variable, as shown in this example:

```
System.out.println("The allowed credit card value: " + visa)
```

Further details about enums are discussed in Chapter 3.

As you know, in a computer program, data is manipulated by holding and operating on it. Whereas the variables discussed so far in this chapter are used to hold the data, the operators allow the operations on data, as discussed next.

Understanding Operations on Data

So far in this chapter, we have been exploring the variables that are used to hold data. The data is often manipulated in a computer program. For example, you may like to change the value of a data item, add two data items and assign the result to another variable, and so on. The piece of data (represented by a variable) that is being operated on is called an *operand*. For example, in the following line of code, x and y (the variables) are operands and the equal sign (=) is an operator:

```
x=y;
```

The execution of this line of code assigns the value of y to x. Operators operate on their operands in a variety of ways. Some operators change the values of their operands, others produce a new value without changing the values of the operands, and yet others simply compare the values of two operands. So, there are different kinds of operators corresponding to different kinds of data manipulation. All of these kinds of operators are discussed in this chapter.

First, let's look at the operators in a rather generic way. From the perspective of the number of operands they operate on, Java operators can be classified into the following three categories:

- *Unary operators*: Require only one operand. For example, ++ increments the value of its operand by one.

- *Binary operators*: Require two operands. For example, + adds the values of its two operands.

- *Ternary operators*: Operate on three operands. The Java programming language has one ternary operator, ?:, which is discussed later in this chapter.

After that very high-level view of the operators, it is time to discuss them in further detail by categorizing them based on their functionality. Let's start with simple arithmetic operators, which we have all used in our elementary school math.

Arithmetic Operators

In mathematics, we are all familiar with the arithmetic operators, which perform arithmetic operations on their operands, and apply to operands of any numeric type. The arithmetic operators supported by the Java programming language are summarized in Table 2-4.

Table 2-4. *Arithmetic Operators Supported by Java*

Operator	Use	Description
+	op1 + op2	Adds the values of op1 and op2
++	++op op++	Increments the value of op by 1
−	op1 − op2	Subtracts the value of op2 from that of op1
--	--op op--	Decrements the value of op by 1
*	op1 * op2	Multiplies value of op1 by that of op2
/	op1 / op2	Divides the value of op1 by that of op2
%	op1 % op2	Computes the remainder of dividing the value of op1 by that of op2

The following sections discuss these operators in detail.

The Unary Arithmetic Operators

The unary operators are of two kinds: those that just change the sign, called the sign unary operators, and those that change the absolute value of the operand, called increment and decrement operators.

The Sign Unary Operators: + and −

These operators do not change the absolute value of the operand, only the sign. The + operator does not have any real effect. The − operator multiplies the value of the operand by -1 before assigning it to another operand. However, it does not change the absolute value of the operand on which it operates. For example, if the value of x is 7, then the execution of the following statement results in the value of y to be -7 and the value of x to remain to be 7:

```
int y = -x;
```

After the execution of the preceding statement, the execution of the following statement results in the value of z to be 7 and the value of y to remain to be -7:

```
int z = -y;
```

There are two unary operators that do change the absolute value of the operand on which they operate: ++ and --.

The Increment and Decrement Operators: ++ and --

The operators ++ and -- increment and decrement the value of an operand by 1. For example, if the current value of an int variable is 7, ++x would change the value of x from 7 to 8, and --x would change the value of x from 7 to 6. Both x++ and ++x would produce the same effect on x. However, note that the result may be different in an expression where an assignment operator is involved. For example, if the value of x is 7, the following code statement results in the value of x to be 8 and the value y to be 7:

```
y = x++;
```

On the other hand, if the value of x is 7, then the following code statement results in the value of x to be 8 and the value of y to be 8 too:

```
y = ++x;
```

The general rule is that if the increment (or decrement) operator is followed by the operand (e.g. ++x), then it operates before the operand takes part in the rest of the expression. On the other hand, if the operand is followed by the operator (e.g. x++), then the operand takes part in the expression before the operator operates on it. Table 2-5 summarizes the examples discussed in this section.

Table 2-5. *Examples of Using Increment and Decrement Unary Operators*

Initial Value of x	Code Statement	Final Value of y	Final Value of x
7	y = ++x;	8	8
7	y = x++;	7	8
7	y = --x;	6	6
7	y = x--;	7	6

Note The unary operators ++ and -- change the absolute value of the operand whereas the sign operators + and – do not.

The most basic arithmetic operations are addition, subtraction, multiplication, and division. Let's look at the Java operators corresponding to these operations.

Basic Arithmetic Operators

Although talking about the basic arithmetic operators may seem unnecessary, you will see that there are some important points that you need to understand regarding these operators from the exam's perspective and, of course, for good programming.

The Multiplication and Division Operators: * and /

Multiplication and division in Java is performed by the operators * and /, respectively, which can operate on all primitive numeric types and the type char. The multiplication and division operations seem simple enough. However, you must be aware of the facts discussed here.

The accuracy of the results is limited to the type. If the result of multiplication of two variables is larger than what the type can hold, the higher bits are dropped. For example, recall that the byte type has the size of 8 bits. Consider the following lines of code:

```
byte a = 70;
byte b = 5;
byte c = (byte) (a*b);
```

The accurate value of c should be 350, which in binary format is 101011110. However, since c is of type byte, only the lower 8 bits, 01011110, would be counted. Therefore, the value actually stored in the variable c would be 94 instead of 350.

Similarly, consider the following lines of code for the int type:

```
int x = 70000;
int y = 70000;
int z = x*y;
```

The accurate value of z should be 4900000000, but the value that would be stored in z is 605032704.

You should also be careful about accuracy while dividing two integers, because the result of dividing an integer by another integer will be an integer—that is, the accuracy will be rounded off to an integer. For example, 66 divided by 7 would be 9, and not 9.43.

Furthermore, in case of integer types (char, byte, short, int, and long), division by zero is not allowed. For example, consider the following lines of code:

```
1.    int x = 2;
2.    int y =0;
3.    int z = x/y;
```

Line 3 would generate ArithmeticException at execution time.

On the contrary, division by zero in case of float and double types does not generate an error. Instead, it would generate POSITIVE_INFINITY or NEGATIVE_INFINITY. The square root of a negative number of float or double type would generate an NaN (Not a Number) value, and will not generate an exception.

In general, an NaN value indicates that the calculation has no meaningful result in ordinary arithmetic. Two NaN values are defined in the java.lang package: Float.NaN, and Double.NaN.

Because NaN means not a sensible value, all the following comparisons would return false for any value of the double variable x, including NaN:

```
x <  Double.NaN
x <= Double.NaN
x >  Double.NaN
x >= Double.NaN
x == Double.NaN
```

As a corollary to the preceding example, consider the following statement:

```
double x = 7.0/0.0;
```

The following comparison will return true:

```
x != Double.NaN
```

■**Caution** Division by zero generates a runtime ArithmeticException only if the operands are integers. In case of float and double, the result of division by zero is infinity.

In some situations in your program, you may be interested only in the remainder of a division. To handle such a situation, Java offers the modulo operator, discussed next.

The Modulo Operator: %

The modulo operator gives the value that is the remainder of a division. For example, the execution of the following statement results in the value of x to be 2:

```
int x = 11%3;
```

For further illustration, some examples for the usage of the % operator are presented in Table 2-6.

Table 2-6. *Examples of Using the Modulo Operator*

Value of x	Value of y	Expression	Final Value of z
11	3	z = x%y	2
11	3	z = x%(-y)	2
11	3	z = -x%y	–2
11	3	z = -x%(-y)	–2
3.8	1.2	z=x%y	0.2

Note that the sign of the result is always the sign of the first (from the left) operand. If the second operand is zero, the result is the same as in division by zero: if the operands are integers, an ArithmeticException results, and if the operands are float or double, the result is an NaN value.

■**Caution** The result of the modulo operator always carries the sign of the first operand; you can ignore the sign of the second operand.

The other two obvious mathematical operations are addition and subtraction. Let's take a look at the Java operators corresponding to these operations.

The Addition and Subtraction Operators: + and −

The addition and subtraction operators perform arithmetic addition and subtraction, respectively. They are not as sophisticated as the division and modulo operators discussed previously. However, remember that if the result overflows, the truncation of bits happens the same way as in multiplication, and an arithmetically incorrect result will be achieved. The second point to note is that the + operator is overloaded in the Java language to concatenate strings. More discussion on this is presented in Chapter 7, which discusses strings.

The data manipulation in a computer program is often done based on some kind of logic; for example, if the score of a student is less than 60, assign a value of fail to the variable that represents the student's grade. Comparing the values of two variables plays an important role in the logic of a program, and the comparison is performed using the relational operators.

Relational Operators

A relational operator, also called a comparison operator, compares the values of two operands and returns a boolean value: true or false. In other words, a comparison operator tests a relationship between two operands to be true or false. For this reason, comparison operators are also called relational operators. The operand could be any of the numeric operands. Table 2-7 summarizes the comparison operators.

Table 2-7. *Comparison Operators*

Operator	Use	Result
>	op1 > op2	true if op1 is greater than op2, otherwise false
>=	op1 >= op2	true if op1 is greater than or equal to op2, otherwise false
<	op1 < op2	true if op1 is less than op2, otherwise false
<=	op1 <= op2	true if op1 is less than or equal to op2, otherwise false
==	op1 == op2	true if op1 and op2 are equal, otherwise false
!=	op1 != op2	true if op1 and op2 are not equal, otherwise false

The comparison operators are commonly used to define conditions in statements such as if(). For example, consider the following lines of code fragment:

```
int i = 9;
int j = 10;
if(i<j){
  System.out.println("i is less than j");
}
if(i<=j){
  System.out.println("i is less than or equal to j");
}
if(i>=j){
  System.out.println("i is greater than or equal to j");
}
```

The output of this code will be

```
i is less than j
i is less than or equal to j
```

■**Caution** The comparison operator to check whether the values of two variables are equal is == and not =. The latter is the assignment operator and not the comparison operator.

So, comparing the values of two variables by using a relational operator represents a condition that may be true or false. A more sophisticated programming logic may require combining two or more conditions together. This is accomplished by using the logical operators.

Logical Operators

Logical operators are used to combine more than one condition that may be true or false. In other words, logical operators deal with connecting the boolean values. Recall that a boolean value is a binary value: true or false. Therefore, it could be conveniently represented by a bit being 1 or 0. This gives the logical operators the power to operate at bit level. You may be making an operation on two binary values to create a third one, or you may just be comparing the two binary values. To handle these two situations, Java offers two kinds of logical operators: bitwise logical operators and short-circuit logical operators.

Bitwise Logical Operators

Java offers some logical operators that are used to manipulate (test, or set) the bits of an integer (byte, short, char, int, long) value. Accordingly, they are called bitwise operators. This section discusses five bitwise logical operators, summarized in Table 2-8. These operators perform the boolean logic on a bit-by-bit basis.

Table 2-8. *Bitwise Logical Operators*

Operator	Use	Operation
&	op1 & op2	AND
|	op1 | op2	OR
^	op1 ^ op2	XOR
~	~op	Bitwise inversion
!	!op	NOT (Boolean inversion)

The following sections further explore each of these operators individually.

The AND Operator: &

This operator performs the boolean AND logic on a bit-by-bit basis. For example, 1&1 produces 1. Every other combination would produce 0. Table 2-9 illustrates this.

Table 2-9. *Illustration of the AND Operator*

op1	op2	op1 & op2
0	0	0
0	1	0
1	0	0
1	1	1

You can implement the bit-by-bit operation shown in Table 2-9 on numbers. For example, consider the following lines of code:

```
byte x = 117;
byte y = 89;
byte z = (byte) (x&y);
System.out.println("Value of z: " + z );
```

The output of this code fragment will be

```
Value of z: 81
```

Here is what happens: The value of x, 117, in binary format is 01110101, and the value of y, 89, in binary format is 01011001. The & operator would operate on these two numbers at bit level:

```
  01110101
& 01011001
-----------
  01010001   =  81.
```

The OR Operator: |

Also called inclusive OR, this operator performs the boolean OR logic on numbers at bit level. As you know, in an OR operation, only one operand has to be true for the result to be true. Given that the bit 1 represents true, if either of the two bits is 1, the result is 1. Table 2-10 illustrates how this operator works.

Table 2-10. *Illustration of the OR Operator*

op1	op2	op1	op2
0	0	0
0	1	1
1	0	1
1	1	1

You can repeat the calculation in the preceding section by replacing & with |:

```
  01110101
| 01011001
-----------
  01111101   =  125.
```

Therefore:

```
117 | 89 = 125.
```

The XOR Operator: ^

This operator performs the `boolean` OR logic on numbers at bit level in an exclusive fashion. That means if one and only one of the two bits is 1, then the final result is 1, otherwise the result is 0. Table 2-11 illustrates this.

Table 2-11. *Illustration of the XOR Operator*

op1	op2	op1^op2
0	0	0
0	1	1
1	0	1
1	1	0

You can repeat the calculation in the previous sections for ^:

```
  01110101
^ 01011001
  -----------
  00101100   =  44.
```

Therefore:

```
117 ^ 89 = 44.
```

The Bitwise Inversion Operator: ~

This unary operator inverts the value of each bit of the operand. That means if the operand bit is 1, the result is 0, and if the operand bit is 0, the result is 1. For example, ~01110101 would result in 10001010.

The Boolean Inversion Operator: !

This unary operator operates on a `boolean` operand and the outcome is the inversion of the value of the operand. For example, if the `boolean` operator op holds `true`, then the outcome of !op would be `false`.

So, the bitwise logical operators are used on numbers at bit level and produce a new value. You will encounter situations in programming in which you just want to test whether both conditions are `true`, or whether one of the two conditions is `true`, and so on. To handle such situations, Java offers short-circuit logical operators.

Short-Circuit Logical Operators

You have just learned how the logical AND operator & and the logical OR operator | operate on numeric types at bit level. Java also offers the counterparts of the & and | operators that operate on the `boolean` types. These operators are called short-circuit logical operators. The outcome of these operators is, of course, a `boolean`. These operators are summarized in Table 2-12.

Table 2-12. *Short-Circuit Logical Operators*

Operator	Name	Usage	Outcome
&&	Short-circuit logical AND	op1 && op2	true if op1 and op2 are both true, otherwise false. Conditionally evaluates op2.
||	Short-circuit logical OR	op1 || op2	true if either op1 or op2 is true, otherwise false. Conditionally evaluates op2.

The following sections discuss these operators individually.

Short-Circuit Logical AND: &&

Logically, the outcome of this operator is true if the first and the second operands are both true. First, the first operand is evaluated. If the first operand turns out to be false, then the second operand is not evaluated because the overall outcome is now known. If the first operand turns out to be true, then the second operand is evaluated.

Short-Circuit Logical OR: ||

Logically, the outcome of this operator is true if either the first or the second operand is true. First, the first operand is evaluated. If the first operand turns out to be true, then the second operand is not evaluated because the overall outcome is now known. If the first operand turns out to be false, then the second operand is evaluated.

The short-circuit logical operators may be used to build powerful conditions based on compound comparison. Consider the following code example:

```
1.  int i = 5;
2.  int j = 10
3.  int k = 15;
4.  if ( (i < j) || ( k++ > j) ) {
5.      System.out.println("First if, value of k: " + k);
6.  }
7.  if ( (i < j) && ( k++ < j) ) {
8.      System.out.println("Second if, value of k: " + k);
9.  }
10.     System.out.println("Out of if, k:" + k);
```

The output of this program will be

```
First if, value of k: 15
Out of if, value of k: 16
```

Here is what happens: Line 4 involves the short-circuit OR operator. First, the expression (i<j) is evaluated and it turns out to be true. Hence, the result of the OR operation is determined to be true without even looking at the second expression. Because the second expression is not evaluated, the value of k is not incremented. As a result, the value of k in the output turns out to be 15.

Line 7 involves the short-circuit AND operator. First, the expression, (i<j) is evaluated and it turns out to be true. However, this alone cannot determine the outcome of the AND operation. Therefore, the second expression needs to be evaluated, which evaluates to false. However, during the evaluation, the value of k is incremented by 1. Because the outcome of the AND operation is false, the body of the second if condition is not executed, and the execution control jumps to line 10 where the changed value of k is printed out.

■**Caution** In case of short-circuit logical AND and OR operations, the second operand is only evaluated if the outcome of the overall operation cannot be determined from the evaluation of the first operand.

You know by now that in a computer program, you operate on data by using the variables; for example, you add two data items by adding two variables that hold those data items. But, how do you make a variable to hold a data item, in the first place? You assign the data item (value) to the variable by using an assignment operator.

Using Assignment Operators

An assignment operator is used to set (or reset) the value of a variable. The most common and obvious assignment operator is =. For example, the following code statement declares a variable x of type int and sets its value to 7:

```
int x = 7;
```

There are two aspects of the assignment operators that you need to understand. First, often in a program, the assignment operators can be combined with other operators, and the resultant operators are called *shortcut assignment operators*. Second, the operands on the two sides of an assignment operator do not have to be of the same type. Let's take a closer look on both of these issues.

Shortcut Assignment Operators

There are several shortcut assignment operators that reduce down to the basic assignment operator =. For example, consider the following statement:

```
x = x + y;    // y is a variable.
```

You can write it in terms of a shortcut operator:

```
x += y;
```

These shortcut assignment operators are summarized in Table 2-13.

Table 2-13. *Shortcut Assignment Operators*

Operator	Use	Equivalent To
+=	op1 += op2	op1 = op1 + op2
-=	op1 -= op2	op1 = op1 - op2
*=	op1 *= op2	op1 = op1 * op2
/=	op1 /= op2	op1 = op1 / op2
%=	op1 %= op2	op1 = op1 % op2
&=	op1 &= op2	op1 = op1 & op2
|=	op1 |= op2	op1 = op1 | op2
^=	op1 ^= op2	op1 = op1 ^ op2
<<=	op1 <<= op2	o1 = op1 << op2
>>=	op1 >>= op2	o1 = op1 >> op2
>>>=	op1 >>>= op2	o1 = op1 >>> op2

The operands on both sides of an assignment operator may not be of the same type. In that case, one value may be transformed to the type of the other operand, as discussed next.

Arithmetic Promotion

When an arithmetic statement involves binary operation between two operands of different types or of types narrower in size than int, the compiler may convert the type of one operand to the type of the other operand, or the types of both operands to entirely different types. This conversion, called *arithmetic promotion*, is performed before any calculation is done. The following list presents the rules that govern arithmetic promotion in Java:

- If both the operands are of a type narrower than int (that is byte, short, or char), then both of them are promoted to type int before the calculation is performed.

- If one of the operands is of type double, then the other operand is converted to double as well.

- If none of the operands is of type double, and one of the operands is of type float, then the other operand is converted to type float as well.

- If none of the operands is of type double or float, and one of the operands is of type long, then the other operand is converted to type long as well.

- If none of the operands is of type double, float, or long, then both the operands are converted to type int, if they already are not.

The result of the operation would be the common type of the two operands achieved (possibly by promotion) before the actual operation occurred. The preceding rules imply that the result of any binary arithmetic operation would be at least of type int. For example, consider the following statements:

```
byte x = 1.0;
byte y = 2.0;
```

The result of operation x/y would be of type int.

For further illustration of these rules, consider the following code fragment:

```
1. byte b = 5;
2. int i = 3;
3. double d = b/i;
```

In line 3, first, b is promoted to type int, then the operation b/i is performed and the result is 1, which is of type int. As a next step, this result is promoted to double before assigning it to d. The value of d would be 1.0.

■Note You will not see questions involving bit shifting and divide by zero on the exam. These topics are covered here for the sake of completeness and flow.

Note that not any type can be converted to any other type. There will be situations in which you explicitly need to use an operator, called the cast operator, to convert one type to another. Java offers casting and a number of advanced operators to handle sophisticated situations in programming, discussed next.

Advanced Operators

In addition to the operators discussed so far in this chapter, Java offers a few more operators, summarized in Table 2-14.

Table 2-14. *Advanced Operators Offered by Java*

Operator	Description
?:	Shortcut if-else statement
[]	Used to declare arrays, create arrays, and access array elements
.	Used to form qualified names of class members
(*<params>*)	Delimits a comma-separated list of parameters; used, for example, in a method declaration
(*<type>*)	Casts (converts) a value to a specified type
new	Creates a new object or a new array
instanceof	Determines whether its first operand is an instance of its second operand

The following sections discuss some of these operators.

The Shortcut if-else Operator: ?:

The ?: operator is a conditional operator that is a shortcut for an if-else statement. For example, consider the following if-else construct:

```
if (x) {
    a=b;
else {
  a=c;
}
```

In short, it could be written as

```
a = x ? b : c;
```

It means if the condition x is true, then a would be set to b, else it would be set to c.

The Cast Operator: (*<type>*)

The cast operator explicitly converts a value to the specified type. For example, consider the following lines of code:

```
1.    byte x = 1;
2.    byte y = 2;
3.    byte z = x/y;
```

Line 3 would generate a compiler error. Due to arithmetic promotion, discussed earlier in this chapter, the right side of line 3 is of type int. A value of type int cannot be assigned to a variable of type byte because byte is narrower (8 bits in size) than int (32 bits in size). Therefore, the value of type int must be converted to type byte before assigning it to a variable of type byte. This can be done by replacing line 3 with the following line:

```
byte z = (byte) (x/y);
```

In technical terms, you say that the result of x/y has been cast to type byte. You will learn more about casting in Chapter 4. Remember that arithmetic promotion is sizing up and casting is sizing down. In sizing up, you do not run the risk of losing information, whereas in sizing down you do. This is why it makes sense to require casting to be explicit and allow arithmetic promotion to be automatic.

The new Operator

The new operator is used to instantiate a class and to create an array. Previous code examples in this chapter have shown the use of this operator.

The instanceof Operator

The instanceof operator determines if a given object is of the type of a specific class. To be more specific, the instanceof operator tests whether its first operand is an instance of its second operand. The test is made at runtime. The first operand is supposed to be the name of an object or an array element, and the second operand is supposed to be the name of a class, interface, or array type. The syntax is

```
<op1> instanceof <op2>
```

The result of this operation is a boolean: true or false. If an object specified by <op1> is an instance of a class specified by <op2>, the outcome of the operation is true, and otherwise is false. The outcome of the operation will also be true if <op2> specifies an interface that is implemented either by the class of the object specified by <op1> or by one of its superclasses.

For example, consider the following code fragment:

```
interface  X{}
class A  implements X {}
class B extends A {}
A a = new A();
B b = new B();
```

Note that class B does not implement the interface X directly, but class A does, and class B extends class A. Given this code, all of the following statements are true:

```
if( b instanceof X)
if (b instanceof B)
if(b instance of A)
if(a instance of A)
if(a instanceof X)
```

Knowing the type of an object at runtime is useful for the following reasons:

- Some invalid casts (explicit type conversions) involving class hierarchies cannot be caught at compile time. Therefore, they must be checked at runtime (using the instanceof operator), to avoid a runtime error.

- You might have a situation where one process is generating various kinds of objects, and the other process is processing them. The other process may need to know the object type before it can properly process it. In this situation the instanceof operator would be helpful, too.

Earlier in the chapter, you read about the equality operator. Next, you find out how testing the equality of primitives is different from testing the equality of objects.

Equality of Two Objects or Two Primitives

When you test the equality in a Java program, always ask two questions: what exactly is being compared and what does equality mean? There are three kinds of elements that can be compared to test the equality:

- Primitive variables
- Reference variables
- Objects

Recall that reference variables refer to objects. Two primitive variables are equal when they hold the same value. Therefore, their equality can be tested with the == operator. For example, the expression a==b returns true if a and b hold the same value, and otherwise returns false.

Just like primitive variables, reference variables can be compared for equality by using the == operator, and two reference variables are considered equal if they hold the same value. However, the value that a reference variables holds is not the data item itself, but rather is the pointer to (the memory address of) the data item, the object. Therefore, if two reference variables pass the equality test, it simply means they point to the same object.

The equality of two objects (including strings) is tested with the equals(…) method of the Object class. This method has the following signatures:

```
public boolean equals(Object <obj>)
```

The implementation of the equals(…) method in the Object class is very shallow—that is, it just uses the == operator for comparison. For example, consider the two objects obj1 and obj2. The code obj1.equals(obj2) returns true if obj1 and obj2 refer to the same object. However, you can override this method in the class that you write and give it a deeper meaning; that is, you can decide what it means that two objects are equal.

You will be revisiting the equals(…) method again in this book, such as when you read about strings in Chapter 7.

Codewalk Quicklet

As discussed in the introduction of this book, you should expect quite a few questions in the exam that involve reading and understanding code. So, it's important that you feel comfortable in reading and understanding chunks of code. The "Codewalk Quicklet" section in each chapter is intended to help you build the code-reading mindset by looking at the code as a process. A process, by definition, has an input, operations on the input, and the resultant output. Almost all the code questions will ask you what the output of this code is. To help you read the code from that perspective, this section presents the concept of process-based codewalk in which you identify the input to the code, the operations on the input, and the resultant output. To elaborate on this concept, Listing 2-3 presents a very simple example.

Listing 2-3. *CodeWalkOne.java*

```
1. class CodeWalkOne {
2.     public static void main(String [] args) {
3.         int [] counts = {1,2,3,4,5};
4.         counts[1] = (counts[2] == 2) ? counts[3] : 99;
5.         System.out.println(counts[1]);
6.     }
7. }
```

The input, operations, and output parts of this code are identified as follows:

- *Input*: An array `counts` is declared and initialized in line 3.
- *Operation*: If the value held by `counts[2]` is equal to 2, then `counts[1]` is set equal to `counts[3]`, else it is set equal to 99 (line 4).
- *Output*: The value of `counts[1]` is printed in line 5.

Looking at the code from this angle, see if you can handle the last question in the upcoming "Review Questions" section based on this code.

The three most important takeaways from this chapter are the following:

- Variables are used to hold data. A primitive variable holds the data value itself, while a reference variable, also called an object reference, holds the memory address that points to the object.
- Each variable is declared to be of a specific data type, and it can only hold data compatible with that type.
- The data held by the variables is manipulated by using operators.

Summary

The manipulation of data, which comprises the core of a typical computer program, involves holding data items and operating on them. The data items are held by variables, and operations on them are made by using operators. Variables have names and data types, which you specify at the time of declaring them. You cannot use Java keywords for naming variables. Java supports eight basic data types, called primitive data types, and also some built-in nonprimitive data types, such as arrays and enums. Java also offers a wide spectrum of operators.

The variables can be local, instance, or static in their scope. Local variables are defined inside a function and only exist during the execution of the function. Instance variables are defined inside a class but outside any function and their scope is the instance. Static variables are the instance variables defined with the `static` modifier and their scope is the class in which they are defined.

The operators let you make arithmetic operations on the values held by the variables, compare the values held by different variables, and assign a value to a variable. Unlike the bitwise logical operators & and |, the short-circuit logical operators && and || operate only on `boolean` operands. Division by zero generates a runtime `ArithmeticException` only if the operands are integers. In case of `float` and `double`, the result of division by zero is infinity. The `==` operator can be used to test the equality of two primitive variables and to test whether two reference variables refer to the same object.

The variables are declared either inside a method or outside of any method, but inside a class. The classes and methods are explored in the next chapter.

EXAM'S EYE VIEW

Comprehend

- A variable holds a value, while an object reference variable points to the memory that holds the object.

- The short-circuit logical operators && and || operate only on `boolean` operands. For example, the expression 9&&7 will not compile. Understand the difference between short-circuit logical operators and bitwise operators.

- If the first expression of a && operator is `false`, the second expression is not evaluated, and if the first expression of a || operator is `true`, the second expression is not evaluated.

Look Out

- Be on guard for words that are only slightly different from the Java keywords, such as `synchronize` instead of `synchronized`, `implement` instead of `implements`, and `protect` instead of `protected`.

- Whether an array stores primitive variables or object references, the array itself is always an object.

- It is illegal to include the array size in the array declaration.

- Division by zero generates a runtime `ArithmeticException` only if the operands are integers. In case of `float` and `double`, the result of division by zero is infinity.

- The result of the modulo operator always carries the sign of the first operand (i.e. the one before the operator); you can ignore the sign of the second operand.

- You cannot instantiate an `enum` by using the `new` operator.

Memorize

- Know the Java language keywords.

- Know the range of values for all primitive data types.

- All primitive data types except `boolean` and `char` are signed.

- The first character of an identifier must be a letter, a dollar sign ($), or an underscore (_). Characters other than the first character in an identifier may be a letter, a dollar sign, an underscore, or a digit.

Review Questions

1. Which of the following are invalid variable names in Java? (Choose all that apply.)

    A. `$char`

    B. `1MyNumber`

    C. `case`

    D. `_int`

2. Consider the following line of code:

    ```
    short  ohMy;
    ```

    What is the range of values that could be assigned to the variable `ohMy`?

    A. 0 to $2^{16} - 1$

    B. 0 to $2^{15} - 1$

    C. $-2^{15} - 1$ to $2^{15} - 1$

    D. $-2^{16} - 1$ to $2^{16} - 1$

    E. -2^{15} to $2^{15} - 1$

    F. -2^{15} to 2^{15}

3. Consider the following line of code:

    ```
    char  ohMy;
    ```

    What is the range of values that could be assigned to the variable `ohMy`?

    A. 0 to $2^{16} - 1$

    B. 0 to $2^{15} - 1$

    C. $-2^{15} - 1$ to $2^{15} - 1$

    D. $-2^{16} - 1$ to $2^{16} - 1$

    E. -2^{15} to $2^{15} - 1$

    F. -2^{15} to 2^{15}

4. Consider the following line of code:

    ```
    byte  ohMy;
    ```

    What is the range of values that could be assigned to the variable `ohMy`?

    A. 0 to $2^{16} - 1$

    B. 0 to $2^{8} - 1$

    C. -2^{7} to $2^{7} - 1$

    D. -2^{7} to 2^{7}

    E. -2^{15} to $2^{15} - 1$

    F. -2^{8} to $2^{8} - 1$

5. Which of the following statements would not produce the compile error?

A. `char my_char = 'c';`

B. `char your_char = 'int';`

C. `char what = 'Hello';`

D. `char what_char = "L";`

E. `char ok = '\u3456';`

6. Consider the following declaration:

```
boolean  iKnow;
```

The variable iKnow will be automatically initialized to which of the following?

A. `true`

B. `false`

7. Consider the following piece of code:

```
float luckyNumber =  1.25;
System.out.println ( "The value of luckyNumber: " + luckyNumber );
```

What is the result?

A. The value of luckyNumber::.

B. The value of luckyNumber: 1.25.

C. This piece of code would not compile.

D. This piece of code would compile, but give an error at execution time.

8. Consider the following code fragment:

```
public class Unary{
    public static void main(String[] args) {
      int x = 7;
      int y = 6*x++;
      System.out.println (" y= " + y);
       int a = 7;
       int b = 6*++a;
          System.out.println (" b=  " + b);
    }
}
```

What is the output of this code fragment?

A. y= 42
   b= 48

B. y= 48
   b= 48

C. y= 48
   b= 42

D. y= 42
   b= 42

9. Consider the following code fragment:

```
int x;
int a = 5;
int b= 8;
x = ++a + b++;
```

After the execution of this code fragment, what is the value of x?

A. 13

B. 14

C. 15

D. Compilation fails.

10. Which of the following expressions are illegal? (Choose all that apply.)

A. int x = 9;

B. int y = !x;

C. double z = 9.00 >> 2;

D. int i = ^7;

11. Consider the following code fragment:

```
1.  public class Unary{
2.    public static void main(String[] args) {
3.      byte x = 7;
4.      byte y = 6*x++;
5.      byte z = x*y;
6.      System.out.println ("z: " + z);
7.    }
8.  }
```

What is the output of this code fragment?

A. z: 42

B. z: 48

C. The code will not compile due to line 4.

D. The code will compile, but will generate a runtime error.

12. Consider the following code fragment:

```
int x = 9;
int y = -2;
System.out.println("output: " + x%y);
```

What is the output of this code fragment?

A. -1;

B. 1;

C. 4.5;

D. 4

13. Consider the following code fragment:

```
1. public class Question{
2.    public static void main(String[] args) {
3.       byte x = 21;
4.       byte y = 13;
5.       int z = x^y;
6.       System.out.println(z);
7.    }
8. }
```

What is the result of this code fragment?

A. 24

B. 29

C. 21

D. 13

E. A compiler error occurs at line 5.

14. Consider the following code fragment:

```
1.  public class LogicTest{
2.    public static void main(String[] args) {
3.       int i = 5;
4.       int j = 10;
5.       int k = 15;
6.       if ( (i < j) || ( k-- > j) ) {
7.            System.out.println("First if, value of k: " + k);
8.       }
9.       if ( (i < j) && ( --k < j) ) {
10.            System.out.println("Second if, value of k: " + k);
11.       }
12.        System.out.println("Out of if, k:" + k);
13.       }
14.    }
```

What is the output of this code fragment?

A. First if, value of k: 14

   Out of if, k: 13

B. First if, value of k: 15

   Out of if, k: 14

C. First if, value of k: 15

   Out of if, k: 13

15. Consider the following code fragment:

```
1.  public class LogicTest{
2.    public static void main(String[] args) {
3.      int i = 5;
4.      int j = 10;
5.      int k = 15;
6.      if ( (i < j) || ( k-- > j) ) {
7.          System.out.println("First if, value of k: " + k);
8.      }
9.      if ( (i > j) && ( --k < j) ) {
10.          System.out.println("Second if, value of k: " + k);
11.     }
12.      System.out.println("Out of if, k:" + k);
13.    }
14.  }
```

What is the output of this code fragment?

A. First if, value of k: 14

   Out of if, k: 13

B. First if, value of k: 15

   Out of if, k: 14

C. First if, value of k: 15

   Out of if, k: 13

D. First if, value of k: 15

   Out of if, k: 15

16. Consider Listing 2-3 in the chapter. What is the result?

A. Compilation fails on line 4.

B. 3

C. 4

D. 2

E. 99

CHAPTER 3

■■■

Classes, Methods, and Interfaces

Exam Objectives

1.1 Develop code that declares classes (including abstract and all forms of nested classes), interfaces, and enums, and includes the appropriate use of package and import statements (including static imports).

1.2 Develop code that declares an interface. Develop code that implements or extends one or more interfaces. Develop code that declares an abstract class. Develop code that extends an abstract class.

1.4 Develop code that declares both static and non-static methods, and—if appropriate—use method names that adhere to the JavaBeans naming standards. Also develop code that declares and uses a variable-length argument list.

1.6 Given a set of classes and superclasses, develop constructors for one or more of the classes. Given a class declaration, determine if a default constructor will be created, and if so, determine the behavior of that constructor. Given a nested or non-nested class listing, write code to instantiate the class.

As described in Chapter 2, a computer program, written in any programming language, is basically made of three elements: data, operations on data, and the logic that determines the operations. Chapter 2 discussed different types of data and the corresponding variables to handle the data. The smallest unit of a program that performs operations on data and holds the logic for these operations is called a function. In procedural languages such as C and Pascal, the data and functions are not closely bound together. The data flows in and out of the functions freely. This not only makes a program highly error prone but also increases its complexity. An object-oriented language, such as Java, offers the promise of binding the data and the operations on data (functions) together. In object-oriented terminology, functions are called methods. Therefore, in Java, the data and the methods that could operate on it are bound together into one entity, called a class.

So, a Java program consists of classes, and a class consists of variables and methods. Chapter 2 explored variables (and operators) that are used to handle data. In this chapter, we explore the methods and the classes. An important feature of any object-oriented programming language is inheritance: you can derive a class from an existing class, and the derived class inherits the nonprivate methods and variables of the original class. However, to keep things simple, Java offers only single inheritance—that is, a class can inherit from only one parent class. The solution to this problem is another element of the Java language, the *interface*.

So, the core issue in this chapter is how the main elements in a Java program work together. To understand this, we explore three avenues: classes, methods, and interfaces. Pay attention to how these three elements are related to each other.

Using Methods

Most modern programming languages offer a feature to create named subprograms inside a program. In procedural languages, such as C, FORTRAN, or Pascal, these subprograms are called subroutines, procedures, or functions. In an object-oriented language, such as Java, they are called methods. Whereas variables represent data, methods represent operations on data and also hold the logic to determine those operations. You can use methods, for example, to set the values of the class variables and retrieve the values.

Using methods offer two main advantages:

- A method may be executed (called) repeatedly from different points in the program. Without the method, you would need to repeat that code at different points in the program, hence increasing the program size and making it more error prone. Also, if a change needs to be made in that piece of code, it must be made in several places, thereby increasing both the effort to maintain the code and the probability for an error.

- Methods help make the program logically segmented, or modularized. A modular program is less error prone, and easier to maintain.

The following sections describe how methods are defined and used in a Java program.

Defining a Method

A method is a self-contained block of code that performs specific operations on the data by using some logic. Defining a method in a program is called *method declaration*. A method consists of the following elements:

- *Name*: The name identifies the method and is also used to call (execute) the method. Naming a method is governed by the same rules as those for naming a variable, discussed in Chapter 2.

- *Parameter(s)*: A method may have zero or more parameters defined in the parentheses immediately following the method name during the method declaration.

- *Argument(s)*: The parameter values passed in during the method call are called arguments and correspond to the parameters defined during the method declaration.

- *Return type*: A method may optionally return a value as a result of a method call. The type of the data returned, such as int, is declared in the method declaration.

- *Access modifier*: Each method has a default or specified access modifier, such as public or private, which determines from where the method can be accessed (called).

The following is the syntax for writing a method in Java:

```
<modifier> <returnType> <methodName> ( <Parameters>) {
// body of the method. The code statements go here.
}
```

The `<modifier>` specifies the method further, such as its visibility, and `<returnType>` defines the data type that will be returned by the method. While zero or more modifiers may be used, `<returnType>` and `<methodName>` are mandatory. The parameters are used to pass data into the method. For example, consider the following method:

```
public int square (int number) {
    return number*number;
}
```

The name of the method is square. It will return a value of type int. The modifier public means it could be called from anywhere. One example of using this method follows:

```
int myNumber = square(2);
```

After executing this statement, the value of the myNumber variable would be 4.

■**Note** The method name and return type are mandatory in a method declaration. Even though you are not required to specify a modifier in a method declaration, the default modifier is assigned to the method if you don't declare one.

From the perspective of visibility within a class, there are two kinds of methods and variables: those that are visible only within an instance of the class, and hence each instance has its own copy of those methods and variables, and those that are visible from all the instances of the class, and hence all the instances share them. The latter kind of methods and variables are called static, which need to be explored further.

The Static Methods and Variables

As you know from Chapter 1, you can create multiple instances, or objects, of a class (called instantiating the class). The static methods and variables are shared by all the instances of a class, and they are declared in the class by using the modifier called, well, static. The static modifier may be applied to a variable, a method, and a block of code inside a method. Because a static element of a class is visible to all the instances of the class, if one instance makes a change to it, all the instances see that change. For example, consider Listing 3-1, which demonstrates the use of a static modifier.

Listing 3-1. *RunStaticExample.java*

```
1. class StaticExample {
2.     static int staticCounter=0;
3.     int  counter=0;
4.     StaticExample() {
5.         staticCounter++;
6.         counter++;
7.     }
8. }
9. class RunStaticExample {
10.    public static void main(String[] args) {
11.        StaticExample se1 = new StaticExample();
12.        StaticExample se2 = new StaticExample();
13.        System.out.println("Value of staticCounter for se1: " +
           se1.staticCounter);
14.         System.out.println("Value of staticCounter for se2: " +
                se2.staticCounter);
15.        System.out.println("Value of counter for se1: " + se1.counter);
16.        System.out.println("Value of counter for se2: " + se2.counter);
17.        StaticExample.staticCounter = 100;
18.         System.out.println("Value of staticCounter for se1: " +
                se1.staticCounter);
19.         System.out.println("Value of staticCounter for se2: " +
                se2.staticCounter);
20.    }
21. }
```

The variable staticCounter is declared static in line 2, and another variable, counter, is declared simply an instance (nonstatic) variable in line 3. When an instance of the class StaticExample is created, both the variables are incremented by 1 (lines 5 and 6). Note that each instance has its own copy of the instance variable counter, but they share the variable staticCounter. A static variable belongs to the class, and not to a specific instance of the class, and therefore it is initialized when the class is loaded. A static variable may be referenced by an instance of the class in which it is declared, or simply by using the class name.

Following is the output from Listing 3-1:

```
Value of staticCounter for se1: 2
Value of staticCounter for se2: 2
Value of counter for se1: 1
Value of counter for se2: 1
Value of staticCounter for se1: 100
Value of staticCounter for se2: 100
```

Note that creating two instances (lines 11 and 12) of the class StaticExample incremented the staticCounter (by 1) twice and set its value to 2, whereas each instance had its own copy of counter and it was incremented by 1, only once for each instance. This explains the first four lines of the output. Line 17 sets the value of the staticCounter variable to 100, which is visible to both instances, and hence the last two lines of the output resulting from lines 18 and 19 in the code.

■**Caution** A static variable is initialized when a class is loaded, whereas an instance variable is initialized when an instance of the class is created.

Like a static variable, a static method also belongs to the class, and not to a specific instance of the class. Therefore, a static method can only access the static members of the class. In other words, a method declared static in a class cannot access the nonstatic variables and methods of the class. Because a static method does not belong to a particular instance of the class in which it is defined, it can be called even before a single instance of the class exists. For example, every Java application has a static method main(), which is the entry point for the application execution. It is executed without instantiating the class in which it exists.

■**Caution** A static method defined in a class cannot access the nonstatic variables and methods of the class. However, it can be called even before a single instance of the class exists.

As an example, consider the following code fragment:

```
1. class MyClass {
2.     String salute = "Hello";
3. public static void main(String[] args){
4.   System.out.println("Salute: " + salute);
5. }
6. }
```

This code generates a compiler error on line 4, because it tries to access a nonstatic variable from inside a static method.

As stated earlier, a class consists of variables and methods. Well, that's true most of the time. However, a class can also have a static code block outside of any method; i.e. the code block does not belong to any method, but only to the class. For example, you may like to execute a task before the class is instantiated, or even before the method main() is called. In such a situation, the static code block will help. For example, consider Listing 3-2.

Listing 3-2. *RunStaticCodeExample.java*

```
1.  class StaticCodeExample {
2.  static int counter=0;
3.  static {
4.      counter++;
5.     System.out.println("Static Code block: counter: " + counter);
6.  }
7.  StaticCodeExample() {
8.         System.out.println("Construtor:  counter: " + counter);
9.  }
10.}
11.  public class  RunStaticCodeExample {
12.  public static void main(String[] args) {
13.        StaticCodeExample sce = new StaticCodeExample();
14.        System.out.println("main: counter:" + sce.counter);
15.  }
16.}
```

When you run the application RunStaticCodeExample, the static variable counter (line 2) is initialized, and the static code block (lines 3 to 6) is executed at the class StaticCodeExample load time. Subsequently, the method main() is executed.

The following is the output from Listing 3-2:

```
Static Code block: counter: 1
Constructor: counter: 1
main: counter: 1
```

This output demonstrates that the static code block was executed before the class was instantiated. The static code block is executed exactly once, at the class load time, regardless of where it appears in the class. It will never be executed again during the execution lifetime of the application.

Now, let's look at methods from a slightly different angle. Assume that you want to write a method that can be called for any number of arguments, such as the following:

```
myMethod(1);
myMethod(1,2);
myMethod(1,2,3);
```

In previous versions of Java, you would need to write three methods corresponding to these three method calls. In J2SE 5.0, you can write a method that will handle all three calls, and more. This type of method is called a method with a variable number of parameters, or a method with variable-length arguments.

Methods with a Variable Number of Parameters

In versions prior to J2SE 5.0, you have to declare a fixed number of parameters in a method. Therefore, the number of arguments that you can pass in during the method call is predetermined. If you want to call a method by passing in, say, two arguments, and then call the same method (not the overloaded version) by passing in, say, three arguments, you cannot do it. This restriction no longer applies in J2SE 5.0, which introduces a new feature that lets you define methods with a variable number of parameters, so that you can make several method calls with a variable number of arguments. These are also called variable-length argument methods.

The rules to define variable-length parameters in a method definition are as follows:

- There must be only one variable-length parameters list.
- If there are individual parameters in addition to the list, the variable-length parameters list must appear last inside the parentheses of the method.
- The variable-length parameters list consists of a type followed by three dots and the name.

A simple but complete example illustrating the use of a variable number of parameters is presented in Listing 3-3.

Listing 3-3. *VarargTest.java*

```
1. import java.io.*;
2. class MyClass {
3.     public void printStuff(String greet, int... values) {
4.         for (int v : values ) {
5.             System.out.println( greet + ":" + v);
6.         }
7.     }
8. }
9.   class VarargTest {
10.        public static void main(String[] args) {
11.            MyClass mc = new MyClass();
12.            mc.printStuff("Hello", 1);
13.            mc.printStuff("Hey", 1,2);
14.            mc.printStuff("Hey you", 1,2,3);
15.        }
16.    }
```

The output from executing this code follows:

```
Hello:1
Hey:1
Hey:2
Hey you:1
Hey you:2
Hey you:3
```

Note that Listing 3-3 invokes the same method `printStuff(…)` with a variable number of `int` arguments. You can also call the method with no argument from the parameters list. For example, the following line of code after line 11 in Listing 3-3 will also work:

```
mc.printStuff("whatever");
```

The `for` loop from line 4 to 6 is called the `for-each` loop and it iterates over the values of v. The `for-each` loop is discussed in Chapter 6. You will get a compiler error if you replace line 3 in Listing 3-3 with the following:

```
public void printStuff(int... values, String greet) {
```

The reason for the error is that the variable-length parameters list must come as the last item in the parentheses.

Also, there can be only one list of variable number of parameters. For example, the following method definition will not compile because it contains two lists of variable number of parameters:

```
public void printStuff(String greet, int... values, double… dnum) {
```

■**Caution** The variable-length parameters list must appear last in the parentheses of a method and it consists of a data type, three dots, and a name, in that order. A method declaration can contain only one variable-length parameters list.

So, once you define a method with a variable-length parameters list, it can be used as a variable-length arguments method, because it can be invoked with a variable number of arguments. The methods with the variable-length parameters are also called vaargs methods.

As mentioned earlier, methods can be used to set the values of the class variables and to retrieve the values. Methods written for these specific purposes are called get and set methods (also known as getter and setter), and programmers conveniently begin the names of these methods with the prefixes get and set. However, in special Java classes, called JavaBeans, the rules for naming the methods (including get and set) are enforced as a standard. Let's take a closer look at this.

JavaBeans Naming Standard for Methods

A JavaBean is a special kind of Java class that is defined by following certain rules, including the naming conventions for its variables and methods. These rules include the following:

- The private variables of a JavaBean called properties can only be accessed through its getter and setter methods. The naming convention for a property is: the first letter of the first word in the name must be lowercase and the first letter of any subsequent word in the name must be uppercase, e.g., myCow.

- Each non-boolean property has a getter method that is used to retrieve the value of the property. The name of the getter method begins with get followed by the name of the property, with the first letter of each word uppercased.

- Each property has a setter method that is used to set the value of the property. The name of the setter method begins with set followed by the name of the property, with the first letter of each word uppercased.

- The getter and setter methods must be public so that anyone who uses the bean can invoke them.

- A setter method must have the void return type and must have a parameter that represents the type of the corresponding property.

- A getter method does not have any parameter and its return type matches the argument type of the corresponding setter method.

The following code fragment illustrates these rules:

```
public class ScoreBean {
 private double meanScore;
 // getter method for property meanScore
  public double getMeanScore() {
     return meanScore;
  }
// setter method to set the value of the property meanScore
  public void setMeanScore(double score) {
     meanScore = score;
  }
}
```

Note that two methods, getMeanScore() and setMeanScore(…), correspond to the variable (property) meanScore. The main motivation for standardizing the naming in JavaBeans is to enable you to use some components (JavaBeans in this case) developed by other developers so that you don't have to develop the whole application code from scratch. The implementation of a naming standard in your application and in the components ensures that the development and deployment tools can recognize and use the components developed by other developers.

So, the methods can be static or nonstatic, and they may have a fixed number of parameters or a variable number of parameters. Just like a variable, a method is a member of a class; in other words, it is written inside a class.

Working with Classes and Objects

The class is the basis for object-oriented programming. The data and the operations on the data are encapsulated in a class. In other words, a class is a template that contains the data variables and the methods that operate on those data variables following some logic. So, the class is the foundation on which the entire Java language is built. All the programming activity happens inside classes.

The data variables and the methods in a class are called class members. Variables, which hold the data (or point to it in case of reference variables), are said to represent the state of an object (that may be created out of the class), and the methods constitute its behavior. In this section, we explore writing classes and creating objects from them.

Defining Classes

A class is declared by using the keyword class. The general syntax for a class declaration is

```
<modifier> class <className> {  }
```

<className> specifies the name of the class, class is the keyword, and <modifier> specifies some characteristics of the class. The <modifier> specification is optional, but the other two elements in the declaration are mandatory.

You can broadly group the modifiers into the following two categories:

- *Access modifiers*: Determine from where the class can be accessed: private, protected, and public. If you do not specify an access modifier, the default access is assumed.

- *Other modifiers*: Specify how the class can be used: abstract, final, and strictfp.

As an example of an access modifier, consider the following class declaration:

```
class MyClass { }
```

■**Note** The keyword class and class name are mandatory in a class declaration. Even though you are not required to specify a modifier in a class declaration, the default modifier is assigned to the class, if you don't declare one.

Because no access modifier is declared in the preceding class declaration, the default access is assumed. As an example of a non-access modifier, you can declare an abstract class by specifying the abstract modifier, as in the following:

```
abstract class MyClass { }
```

Chapter 4 explores the details of abstract classes and modifiers, including the default modifier.

The class code that contains the class members (variables and methods) is written inside two curly braces. Listing 3-4 presents an example of a full definition (declaration plus code) of a simple class.

Listing 3-4. *ClassRoom.java*

```
1. class ClassRoom {
2 . private String roomNumber;
3.  private int totalSeats = 60;
4.  private static int totalRooms = 0;

5.   void setRoomNumber(String rn) {
6.     roomNumber = rn;
7.   }
8.   String getRoomNumber() {
9.     return roomNumber;
10.  }
11.  void setTotalSeats(int seats) {
12.     totalSeats = seats;
13.  }
14.  int getTotalSeats() {
15.     return totalSeats;
16.  }
17. }
```

The class defined in Listing 3-4 has the following class members:

- The instance variables roomNumber and totalSeats

- The class (static) variable totalRooms

- The methods setRoomNumber(…), getRoomNumber(), setTotalSeats(…), and getTotalSeats()

In object-oriented programming, a problem is solved by creating objects in a program that correspond to the objects in the real problem, such as student and classroom. A class is a template or a blueprint for creating objects.

Creating Objects

When you write a class, you must keep in mind the objects that will be created from it, which correspond to the objects in the problem that is being solved by the program. You may also look upon the classes as data types. You know from Chapter 1 that you can declare a variable, for example, of a primitive data type and assign it a value, as follows:

```
int i=0;
```

Similarly, you can declare a variable (a reference variable) of a class and assign it a value with the following syntax:

```
<className>  <variableName> = new <classConstructor>
```

<variableName> in this case is the name of the object reference that will refer to the object that you want to create, and you choose this name. <className> is the name of an existing class, and <classConstructor> is a constructor of the class. The right side of the equation creates the object of the class specified by <className> with the new operator, and assigns it to <variableName> (i.e. <variableName> points to it). Creating an object from a class this way is also called instantiating the class. For example, consider the following code fragment:

```
class ClassRoomManager {
   public static void main(String[] args)
   {
      ClassRoom  roomOne  =  new ClassRoom();
      roomOne.setRoomNumber("MH227");
      roomOne.setTotalSeats(30);

      System.out.println("Room number: " + roomOne.getRoomNumber());
      System.out.println("Total seats: " + roomOne.getTotalSeats());
   }
}
```

This program instantiates the ClassRoom class presented in Listing 3-4 and invokes its methods. If you compile both classes, ClassRoom and ClassRoomManager, and execute ClassRoomManager, the following will be the output:

```
Room number: MH227
Total seats: 30
```

The object is created in the following line of code:

```
ClassRoom  roomOne  =  new ClassRoom();
```

Here is what happens:

- The left side declares a reference variable roomOne of class ClassRoom.

- The right side creates an object of class ClassRoom with the operator new.

- The assignment operator = assigns the newly created object to the reference variable roomOne.

Note that the variable roomOne does not hold the object; it is only a reference to the object, and therefore is called a reference variable, or object reference. However, for brevity, the object references are also called objects, which is the convention used in this book. But always remember that what you have is not the real object, but a reference variable that points to a real object.

Let's summarize some terminology here: You instantiated the *class* ClassRoom inside another class called ClassRoomManager, you declared an *object reference* roomOne that points to the newly created *object*, and then you invoked methods on the object roomOne (the object reference), which is of *type* ClassRoom. *Instantiating* a class and invoking its methods is called *accessing* a class (or object) and its methods.

The new operator creates the object dynamically, which means that it creates it at runtime, not at compile time. When the Java runtime system executes the statement with the operator new, it allocates memory for the instance (object) of class ClassRoom, and then calls the constructor ClassRoom() to initialize this memory. This book uses the terms *instance* and *object* interchangeably; they mean the same thing.

You may create more than one *instance* of a class. Each instance would have its own copy of the nonstatic variables of the class. For this reason, the nonstatic data members of a class are also called *instance variables*, but they share the static variables of the class. Changing the value of an instance variable in one object of a class does not change the value of the same variable in another object of the same class. But if you change the value of a static variable of the class in one object, the change will be visible from all the objects.

You know by now that a class consists of variables and methods. However, there are special classes that can also contain one or more other classes inside them as class members, in addition to variables and methods. Such classes are called nested classes.

Nested Classes

All the classes discussed so far fall into a category called top-level classes. Java also allows you to define a class inside a top-level class. This kind of class is called a nested class. In this context, the top-level class is also called an outer class or enclosing class.

A nested class is a member (like a variable or a method) of another class. It would look like the following:

```
class <OuterClassName> {
  // variables and methods for the outer class
  …
     class  <NestedClassName> {
        // variables and methods for the nested class
        …
        }
}
```

As you already know, a class member can be static or nonstatic. A nonstatic nested class is also called an inner class, while a static nested class is called, well, a static nested class.

■**Note** A nested class is a class that is a member of another class. A nonstatic nested class is called an inner class, and its instance has direct access to instance variables and methods of the outer class instance.

As illustrated in Figure 3-1, an instance of an inner class can only exist within an instance of its outer class and therefore it has direct access to all the instance variables and methods of the outer instance.

Figure 3-1. *The instance of an inner class has direct access to the instance variables and methods of an instance of the outer class.*

You write inner classes only when a relationship between two objects in the real problem requires it—for example, when the inner class makes sense only in the context of the outer class, or it depends upon the outer class in its functionality.

Following are the salient features of the nested classes:

- An inner class (nonstatic nested class) is associated with an instance of its outer class.

- Unlike an external class, an inner class has unlimited access to the members of the outer class, including the private members, because the inner class itself is a member of the outer class.

- Just like the static variables and methods of the outer class (also called class variables and methods), the scope of the static nested class is the outer class, and not just one instance. Therefore, just like static methods in the outer class, you cannot access directly the nonstatic variables or methods of the outer class from inside the static nested class.

- Because an inner class, being a nonstatic member, is associated only with an instance of its outer class, you cannot define a static member inside an inner class.

- An instance of an inner class can only exist within an instance of its outer class, just like any other nonstatic member of the outer class.

- Nested classes can be declared abstract or final, just like any other class and with the same meaning.

- The access modifiers, such as public, private, and protected, can be used for inner classes just like with other members of the outer class and with the same meaning. The modifiers were introduced in Chapters 1 and 2 and are discussed in detail in Chapter 4.

- Any nested class can be declared in any block of code such as a class or a method.

- A nested class declared within any block of code, such as a method, will have access to any local (including final) variables within the scope of the block.

Listing 3-5 presents an example that contains two nested classes: a static nested class MyNested and an inner class MyInner.

Listing 3-5. *TestNested.java*

```
1. class TestNested {
2.   public static void main(String[] args) {
3.     String ext = "From external class";
4.     MyTopLevel mt = new MyTopLevel();
5.     mt.createNested();
6.     MyTopLevel.MyInner inner = mt.new MyInner();
7.     inner.accessInner(ext);
8.   }
9. }
10.  class MyTopLevel{
11.    private String top = "From Top level class";
12.    MyInner minn = new MyInner();
13.    public void createNested() {
14.        minn.accessInner(top);
15.    }
16.    class MyInner {
17.        public void accessInner(String st) {
18.            System.out.println(st);
19.        }
20.    }
21.  }
```

The output from executing Listing 3-5 follows:

```
From Top level class
From external class
```

Note how an inner class is instantiated from an external class:

```
MyTopLevel mt = new MyTopLevel();
MyTopLevel.MyInner inner = mt.new MyInner();
```

First you instantiate the outer class, and then you use the new operator on its instance to instantiate the inner class. Also, you include the name of the outer class when you are declaring the object reference for the inner class. These two lines of code could also be written in the following line if MyInnerClass were not static:

```
MyTopLevel.MyInner inner = new MyTopLevel().new MyInner();
```

Also note the instantiation of the inner class from its outer class in Listing 3-5 (line 12). The corresponding instantiations of a static nested class are very similar, as demonstrated in Listing 3-6.

Listing 3-6. *TestStaticNested.java*

```
1.  class TestStaticNested {
2.      public static void main(String[] args) {
3.          String ext = "From external class";
4.          new MyTopLevel().gateToStatic();
5.          MyTopLevel.StaticNested sn = new MyTopLevel.StaticNested();
6.          sn.accessStaticNested(ext);
7.      }
8.  }
9.   class MyTopLevel{
10.      private static String top = "From top level class";
11.      public static void gateToStatic(){
12.          StaticNested s = new StaticNested();
13.           s.accessStaticNested(top);
14.      }
15.      static class StaticNested {
16.          public void accessStaticNested(String st) {
17.              System.out.println(st);
18.          }
19.      }
20.  }
```

As you learned in this section, a nested class is a member of its outer class. Java offers a special element called enum that can be used like a class, an inner class, or a data type.

Understanding Enums

As briefly discussed in Chapter 2, the data type enum, introduced in J2SE 5.0, is useful when you want a variable to hold only a predetermined set of values. You should use enums any time you need a fixed set of constants, including natural enumerated types such as days of the week. You define an enum variable in two steps:

1. Define the enum type with a set of named values.

2. Define a variable to hold one of those values.

Following is an example:

```
The enum AllowedCreditCard {VISA, MASTER_CARD, AMERICAN_EXPRESS};
```

```
AllowedCreditCard visa = AllowedCreditCard.VISA;
```

You can think of enum as an alternative to defining a regular class, or you can think of it as a special kind of class. In other words, it has differences and similarities with the regular Java class. The preceding code defines a class named AllowedCreditCard with the restriction that you can create only three instances (a regular class does not have such a restriction) of this class, corresponding to each value defined in the curly braces. However, just like a normal class, a public enum must be in a file named after the enum name. A value stored in an instance of an enum is retrieved by referring to it just like a variable, as shown in this example:

```
System.out.println("The allowed credit card value: " + visa)
```

Any enum type you declare inherits some methods that you can use.

Methods of the Enum Class

All enum types are inherently subclasses of the Java class Enum and therefore inherit its methods, some of which are listed in Table 3-1.

Table 3-1. *Some Methods of the Enum Class*

Method	Description
final boolean equals(Object obj)	Returns true if the object passed in as an argument is equal to this enum constant.
final String name()	Returns the name of this enum constant exactly as in the enum declaration.
String toString()	Returns the name of this enum constant exactly as in the enum declaration. You can override this method, but not the name() method.
static Enum valueOf(Class enumClass, String name)	Returns the enum constant of the specified enum class with the specified name.

In addition to these methods, each enum type has a static method that returns an array containing all the values of the enum type in the order in which they are declared. This method can be used in combination with the for-each loop when you want to iterate over the values of an enumerated type. The for-each loop is a loop that presents a robust way of iterating over the elements of a list. You will learn about the for-each loop in Chapter 6.

Some of the enum methods are used in this section. For example, continuing with our AllowedCreditCard example, the following line of code retrieves an array of values of the enumeration by using the values() method:

```
AllowedCreditCard[] allValues = AllowedCreditCard.values();
```

So far, you have seen a rather simple example of enum, AllowedCreditCard, which looks very similar to enumerations defined in some other languages. However, in Java, enum is a much more powerful concept. You can define an enum as a full-fledged class that contains its own methods, constructors, and fields, implements interfaces, and so on.

Constructors, Methods, and Variables in an enum

Just like a class, an enum can have constructors, methods, and variables in addition to the constants. For example, Listing 3-7 implements an enum named Quark (lines 17 through 36), which has a constructor (lines 26 through 29) that takes two arguments of types char and double. The possible values for these arguments are declared in terms of constants, such as UP and DOWN (lines 18 through 23), which will be passed when an instance of enum is constructed (line 9). This enum also has two final variables, symbol and charge (lines 24 and 25), and two methods, getSymbol() and getCharge().

Listing 3-7. *EnumTest.java*

```
1. public class EnumTest {
2.  public static void main(String[] args) {
3.      int nargs=args.length;
4.      if(nargs < 1){
5.          System.out.println("There must be an argument in the command: UP,
            DOWN, STRANGE, CHARM, TRUTH, or BEAUTY");
6.          System.out.println("Example: java EnumTest BEAUTY");
7.          System.exit(0);
```

```
8.        }else {
9.            Quark q = Enum.valueOf(Quark.class, args[0].toUpperCase());
10.            char symbol = q.getSymbol();
11.            double charge = q.getCharge();
12.            System.out.println("The electric charge for quark " + symbol +
                ": " + charge);
13.            System.out.println("The name of the quark: " + q.name());

14.      }

15.    }
16.  }

17.  enum Quark {
18.    UP('u', 2.0/3.0),
19.    DOWN('d', -1.0/3.0),
20.    CHARM('c', 2.0/3.0),
21.    STRANGE('s', -1.0/3.0),
22.    TRUTH('t', 2.0/3.0),
23.    BEAUTY('b', -1.0/3.0);

24.    private final char symbol;
25.    private final double charge;
26.    Quark(char symbol, double charge){
27.      this.symbol = symbol;
28.      this.charge = charge;
29.    }
30.    public char getSymbol(){
31.      return symbol;
32.    }
33.    public double getCharge(){
34.      return charge;
35.    }
36.  }
```

First note how the enum constants, variables, enum constructor, and the methods are declared in the enum (lines 17 through 36). The enum constants are declared first and terminated with a semicolon before declaring the variable, enum constructors, and methods. The enum Quark is instantiated and used in the class EnumTest (lines 1 through 16). Note the use of the valueOf(…) method of the Enum class, which returns the enum constant of the specified enum type (first argument) with the specified name (second argument). Another useful method of the Enum class is the name() method (line 13), which returns the name of the enum constant as a string, exactly as it is declared in its enum declaration. Here is an example of how to execute this program:

```
java EnumTest  charm
```

It generates the following output:

```
The electric charge for quark c: 0.6666666666666666
The name of the quark: CHARM
```

Although we are using the terminology of instantiating an enum, note that no new operator is used to create an instance of an enum.

Through Listing 3-7, you learned how to declare enums outside a class and then use them in the class. They can also be declared inside a class. For an example, consider Listing 3-8.

Listing 3-8. *EnumColorTest.java*

```
1. public class EnumColorTest {
2.   public static void main(String[] args) {
3.       Colors c = new Colors();
4.       c.color = Colors.ThreeColors.RED;
5.       System.out.println(c.color);
6.   }
7. }
8. class Colors {
9.     enum ThreeColors {BLUE, RED, GREEN}
10.    ThreeColors  color;
11.}
```

The output of this code follows:

RED

The point is that an enum can be declared either as its own class or inside another class just like an inner class. However, an enum cannot be declared within a method.

■**Caution** An enum cannot be declared within a method.

Listing 3-9 shows how to declare constants with arguments. These arguments are passed to the constructor automatically.

Listing 3-9. *Waist.java*

```
1.  public class Waist {
2.    WaistSize size;
3.    public static void main(String[] args) {
4.        Waist w1 = new Waist();
5.        Waist w2 = new Waist();
6.        w1.size = WaistSize.SMALL;
7.        w2.size = WaistSize.LARGE;
8.        System.out.println(w1.size + " " + w2.size);
9.          System.out.println("Small size: " + w1.size.getSize());
10.   }
11.}
12. enum WaistSize {
13.    SMALL(30), MEDIUM(34), LARGE(40);  //First define the enum constants.
14.    private int size;  //The instance variables, constructors,
                                     and methods may follow.
15.    WaistSize(int size) {
16.     this.size = size;
17.    }
18.    public int getSize() {
19.     return size;
20.    }
21.  }
```

The output of Listing 3-9 follows:

```
SMALL LARGE
Small size: 30
```

Note that at lines 6 and 7 the arguments 30 and 40 for SMALL and LARGE are passed along. That's how you get the second line of output from line 9 in the code.

Following is a summary of the important points you should remember about an enum: .

- You use the keyword enum and not class to declare an enum.

- Just like a class, an enum can have constructors, methods, and fields.

- When you compile, an enum goes into a .class file just like any other class.

- You cannot instantiate an enum with the new operator.

- The enums do not participate in class hierarchy: they cannot extend and they cannot be extended.

- You cannot directly call an enum constructor.

- An enum may have a main() method and therefore can be executed by name from the command line like an application.

- You can use an enum as a valid argument in a switch statement. You will learn about the switch statements in Chapter 6.

■Caution Unlike a class, you never invoke the constructor of an enum directly. It will be invoked automatically behind the scenes with the appropriate arguments.

As you have seen, a class can use another class (or enum) as a data type. There is another relationship that can be set up between classes, and that is called inheritance.

Inheritance

Inheritance is a fundamental feature of object-oriented programming. It enables the programmer to write a class based on an already existing class. The already existing class is called the parent class, or superclass, and the new class is called the subclass, or derived class. The subclass inherits (reuses) the nonprivate members (methods and variables) of the superclass, and may define its own members as well.

Inheritance facilitates the reuse of code and helps to adapt programming to real-world situations. For example, consider a class named ClassRoom whose members represent general properties (and behavior) of a classroom. A specific classroom may have additional members to further specify the classroom. For example, a computer lab used by a teacher for a hands-on class is a classroom. So is a lecture hall with no computers in it. Instead of writing the class ComputerLab from scratch, you can derive it from the class ClassRoom. The keyword to derive a class from another class is extends. The declaration looks like this:

```
class ComputerLab extends ClassRoom {
}
```

A full code example is presented in Listing 3-10.

Listing 3-10. *TestComputerLab.java*

```
1. class TestComputerLab {
2.  public static void main(String[] args) {
3.    ComputerLab cslab = new ComputerLab();
4.    cslab.printSeatInfo();
5.    System.out.println("Total seats in the class room:
          "+cslab.getTotalSeats());
6.   }
7. }

8. // Class ComputerLab
9.   class ComputerLab extends ClassRoom {
10.     int  totalComputers = 30;
11.     String labAssistant="TBA";
12.    void printSeatInfo() {
13.        System.out.println("There are " + getTotalSeats() + " seats, and "+
               totalComputers + "  computers in this computer lab.");
15.    }
16.    String getLabAssistant(){
17.        return labAssistant;
18.    }
19.    void setLabAssistant(String assistant){
20.        this.labAssistant = assistant;
21.    }
22. }
```

In line 9, the ComputerLab class extends the ClassRoom class. The TestComputerLab class (lines 1 to 7) is used to test the ComputerLab class, which uses an inherited method of the ClassRoom class (getTotalSeats() in line 13) and defines a couple of its own methods: getLabAssistant() and setLabAssistant(). The output from executing Listing 3-10 follows:

```
There are 60 seats, and 30 computers in this computer lab.
Total seats in the class room: 60
```

In line 4 of Listing 13-10, the method printSeatInfo() of the class ComputerLab is invoked. This method, in turn, invokes the inherited method, getTotalSeats(), in line 13. This is an example of how the inherited members can be used inside the class that inherits them: just like any other member of the class.

In line 5 of Listing 3-10, the method getTotalSeats() is invoked on an instance of the class ComputerLab. This is an example of how the inherited methods of a class are used from outside the class: just like any other method of the class.

A couple of final notes on inheritance are in order:

- A subclass inherits only nonprivate members of the superclass—that is, the members that do not have an access modifier of private. You will learn more about modifiers in Chapter 4.

- A class can inherit only from one other class and no more. This is called single inheritance.

As an example of the second point, the following code fragment is invalid and will generate a compiler error because class C attempts to inherit from two classes, B and A:

```
class C extends  B, A {
}
```

In other words, Java supports single inheritance, and not multiple inheritance. On one hand, single inheritance simplifies the programs. On the other hand, while designing a Java application, you may run into a situation where multiple inheritance is a good idea. A Java feature called an *interface* comes to your rescue in such situations. Interfaces are discussed later in this chapter. First, let's explore a special method in a class called a constructor.

Writing and Invoking Constructors

When you instantiate a class, the resulting object is stored in memory. Two elements are involved in allocating and initializing memory for an object in Java: the new operator, and a special method called a constructor. The constructor of a class has the same name as the class and has no explicit return type. When the Java runtime system encounters a statement with the new operator, it allocates memory for that instance. Subsequently, it executes the constructor to initialize the memory. For example, consider the following line of code:

```
ComputerLab csLab = new ComputerLab();
```

This statement includes the operator new and a special method ComputerLab(), which has the same name as the class ComputerLab. This special method is called a constructor, the default no-argument constructor of a class. When the Java runtime system encounters this statement, it does the following, and in this order:

1. Allocates memory for an instance of class ComputerLab

2. Initializes the instance variables of class ComputerLab

3. Executes the constructor ComputerLab()

Did you notice that there is no constructor ComputerLab() in the class ComputerLab defined in Listing 3-10 If a class does not have any constructor defined, the compiler provides the constructor with no parameters, called the default constructor. If a class has at least one constructor defined, the compiler does not provide the default constructor.

■**Caution** If you do not provide any constructor for a class you write, the compiler provides the default constructor for that class. If you write at least one constructor for the class, the compiler does not provide a constructor.

In addition to the constructor (with no parameters), you can also define nondefault constructors with parameters. However, the constructor name stays the same: the class name. The constructor may be called from inside the class where it is defined or from outside the class, using the following rules:

- Outside of the class in which a constructor is defined, the constructor can be called only with the new operator, that is, when you want to create an instance of the class. For example, a code expression new A() in the class B will create an instance of the class A.

- Inside the class where a constructor is defined, the constructor can be called from within another constructor, and not from anywhere else.

From inside a constructor of a class, you can call another constructor of the same class, or a constructor of the superclass. You use the keyword this to call another constructor in the same class, and use the keyword super to call a constructor in the superclass. If you use either this or super, it must appear in the beginning of the code block of the constructor.

If you add your own super or this call, then the compiler will not add the line super(). With regard to including super or this in the constructor, three possible cases exist:

- If you include neither a super call nor a this call, the compiler places a super call in the beginning of the constructor's body.

- If you include a super call with or without arguments, the compiler adds no super call to the code.

- If you include this to make a call to another constructor in the same class, the other constructor would have either an explicit this call in the beginning of the code block or an explicit or implicit (added by the compiler) super call. If the other constructor had a this call, then at the end of this chain, a super call would be made eventually.

The preceding discussion shows that before executing the body of a constructor in a class that is being instantiated, a constructor in the superclass must be executed. In other words, the superclass is initialized before executing the body of the constructor in the class that is being instantiated. This would make sure that the instance variables of both the current class and the superclass are initialized before the constructor body is executed.

■**Note** If you don't make a this or super call in the beginning of a constructor, the compiler places a super call there.

To illustrate some of these points, consider Listing 3-11.

Listing 3-11. *TestConstructors.java*

```
1.   class TestConstructors {
2.       public static void main(String[] args) {
3.           new MySubSubClass();
4.       }
5.
6.   }
7. // Class MySuperClass
8.   class MySuperClass {
9.       int superVar = 10;
10.      MySuperClass(){
11.      System.out.println("superVar: " + superVar);
12.      }
13.      MySuperClass(String message) {
14.        System.out.println(message + ": " + superVar);
15.      }
16.  }
17.  // Class MySubClass inherits from MySuperClass
18.    class MySubClass extends MySuperClass {
19.        int subVar = 20;
20.      MySubClass() {
21.         super("non default super called");
22.         System.out.println("subVar: " + subVar);
23.      }
24.    }
25.  // Class MySubSubClass inherits from MySubClass
26.    class MySubSubClass extends MySubClass {
27.       int subSubVar = 30;
28.      MySubSubClass() {
29.        this("A non-deafult constructor of MySubSubClass");
30.        System.out.println("subSubVar: " + subSubVar);
```

```
31.            }
32.            MySubSubClass(String message){
33.                System.out.println(message);
34.            }
35.        }
```

In Listing 3-11, the class MySubSubClass (line 26) extends MySubClass (line 18), which in turn extends MySuperClass (line 8). The class MySubSubClass is instantiated (line 3) in the class TestConstructors (line 1). If you compile and execute this code, you receive the following output:

```
non default super called:10
subVar: 20
A non default constructor of MySubSubClass
subSubVar: 30
```

Now, let's see what happened to generate this output. As a result of executing line 3, the MySubSubClass() constructor (line 28) was called, which in turn called the MySubSubClass(String message) constructor (line 32) due to the this call (line 29). Because the MySubSubClass(String message) constructor had no this or super call in the beginning of its body, the compiler placed a super() call there. As a result, this constructor first calls the MySubClass() constructor (line 20), which, due to a super call (line 21), calls the MySuperClass(String message) constructor, which in turn produces the first line of output. After that, the execution control returns to line 22, which generates the second line of the output. Subsequently, lines 33 and 30 are executed, generating the third and fourth lines of the output, respectively. .

It is important to understand the flow of execution control from constructor to constructor when a class is instantiated. There is another very interesting scenario to consider. Assume that you write a superclass only with a constructor with parameters (therefore, the compiler will not provide the default constructor). Now, if a constructor in the subclass of this superclass makes the super() call, it will generate a compiler error, because the default constructor of the superclass does not exist. For example, consider the following code fragment:

```
class A {
    int myNumber;
  A(int i) {
    myNumber =  i;
  }
}
class B extends A {
    String myName;
  B (String name) {
    myName = name;
  }
}
```

This code will generate a compiler error, and here is why. The compiler will add the super() call in the beginning of the code body of the constructor B(String name) of class B. This would be a call to the default constructor of class A. However, the compiler did not create the default constructor for A because A already had a nondefault constructor. Therefore, the compiler will generate an error. One way to fix this problem is to add a default constructor to class A manually.

The key points about constructors are summarized here:

- A constructor of a class has the same name as the class, and has no explicit return type.

- A class may have more than one constructor. If the programmer defines no constructor in a class, the compiler will add the default constructor with no arguments. If there are one or more constructors defined in the class, the compiler will not provide any constructor.

- A constructor may have zero or more parameters.

- From outside the class, a constructor is always called with the new operator. From inside the class, it may be called from another constructor with the this or super operator—this to call another constructor of the same class, super to call a constructor of the superclass. The super or this call is always made in the beginning of the constructor body.

- Unlike other methods, the constructors are not inherited. If the superclass has constructors and the subclass does not, the compiler assumes that the subclass does not have any constructor and creates the default constructor.

- If there is no super call in a constructor, the default super call is placed by the compiler, that is, a call to the default constructor of the superclass.

A key point to remember here is that before the variables of a class are initialized, the variables of its parent class must be initialized, and this is accomplished by a chain of constructor calls. As you already know by now, a class can inherit only from one class, but it can inherit from more than one interface.

Writing and Using Interfaces

Java supports single inheritance. That means a subclass in Java can have only one superclass. However, if multiple inheritance is needed, Java provides a solution: use an interface. While a subclass can inherit only from one superclass, it can also inherit from one or more interfaces in addition to the superclass. An interface is a template that contains some method declarations. The interface provides only declarations for the methods, and no implementation. The class that inherits from an interface must provide the implementation for the methods declared in the interface.

Note An interface contains method declarations, and a class that implements the interface must provide implementation for its methods.

You define an interface by using the keyword interface, as shown in the following:

```
interface <InterfaceName> {
<dataType1> <var1>;
<dataType2> <var2>;
<ReturnType1> <methodName1> ( );
<ReturnType2> <methodName2>(<parameters>);
} // interface definition ends here.
```

The methods declared in an interface are implicitly public and abstract. Therefore, when you implement them in a class, you must declare them public. The data variables declared in an interface are inherently constants and are visible from all the instances of the class that implements the interface. In other words, they are inherently public, final, and static.

Caution When you implement a method of an interface, you must declare it public in your class, because all the interface methods are implicitly public. The data variables in an interface are inherently public, final, and static.

There are a few more features of interfaces related to inheritance and implementation:

- A class can extend (inherit from) another class (only one) by using the keyword extends, but it can inherit from one or more interfaces by using the keyword implements.

- Just like a class, an interface can also extend one or more interfaces by using the keyword extends.

- An interface cannot implement any interface or class.

Listing 3-12 demonstrates some of the interface features discussed in this section.

Listing 3-12. *TestInterface.java*

```
1.  interface ParentOne {
2.    int pOne = 1;
3.    void printParentOne();
4.  }
5.  interface ParentTwo {
6.    int pTwo = 2;
7.    void printParentTwo();
8.  }
9.  interface Child extends ParentOne, ParentTwo{
10.        int child = 3;
11.        void printChild();
12. }
13.
14. class InheritClass implements Child {
15.     public void printParentOne(){
16.         System.out.println(pOne);
17.     }
18.     public void printParentTwo(){
19.         System.out.println(pTwo);
20.     }
21.     public void printChild(){
22.         System.out.println(child);
23.     }
24. }
25.  class TestInterface {
26.     public static void main(String[] args){
27.         InheritClass ic = new InheritClass();
28.         ic.printParentOne();
29.         ic.printParentTwo();
30.         ic.printChild();
31.     }
32.  }
```

The following is the output from this code:

```
1
2
3
```

Note how the Child interface extends two interfaces, ParentOne and ParentTwo (line 9):

```
interface Child extends ParentOne, ParentTwo {}
```

If class A extends another class, B, and implements an interface, C, the syntax will be

```
class  A extends B implements C {}
```

Note that extends must come before implements. Also note that the methods declared in the interfaces are declared public in the class InheritClass in which they are implemented (lines 15, 18, and 21). If you remove the keyword public from any of these methods, the code will not compile. If you, for example, prepend the method declaration for printParentOne (line 3) with the modifier protected or private, the code will not compile, either. However, if you prepend the declaration with the modifier public, the code will compile; but you don't need to do that because a method declared in an interface is inherently public.

The important points about interfaces are summarized here:

- An interface must be declared with the keyword interface.

- All interface variables are inherently public, static, and final.

- All interface methods are inherently public and abstract. This means they must be implemented in the class that implements the interface and declared public in there. That is, all the interface methods must be implemented by the class that implements the interface unless the class is abstract.

- Because interface methods are inherently abstract, they cannot be declared final, native, strictfp, or synchronized.

- A class can extend another class and implement one or more interfaces at the same time.

- An interface can extend one or more interfaces. An interface cannot extend a class, just another interface.

- An interface cannot implement another interface or class.

■**Caution** A class can extend another class by using the keyword extends, implement one or more interfaces by using the keyword implements, or do both. An interface can extend another interface but cannot implement it. Also, an interface cannot implement any class.

Table 3-2 shows some legal and illegal cases for the use of extends and implements.

Table 3-2. *Examples of Legal and Illegal Use of extends and implements for Classes C1 and C2 and Interfaces I1 and I2*

Example	Legal?	Reason
class C1 extends C2 { }	Yes	A class can extend another class.
interface I1 extends I2 { }	Yes	An interface can extend another interface.
class C1 implements I1 { }	Yes	A class can implement an interface.
class C1 implements I1, I2 { }	Yes	A class can implement multiple interfaces.
class C1 extends I1 { }	No	A class cannot extend an interface; it has to implement it.
class C1 extends C2, C3 { }	No	A class cannot extend multiple classes.
interface I1 implements I2 { }	No	An interface cannot implement another interface.
interface I1 extends I2 { }	Yes	An interface can extend an interface.

Example	Legal?	Reason
`interface I1 extends I2, I3 { }`	Yes	An interface can extend multiple interfaces.
`interface I1 extends C1 { }`	No	An interface cannot extend a class.
`interface I1 implements C1 { }`	No	An interface cannot implement a class.
`class C1 extends C2 implements I1 { }`	Yes	A class can extend one other class and implement one or more interfaces.
`class C1 implements I1 extends C2 { }`	No	`extends` must come before `implements`.

So, a class can inherit from one or more interfaces in addition to inheriting only from one class, and an interface can also inherit from one or more interfaces. However, an interface cannot implement anything: neither a class nor another interface.

Codewalk Quicklet

The code for the codewalk quicklet exercise in this chapter is presented in Listing 3-13.

Listing 3-13. *CodeWalkTwo.java*

```
1. class CodeWalkTwo{
2.     int x = 3;
3.     static int y = 3;
4.     public static void main(String [] args) {
5.         int x = 10;
6.         int y = 10;
7.         CodeWalkTwo boardWalk = new CodeWalkTwo();
8.         boardWalk.printIt();
9.         boardWalk.printIt(y);
10.    }
11.        { x = x+1; }
12.        static { y += y;}
13.    void printIt() {
14.        System.out.print(++x);
15.    }
16.    void printIt(int y) {
17.        System.out.print(" " + ++y);
18.    }
19. }
```

To get you started on this exercise, following are some hints:

- *Input*: Lines 2, 3, 5, and 6
- *Operations*: Lines 11, 12, 14, and 17
- *Output*: Lines 14 and 17
- *Rules*: Behavior of static and instance variables

Looking at the code from this angle, see if you can handle the last question in the "Review Questions" section based on this code.

The three most important takeaways from this chapter are the following:

- A Java program consists of classes, and a class usually consists of methods and variables, but it can also contain another class, called a nested class.

- The methods in a class can be static or nonstatic, and a static method can only access the static members of the class.

- A class can extend only one class, but it can implement one or more interfaces in addition to extending one class. An interface can extend one or more interfaces, but it cannot implement any interface or class.

Summary

A Java program consists of classes, and a class consists of variables, methods, and possibly one or more other classes and nested classes. A class is a template out of which you can create objects. A method contains variables, operations on variables, and the logic for the operations. Whereas a nonstatic method belongs to a particular object of the class (that is, each object has its own copy of the method), a static method belongs to the class (that is, it is shared by all the objects of the class). For this reason, a static method cannot access the nonstatic members (variables and methods) of the class.

An interface is a template that contains only variables and method declarations. The variables of an interface are inherently `public`, `final`, and `static`, while the methods in an interface are inherently `public` and `abstract`. Because the methods in an interface are inherently `abstract`, any class that implements the interface must provide implementation for all the interface methods, if the class itself is not `abstract`.

By now, you may be wondering about the other modifiers that have not been discussed yet, and what the rules are to put together a number of classes into a program, compile the program, and execute it. You will find answers in the next chapter, which explores the fundamentals of the Java language.

EXAM'S EYE VIEW

Comprehend

- The method name and return type are mandatory in a method declaration. Even though you are not required to specify a modifier in a method declaration, the default modifier is assigned to the method, if you don't declare one.

- A static variable belongs to the class and not to a particular instance of the class, and therefore is initialized when the class is loaded, and before the class is instantiated.

- Because a static method belongs to a class and not to a particular instance of the class, it cannot access the nonstatic methods and variables of the class in which it is defined.

- An instance of an inner class can only exist in an instance of the outer class, and has direct access to all the instance variables and methods of the outer instance.

- If you make a `super` call or a `this` call, it must be in the beginning of a constructor. That means you can make either a `super` call or a `this` call, but not both.

Look Out

- The variable-length parameters list must appear last in the parentheses of a method and it consists of a data type, three dots, and a name, in that order.

- A Java class cannot inherit from more than one class, but it can inherit from one class and one or more interfaces.

- The class that inherits from an interface must provide implementation for all the methods that are declared in the interface if the class is not `abstract`.

- An interface can extend another interface but it cannot implement another interface or a class.

Memorize

- If you do not provide any constructor for a class you write, the compiler provides the default constructor for that class. If you write at least one constructor for the class, the compiler provides no constructor.

- If you do not make a `this` or a `super` call in the beginning of a constructor, the compiler places a `super()` call there.

- You use the keyword `extends` to write a derived class that inherits from a parent class, and use the keyword `implements` to write a class that inherits from an interface.

- The methods in an interface are inherently `public` and `abstract`, and the variables in the interface are inherently `public`, `final`, and `static`.

Review Questions

1. Consider the following code:

```
1. class MyClass {
2.  String hello = "Hello, Dear.";
3.   void printMessage() {
4.     System.out.println(hello);
5.   }
6. }
7.  class TestMyClass {
8.      public static void main(String[] args) {
9.        MyClass mc = new MyClass();
10.        mc.printMessage();
11.      }
12.    }
```

What is the output of this code? (Choose one.)

A. A compiler error occurs at line 9 because no such method (constructor) for class MyClass has been declared.

B. A runtime exception occurs at line 4.

C. The code compiles and executes fine, and the output is Hello, Dear.

D. The code compiles and executes fine, and there is no output.

2. Consider the following code:

```
public class MyOuterClass {
    public static class MyNestedClass {
    }
}
```

Which of the following is a correct statement to instantiate MyNestedClass from a class outside of MyOuterClass? (Choose all that apply.)

A. MyNestedClass mn = new MyOuterClass.MyNestedClass();

B. MyOuterClass.MyNestedClass mn = new MyOuterClass.MyNestedClass();

C. MyOuterClass.MyNestedClass mn = new MyNestedClass();

D. MyOuterClass mo = new MyOuterClass();
   MyOuterClass.MyNestedClass mn = mo.new MyNestedClass();

3. Consider the following code:

```
1.  class A {
2.      A(String message) {
3.          System.out.println(message + " from A.");
4.      }
5.  }
6.    class B extends A{
7.        B() {
8.              System.out.println("Hello from B.");
9.        }
10. }
11. class RunSubClass {
12.    public static void main(String[] args) {
13.        B b = new B();
14.    }
15. }
```

What is the output of this code?

A. Hello from B.

B. A compiler error occurs at line 2.

C. A compiler error is triggered by the call made at line 13.

D. It compiles fine but throws a runtime exception.

4. Which of the following is true about an interface? (Choose all that apply.)

A. You can declare a method with the private modifier in an interface.

B. You must use the public modifier while declaring a method in an interface.

C. You can declare variables inside an interface, and change their values in a class that implements the interface.

D. You can declare variables inside an interface, but you cannot change their values in a class that implements the interface.

E. You cannot declare a variable inside an interface.

5. Consider the following code:

```
1. class MyClass {
2.   int i = 5;
3.   static int j = 7;
4.   public static void printSomething () {
5.     System.out.println("i: " + i);
6.     System.out.println("j: " + j);
7. }
8. }
```

What is the result if the printSomething() method of MyClass is called from another class?

A. i: 5

   j: 7

B. A compiler error occurs at line 5.

C. A compiler error occurs at line 6.

D. A runtime exception is thrown.

6. Consider the following class definition:

```
public class SubClass extends SuperClass {
public    SubClass ( int i){
}
public    SubClass(int i,  int j) {
    super(i, j);
}
public SubClass (int i, int j, int k) {
}}
```

Which of the following forms of constructors must exist in the SuperClass? (Choose all that apply.)

A. SuperClass(int i) {}

B. SuperClass(int i, int j) {}

C. SuperClass() {}

D. SuperClass(int i, int j, int k) {}

7. Consider the following class definition:

```
1.  class MyClass {
2.  MyClass (int i ) {
3.  }
4.  void printTheThing(String message) {
5.    System.out.println(message);
6.  }
7.  }
8. class Test {
9. public static void main(String[]  args) {
10.    MyClass myClass = new MyClass ( );
11.    myClass.printTheThing("Hello, I did not crash!");
12. }
13. }
```

Which of the following is a true statement about this code?

A. A compiler error occurs at line 10.

B. A compiler error occurs at line 2.

C. The code compiles but generates a runtime exception.

D. The code compiles and runs fine and produces the output Hello, I did not crash!.

8. Consider the following code fragment:

```
class SuperClass {
  SuperClass(){}
  SuperClass(int i) {
    System.out.println ("The value of i is " + i);
  }
}
  class SubClass extends SuperClass {
    SubClass(int j) {
      System.out.println ("The value of j is " + j );
      super(j);
    }
  }
```

```
class Test {
 public static void main(String args[]) {
    SubClass sub = new SubClass(5);
 }
}
```

What output is generated when the class Test is run?

A. The value of i is 5.

B. The value of j is 5.

C. The value of i is 5 The value of J is 5.

D. A compiler error occurs.

E. An exception is thrown at execution time.

9. Which of the following are true statements? (Choose all that apply.)

A. A class can inherit from more than one class by using the keyword extends.

B. An interface can inherit from more than one interface by using the keyword extends.

C. A class can inherit from more than one interface by using the keyword extends.

D. A class can inherit from more than one interface by using the keyword implements.

10. Which of the following are illegal enum definitions?

A. enum Day {Sunday, Monday, Tuesday}

B. enum Day {Sunday, Monday, Tuesday,
       private String holiday;
    }

C. enum Day {Sunday, Monday, Tuesday;
       private String holiday;
    }

D. enum Day {private String holiday;
            Sunday, Monday, Tuesday;

    }

E. enum Day {Sunday, Monday, Tuesday;
        private String holiday;
        Day(){
           System.out.println("Hello");
        }
    }

11. Consider Listing 3-13. What is the output?

A. 5 11

B. 11 11

C. 5 5

D. Compilation fails at line 17.

E. Compilation fails at lines 5 and 6.

■■■

Java Language Fundamentals

Exam Objectives

1.1 Develop code that declares classes (including abstract and all forms of nested classes), interfaces, and enums, and includes the appropriate use of package and import statements (including static imports).

7.1 Given a code example and a scenario, write code that uses the appropriate access modifiers, package declarations, and import statements to interact with (through access or inheritance) the code in the example.

5.3 Explain the effect of modifiers on inheritance with respect to constructors, instance or static variables, and instance or static methods.

7.2 Given an example of a class and a command-line, determine the expected runtime behavior.

7.3 Determine the effect upon object references and primitive values when they are passed into methods that perform assignments or other modifying operations on the parameters.

7.4 Given a code example, recognize the point at which an object becomes eligible for garbage collection, and determine what is and is not guaranteed by the garbage collection system. Recognize the behaviors of System.gc and finalization.

7.5 Given the fully-qualified name of a class that is deployed inside and/or outside a JAR file, construct the appropriate directory structure for that class. Given a code example and a classpath, determine whether the classpath will allow the code to compile successfully.

In the previous chapter, you learned about classes, methods, and interfaces. In this chapter, we explore various aspects of a class and its members (variables and methods). You will learn how to organize your classes into an application. You will also learn what can happen to variables when you pass them as arguments in a method call. Another important issue covered in this chapter is from where in the application you can access a class or its members. This depends upon the access modifiers assigned to a class or its members. Modifiers modify (further specify) the behavior of a class or its members, and you can specify them when you write the code. Finally, you'll learn how memory management is performed in Java. You instantiate a class into an object, and the object occupies some memory. You can free the memory from the object when you no longer need it, which is called garbage collection in Java.

So, the core issue in this chapter is nothing other than the fundamentals of the Java language. To enable you to put your arms around this issue, we explore three avenues: organizing your Java application, modifiers, and garbage collection.

Organizing Your Java Application

A Java application is composed of a set of files generally distributed in a directory structure. This set of files may comprise groups of files, called packages, based on their functionalities. Here are some bare-bones facts about these files:

- The files that contain the original source code are called source files and have the extension .java. All the code goes into classes, which are defined inside the .java files.

- When you compile a .java file, it produces a .class file corresponding to each class declared (defined) in the .java file, including nested classes and interfaces.

- The .class file has the same name as the class in the .java file to which it corresponds.

- The compiler searches for a class file when it encounters a reference to a class in a .java file. Similarly, the interpreter, during runtime, searches the .class files.

- Both the compiler and the interpreter search for the .class files in the list of directories listed in the classpath variable.

In order to compile and execute an application correctly, you need to understand the relationship between the class name, classpath, and package name and how these three elements determine the directory structure in which you are supposed to store the .class files.

We cover all of these concepts in this section. Let's begin by identifying the point in your application where the execution starts.

Entering Through the Main Gate

When you issue a command to execute a Java application, the Java virtual machine (JVM) loads the class mentioned in the command, and invokes the main(…) method of this class. In other words, the main(…) method of a class in a Java application is the starting point for the execution control. You write the application by writing the Java source (.java) files. A source file may contain interfaces or classes. One of the classes in the application must have the main(…) method with the signature:

```
public static void main (String[] args) {
}
```

The method main(…) must be declared public, static, and void. These keywords are explained here:

- public: The method can be accessed from the code outside the class in which it is defined (remember, it is invoked by the JVM, which exists outside the class in which it is defined).

- static: The method can be accessed without instantiating the class in which it is declared. Again, this keyword also allows the JVM to invoke this method without instantiating the class.

- void: The method does not return any data.

A source file may have one or more classes defined in it. Out of these classes, only one class at most may be declared public. If there is one class declared public in the file, then the file name must match the name of this public class. When the source file is compiled, it generates one class file (a file with the .class extension) corresponding to each class in the source file. The name of the generated class file matches the name of the corresponding class in the source file.

The parameter of type array in the main(…) method indicates that you can pass arguments to this method. You provide those arguments in the command line when you execute the application by specifying the class that contains the main(…) method. For example, consider Listing 4-1.

Listing 4-1. *TestArgs.java*

```
1. public class TestArgs {
2.  public static void main (String [] args) {
3.    System.out.println("Length of arguments array: " + args.length);
4.    System.out.println("The first argument: " + args[0]);
5.    System.out.println("The second argument: " + args[1]);
6.  }
7. }
```

You can compile this code by issuing the following command from the command line:

```
javac TestArgs.java
```

This generates a file called TestArgs.class. You can execute this program and pass in the arguments for the main(...) method. For example, you could issue the following command:

```
java  TestArgs  Ruth Srilatha
```

The output of execution follows:

```
Length of arguments array: 2
The first argument: Ruth
The second argument: Srilatha
```

■**Note** In the javac command, you include the file extension .java in the name of the file that you want to compile. However, you do not use any file extension when issuing the execution command, java.

If you do not provide all the arguments in the command line that the main(...) method is expecting, you receive a runtime exception. Note the following two facts regarding the arguments of the main(...) method:

- The length of the arguments array is not fixed. It becomes equal to the number of arguments that you pass.

- The parameter name in the main(...) method does not have to be args; it could be any valid variable name. However, its type must be a String array.

Important points about the names are summed up here:

- A .java file name should match the name of a class in the file. If one of those classes is declared public, then the name of the .java file must match the name of the public class.

- There can be only one public class at maximum in a source file.

- The compiler generates a file with extension .class corresponding to each class in the source file that is compiled.

- The name of the .class file matches the name of the corresponding class.

■**Caution** The name of a .java file must match the name of a class in the file. If the file has a public class, the file name must match the name of the public class.

And there is more to names.

What Is in a Name?

A beginner in Java usually runs into compiler and execution errors related to finding the classes. These errors arise due to the confusion about the namespace. So, if it happens to you, rest assured that you are not the only one. The package name, the class name, and the classpath variable are the three players that you must be familiar with to avoid any confusion in the namespace area.

You know from the previous section that the .class file name matches the name of the class. You can bundle related classes and interfaces into a group called a package. You store all the class files related to a package in a directory whose name matches the name of the package. How do you specify to which package a class belongs? You specify it in the source file in which you write the class by using the keyword package. There will be at most one package statement in a .java file. For example, consider a class Student defined in a file, as shown in Figure 4-1.

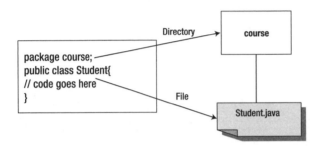

Figure 4-1. *The Student class is specified to be in the package course.*

The file name of the file in which the class Student exists will be Student.java, which will exist inside a directory named course, which may exist anywhere on the file system. The qualified name for the class is course.Student, and the path name to it is course/Student.java.

You can use this class in the code by specifying its qualified name, as in this example:

```
course.Student student1 = new course.Student();
```

However, it is not convenient to use the qualified name of a class over and over again. The solution to this problem is to import the package in which the class exists, and use the simple name for the class, as shown here:

```
import course.Student;
```

You place the import statement in the file that defines the class in which you are going to use the Student class. The import statement must follow any package statement and must precede the first class defined in the file. After you have imported the package this way, you can use the Student class by its simple name:

```
Student student1 = new Student();
```

You can import all the classes in the package by using the wildcard character *:

```
import  course.*;
```

However, you cannot use the wildcard character in specifying the names of the classes. For example, the following statement to refer to the class Student will generate a compiler error:

```
import course.Stud*;
```

You can have more than one import statement in a .java file. Bundling related classes and interfaces into a package offers the following advantages:

- It makes it easier to find and use classes.

- It avoids naming conflicts. Two classes with the same name existing in two different packages do not have a name conflict, as long as they are referenced by their fully qualified name.

- It provides access control. You will learn more about access control when access modifiers are discussed later in this chapter.

So, the files in a directory may be composed into a package by the declaration with keyword package:

```
package  <PackageName>;
```

Then you may use this package in another file by the statement with keyword import:

```
import <PackageName>;
```

In a file, package declaration must precede the import statement, which must precede the class definition. For example, the .java file with the following code will not compile because the import statement appears before the package statement:

```
import otherPackage;
package thisPackage;
class A { }
```

Caution In a Java file, the package declaration, the import statement, and the class definition must appear in this order.

You need to manage your source and class files in such a way that the compiler and the interpreter can find all the classes and interfaces that your program uses. Companies usually follow the convention of stating the package names with the reversed domain name. For example, the full package name of course in a fictitious company netalong.com will be com.netalong.course. Each component of a package name corresponds to a directory. In our example, the directory com contains the directory netalong, which in turn contains the directory course, and the Student file is in the course directory. This relationship is shown in Figure 4-2.

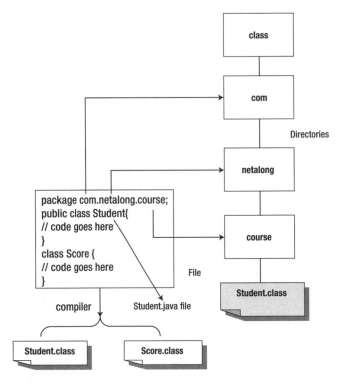

Figure 4-2. *Relationship between a package name and the corresponding directory structure*

The directory structure corresponding to the package name goes into a directory called the top-level directory. We assume in this example that the com directory is in the class directory. When you compile the source file Student.java, it will produce two class files, named Student.class and Score.class. It's a good practice to keep the class files separate from the source files. Let's assume that we put the class files in the class/com/netalong/course directory, and that the source and the class directories exist in the C:\app directory on a Microsoft Windows machine. So, the top-level directory for our package is

```
c:\app\class
```

When the compiler encounters a class name in your code, it must be able to find the class. In fact, both the compiler and the interpreter must be able to find the classes. As said earlier, they look for classes in each directory or a JAR (Java Archive) file listed in the classpath: an environment variable that you defined after installing JDK. In our example, the classpath must include this path name:

```
c:\app\class
```

■**Note** A classpath is an environment variable whose value is a list of directories or JAR files in which the compiler and the interpreter searches for the class files. Following is an example of a classpath:

```
c:\jdk1.5.0_01; c:\jdk1.5.0_01\bin; c:\myclasses
```

Note that the directories are separated by a semicolon (;).

So, each directory listed in the classpath is a top-level directory that contains the package directories. The compiler and interpreter will construct the full path of a class by appending the package name to the top-level directory name (in the classpath) followed by the class name, as shown in Figure 4-3.

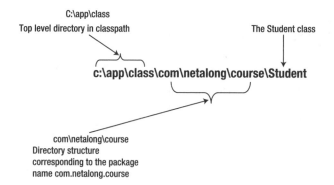

Figure 4-3. *This is how the compiler and the interpreter construct a full path name for a class mentioned with the name Student in a code file that imports the package com.netalong.course.*

The .java files and .class files live in directories. All the directories of an application can be compressed into what is called a JAR file.

The JAR Files

When the compiler (or the interpreter) encounters a class name in your code, it looks for that class in each directory or a JAR (Java Archive) file listed in the classpath. You can think of a JAR file as a tree of directories. Using the JAR facility of Java, the whole application (a number of source files and class files in a number of folders) can be compressed into one file, the JAR file. The file extension of a JAR file is .jar, and can be created with the jar command. For example, consider the following command:

```
jar  cf  myApp.jar topDir
```

This command will compress the whole directory tree (along with files in the directories) with topDir as the root directory into one file named myApp.jar. You can look at the list of directories and files in this JAR file by issuing the following command:

```
jar  -tf  myApp.jar
```

You can even execute your application contained in the JAR file by issuing the following command:

```
java  -jar   myApp.jar
```

When you specify the path to a JAR file, you must include the JAR file name at the end of the path, such as the following:

```
c:\jdk1.5.0\jre\lib\charsets.jar
```

■**Caution** To make the `java -jar` command work, you need to specify which class contains the `main(…)` method by adding an entry like the following to the `MANIFEST.MF` file:

```
Main-Class: MyClass
```

In this entry, `MyClass` is the name of the class (and also the name of a `.class` file) that contains the `main(…)` method.

To the contrary, when you mention a directory name in a path, all the files in the directory will automatically be included in the path. By including a JAR file in the `classpath`, you can use the classes in it that may be referred to by another application. Another way of including the external classes in your application is by importing them, as discussed earlier in the chapter. J2SE 5.0 introduces a special kind of import called *static import.*

The Static Import

Assume that you have imported a package that contains a class, A. If you want to use a `static` member of that class, say a variable `v`, you need to refer to it as `A.v`. The *static import* feature introduced in J2SE 5.0 lets you import the `static` variables of a class so that you can refer to them without having to mention the class—that is, just as `v` instead of as `A.v` in our example.

As an example, consider Listing 4-2 without static import and Listing 4-3 with static import. Lines 3 and 4 of Listing 4-2 refer to `PI` and `E`, two `static` fields of the class `Math`, as `Math.PI` and `Math.E`. If you exclude the word `Math`, you will get a compiler error. Remember that the class `Math` is in the `java.lang` package, which is automatically imported when you compile your application.

Listing 4-2 imports the `static` members `PI` and `E` of the `Math` class in the `java.lang` package (lines 1 and 2). Now, you can use the imported `static` members without qualifying them with the class name (lines 5 and 6).

Listing 4-2. *NoStaticImport.java*

```
1. class NoStaticImport{
2.   public static void main(String[] args) {
3.     System.out.println("Pi:" + Math.PI);
4.     System.out.println("E:" + Math.E);
5.   }
6. }
```

Listing 4-3. *StaticImportTest.java*

```
1. import static java.lang.Math.PI;
2. import static java.lang.Math.E;
3. class StaticImportTest{
4.   public static void main(String[] args) {
5.     System.out.println("Pi:" + PI);
6.     System.out.println("E:" + E);
7.   }
8. }
```

The output from both Listing 4-2 and Listing 4-3 is the same:

```
Pi:3.141592653589793
E:2.718281828459045
```

Remember that you can use the static import feature for the classes that you write, as well, without inheriting them from those classes. Note that the static import declaration is very similar to the normal import declaration. A normal import declaration imports classes from a package, enabling you to use a class without package qualification (that is, without referring to the package name in the code), whereas a static import declaration imports static members from a class, enabling you to use the static members without class qualification (that is, without referring to the class name in the code).

Remember the following while using the static import feature:

- It is an import statement: import comes before static, even though the name of the feature is static import.

- You can use the wildcard * to import all the static members of a class just as you can use it to import all the classes of a package.

- You can use static import to import static variables, static object references, and static methods.

So, a Java application is a collection of packages, which in turn are collections of classes. The classes are composed of data and methods that operate on data using some logic. One of the ways to pass data to a method is through its arguments.

Passing Arguments into Methods

You learned in Chapter 3 that a method declaration may have parameters defined in the parentheses following the method name. The values of these parameters are called *arguments* and can be passed during a method call. These parameters may be either primitive variables or reference variables. Assume you declare a variable in your method, and then you pass that variable as an argument in a method call. The question is: What kind of effect can the called method have on the variable in your method?

The key point to remember is that regardless of whether the passed variable is a primitive or a reference variable, it is always the copy of the variable, and not the original variable itself. Technically speaking, it is pass-by-value and not pass-by-reference within the same virtual machine.

Passing a Primitive Variable

Recall that a primitive variable holds a data item as its value. When a primitive variable is passed as an argument in a method call, only the copy of the original variable is passed. Therefore any change to the passed variable in the called method will not affect the variable in the calling method.

As an example, consider Listing 4-4. An integer variable score is defined in the main(…) method (line 3) and is passed as an argument in a method call to the modifyStudent(…) method (line 5). The value of the passed variable is changed in the called method (line 9).

Listing 4-4. *Student.java*

```
1. class Student {
2. public static void main (String [] args) {
3.   int score = 75;
4.   Student st = new Student();
```

```
5.    st.modifyStudent(score);
6.    System.out.println("The original student score: " + score);
7.  }
8.  void modifyStudent(int i){
9.     i = i+10;
10.    System.out.println("The modified student score: " + i);
11. }
12.}
```

The output from the execution of Listing 4-4 follows:

```
The modifed student score: 85
The original student score: 75
```

This demonstrates that the change in value of the passed variable in the called method did not affect the value of the original variable in the calling method. What if we pass a reference variable as an argument in a method call?

Passing a Reference Variable

Recall that an object reference variable points to an object, and it is not the object itself. When you pass a reference variable in a method, you pass a copy of it and not the original reference variable. Because the copy of the reference variable points to the same object to which the original variable points, the called method can change the object properties by using the passed reference. Now, changing the object and the reference to the object are two different things, so note the following:

- The original object can be changed in the called method by using the passed reference to the object.

- However, if the passed reference itself is changed in the called method, for example, set to null or reassigned to another object, it has no effect on the original reference variable in the calling method. After all, it was a copy of the original variable that was passed in.

As an example, consider Listing 4-5.

Listing 4-5. *TestRefVar.java*

```
1.   class TestRefVar {
2.    public static void main (String [] args) {
3.      Student st = new Student("John", 100);
4.      System.out.println("The original student info:");
5.      System.out.println("name: " + st.getName() + " score: " +
6.      st.getScore());
7.      TestRefVar tr = new TestRefVar();
8.      tr.modifyRef(st);
9.      System.out.println("The modified student info in the calling method:");
10.        System.out.println("name: " + st.getName() + " score: " + st.getScore());
11. }
12. void modifyRef(Student student){
13.        student.setScore(50);
14.        student = new Student("Mary", 75);
15.        System.out.println("The modified student info in the called method:");
16.        System.out.println("name: " + student.getName() + " score: " +
                  student.getScore());
17. }
18. }
```

```
19. class Student {
20.  int score;
21.  String name;
22.  Student(String st, int i){
23.   score=i;
24.   name=st;
25. }
26. String getName(){
27.     return name;
28. }
29. int getScore(){
30.  return score;
31. }
32. void setScore(int i){
33.  score = i;
34. }
35.}
```

The following is the output from the execution of Listing 4-5:

```
The original student info:
name: John score: 100
The modified student info in the called method:
name: Mary score: 75
The modified student info in the calling method:
name: John score: 50
```

The output demonstrates that the called method used the passed reference to change the score of the existing student John (line 13). Then the called method re-pointed the passed reference to the new student named Mary (line 14). However, it did not affect the reference in the calling method, which is still pointing to John (line 10).

You already know about classes and packages containing groups of classes. The next question to ask is: From where can these classes and their members (variables and methods) be accessed? This is determined by the access modifiers that you can assign to the classes and their members when you write the classes.

Using Access Modifiers

Access modifiers, also called visibility modifiers, determine the accessibility scope of the Java elements they modify. If you do not explicitly use an access modifier with a Java element, the element implicitly has the default access modifier. The explicit access modifiers may be used with a class and its members (that is, instance variables and methods). They cannot be used with the variables inside a method.

■**Caution** Data members of a method cannot explicitly use access modifiers.

The Java language offers three explicit access modifiers, public, protected, and private, and a default modifier, which is enforced when you do not specify a modifier.

The public Modifier

The public modifier makes a Java element most accessible. It may be applied to classes and to their members (that is, instance variables and methods). A class, variable, or method, declared as public, may be accessed from anywhere in the Java application. For example, you declare the main(...) method of any application public so that it may be invoked from any Java runtime environment. Other public methods may be called from anywhere inside the application. However, generally speaking, it is not a good object-oriented programming practice to declare the instance variables public. If you declare them public, they could be accessed directly, whereas they should always be accessed through the class methods. For example, consider the code fragment in Listing 4-6.

Listing 4-6. *InstanceTest.java*

```
1. class MyClass {
2.    public int  myNumber = 10;
3.       public int getMyNumber(){
4.          return myNumber;
5.       }
6.  }
7.  class InstanceTest {
8.     public static void main(String[] args) {
9.         MyClass  mc = new MyClass();
10.        System.out.println (" The value of myNumber is " + mc.myNumber);
11.        System.out.println (" The value returned by the method is " +
               mc.getMyNumber());
12.    }
13.  }
```

The output of Listing 4-6 follows:

```
The value of myNumber is 10
The value returned by the method is 10
```

Note that the myNumber variable is directly accessed in line 10, and also accessed using a method in line 11. If you replace the access modifier public with private in line 3 and try to recompile it, line 10 will generate the compiler error because you cannot directly access a private class member from outside the class.

The private Modifier

The private modifier makes a Java element (a class or a class member) least accessible. The private modifier cannot be applied to a top-level class. It can be applied only to the members of a top-level class—that is, instance variables, methods, and inner classes. Recall that a class that is not defined inside another class is called a top-level class. A private member of a class may only be accessed from the code inside the same class in which this member is declared. It can be accessed neither from any other class nor from a subclass of the class in which it is declared.

■**Caution** A top-level class cannot be declared private; it can only be public, or default (that is, no access modifier is specified).

As an example, consider Listing 4-7.

Listing 4-7. *TestPrivateTest.java*

```
1. class PrivateTest {
2.
3.    // public int  myNumber = 10;
4.    private int  myNumber = 10;
5.   public int getMyNumber(){
6.      return myNumber;
7.    }
8. }
9. class SubPrivateTest extends PrivateTest {
10.    public void printSomething(){
11.      System.out.println (" The value of myNumber is " + this.myNumber);
12.      System.out.println (" The value returned by the method is " +
                this.getMyNumber());
13.    }
14. }
15. class TestPrivateTest{
16.   public static void main(String[] args) {
17.       SubPrivateTest spt = new SubPrivateTest();
18.       spt.printSomething();
19.   }
20. }
```

This code will not compile because line 11 will generate a compiler error. You cannot access a private data variable of the parent class directly, as the private class members are not inherited. If you comment out line 11 and then compile and execute the program, the output of Listing 4-7 follows:

```
The value returned by the method is 10.
```

In Listing 4-7, by declaring the data variable myNumber private, you have disabled the direct access to it from outside the class in which it is declared, and have enforced the rule that this data variable may only be accessed from inside the class, for example, through the method getMyNumber(). This is a good programming practice in the world of object-oriented programming.

The fact that you cannot directly access the private members of a class from its subclass can be looked upon this way: a subclass does not inherit the private members of its parent class. The public and private access modifiers are on the two extremes of access: access from everywhere and access from nowhere outside of the class. There is another access modifier called protected that covers the middle ground between these two extremes.

The protected Modifier

The protected modifier makes a class member more accessible than the private modifier would, but still less accessible than public. This modifier may be applied only to class members—that is, the variables, methods, and inner classes—but not to the class itself. A class member declared protected is accessible to the following elements:

- All the classes in the same package that contains the class that owns the protected member.
- All the subclasses of the class that owns the protected member. These subclasses have access even if they are not in the same package as the parent class.

For example, consider these two code fragments:

```
1. package networking;
2. class Communicator {
3.        void sendData() {}
4.        protected void receiveData() {}
5. }
```

```
1. package internetworking;
2. import networking.*;
3. class Client extends Communicator {
4.    void  communicate(){
5.       receiveData();
6.    }
7. }
```

The class Client is a subclass of the class Communicator. But both classes are in different packages. The method receiveData() is declared protected in the class Communicator. It may be called from the class Client (line 5), even though Communicator and Client are in different packages. This is because Client is a subclass of Communicator.

■**Caution** You cannot specify any modifier for the variables inside a method, and you cannot specify the protected modifier for a top-level class.

You don't have to specify an access modifier for a class or a class member, in which case the access is assumed to be default.

The Default Modifier

You cannot specify any modifier for the variables inside a method, and you cannot specify the protected modifier for a class. The compiler only tells you what access modifier you cannot specify for a given element; however, it does not require you to specify any access modifier for any element. When you do not specify any access modifier for an element, it is assumed that the access is default. In other words, there is no keyword default for the default modifier. If an element does not explicitly use any modifier, the default access is implied. It may be applied to a class, a variable, or a method.

■**Caution** Although there is no keyword default for the default modifier, there is a Java keyword default related to the switch statement, as discussed in Chapter 6.

A class or a class member declared default (no access modifier specified) is accessible from anywhere (classes or subclasses) in the same package in which the accessed class exists. As an example, consider the following code fragment:

```
1. package internetworking;
2. import networking.*;
3. class Client extends Communicator {
4.    void  communicate(){
5.       receiveData();
6.       sendData();  // compiler error.
7.    }
8. }
```

Line 5 would generate a compiler error, because the method `sendData()` is declared default in the class `Communicator`, which is in a different package:

```
1. package networking;
2. class Communicator {
3.        void sendData() {}
4.        protected void receiveData() {}
5. }
```

Note the difference between the `protected` modifier and the default modifier. A member with a default access can be accessed only if the accessing class belongs to the same package, whereas a member with the `protected` modifier can be accessed not only from the same package but also from a different package if the accessing class is a subclass of the accessed class.

■**Note** A method cannot be overridden to be less public.

The final word about access modifiers: a method may not be overridden to be less accessible. For example, a `protected` method may be overridden as `protected` or `public`, but not as `private` or default. Recall that overriding a method means reimplementing a method inherited from a class higher in the hierarchy. You will learn more about method overriding in Chapter 5.

In a nutshell, you can use access modifiers to protect both variables and methods of a class. The Java language supports four distinct access levels for member variables and methods by offering four access modifiers: `private`, `protected`, `public`, and default (i.e. left unspecified). These access modifiers are summarized in Table 4-1.

Table 4-1. *Access Level that a Class Has Granted to Other Classes by Using Different Modifiers*

Access Modifier	Class	Subclass	Package	World
private	Yes	No	No	No
protected	Yes	Yes	Yes	No
public	Yes	Yes	Yes	Yes
Default	Yes	No	Yes	No

The first column in Table 4-1 specifies the possible access modifiers of a class member. The headings of the other columns identify the elements that are trying to access this member. The value Yes means an element has access to the member with the specified access modifier. For example, the second column indicates that a class always has access to its own members regardless of what access modifier they have. The third column indicates whether the subclasses of the class, regardless of which package they are in, have access to the class members with different modifiers. The fourth column indicates whether another class in the same package as the class in question has access to the class members. The fifth column indicates whether all other classes have access to the class members with different access modifiers.

So, the decision to use the modifiers is generally driven by striking a balance between accessibility and security. The underlying effect of any modifier, in general, is to modify (or further specify) the behavior of a class or a class member. The access modifiers specify the access behavior, while there are some non-access modifiers that specify how a class or a class member can be used. I call them *usage modifiers* in this book.

Understanding Usage Modifiers

There are some modifiers that are not access modifiers but still modify the way a class or a class member is to be used. Collectively, we call these modifiers the *usage modifiers*. Some of them, such as final, abstract, and static, may be more familiar than others to a beginner.

The final Modifier

The final modifier may be applied to a class, a method, or a variable. It means, in general, that the element is final. The specific meaning slightly depends upon the element it applies to. If the element declared final is a variable, that means the value of the variable is constant, and cannot be changed. If a class is declared final, it means the class cannot be extended, and a final method cannot be overridden.

For example, consider Listing 4-8. The variable dime in the class Calculator is declared final. Also, the object reference calc in class RunCalculator is declared final. The code lines 11 and 13 will generate compiler errors because they attempt to modify the values of the final variables calc and dime, respectively. However, note that line 12 will compile fine, which shows that the final object reference may be used to modify the value of a non-final variable.

Listing 4-8. *RunCalculator.java*

```
1. class Calculator {
2.   final int dime = 10;
3.   int count = 0;
4.   Calculator (int i) {
5.     count = i;
6.   }
7. }
8. class RunCalculator {
9.     public static void main(String[] args) {
10.      final Calculator calc = new Calculator(1);
11.      calc = new Calculator(2); // compiler error.
12.      calc.count = 2;   //ok
13.      calc.dime  = 11; // compiler error.
14.     System.out.println("dime: " + calc.dime);
15.   }
16.  }
```

If you comment out lines 11 and 13, the code will compile, and the result of execution will be as follows:

```
dime: 10
```

■**Caution** Although a final object reference may not be modified, it can be used to modify the value of a non-final variable in the object to which the final object reference refers.

If you declare a final method inside a non-final class, it will be legal to extend the class, but you cannot override the final method of the parent class in the subclass. Similarly, you can pass the final variable to a method through arguments, but you cannot change their value even inside the method.

So, the final modifier is related to changing the value of a variable. There is another property of a variable, and that is visibility: from where can you see the value (or a change in value) of a variable?

The static Modifier

The static modifier can be applied to variables, methods, and a block of code inside a method. The static elements of a class are visible to all the instances of the class. As a result, if one instance of the class makes a change to a static element, all the instances will see that change.

Consider Listing 4-9. The variable instanceCounter is declared static in line 2, and another variable, counter, is not declared static in line 3. When an instance of the class StaticExample is created, both variables are incremented by one (lines 5 and 6). Each instance has its own copy of the variable counter, but they share the variable instanceCounter. A static variable belongs to the class, and not to a specific instance of the class, and therefore is initialized when the class is loaded. A static variable may be referenced by an instance of the class (lines 13 and 14) in which it is declared, or by the class name itself (line 15).

Listing 4-9. *RunStaticExample.java*

```
1. class StaticExample {
2.   static int instanceCounter = 0;
3.   int  counter = 0;
4.   StaticExample() {
5.         instanceCounter++;
6.         counter++;
7.   }
8. }
9. class RunStaticExample {
10.   public static void main(String[] args) {
11.         StaticExample se1 = new StaticExample();
12.         StaticExample se2 = new StaticExample();
13.         System.out.println("Value of instanceCounter for se1: " +
                    se1.instanceCounter);
14.         System.out.println("Value of instanceCounter for se2: " +
                    se2.instanceCounter);
15.         System.out.println("Value of instanceCounter: " +
                    StaticExample.instanceCounter);
16.         System.out.println("Value of  counter for se1: " + se1.counter);
17.         System.out.println("Value of  counter for se2: " + se2.counter);
18.   }
19.}
```

The following is the output from Listing 4-9:

```
Value of instanceCounter for se1: 2
Value of instanceCounter for se2 2
Value of instanceCounter: 2
Value of  counter for se1: 1
Value of  counter for se2 1
```

The following line of code outside the StaticExample class will set the value of instanceCounter to 100 for all the instances of the class StaticExample:

```
StaticExample.instanceCounter = 100;
```

Just like a static variable, a static method also belongs to the class in which it is defined, and not to a specific instance of the class. Therefore, a static method can only access the static members of the class. In other words, a method declared static in a class cannot access the non-static variables and methods of the class. Because a static method does not belong to a particular instance of the class in which it is defined, it can be called even before a single instance of the class exists. For example, every Java application has a method main(...), which is the entry point for the application execution. It is executed without instantiating the class in which it exists. Also, a static method may not be overridden as non-static and vice versa.

■**Note** A static method cannot access the non-static variables and methods of the class in which it is defined. Also, a static method cannot be overridden as non-static.

In addition to static variables and static methods, a class may have a static code block that does not belong to any method, but only to the class. For example, you may like to execute a task before the class is instantiated, or even before the method main(...) is called. In such a situation, the static code block will help because it will be executed when the class is loaded.

Consider Listing 4-10. When you run the application RunStaticCodeExample, the static variable counter (line 2) is initialized, and the static code block (lines 3 to 6) are executed at the class StaticCodeExample load time. Then, the method main(...) is executed.

Listing 4-10. *RunStaticCodeExample.java*

```
1.  class StaticCodeExample {
2.  static int counter=0;
3.  static {
4.      counter++;
5.      System.out.println("Static Code block: counter: " + counter);
6.  }
7.  StaticCodeExample() {
8.          System.out.println("Constructor:  counter: " + counter);
9.  }
10.  static {
11.              System.out.println("This is another static block");
12.              }
13.}
14.  public class  RunStaticCodeExample {
15.  public static void main(String[] args) {
16.      StaticCodeExample sce = new StaticCodeExample();
17.      System.out.println("main: " + sce.counter);
18.  }
19.}
```

The output from Listing 4-10 follows:

```
Static Code block: counter: 1
This is another static block
Constructor: counter: 1
main: counter: 1
```

This output demonstrates that the static code block is executed exactly once, and before the class constructor is executed—that is, at the time the class is loaded. It will never be executed again during the execution lifetime of the application. Note that all the static blocks will be executed in order before the class initialization regardless of where they are located in the class.

So, remember these points about the static modifier:

- The static elements (variables, methods, and code fragments) belong to the class and not to a particular instance of the class.

- Any change in a static variable of a class is visible to all the instances of the class.

- A static variable is initialized at class load time. Also, a static method and a static code fragment are executed at class load time.

- A static method of a class cannot access the non-static members of the class.

- You cannot declare the following elements as static: constructor, class (that is, the top-level class), interface, inner class (the top-level nested class can be declared static), inner class methods and instance variables, and local variables.

- It is easier to remember what you can declare static: top-level class members (methods and variables), the top-level nested class, and code fragments.

The static modifier cannot be applied to a top-level class or a class constructor. However, you can apply the final modifier to a class, which means the class cannot be extended. You may face the opposite situation, where you want the class to be extended before it can be instantiated. This situation is handled by the abstract modifier.

The abstract Modifier

The abstract modifier may be applied to a class or a method, but not to a variable. A class that is declared abstract cannot be instantiated. Instantiation of an abstract class is not allowed, because it is not fully implemented yet.

There is a relationship between an abstract class and an abstract method. If a class has one or more abstract methods, it must be declared abstract. A class may have one or more abstract methods in any of the following ways:

- The class may have one or more abstract methods originally defined in it.

- The class may have inherited one or more abstract methods from its superclass, and has not provided implementation for all or some of them.

- The class declares that it implements an interface, but does not provide implementation for at least one method in the interface.

In any of the preceding cases, the class must be declared abstract. However, if there is no abstract method in the class, it could still be declared abstract. Even in this case, it cannot be instantiated, obviously.

Note A class with one or more abstract methods must be declared abstract. However, a class with no abstract method may also be declared abstract. An abstract class cannot be instantiated.

Consider Listing 4-11, in which the method draw() in class Shape is abstract. Note its signatures:

```
abstract void draw();
```

Each of the subclasses of Shape (that is, Cone and Circle) implements its own version of the method draw(). Therefore, when the method draw() is called from main(…) in class RunShape, its action depends upon which implementation of draw() is invoked.

Listing 4-11. *RunShape.java*

```
1. abstract class Shape {
2.    abstract void draw();   //Note that there are no curly braces here.
3.    void message() {
4.        System.out.println("I cannot live without being a parent.");
5.    }
6. }
7.  class Circle extends Shape {
8.   void draw() {
9.        System.out.println("Circle drawn.");
10.   }
11. }
12. class Cone extends Shape {
13.   void draw() {
14.        System.out.println("Cone drawn.");
15.   }
16. }
17.  public class RunShape {
18.   public static void main(String[] args) {
19.        Circle circ = new Circle();
20.        Cone cone = new Cone();
21.        circ.draw();
22.        cone.draw();
23.        cone.message();
24.   }
25. }
```

The output from Listing 4-11 follows:

```
Circle drawn.
Cone drawn.
I cannot live without being a parent.
```

Notice that the effect of calling the same method draw() depends upon the caller. This feature of an object-oriented language is called *polymorphism*. Note that you can also implement polymorphism by simply overriding the method of the parent class in the subclasses. (You will learn more about polymorphism in Chapter 5.) However, in case of an abstract method, the overriding is enforced. If a subclass leaves at least one method unimplemented that was declared abstract in the parent class, it cannot be instantiated. Also note the difference between an abstract class and an interface from the perspective of a subclass. A subclass that extends an abstract class only has to implement all the unimplemented methods of the abstract class if you need to instantiate the subclass, whereas a subclass implementing an interface has to provide implementation for all the interface methods.

The abstract class is to some extent opposite to the final class. A final class cannot be extended, whereas an abstract class must be extended (before it can be instantiated). An abstract class or an abstract method means it's not fully implemented yet. So, if you want to use it, you have to implement it. In case of a method, there is another way of saying the same thing when the implementation is not the responsibility of the programmer who extends the class: the native modifier.

The native Modifier

In your applications, sometimes you will want to use a method that exists outside of the JVM. In this case, the native modifier can help you. The native modifier can only apply to a method. Like abstract, the keyword native indicates that the implementation of the method exists elsewhere. In case of abstract, the implementation may exist in a subclass of the class in which the abstract method is declared. In case of native, the implementation of the method exists in a library outside of the JVM.

The native method is usually implemented in a non-Java language such as C or C++. Before a native method can be invoked, a library that contains the method must be loaded. The library is loaded by making the following system call:

```
System.loadLibrary("<libraryName>");
```

For example, the following code fragment presents an example of loading a library named NativeMethodsLib that contains a method (function) named myNativeMethod():

```
1. class MyNativeExample {
2.     native void myNativeMethod();
3.     static {
4.         System.loadLibrary("NativeMethodLib");
5.     }
6. }
```

Notice that the library is loaded in a static code block (lines 3 to 5). Therefore, the library is loaded at the class load time, so it is there when a call to the native method is made. You can use the native method in the same way as you use a non-native method. For example, the following two lines of code would invoke the native method:

```
MyNativeExample myNative  = new MyNativeExample();
myNative.myNativeMethod();
```

■**Note** The exam does not require you to know how to use the native methods. Just remember that it is a modifier (and hence a Java keyword) and that it can only be applied to methods.

The native modifier applies only to methods, while another modifier called transient applies only to variables.

The transient Modifier

When an application is running, the objects live in the random access memory (RAM) of the computer. This limits the scope and life of the object. However, an object may be stored in persistent storage (say disk) outside of the JVM, for later use by the same application, or by a different application. The process of storing an object is called *serialization*. For an object to be serializable, the corresponding class must implement the interface Serializable, or Externalizable.

So, the transient modifier is related to storing an object on the disk. Such storage is called the object's *persistent state*. A variable declared transient is not stored, and hence does not become part of the object's persistent state. One use of transient is to prevent a security-sensitive piece of data from copying to a file where there is no security mechanism in effect.

The transient modifier can only be applied to instance variables. When you are declaring an instance variable transient, you are instructing the JVM not to store this variable when the object in which it is declared is being serialized.

In a multithreaded environment, more than one process may try to access the same class element concurrently. To handle that situation, there are a couple of modifiers that you need to know about.

The Thread-Related Modifiers

A computer program may have launched more than one process executing concurrently. This is called *multithreaded programming,* and you will learn more about it in Chapter 10. But for now, just imagine that if there are more than one process in a program executing concurrently, they may attempt to access a class element at the same time. There are a couple of modifiers that relate to such a situation.

The volatile Modifier

Like the transient modifier, the volatile modifier only applies to instance variables. The variables declared volatile are subject to asynchronous modifications. In other words, declaring a variable volatile informs the compiler that this variable may be changed unexpectedly by other parts of the program. So, the compiler takes some special precautions to keep this variable properly updated. The volatile variables are generally used in multithreaded or multiprocessor environments. The volatile modifier tells the accessing thread that it should synchronize its private copy of the variable with the master copy in the memory.

The synchronized Modifier

The synchronized modifier is used in multithreaded programming to control access to critical sections in the program. This modifier is discussed in detail in Chapter 10 in conjunction with threads.

You have explored a multitude of modifiers. Let's take a look at the big picture.

Modifiers: The Big Picture

As you have noticed, not all modifiers can be applied to all Java elements such as classes, methods, and variables. For example, classes cannot be declared private and methods cannot be declared transient or volatile. Table 4-2 summarizes the use of different modifiers by Java classes and class members. Note that the constructors can use only access modifiers and no other type of modifiers. To the contrary, a code block cannot use any explicit access modifier. To be specific, it can only use static or synchronized modifiers.

Table 4-2. *Summary of Modifiers Used by Java Classes and Class Members*

Modifier	Top-Level Class	Variable	Method	Constructor	Code Block
public	Yes	Yes	Yes	Yes	No
private	No	Yes	Yes	Yes	No
protected	No	Yes	Yes	Yes	No
Default	Yes	Yes	Yes	Yes	N/A
final	Yes	Yes	Yes	No	No
static	No	Yes	Yes	No	Yes
abstract	Yes	No	Yes	No	No
native	No	No	Yes	No	No
transient	No	Yes	No	No	No
volatile	No	Yes	No	No	No
synchronized	No	No	Yes	No	Yes

All of these modifiers are specified with different Java elements in a Java application. Applications running on a computer use memory, which makes memory management a significant issue for any programming language. Because Java is a relatively high-level language, the memory management in Java is automatic. However, to make it more efficient, you need to understand *garbage collection*—that is, freeing memory from objects that are no longer in use.

Understanding Garbage Collection in Java

When you create an object by instantiating a class, the object is put on the heap; in other words, it uses some memory. A Java application creates and uses objects. After an object in memory has been used and is no longer needed, it is sensible to free memory from that object. The process of freeing memory from the used objects is called *garbage collection*. How do you accomplish this in Java?

In Java, garbage collection is done automatically by what is called the *garbage collector*.

Understanding the Garbage Collector

The garbage collector in Java automates memory management by freeing up the memory from objects that are no longer in use. The advantage of this is that you do not need to code the memory management into your application. The price you pay for this service is that you have no control over when the garbage collector runs. There are two things that you can do in the code to help memory management:

- Make an object eligible for garbage collection, because a garbage collector will only free up memory from an eligible object.

- Make a request for garbage collection by making a system call to the garbage collector: System.gc();.

You can also invoke the gc() method by using an instance of the Runtime class that a running application always has. You get hold of this instance by calling the static method getRuntime() of the Runtime class:

```
Runtime rt = Runtime.getRuntime();
```

Then, you can use this instance to invoke methods in order to perform some runtime tasks, such as to get memory information or to run the garbage collector:

```
rt.gc();
rt.getTotalMemory() // Returns the total amount of memory allocated to the JVM.
rt.freeMemory()     // Returns the amount of free JVM memory.
```

These uses of the Runtime class are demonstrated in Listing 4-12.

Listing 4-12. *RuntimeTest.java*

```
1. class RuntimeTest {
2.   public static void main (String [] args) {
3.     Runtime rt = Runtime.getRuntime();
4.     System.out.println("JVM free memory before running gc: " + rt.freeMemory());
5.     rt.gc();
6.     System.out.println("JVM free memory after running gc: " + rt.freeMemory());
7.   }
8. }
```

Remember that an application cannot create its own instance of the Runtime class. Therefore the following code will be invalid:

```
new Runtime().gc();
```

A call to the garbage collector is no guarantee that the memory will be free. It is possible, for example, that the JVM *in which* your program is running did not even implement the gc() method. The Java language specification allows a dummy gc() method.

The basic requirement for garbage collection is that you must make your object eligible for garbage collection. An object is considered eligible for garbage collection when there is no reference pointing to it. You can remove the references to an object in two ways:

- Set the object reference variable pointing to the object to null; for example:

```
myObject = null;
```

- Reassign a reference variable of an object to another object. For example, if a reference variable myObject is pointing to an object of the MyClass class, you can free this object from this reference by pointing the reference to another object:

```
myObject = new YourClass();
```

Now, the object reference myObject is pointing to an object of the class YourClass and not to an object of MyClass, to which it was pointing previously.

What if you want an object to clean up its state before it is deleted? Well, you can declare the finalize() method in the class, and this method will be called by the garbage collector before deleting any object of this class.

The finalize() Method

The object that has no object references pointing to it can be deleted by the garbage collector to reclaim the memory. If the object has a finalize() method, it will be executed before reclaiming the memory in order to give the object a last chance to clean up after itself—for example, to release the resources that the object was using.

The finalize() method is inherited from the Object class by any class you define. The signature of the finalize() method in the object class is shown here:

```
protected void finalize()
```

You can override this method in your class. The Java programming language specifies that the finalize() method will be called before the object memory is reclaimed, but it does not guarantee exactly when it will happen. Remember that the finalize() method that your class inherited does not do anything. If you want your object to clean up after itself, you have to override the finalize() method. Then, what is the point of putting the finalize() method in the Object class? It makes it safe for the finalize() method of any class to invoke the finalize() of the superclass, as shown here:

```
protected void finalize() {
  super.finlaize();
  // clean up code follows.
}
```

This is generally a good practice.

■**Note** Unlike a constructor, a finalize() method in any class will not automatically call the finalize() method of the super class. You need to call it explicitly, if you want to.

When an object is instantiated from a class, it is called *reachable* and *unfinalized*. When no reference is pointing to an object, the object can only be reached by the finalize() method, and hence it is called *finalizer reachable*. However, it is possible to make the object reachable again for any live thread by creating a reference to this object in its finalize() method. The finalize() method for an object is only run once. If you make an object ineligible for garbage collection in its finalize() method, it does not mean that the object will never be garbage collected because its finalize() method now will never be called. The object can still become eligible for garbage collection when it has no reference pointing to it. The only difference is that, this time, the garbage collector will remove it without calling its finalize() method, because it has already been called. The garbage collector is not guaranteed to be invoked, and thus the finalize() method is not guaranteed to be called. It is a good practice for you, the programmer, to free up the resources when they are no longer required.

Codewalk Quicklet

The code for the codewalk quicklet exercise in this chapter is presented in Listing 4-13.

Listing 4-13. *CodeWalkThree.java*

```
1.   class CodeWalkThree {
2.       public static void main(String [] args) {
3.           CodeWalkThree cw = new CodeWalkThree();
4.           CodeWalkThree cw2 = new CodeWalkThree();
5.           System.out.print(cw == cw2);
6.           cw2 = operate(cw,cw2);
7.           System.out.print(" " + (cw == cw2));
8.       }
9.       static CodeWalkThree operate(CodeWalkThree cw1, CodeWalkThree cw2) {
10.          CodeWalkThree cw3 = cw1;
11.          cw1 = cw2;
12.          return cw3;
13.      }
14.  }
```

To get you started on this exercise, following are some hints:

- *Input*: Lines 3, 4, and 10

- *Operations*: Lines 5, 6, 7, and 11

- *Output*: Lines 5 and 7

- *Rules*: The effect of a method call on object references

Looking at the code from this angle, see if you can handle the last question in the "Review Questions" section based on this code.

The three most important takeaways from this chapter are the following:

- The full path name to a class is constructed from the classpath followed by the package name followed by the class name.

- You specify access modifiers in order to strike a balance between security and access.

- You can make an object eligible for garbage collection by making sure that no reference is pointing to it. But you have no control over when the garbage collector will collect an eligible object.

Summary

A Java application is composed of classes, which are written in source files with the `.java` extension. The related classes and interfaces can be bundled together into a package by using the `package` keyword in the source files in which classes are written. A package can be imported into another source file by using the keyword `import`. In a source file, the package declaration, the `import` statement, and the class definition must appear in this order. The compiler generates a `.class` file corresponding to each class in the source file, and the name of the `.class` file matches the corresponding class. The compiler and the interpreter make the full path of a directory in which a class file exists by appending the package name to the `classpath`.

From where a class or a class member can be accessed is determined by its access modifier. A class or a class member declared `public` can be accessed from anywhere inside the application. A private member of a class may only be accessed from the code inside the same class in which that member is declared. It can be accessed neither from any other class nor from a subclass of the class in which it is declared. For this reason, a top-level class can never be declared `private`, but its members can be. A class member declared `protected` can be accessed from any other class in the same package as the accessed class, or from a subclass of the accessed class in any package. A class or a class member with a default access (which means no access modifier is specified) can be accessed only if the accessing class belongs to the same package as the accessed class.

When you pass a variable in a method call, only a copy of the variable is passed and not the original variable, regardless of whether the variable is a primitive variable or a reference variable. Therefore, any change in the passed variable in the called method does not affect the variable in the calling method. However, in case of a reference variable, the called method can use the passed variable to change the properties of the object to which the passed variables refers.

Memory management in Java is automatic. The Java garbage collector automatically frees up the memory from objects that are no longer being used. In order to get an object garbage collected, you must make it eligible by making sure no reference is pointing to it. The garbage collector calls the `finalize()` method on the object before freeing up its memory. The `finalize()` method is inherited by your class from the `Object` class, but you can override it to clean up after the object (for example, to release resources). However, there is no way to guarantee when the garbage collector will be invoked.

In this chapter, we explored the fundamentals of Java, which is an object-oriented language. In the next chapter, we explore some salient features of object-oriented programming implemented in Java.

Comprehend

- Only eligible objects will be removed by the garbage collector. An object is eligible for garbage collection if no reference points to it.

- A member with a default access can be accessed only if the accessing class belongs to the same package, whereas a member with the `protected` modifier can be accessed not only from the same package but also from a different package if the accessing class is a subclass of the accessed class.

- It is legal to use the `final` object reference to change the value of a non-final variable of the object.

- An `abstract` class can be extended but cannot be instantiated. You must implement all of its `abstract` methods in a subclass before you can instantiate the subclass.

- A `final` class can be instantiated but cannot be extended.

Look Out

- The name of a `.java` file must match the name of a class in the file. If the file has a `public` class, the file name must match the name of the `public` class.

- In a `.java` file, the package declaration, the `import` statement, and the class definition must appear in this order.

- Variables inside a method cannot have explicit access modifiers such as `public`, `private`, and `protected` assigned to them.

- A top-level class cannot be declared `private`; it can only be `public` or default (that is, no access modifier specified).

- There is no such modifier named `default`, but the default access is assumed if no modifier is specified.

- A `static` method of a class cannot access non-static members of the class.

- It is possible to make an object ineligible for garbage collection by creating references to it in its `finalize()` method.

- The called method can change the properties of the object to which a passed reference to the method points. However, any change in the reference in the called method will not affect the reference in the calling method.

Memorize

- You cannot change the value of a `final` variable, you cannot extend the class that is declared `final`, and you cannot override a `final` method.

- A variable cannot be declared `abstract`.

- While the `native` modifier only applies to methods, the `transient` and `volatile` modifiers only apply to instance variables.

- Executing `System.gc()` does not necessarily mean that memory will be made free; that is, you cannot force the garbage collection.

- In a method call, it is always the copy of a variable that is passed, regardless of whether the variable is a primitive variable or a reference variable.

Review Questions

1. Which of the following declarations will result in compiler error? (Choose all that apply.)

   A. `abstract final class MyClass {};`

   B. `abstract int i;`

   C. `default class MyClass {};`

   D. `native myMethod();`

2. Which of the following statements is false?

   A. An abstract class must have at least one `abstract` method.

   B. An abstract class cannot have a `finalize()` method.

   C. A `final` class cannot have abstract methods.

   D. A top-level class cannot be declared `private`.

3. Assume that a variable exists in a class and that the variable must not be copied into a file when the object corresponding to this class is serialized. What modifier should be used in the declaration of this variable?

   A. `private`

   B. `protected`

   C. `public`

   D. `transient`

   E. `native`

4. Which of the following statements is true about the `static` modifier?

   A. A `static` variable cannot change its value.

   B. A `static` method cannot be overridden to be non-static.

   C. A `static` method is often written in a non-Java language and exists outside of JVM.

   D. The `static` code lies outside of any class.

5. Consider the following code fragment:

```
1. class MySuperClass {
2.    public void message() {
3.        System.out.println("From the super class!");
4.    }
5. }
6. public class MySubClass extends MySuperClass {
7.    void message() {
8.      System.out.println("From the subclass!");
9.    }
10.   public static void main(String args[]) {
11.     MySubClass mysub = new MySubClass();
12.     mysub.message();
13.   }
14. }
```

Which of the following statement is true about this code?

A. The code would compile and execute, and generate the output: `From the subclass!`.

B. The code would compile and execute, and generate the output: `From the super class!`.

C. Line 7 would generate a compiler error.

D. Line 11 would generate a compiler error.

6. Consider the following code fragment:

```
1. class MySuperClass {
2.    static void message() {
3.         System.out.println("From the super class!");
4.    }
5. }
6. public class MySubClass extends MySuperClass {
7.    void message() {
8.      System.out.println("From the subclass!");
9.    }
10.    public static void main(String args[]) {
11.       MySubClass mysub = new MySubClass();
12.       mysub.message();
13.    }
14. }
```

Which of the following modifiers placed in the beginning of line 7 will make the code compile and execute without error?

A. `static`

B. `public`

C. `protected`

D. `transient`

7. Which of the following statements is true?

A. The `final` variable may only be used with a variable or a method.

B. The `final` variable may not be copied to a file during object serialization.

C. The `final` method may not be overridden.

D. The class that has a `final` method may not be extended.

8. Consider the following code fragment:

```
1.    class MyClass {
2.        public void message (int i) {
3.           public   int j= i;
4.           System.out.println("Value of  j: " + j);
5.        }
6.        public static void main(String[] args) {
7.            MyClass ma = new MyClass();
8.            ma.message(15);
9.        }
10. }
```

Which of the following statements is true about this code?

A. The code will compile and execute fine, and the output will be Value of j: 15.

B. Line 2 will generate a compiler error.

C. The code will compile but give an error at execution time.

Consider the following code fragment for questions 9 and 10:

```
package robots;
public class FunnyRobot {
protected void dance () {
    System.out.println("The funny robot is dancing!");
}
void shyAway () {
  System.out.println("The funny robot is shying away!");
}
private void freeze () {
  System.out.println("The robot has come to a stop!");
}
}
```

9. Consider the following code fragment:

```
1. package  RobotDrivers ;
2. import robots.*;
3. public class RobotPlayer extends FunnyRobot {
4.         static int i =5;
5.    public static void main(String[] args){
6.                 i = 6;
7.         RobotPlayer rp = new RobotPlayer();
8.         rp.dance();
9.   }
10. }
```

Which of the following statements is true about this code fragment?

A. The code will compile and execute correctly, and generate the output: The funny robot is dancing!.

B. There would be a compiler error at line 7 because the method dance() is protected and the classes RobotPlayer and FunnyRobot are in different packages.

C. There would be a compiler error at line 6.

D. The code will compile, but will generate a runtime exception.

10. Consider the following code fragment:

```
1. package  RobotDrivers ;
2. import robots.*;
3.  public class RobotPlayer{
4.         static int i =5;
5.    public static void main(String[] args){
6.         i = 6;
7.         FunnyRobot fr = new FunnyRobot();
8.         fr.dance();
9.  }
10. }
```

Which of the following statements is true about this code fragment?

A. The code will compile and execute correctly, and generate the output: The funny robot is dancing!.

B. There would be a compiler error at line 7 because the method dance() is protected and the classes RobotPlayer and FunnyRobot are in different packages.

C. There would be a compiler error at line 6.

D. The code will compile, but will generate a runtime exception.

11. Consider the code in Listing 4-13. What is the result?

A. false false

B. true true

C. false true

D. true false

E. Compilation fails.

CHAPTER 5

■■■

Object-Oriented Programming

Exam Objectives

5.1 Develop code that implements tight encapsulation, loose coupling, and high cohesion in classes, and describe the benefits.

5.2 Given a scenario, develop code that demonstrates the use of polymorphism. Further, determine when casting will be necessary and recognize compiler vs. runtime errors related to object reference casting.

5.4 Given a scenario, develop code that declares and/or invokes overridden or overloaded methods and code that declares and/or invokes superclass, overridden, or overloaded constructors.

1.5 Given a code example, determine if a method is correctly overriding or overloading another method, and identify legal return values (including covariant returns), for the method.

5.5 Develop code that implements "is-a" and/or "has-a" relationships.

Java is an object-oriented language that adapts itself to the real-world problem being solved as opposed to a procedural language that adapts the problem to itself. In this chapter, we explore some features of Java that make it possible to adapt the programs to the problem rather than the other way around. The real world and its problems are composed of objects such as a room, a classroom, a cow, and the cow's tail. The objects in the real world also have relationships among themselves; for example, the classroom is a room, and the cow has a tail. You will see in this chapter how Java supports these object-oriented relationships.

The hierarchical relationships (such as all cows are animals but not all animals are cows) lead to a degree of freedom that lets you provide different interpretations of the same thing. This capability in Java is called *polymorphism*, which involves converting the data type of a variable: primitive or object reference. If the conversion is automatic, it is called *implicit conversion*, and if it is enforced by the programmer, it is called *explicit conversion* or *casting*. In this chapter, we explore different programming situations in which this conversion happens.

Another salient feature of an object-oriented language is *inheritance*, which allows a programmer to derive a subclass from a parent class, also called superclass. You can rewrite the inherited method of the superclass in the subclass, a process called *overriding*. You can also write different versions of the same method in a given class in order to solve slightly different but related problems, a process called *overloading*.

So, the focus of this chapter is to understand the object-oriented features of Java. To accomplish that, we explore three avenues: object-oriented relationships, data type conversion, and overriding/overloading methods.

Understanding Object-Oriented Relationships

In an application, the classes and class members are related to each other. For example, a class has a data variable defined in it. So the relationship in this example is that the class has the data variable in it. The classes themselves are related to each other; e.g. a class is derived from another class. There are two kinds of relationships that the classes inside an application may have, and these kinds correspond to the two properties of classes: inheritance and data abstraction.

The is-a Relationship

The *is-a* relationship corresponds to inheritance. Consider this statement: a boombox is a stereo. In Java, this statement may be translated to the following code:

```
class Stereo {
}
class Boombox extends Stereo {
}
```

In Java, this relationship is represented by the keyword extends, whereas in plain English this is an *is-a* relationship. When we say Boombox *is-a* Stereo, we mean all the following statements:

- Boombox is a subclass of Stereo.
- Stereo is a superclass of Boombox.
- Boombox inherits from Stereo.
- Boombox is derived from Stereo.
- Boombox extends Stereo.

A rule of thumb to recognize an *is-a* relationship is that every object of the subclass is also an object of the superclass and not vice versa. For example, every cow on the planet is an animal, but not every animal is a cow. Also remember that a class is in an *is-a* relationship with any class up in its hierarchy tree. For example, if A extends B, and B extends C, then C is B, and also C is A.

So, a class can relate to another class by inheriting from it. There is another way in which two classes can be related to each other: the *has-a* relationship.

The has-a Relationship

The *has-a* relationship corresponds to an object-oriented characteristic called encapsulation, which means the data and the methods are combined into a structure called a class. Consider a class CDPlayer. Now, consider this statement: the boombox *is-a* stereo and it *has-a* CD player. In Java, this statement may be translated to the following:

```
class Stereo {
}
class Boombox extends Stereo {
     CDPlayer cdPlayer = new CDPlayer();
}
class CDPlayer {
}
```

Following are some other examples of *is-a* and *has-a* relationships:

- A city has a community center. A community center is a building.
- A classroom has a whiteboard. The classroom is a room.
- A country has citizens. The president is a citizen.

■**Caution** The exam expects you to understand *is-a* and *has-a* relationships in context of the real world. For example, be prepared to see statements such as a cow is an animal and it has a tail, or a boombox is a stereo and has a CD player. Be able to interpret such statements in terms of inheritance and instantiation even if no Java code is given.

So, a class X *has-a* class Y, if the class X has a reference to class Y.

The classes can have *is-a* or *has-a* relationships with each other. A given class is also related to its class members: variables and methods. The methods and variables are encapsulated in a class.

Encapsulation and Data Abstraction

Encapsulation facilitates *data abstraction*, which is the relationship between a class and its data members. Encapsulation refers to the fact that the data variables (also called the properties) and the methods (also called the behavior) are encapsulated together inside a template called a class. The data members encapsulated inside a class may be declared public, private, or protected. However, good object-oriented programming practice requires tight encapsulation. That means all data members of the class should be declared private. That is, the code outside of the class in which the data members are declared can access them only through method calls, and not directly. This is called data abstraction (or data hiding), because now the data is hidden from the user, and the user can have access to it only through the methods.

Encapsulation (and data abstraction) makes the code more reliable, robust, and reusable. This is so because the data and the operations on it (methods) are encapsulated into one entity (the class), and the data member itself and the access to it are separated from each other (tight encapsulation or data abstraction). For example, in tight encapsulation, where your data members are private, if you change the name of a data variable, the access code will still work as long as you don't change the name of the parameters of the method that is used to access it.

Consider the code example in Listing 5-1.

Listing 5-1. *TestEncapsulateBad.java*

```
1. public class TestEncapsulateBad {
2.   public static void main(String[] args) {
3.     EncapsulateBad eb = new EncapsulateBad();
4.     System.out.println("Do you have a headache? " + eb.headache);
5.   }
6. }
7. class EncapsulateBad {
8.   public boolean headache = true;
9.   public int doses = 0;
10.}
```

The output from this code follows:

```
Do you have a headache? true
```

Note that in line 4, the data variable of class EncapsulateBad is accessed directly by the code piece eb.headache. This is only possible because the variable headache is declared public in the class EncapsulateBad. If you declare this variable private, line 4 will cause a compiler error. Let's say you keep it public, and then you change the name of the variable headache in the EncapsulateBad class to something else. In this case, line 4 will again generate an error, because you need to change the name of the variable headache in line 4 to the new name as well.

However, a better solution is to separate the data variable from the access by declaring it private and provide access to it through methods, as shown in Listing 5-2.

Listing 5-2. *TestEncapsulateGood.java*

```
1. public class TestEncapsulateGood {
2.   public static void main(String[] args) {
3.     EncapsulateGood eg = new EncapsulateGood();
4.     eg.setHeadache(false);
5.     System.out.println("Do you have a headache? " + eg.getHeadache());
6.   }
7. }
8. class EncapsulateGood {
9.   private boolean headache = true;
10.  private int doses = 0;
11.  public void setHeadache(boolean isHeadache){
12.    this.headache = isHeadache;
13.  }
14.  public boolean getHeadache( ){
15.    return headache;
16.  }
17. }
```

The output from this code follows:

```
Do you have a headache? false
```

Note that the variable headache is now declared private (line 9), and it can be accessed through methods setHeadache(…) and getHeadache(), which are declared public (lines 11 and 14). The world can still access your data, but this access process is separated from the details of the data—the data variable name, how the change is made to it, and so forth. This hiding of the data details from the access procedure is called data abstraction. In an application, it means you can make changes to the data variables in your class without breaking the API. Such protection also makes the code more extendible and easier to maintain. So, the benefits of encapsulation are: hard-to-break reliable code, easy maintenance, and extensibility.

■**Note** The *has-a* relationship is associated with encapsulation, whereas the *is-a* relationship is associated with inheritance.

So, encapsulation (or a lack of it) determines how the classes interact with each other, a property also called *coupling*. Actually, there are two more characteristics that good object-oriented programming should exhibit: loose coupling and cohesion.

Coupling and Cohesion

Good object-oriented programming demands cohesive classes, which may be loosely coupled to each other. *Loose coupling* refers to minimizing the dependence of an object on other objects. In other words, you can change the implementation of a class without affecting the other classes. These properties make the code extensible and easy to maintain.

For example, consider two classes, A and B. If they do not use each other at all (neither of them instantiates the other, invokes a method on the other, and so on), they are not coupled. If A uses B (for example, instantiates B) but B does not use A, then they are loosely coupled. If both A and B use each other, then they are tightly coupled.

Another criterion of loosely coupled classes is how they access each other's members. Loose coupling demands that a class keep its members `private` and that the other class access them through getters and setters (recall encapsulation). *Tight coupling* is exhibited by accessing the `public` member of another class directly, as shown in Listing 5-3.

Listing 5-3. *TightlyCoupledClient.java*

```
1. public class TightlyCoupledClient{
2.   public static void main(String[] args) {
3.    TightlyCoupledServer server = new TightlyCoupledServer();
4.    server.x=5;  //should use a setter method
5.      System.out.println("Value of x: "  + server.x);
          //should use a getter method
6.   }
7. }
8.  class TightlyCoupledServer {
9.   public int x = 0;  //should be private
10. }
```

Whereas coupling refers to how two classes interact with each other, *cohesion* refers to how a class is structured. A cohesive class is a class that performs a set of closely related tasks, or just one task (think of modular programming). If a class is performing a set of unrelated tasks (a noncohesive class), you should consider writing multiple classes (cohesive classes) or reshuffling the tasks (during design phase) until each class has a set of related tasks, or just one main task.

As previously described, the *has-a* relationship is associated with encapsulation, whereas the *is-a* relationship is associated with inheritance. Next, you will see how the *is-a* relationship leads to polymorphism, another important characteristic of an object-oriented language.

Implementing Polymorphism

The *is-a* relationship between a superclass and a subclass has a profound implication. For example, the fact that a cow is an animal means that all cows are animals. It further means that you can substitute an object of the subclass Cow for an object of the superclass Animal, because a cow is, after all, an animal. For example, the following code is valid:

```
Animal a = new Animal();  // Variable a points to an object of Animal
a = new Cow(); // Now, a points to an object of Cow.
```

However, note that the reverse is not true: not all animals are cows. Therefore, the following line of code is not valid:

```
Cow c = new Animal(); // not valid
```

Now, a superclass can have multiple subclasses. For example, if a cow is an animal so is a buffalo. This means you can substitute either a cow or a buffalo for an animal. This is an example of *polymorphism*, which means giving different meaning to the same thing. For example, consider the code in Listing 5-4.

Listing 5-4. *TestPoly.java*

```
1.  public class TestPoly {
2.    public static void main(String [] args) {
3.     Animal heyAnimal = new Animal();
```

```
4.     Cow c = new Cow();
5.     Buffalo b = new Buffalo();
6.     heyAnimal=c;
7.     heyAnimal.saySomething();
8.     heyAnimal=b;
9.     heyAnimal.saySomething();
10. }
11.}
12.class Animal {
13.  public void saySomething() {
14.     System.out.println("Umm...");
15.  }
16.}
17. class Cow extends Animal {
18.   public void saySomething() {
19.//     super.saySomething();
20.     System.out.println("Moo!");
21.  }
22.  }
23. class Buffalo extends Animal{
24.   public void saySomething() {
25.  // super.saySomething();
26.     System.out.println("Bah!");
27.  }
28. }
```

The output from this code follows:

```
Moo!
Bah!
```

Note that invoking two calls from the same object to the same method (lines 7 and 9), saySomething(), has different effects. This is made possible by assigning objects of different subclasses of Animal, cow and buffalo, to the object reference of Animal, and by having different implementations of the saySomething() method in the subclasses (lines 18 and 24). Lines 19 and 25 are commented out for use in an upcoming section.

■Note The compiler only knows about the declared object reference types. However, at runtime, the JVM knows what the referred object really is.

It should be obvious by the definition of the static modifier (discussed in the previous chapter) that polymorphism does not apply to the static class members. For example, if you have a static method with identical signatures defined in the parent class and its subclass, and you assign an instance of the subclass to the reference variable of the parent class, and the variable invokes this static method, the parent version of the method will be executed.

Note that the capability to convert an object reference from one type (Animal in our example) to another type (say Cow) is at the heart of polymorphism. This conversion can happen to both kinds of data types: primitives and object references.

Conversion of Primitive Data Types

You know from Chapter 2 that each data variable in Java has a type. For example, there are primitive data types such as boolean, byte, char, short, int, long, float, and double. Furthermore, classes in Java are also data types. Therefore, the number of data types associated with object references is infinite. As you know, data held in memory is referred to by using the primitive variable names. A variable is declared of a certain type corresponding to the type of the data it will hold or refer to. During data manipulation, the data values may change their types. This is called *type conversion*.

Type conversion in Java can happen in two ways:

- *Implicit type conversion*: The programmer does not make any attempt to convert the type; rather, the type is automatically converted by the system under certain circumstances.

- *Explicit type conversion*: Conversion is initiated by the programmer by making an explicit request for conversion. This is also known as *type casting*.

In this and the next section, you will become familiar with the conversion rules.

Implicit Conversion of Primitive Data Types

Implicit conversion happens when a data value of a given type is being assigned to a variable of a different but compatible data type. In case of primitive data types, all the information to determine the validity of a conversion is available at compile time. Therefore, all conversion takes place at compile time. This means that if a conversion rule is being violated, the compiler generates an error. Implicit conversion of primitive data types takes place in three situations, discussed in this section.

■Note In case of primitive data types, all the information to determine the validity of a conversion is available at compile time. Therefore, violation of a conversion rule in this case generates a compiler error.

You have already encountered implicit conversion in the form of arithmetic promotion, discussed in Chapter 2. There are two other ways that implicit conversion can happen: when you assign a value to a variable of a different type, and when you pass an argument in a method call corresponding to a parameter of a different type.

Assignment Conversion

The assignment conversion may take place when a value is assigned to a variable using an assignment operator and the two operands do not have identical types. For example, consider the code fragment shown here:

```
1    public class ConversionToNarrower{
2.      public static void main(String[] args) {
3.        int i = 15;
4.        short s = 10;
5.        s = i;     //compiler error
6.        System.out.println("Value of s: "  + s );
7.      }
8.    }
```

At line 5, the int value is being assigned to the variable s of type short. Recall that the int value is stored in 32 bits, while the variable s of type short refers to a memory slot that has only 16 bits. It is impossible to store the value that takes 32 bits into a memory slot of 16 bits. Therefore, line 5 would generate a compiler error.

So, here you get a rule: implicit conversion to a narrower type is not allowed, but implicit conversion to a wider type is allowed. For example, consider the following code fragment:

```
1. public class ConversionToWider{
2.     public static void main(String[] args) {
3.         int i = 15;
4.         short s = 10;
5.         i = s;
6.          System.out.println("Value of i: " + i );
7.     }
8. }
```

In line 5, the value of type short is being assigned to a variable i of type int. The int type is 32 bits in size and can easily accommodate a value of short type, which is 16 bits in size. Therefore, the value of s is converted into int before assigning it to the variable i, and there is no compiler error. The output of this code fragment follows:

```
Value of i: 10
```

Two general rules for implicit primitive type conversion are the following:

1. There is no conversion between boolean and non-boolean types.

2. A non-boolean type can be converted into another non-boolean type only if the conversion is not narrowing—that is, the size of the target type is greater than or equal to the size of the source type.

The definition of widening (that is, not narrowing) conversion is illustrated in Figure 5-1. Identify the source type and the target type of conversion in Figure 5-1. If you can reach from the source type to the target type by following the arrows, then the conversion is allowed; otherwise, the conversion is not allowed.

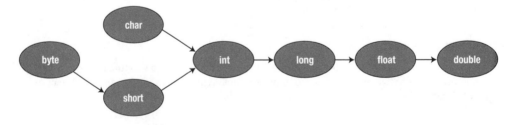

Figure 5-1. *Allowed conversions for primitive data types (arrows indicate paths of allowed conversion)*

For example, note that implicit conversion from short to char is not allowed because we cannot reach char from short by following the arrows. For the same reason, conversion from float to integer is also not allowed. However, conversion from long to float is allowed because we could reach float from long by following the arrows in Figure 5-1. The following code fragment illustrates this example:

```
1. public class ConversionTest{
2.     public static void main(String[] args) {
3.         short s = 10;
4.         char c = 'a';
5.         long l = 16;
6.         float f = 1.2f;
7.         f = l;      //ok
8.         c = s;    // compiler error
9.         i = f;      // compiler error
10.        System.out.println("Value of f: "  + f );
11.    }
12. }
```

Line 7 is legal, while lines 8 and 9 will generate compiler errors. If lines 8 and 9 are commented out, the output of this code fragment would be:

```
Value of f: 16.0
```

Note that the long value 16 is converted to type float before being assigned to the float variable f. The information in Figure 5-1 is outlined in Table 5-1.

■**Caution** Although short and char are both 16-bit integers, implicit conversion between them is not allowed. Recall that short is a signed integer, whereas char is an unsigned integer.

Table 5-1. *Allowed Implicit Conversion Among Primitive Data Types*

Primitive Data Type	Allowed Implicit Conversion To
byte	short, int, long, float, double
short	int, long, float, double
char	int, long, float, double
int	long, float, double
long	float, double
float	double

In implementing the rules discussed so far, you need to take extra precaution when dealing with the literal numeric values. Remember that by default, a literal value with a decimal, for example 1.2, is considered of type double, and a literal value without a decimal, for example 9, is considered of type int. Therefore, the following line of code will generate a compiler error:

```
float f = 1.2;
```

The error will occur because 1.2 is a double, and you cannot implicitly convert a double to a float.

By the same token, you would expect the following lines of code to all generate compiler errors because a value of type int is being converted into narrower types:

```
byte b = 9;
short s = 9;
char c = 9;
```

However, all three lines will be compiled without an error because the conversion rule is relaxed when a literal int value is assigned to a variable of type byte, short, or char, provided the value falls within the range of the target type. For example, consider the following line of code:

```
byte b = 158;
```

This will generate a compiler error because the literal value 158 exceeds the legal range of byte, which is from -128 to 127.

■**Caution** Generally speaking, implicit conversion to a narrower type is not allowed. However, this rule is relaxed for literal integer value assignment. A literal integer value can be assigned to variables of type byte, short, or char, provided that the value is within the legal range of the variable type.

Another way a value with one type may be assigned implicitly to a variable of a different type is by sending values in a method call as arguments.

Method Call Conversion

Recall that in a method definition, you define parameters, which are simply declarations of variables. During a method call, you pass in the arguments, which are simply the values for the variables defined in the method definitions—that is, the parameters. Method call conversion happens if the argument passed in the method call is of a different type from the corresponding parameter type specified in the method definition.

Consider the code example in Listing 5-5.

Listing 5-5. *MethodCallTest.java*

```
1.  public class MethodCallTest{
2.      public static void main(String[] args) {
3.          int i = 15;
4.          long j = 16;
5.          byte b = 8;
6.          short s = 9;
7.          float f = 1.2f;
8.          double d = 2.56d;
9.          int result1, result2;
10.         MethodCallTest mct = new MethodCallTest();
11.         result1 = mct.add(f, d);
12.         result2 = mct.add(b, s);
13.          System.out.println("result2: "  + result2 );
14.     }
15.     public int add(int i, int j) {
16.             return (i+j);
17.     }
18. }
```

In line 15, the method definition declares two parameters, i and j of type int. In line 11, the value float is being passed for int i, and the value double is being passed for int j. However, neither float nor double could be implicitly converted to int. Therefore, line 11 will generate a compiler error. In line 12, a value of type byte is being passed in as an argument for int i, and a value of type short is being passed in for int j. Both byte and short can be implicitly converted to int. Therefore, there will be no compiler error on line 12. If you comment out line 11, the output of the code example in Listing 5-5, as expected, will be

```
result2: 17
```

In a method call, a value passed as an argument is being assigned to the corresponding variable (parameter) declared in the method definition. Therefore, method call conversion is a special kind of assignment conversion. As a result, all the rules of assignment conversion apply to method call conversion as well.

Arithmetic Promotion

Arithmetic promotion is the primitive type conversion that takes place in an arithmetic statement involving operands of different types. The operators involved may be unary (operating only on one operand) or binary (operating on two operands).

In case of unary operators, the following conversion rules apply:

- If the unary operator is neither ++ nor --, and if the operand (on which the unary operator is operating) is of type byte, short, or char, the operand is converted into type int.

- If the operator is either ++ or --, no conversion takes place.

- If the operand type is not one of byte, short, or char, no conversion takes place.

For example, the following code is legal:

```
short x = 9;
x = ++x;
```

This is legal because ++x is of the same type as x.

However, the following code is illegal and will generate the compiler error:

```
short x = 9;
x = +x;
```

This is illegal because the value on the right side is promoted to be an integer before making the assignment, and an integer cannot be implicitly converted to a short.

In case of binary operators, the following conversion rules apply:

- If one of the operands is of type double, the other operand is converted into type double before the operation.

- If one of the operands is of type float, and the other operand is not of type double, the other operand is converted into type float before the operation.

- If one of the operands is of type long, and the other operand is not of type double or float, the other operand is converted into type long before the operation.

- If none of the operands is of type double, float, or long, both operands are converted into type int before the operation.

These rules are illustrated in the flow diagram presented in Figure 5-2.

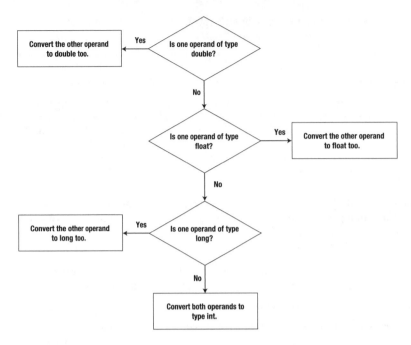

Figure 5-2. *Rules for arithmetic conversion of operands for a binary operator*

As a demonstration, consider Listing 5-6.

Listing 5-6. *ArithmeticConversion.java*

```
1.  public class ArithmeticConversion{
2.     public static void main(String[] args) {
3.        byte b = 5;
4.        int i = 15;
5.        float f =   2.0f;
6.        double d = 10.5d;
7.        if ( (d - f ) >= (-b*i) ) {
8.           System.out.println("The condition >= is true.");
9.        } else {
10.           System.out.println("The condition >= is false.");
11.        }
12.     }
13. }
```

The following is what happens at line 7 of this code:

1. The value of variable b is promoted to the int type and is negated. Remember that this is done just for line 7. The original variable b remains of type byte.

2. The result of step 1 (that is, -5) is multiplied by the value of int i.

3. The value of float f is converted to type double.

4. The result of step 3 is subtracted from the value of double d.

5. The condition is tested to be true.

The output of the code in Listing 5-6 follows:

```
The condition >= is true.
```

In some situations, even if implicit conversion is not possible, the programmer can force the conversion by using what is called *explicit conversion* or casting.

Explicit Conversion of Primitive Data Types

The previous section discussed implicit conversion of primitive data types. It is called *implicit* conversion because you, the programmer, do not need to explicitly ask the compiler for conversion. However, implicit conversion takes place only if the conversion is a widening conversion (except the assignment of literal int values to byte, short, or char). If the conversion is narrowing, then you need to explicitly request the compiler to do the conversion. Explicit conversion is also called *casting*.

Consider the casting example in Listing 5-7.

Listing 5-7. *Casting.java*

```
1. public class Casting{
2.    public static void main(String[] args) {
3.        long l = 10;
4.        int i = (int) l;
5.        short s = 175;
6.        byte  b = (byte) s;
7.        System.out.println("Value of i: " + i );
8.        System.out.println("Value of b: " + b);
9.    }
10. }
```

Consider the statement in line 4:

```
int i = (int)l;
```

We first cast the value of type long l into type int, and then assign it to the int variable i. The casting is done by preceding the variable (or value) of the source type with the name of the target type in the parentheses. Assume that we replace line 4 with the following:

```
int i = l;
```

This will generate a compiler error. You should be aware that in casting you could lose precision and also get wrong results. For example, consider lines 5 and 6 in Listing 5-7. The value of short s is 175, which is 0000000010101111 in binary. In line 6, this number is cast into a byte. A byte is 8 bits in size. Therefore, the highest 8 bits in the number would be thrown away, and the converted number would be 1010111, which is a negative number with the value -81.

The output of the code fragment in Listing 5-7 follows:

```
Value of i: 10
Value of b: -81
```

Note that the value of b is inaccurate. Now you understand why it makes sense that the compiler will not make this (narrowing) conversion implicitly.

■**Caution** In a narrowing conversion, casting is mandatory. However, casting to a narrower type runs the risk of losing information and generating inaccurate results.

In a narrowing conversion, the casting is mandatory. In a widening conversion, the casting is not necessary because implicit conversion will kick in, but it could be used to make the code more readable.

Casting of primitive data types may be summarized into the following rules:

- You can cast any non-boolean data type to any other non-boolean data types. The cast may be narrowing or widening.

- You cannot cast a boolean to a non-boolean type.

- You cannot cast a non-boolean type to a boolean type.

Now that you know how the primitive types are converted explicitly and implicitly, an obvious question will be: how about the conversion of reference types?

Conversion of Object Reference Types

As you learned in Chapter 2, in addition to primitive data types in Java there are nonprimitive data types called objects or object references. The name object reference owes to the fact that you handle an object by using a variable that points (refers) to the object (data), as opposed to a primitive variable, which holds the value (data) itself. Just like primitive types, object reference types can also go through conversion in two ways: implicit and explicit.

Implicit Conversion of Object Reference Types

Before understanding the conversion, you should know that there are three kinds of object reference types:

- A class

- An interface

- An array

Like the primitive variables, implicit type conversion of object reference variables takes place in assignments and in method calls, and the rules are the same for both situations. Unlike the primitive variables, the object reference variables do not participate in arithmetic promotion, simply because the object reference variables cannot be arithmetic operands. For example, if cow is an object of the Cow class and buffalo is an object of the Buffalo class, cow + buffalo is not defined.

Assignment Conversion

Implicit conversion of an object reference type in an assignment operation typically looks like the following:

```
<sourceType> s  = new <sourceType>();
<targetType> t  = s;    // Implicit conversion of <sourceType> to <targetType>.
```

This is the general form of implicit conversion from <sourceType> to <targetType> in assignment. The <sourceType> and <targetType> may be a class, an interface, or an array. This creates nine possible cases for conversion. The rules for these nine cases are summarized in Table 5-2.

Table 5-2. *Rules for Implicit Conversion of Object Reference Types*

<table>
<tr><td rowspan="2">Target Type</td><td></td><td colspan="3" align="center">Source Type</td></tr>
<tr><td></td><td>Class</td><td>Interface</td><td>Array</td></tr>
<tr><td></td><td>Class</td><td>Source type must be a subclass of target type.</td><td>Target type must be an <code>Object</code>.</td><td>Target type must be an <code>Object</code>.</td></tr>
<tr><td></td><td>Interface</td><td>Source type must implement the interface of target type.</td><td>Source type must be subinterface of target type.</td><td>Target type must be <code>Cloneable</code> or <code>Serializable</code>.</td></tr>
<tr><td></td><td>Array</td><td>Compiler error.</td><td>Compiler error.</td><td>Source type must be an array of an object reference type. It must be legal to convert that object reference type to the type of elements contained in the the target type array.</td></tr>
</table>

Table 5-2 depicts the following rules for implicit conversion of object reference types:

- A class type may be converted to another class type if one of the following is true:
  - The <sourceType> is a subclass of the <targetType>.
  - The <sourceType> implements the <targetType>.
- An interface type may be converted to one of the following:
  - Another interface if the <sourceType> is a subinterface of the <targetType>.
  - The Object type if the <targetType> is an object.
- An array may be converted to one of the following:
  - Another array if the following conditions are true: both <sourceType> and <targetType> are arrays of object reference types, and the object reference type of <sourceType> array elements is convertible to the object reference types of <targetType> array elements.
  - The interface: Cloneable or Serializable.
  - The class Object.

Note Implicit conversion of a class type or an interface type into an array is not allowed.

As an example, the class hierarchy in Figure 5-3 illustrates some of the rules for implicit conversion of object reference types. The classes Lab, LectureHall, and Auditorium are derived from the class ClassRoom, which in turn is derived from the class Room. Furthermore, the class ClassRoom implements the interface Facilities.

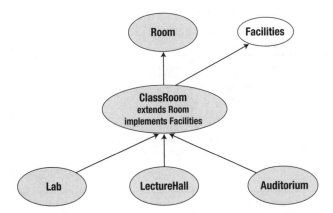

Figure 5-3. *Hierarchy of classes to illustrate the conversion rules*

As an example, consider the following lines of code:

```
Lab  lab1 =  new Lab();
ClassRoom csroom = lab1;
```

This code would work because the class `Lab` is being converted into the class `ClassRoom`, and `Lab` is a subclass of `ClassRoom`. On the other hand, the following code will generate a compiler error:

```
ClassRoom croom = new ClassRoom();
Lab cslab = croom;     // compiler error.
```

The compiler error will be generated because an attempt is being made to convert `ClassRoom` into `Lab`, but `ClassRoom` is not a subclass of `Lab`.

Further, consider the following code:

```
1. LectureHall  lh174 = new LectureHall();
2. Facilities facil174 = lh174;
3. LectureHall lh158 = facil174;  // compiler error.
```

Line 2 will work because the class `LectureHall` is being converted into the interface `Facilities`, `LectureHall` extends `ClassRoom`, and `ClassRoom` implements `Facilities`. However, line 3 would generate a compiler error because the interface `Facilities` is being converted into `LectureHall`, and `Facilities` is not a subinterface of `LectureHall`.

Finally, consider a full code example in Listing 5-8.

Listing 5-8. *ObjectRefConversion.java*

```
1. public class ObjectRefConversion{
2.   public static void main(String[] args) {
3.         ClassRoom[] crooms = new ClassRoom[10];
4.         Room[] rooms;
5.         Lab[] labs;
6.       for (int i = 0; i<5; i++) {
7.           crooms[i] = new ClassRoom();
8.       }
9.          rooms = crooms;
10.         labs = crooms;  // compiler error
11.   }
12.  }
13.
```

```
14.  interface Facilities {
15.  }
16. class Room {
17. } .
18. class ClassRoom  extends Room implements Facilities{
19. }
20. class Lab extends ClassRoom {
21. }
```

The conversion in line 9 will work because rooms and crooms are both arrays and the element type of crooms (that is, ClassRoom) is convertible to the element type of rooms (that is, Room). On the other hand, line 10 will generate a compiler error because the type of elements of array crooms (that is, ClassRoom) is not convertible to the type of elements of array labs (that is, Lab).

Just as with primitive types, implicit conversion of reference types can happen during method calls.

Method Call Conversion

The rules for method call conversion are the same as the rules for assignment conversion. The point to remember here is that the passed-in argument types are converted into the method parameter types when the conversion is valid.

In some situations, even if implicit conversion is not possible, the programmer can force conversion by using what is called casting, or explicit conversion.

Explicit Conversion of Object Reference Types

Explicit conversion of object reference types is also called *object reference casting*. Its syntax is the same as that of primitive data type casting. Any conversion that is allowed implicitly is also allowed explicitly. However, explicit conversion exhibits its real power when we use it for conversions that are not allowed implicitly.

To understand explicit conversion of object references, you must understand that complete information may not be available at compile time, unlike with the primitive types. For example, consider the following lines of code:

```
Lab  lab1 =  new Lab();
ClassRoom csroom = lab1;
```

Here, csroom is an object reference of type ClassRoom. This information is available at compile time. However, it refers to the object lab1, which will be created at runtime. Therefore, at compile time we do not know to which object type this reference variable csroom refers. Because object reference conversion may involve reference types and object types, the rules of object reference casting are much broader:

- Some of the casting rules relate to the reference type (which is known at compile time) and therefore can be enforced at compile time.

- Some of the casting rules relate to the object type (which is not known at compile time) and therefore can only be enforced at runtime.

At compile time, the following rules must be obeyed:

- When both the source type and target type are classes, one class must be a subclass of the other.

- When both the source type and target type are arrays, the elements of both the arrays must be object reference types and not primitive types. Also, the object reference type of the source array must be convertible to the object reference type of the target array.

- The casting between an interface and an object that is not final is always allowed.

If a casting passes the compilation, then the following rules are enforced at runtime:

- If the target type is a class, then the class of the expression being converted must be either the same as the target type or its subclass.

- If the target type is an interface, then the class of the expression being converted must implement the target type.

As an example, consider the following code fragment:

```
1. Auditorium a1,a2;
2. ClassRoom c;
3. LectureHall lh;
4. a1 = new Auditorium();
5. c = a1;        //legal implicit conversion.
6. a2  = (Auditorium) c;    // Legal cast.
7. lh = (LectureHall) c;    // Illegal cast.
```

First, note that the code fragment has four object references, namely a1, a2, c, and lh. However, only one object is created and assigned to the reference a1 in line 4. The assignment in line 5 represents a legal conversion because the class of a1 is a subclass of the class of c. In line 6, the compiler cannot determine the class of the object to which c refers. Therefore, line 6 would be fine at compile time because the compiler would look at c as a ClassRoom, and Auditorium is a subclass of ClassRoom. Line 6 will also be fine at execution time because c already refers to an object of Auditorium, and a2 is also of type Auditorium. In line 7, again the compiler cannot determine the class of the object to which c refers. However, c is an abject reference of class ClassRoom, and LectureHall is a subclass of ClassRoom. Therefore, line 7 will be fine at compile time. However, at execution time, the JVM knows that c refers to an object of class Auditorium (due to line 5). Auditorium type cannot be converted to LectureHall. Thus, the conversion in line 7 is illegal, and will generate an exception at runtime. For this to be legal, the class of the object to which c refers has to be either LectureHall or a subclass of it.

■Caution When an attempt to cast a reference variable to a type is illegal, the JVM throws the ClassCastException. You will learn about throwing exceptions in Chapter 7.

You have seen how object reference type conversion is related to inheritance. A subclass inherits the non-private members of its superclass, including methods. An inherited method can be rewritten to meet the requirements of the subclass, which is called *overriding*. You can also write several versions of the same method in a class, called *overloading*. You need to understand the rules that you must follow while overriding or overloading a method.

Using Method Overriding and Overloading

Overriding and overloading are two salient features of Java. Overriding allows you to modify the behavior of an inherited method to meet the specific needs of a subclass, while overloading allows you to use the same method name to implement different (but related) functionalities. Therefore, overriding and overloading facilitate code extensibility and flexibility.

Method Overriding

You know that a subclass inherits all the (non-private) methods and variables of the superclass. In some situations, you might need to change the behavior of an inherited method, such as when implementing polymorphism, as explored earlier in the chapter. In that case, you would redefine the method by keeping the same signature but rewriting the body. This is exactly what is called method overriding. In other words, *method overriding* is a feature of Java that lets the programmer declare and implement a method in a subclass that has the same signature as a method in the superclass. The same signature in this case means the same name and the same number of parameters and their types appearing in the same order. While the signature must be the same, the code in the method body may be, and generally is, different.

The body of the overriding method may or may not include a call to the overridden method. That is, you can specifically invoke the overridden method from the body of the overriding method, if you want to. As an example, consider again the code example in Listing 5-4. Uncomment lines 19 and 25, which invoke the overridden method saySomething() of the superclass Animal from the subclasses Cow and Buffalo. If you compile and execute the code, the following is the output:

```
Umm...
Moo!
Umm...
Bah!
```

The overridden version and the overriding versions of saySomething() were executed.

The following are the rules for overriding a method:

- You cannot override a method that has the final modifier.

- You cannot override a static method to make it non-static.

- The overriding method and the overridden method must have the same return type. J2SE 5.0 allows a covariant return type as well, as discussed a bit later in this section.

- The number of parameters and their types in the overriding method must be same as in the overridden method and the types must appear in the same order. However, the names of the parameters may be different.

- You cannot override a method to make it less accessible. For example, overriding a public method and declaring it protected will generate a compiler error, whereas overriding a protected method and declaring it public will be fine.

- If the overriding method has a throws clause in its declaration, then the following two conditions must be true:

  - The overridden method must have a throws clause, as well.

  - Each exception included in the throws clause of the overriding method must be either one of the exceptions in the throws clause of the overridden method or a subclass of it.

- If the overridden method has a throws clause, the overriding method does not have to.

The throws clause has to do with the execution flow when an error happens in the executing program. You will learn more about this topic in Chapter 7. Do not forget the obvious rule that if you cannot inherit a method, you cannot override it either. For example, you cannot override a private method of the superclass because you cannot inherit it. Of course, you can write a method in the subclass with the same signatures (method name and parameters) as a private method in the superclass. But it will not be considered as an overriding. Note that violating any of the overriding rules mentioned here will generate a compiler error.

To elaborate on some of the rules for overriding, consider the following method signature of a superclass:

```
protected int aMethod(String st, int i, double number);
```

Table 5-3 presents some examples of valid and invalid overriding of this method in a subclass.

Table 5-3. *Examples of Valid and Invalid Overriding of the Method protected int aMethod(String st, int i, double number)*

Method Signature in a Subclass	Validity	Reason
`protected int aMethod(String st, int i, double number)`	Valid	Same signature
`protected int aMethod(String st, int j, double num)`	Valid	Same signature
`protected double aMethod(String st, int i, double number)`	Invalid	Different return type
`protected int aMethod(int i, String st, double number)`	Invalid	Argument types are in different order
`protected int aMethod(String st, int i, double number, int j)`	Invalid	Different number of types
`protected int aMethod(String st, int i)`	Invalid	Different number of types
`int aMethod(String st, int i, double number)`	Invalid	Default modifier is less public than `protected`

Prior to J2SE 5.0, the return type of the overriding method must be identical to the return type of the overridden method. Starting with J2SE 5.0, however, the return type of the overriding method can also be a subclass of the return type of the overridden method. This return type of the overriding method is called a *covariant return type.*

■Note A covariant return type of an overriding method is a subclass of the return type of the overridden method, and is legal.

For example, consider the following method:

```
public Number myMethod();
```

In J2SE 5.0, it can be legally overridden by the following method:

```
public Double myMethod();
```

Note that this overriding is legal because Double is a subclass of Number.

So, overriding is rewriting a method that a subclass inherits from its superclass. It does not, however, overwrite the superclass method; you can still invoke the original version of the inherited method by using the keyword super. So after overriding, two versions of a method co-exist. You can also write multiple versions of a method in the same class in order to meet the business requirements of using basically the same functionality but in slightly varying ways. This is called method overloading.

Method Overloading

Method overloading is helpful when the same task is to be performed in slightly different ways under different conditions. So, method overloading is a feature of Java that facilitates defining multiple methods in a class with identical names. In contrast to overriding methods, no two overloaded methods could have the same parameter types in the same order. The return types in overloaded methods may be the same or different, while the return type of an overriding method must match that of the overridden method.

■**Note** No two overloaded versions of a method can have an identical list of parameter types, while an overridden and the overriding methods must have an identical list of parameter types. The return types of any two overloaded versions of a method can be different or the same, while the return type of an overriding method must be the same as that of the overridden method or a subclass of it.

For example, assume that we want to write a class for calculating the area of different shapes such as a triangle, a rectangle, and a square. All of these tasks are the same to the extent that they all relate to calculating the area, but they are performed differently because the formulae to calculate the area in all of these cases would differ and would require different input. To perform this task, we write three versions of an overloaded method calculateArea(…) inside the class AreaCalculator in Listing 5-9.

Listing 5-9. *TestAreaCalculator.java*

```
1. class TestAreaCalculator {
2.    public static void main(String[] args) {
3.    AreaCalculator ac = new AreaCalculator();
4.    System.out.println("Area of a rectangle with length 2.0, and width 3.0:
      " + ac.calculateArea(2.0f, 3.0f));
5.    System.out.println("Area of a triangle with sides 2.0, 3.0, and 4.0: "
         + ac.calculateArea(2.0, 3.0, 4.0));
6.    System.out.println("Area of a circle with radius 2.0: " +
         ac.calculateArea(2.0));
7.    }
8.  }
9. class AreaCalculator {
10.    float  calculateArea(float length, float width) {
11.        return length*width;
12.    }
13.    double calculateArea(double radius) {
14.        return ((Math.PI)*radius*radius);
15.    }
16.    double  calculateArea(double a, double b, double c) {
17.        double s = (a+b+c)/2.0;
18.        return  Math.sqrt(s*(s-a)*(s-b)*(s-c));
19.    }
20. }
```

The output from this code follows:

```
Area of a rectangle with length 2.0, and width 3.0: 6.0
Area of a triangle with sides 2.0, 3.0, and 4.0: 2.9047375096555625
Area of a circle with radius 2.0: 12.566370614359172
```

Note that lines 4, 5, and 6 make identical method calls except the list of arguments and return types. Recall that no two versions of an overloaded method are allowed to have the same parameter types in the same order. This is because the compiler determines which of the overloaded methods to call by looking at the argument list of the method call. One final point: a method in a subclass inherited from its superclass may also be overloaded. To elaborate the rules of method overloading, consider this code fragment:

■Caution A method in a subclass inherited from its superclass can be both overridden and overloaded. Look out for this situation in the exam questions.

```
class VolumeCalculator extends AreaCalculator {
  int  calculateArea (int i, int j) {
  }
  double calculateVolume (double x, int y, double z);
  }
}
```

In the class VolumeCalculator, calculateArea(…) is an overloaded version of the inherited methods, and the method calculateVolume(…) is a new method of the VolumeCalculator class. In terms of overriding, you may think that the calculateArea(int i, int j) method is invalid because its parameter types do not match those of the corresponding methods in the superclass. However, if you recall that the subclass VolumeCalculator inherits all the methods of its superclass, and think of calculateArea(…) as another overloaded version of these inherited methods, then you will realize that it is a valid method. Table 5-4 presents some examples of methods that could or could not be added to the class VolumeCalculator.

Table 5-4. *Some Examples of Permitted and Prohibited Methods in the VolumeCalculator Class Derived from the AreaCalculator Class*

Method	Validity	Reason
int calculateArea(float a, float b)	Invalid	The method has the same name as methods inherited from the superclass CalculateArea. But this method is neither correctly overridden nor correctly overloaded. Hence the compiler will generate an error on this.
double calculateVolume (double x, double y, int z)	Valid	Same set of argument types but in different order. Therefore it is a valid overloading of the existing method.
int calculateVolume (double x, int z, double y)	Invalid	Same set of argument types in the same order as the previously defined method with the same name. Therefore, invalid overloading. It cannot be overridden because the superclass does not have it. It will generate a compiler error.
void CalculateVolume()	Valid	Different set of argument types from the existing method. Therefore valid overloading.

■Caution When determining the validity of a method in a class, consider both cases: overriding and overloading. If either of the two is valid, then the method is valid. In the exam, look out for traps in questions where a method will be a valid overloading but an invalid overriding or vice versa.

The key points about method overloading are summarized here:

- Two or more methods in the same class with the same name are called overloaded if they have either different sets of parameter types or the same set of parameter types in different order.

- The return type of two overloaded methods can be different or the same.

- Overloaded methods are effectively independent of each other.

- The compiler determines which of the overloaded methods to call by looking at the argument list of the method call.

- Any of the methods inherited from the superclass can also be overloaded.

- Overloaded versions of a method can have different or the same checked exceptions in the throws clauses. You will learn about exceptions in Chapter 7.

- Overloaded versions of a method can have different modifiers.

As a summary, overriding and overloading are compared in Table 5-5.

Table 5-5. *Comparison of Overriding and Overloading*

Characteristic	Overriding	Overloading
Name	Must have the same method name.	Must have the same method name.
Access modifiers	The overriding method cannot be less public than the overridden method.	Different versions can have different access modifiers.
Parameter types	Identical list of parameter types.	The set of parameter types of any two versions must be different or should appear in a different order.
Return types	Must be the same.	Can be the same or different.
Checked exceptions	Any exception declared in the overriding method must be the same as or a subclass of an exception declared in the overridden method.	No restriction on exception.

Now that you know about method overriding and method overloading, you can consider those method-like creatures called constructors, and ask the question: Can I override or overload a constructor? You know from Chapter 3 that constructors cannot be inherited. That means you cannot override constructors, but you can overload them.

Constructor Overloading

Recall some facts about constructors from Chapter 3:

- A constructor of a class has the same name as the class, and has no explicit return type; it can have zero or more parameters.

- A class may have more than one constructor. If the programmer defines no constructor in a class, the compiler adds the default constructor with no arguments. If one or more constructors are defined in the class, the compiler does not provide any constructor.

When we say a constructor must have the same name as the class, but we can have multiple constructors for a class, we are obviously talking about constructor overloading. Constructor overloading provides flexibility in how you want your constructor to be instantiated and initialized. Inside a constructor, you can call another constructor.

The keyword this is used to call another constructor of the same class, and the keyword super is used to call a constructor of the superclass. If either this or super is used, it must appear in the beginning of the code block of the constructor. If we add our own super or this call, then the compiler will not add this line.

As an example, consider the code in Listing 5-10.

Listing 5-10. *ConstOverload.java*

```
1. public class ConstOverload{
2.   public static void main(String[] args) {
3.       new A();
4.   }
5. }
6. class A {
7.    int x=0;
8.    A(){
9.      this(5);
10.     System.out.println("A() ");
11.   }
11.   A(int i){
12.     //   this();
13.       System.out.println(i);
14.   }
15. }
```

Note that line 12 is commented. The output from Listing 5-10 follows:

```
5
A( )
```

If you uncomment line 12, depending upon a specific compiler, you may get a compiler error. But if you don't, your program will execute in a loop. This is because class A has only two constructors, and both have the this statement in the beginning, so the compiler does not place any super() call. So, both constructors would keep calling each other.

Remember the following two things relevant to constructor overloading:

- The first line in a constructor must be a super() or a this() call. If (and only if) you do not place either of these calls, the compiler will place the super() call.

- If (and only if) you do not define a constructor for a class, the compiler will place a no-argument default constructor for you.

Codewalk Quicklet

The code for the codewalk quicklet exercise in this chapter is presented in Listing 5-11.

Listing 5-11. *CodeWalkFour.java*

```
1. class CodeWalkFour {
2.    public static void main(String[] args){
3.        Car c = new Lexus();
4.        System.out.print(c.speedUp(30) + " ");
5.        Lexus l = new Lexus();
```

```
6.         System.out.print(l.speedUp(30, 40, 50));
7.     }
8.  }
9.  class Car {
10.     private int i=0;
11.     int speedUp(int x){
12.         return i;
13.     }
14. }
15. class Lexus extends Car {
16.     private int j = 1;
17.     private int k = 2;
18.       int speedUp(int y){
19.       return j;
20.     }
21.     int speedUp(int... z){
22.         return k;
23.       }
24.  }
```

To get you started on this exercise, following are some hints:

- *Input*: Lines 10, 16, and 17.

- *Operations*: Lines 12, 19, and 22.

- *Output*: Lines 4 and 6.

- *Rules*: How do the vararg methods work?

Looking at the code from this angle, see if you can handle the last question in the "Review Questions" section based on this code.

The three most important takeaways from this chapter are the following:

- A subclass is in an *is-a* relationship with its parent class, and a class is in a *has-a* relationship with another class if it contains an object reference for that class. For example, a lab is a room, and a lab has a microscope.

- A primitive as well as an object reference variable can be converted from one data type to another implicitly or explicitly by following certain rules.

- Method overriding means modifying the method inherited from the parent class, while method overloading means writing several versions of the same method of the class. An inherited method can be overloaded too.

Summary

An object-oriented language such as Java contains some special features such as object-oriented relationships, encapsulation, polymorphism, and method overriding. The *is-a* relationship is implemented through inheritance by deriving a subclass from a superclass, and the *has-a* relationship between two classes is implemented by having a reference to a class (object reference variable) in another class. Encapsulation refers to the fact that in an object-oriented language, the data and the operations on the data (methods) are encapsulated in the class. Tight encapsulation (or data abstraction) is achieved by making the data members of a class `private` and providing access to them through methods. Polymorphism means giving different meanings to the same thing, and is an implication of an *is-a* relationship in Java, which in turn is related to inheritance. The ability to convert an object reference from one type to another type is at the heart of polymorphism.

During data handling, the data variables (both primitive and object reference) are often converted from one type to another. This conversion can happen implicitly, or it can be enforced by the programmer, which is called casting. No conversion is allowed between a boolean and a non-boolean type. Also, an implicit conversion to a narrower type is not allowed. Casting (explicit conversion) to narrower types is possible but runs the risk of losing accuracy.

You can rewrite an inherited method in the subclass, which is called overriding. You can also write a different version of a method in the same class, called overloading. An overriding method has the same name as the overridden method. Also, all the versions of an overloaded method have the same name. However, no two overloaded versions of a method can have an identical list of parameter types, while an overridden and the overriding methods must have an identical list of parameter types. The return types of any two overloaded versions of a method can be different or the same, while the return types of an overriding and the overridden methods have to be same.

When a method calls another method, the execution control is transferred to the other method, and returns back to the calling method after it's done with the called method. Every programming language has to offer some constructs for controlling the flow of execution. This is the topic of the next chapter.

EXAM'S EYE VIEW

Comprehend

- The *is-a* relationship is associated with inheritance. For example, if the class Cow is derived from the class Animal, then a cow (an instance of the Cow class) is an animal (an instance of the Animal class).

- The *has-a* relationship is associated with encapsulation; that is, the class members (data and methods) are encapsulated into the class. For example, if the Cow class has a data variable tail in it, then you can say a cow has a tail.

- An invalid implicit conversion will generate a compiler error because all the information needed to determine the validity of an implicit conversion is available at compile time.

Look Out

- No two overloaded versions of a method can have an identical list of parameter types, while an overridden and the overriding methods must have an identical list of parameter types.

- The return types of any two overloaded versions of a method can be different or the same, while the return types of an overriding and the overridden methods have to be same.

- An inherited method can also be overloaded.

- You cannot override a final method, and you cannot override a static method to make it non-static.

- Generally speaking, implicit conversion to a narrower type is not allowed. However, a literal integer value can be assigned to variables of type byte, short, or char provided the value is within the legal range of the variable type.

Memorize

- No conversion between boolean and non-boolean types is allowed.

- Implicit conversion of a non-boolean type to a narrower type is not allowed.

- A decimal numeric value is considered of type double and a literal non-decimal value is considered of type int.

- Implicit conversion of a class type or an interface type into an array is not allowed.

Review Questions

1. Consider the following line of code:

```
short s = 9L;
```

What would be the output? (Choose all that apply.)

A. Compiler error

B. Runtime error

C. No error

D. Loss of accuracy

2. Which of the following statements is true?

A. Only primitive data types, and not the object references, can be converted implicitly.

B. Only the object references, and not the primitive data types, can be cast (converted explicitly).

C. Both object references and primitive data types may be converted implicitly and explicitly.

D. Casting primitive data types is checked only at execution time.

3. Consider the following line of code:

```
short s = 9;
```

What would be the output of this line of code? (Choose all that apply.)

A. Compiler error

B. Runtime error

C. No error

D. Loss of accuracy

4. Consider the following line of code:

```
byte b  = 335;
```

What would be the output of this line of code?

A. Compiler error

B. Runtime error

C. No error

D. Loss of accuracy

5. If the following code works correctly, what are the possible types of variable c?

```
byte a = 7;
short  b =  3;
c = a * ++b;
```

A. short, int, long, float, double

B. short, char, int, float, double

C. byte, short, int, long, float, double

D. int, long, float, double

6. Consider the following code fragment:

```
1. class Student {
2.    private int studentId  =  0;
3.    void setStudentID (int sid) {
4.    studentId = sid;
5.    System.out.println("Student ID has been set to " + sid);
6.    }
7.    public static void main(String args[]) {
8.        short s = 420;
9.        Student st1 = new Student();
10.       st1.setStudentID(s);
11.  }
12. }
```

Which of the following statements about this code is true?

A. Line 10 will generate a compiler error because the method setStudentID(…) takes an int argument, and not a short argument.

B. The code will compile but will throw an exception at execution time due to line 10.

C. The code will compile, execute, and produce the output Student ID has been set to 420.

D. Line 8 will generate a compiler error.

7. Which of the following statements about object reference conversion is true?

A. Object references can never be converted.

B. Object references can never be converted in method calls.

C. Object references can be converted both in method calls and in assignments, but the rules for both are different.

D. Object references can be converted both in method calls and in assignments, and the rules for both are the same.

8. Consider the following code fragment:

```
1. class StudentProb {
2.    private int studentId  =  0;
3.    void setStudentID(int sid) {
4.        student_id = sid;
5.        System.out.println("Student ID has been set to " + sid);
6.    }
7.    public static void main(String args[]) {
8.        int i = 420;
9.        Object ob1;
10.       StudentProb st1 = new StudentProb();
11.       ob1 = st1;
12.       st1.setStudentID(i);
13.   }
14. }
```

Which of the following statements is true about this code?

A. A compiler error will occur due to line 9.

B. A compiler error will occur due to line 11.

C. An exception will occur during execution due to line 11.

D. The code will compile, execute, and produce the output Student ID has been set to 420.

For questions 9 and 10, consider the class hierarchy shown in the Exhibit:

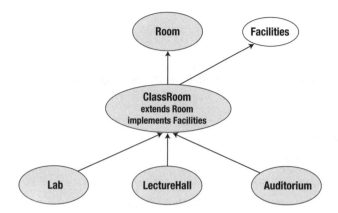

9. Consider the following code fragment:

```
1.    LectureHall lh = new LectureHall();
2.    Auditorium a1;
3.    Facilities f1;
4.
5.    f1 = lh;
6.    a1 = f1;
```

What of the following is the true statement about this code?

A. The code will compile and execute without any error.

B. Line 5 will generate a compiler error because an explicit conversion (cast) is required.

C. Line 6 will generate a compiler error because an explicit conversion (cast) is required to convert Facilities to Auditorium.

10. Consider the following code fragment:

```
1.    LectureHall lh = new LectureHall();
2.    Auditorium a1;
3.    Facilities f1;
4.
5.    f1 = lh;
6.    a1 = (Auditorium) f1;
```

What of the following is the true statement about this code?

A. The code will compile and execute without any error.

B. Line 5 will generate a compiler error because an explicit conversion (cast) is required.

C. Line 6 will generate a compiler error because an interface cannot be converted to the class that implements the interface.

D. Line 6 will compile fine, but an exception will be thrown during the execution time.

11. Consider the following class:

```
1.  class MyClass {
2.    public int myMethod (double a, int  i) {
3.    }
4.
5.  }
```

Which of the following methods, if added at line 4 independently, would be valid?

A. `public int myMethod(int i, double a) { }`

B. `public double myMethod(double b, int j){ }`

C. `public int myMethod(double a, double b, int i){ }`

D. `public int yourMethod(double a, int i) { }`

12. You have been given a design document for implementation in Java. It states:

A room has a table, and a chair. A classroom is a room that has a teacher and students. Assume that the Room *class has already been defined.*

Which of the following data members would be appropriate to include in the class `ClassRoom`?

A. `Room aRoom;`

B. `Table aTable;`

C. `Chair aChairbb;`

D. `Teacher aTeacher;`

E. `Student aStudent;`

13. Which of the following statements are true?

A. Inheritance represents an *is-a* relationship.

B. Inheritance represents a *has-a* relationship.

C. An instance represents an *is-a* relationship.

D. An instance represents a *has-a* relationship.

E. A method represents an *is-a* relationship.

14. A laptop is a specific kind of computer, and it has a network card installed on it. A desktop is also a specific kind of computer. Which of the following statements are true?

A. A laptop *is-a* computer.

B. A computer *is-a* laptop.

C. A laptop *has-a* network card.

D. A computer *is-a* desktop.

15. Consider the following classes defined in separate source files:

```
class SuperClass {
SuperClass() {
   System.out.print(" I was in Super Class." );
}
  public void aMethod (int i) {
     System.out.print (" The value of i is " + i );
  }
}
  class SubClass extends SuperClass {
  public void aMethod(int j) {
     System.out.print (" The value of j is " +  j );
  }
}
class Test {
 public static void main(String args[]) {
    SubClass sub = new SubClass();
    sub.aMethod(5);
  }
}
```

What output is generated when the class Test is run?

A. The value of i is 5.

B. The value of j is 5.

C. I was in Super Class. The value of i is 5.

D. I was in Super Class. The value of j is 5.

16. Consider the code in Listing 5-11. What is the result?

A. 30 30 40 50

B. 0 1

C. 0 2

D. 1 2

E. Compilation fails.

CHAPTER 6

Execution Flow Control in Java

Exam Objectives

2.1 Develop code that implements an if or switch statement; and identify legal argument types for these statements.

2.2 Develop code that implements all forms of loops and iterators, including the use of for, the enhanced for loop (for-each), do, while, labels, break, and continue; and explain the values taken by loop counter variables during and after loop execution.

The order in which the code statements will be executed is an important component of the internal architecture of a program. In a given block, the program is executed sequentially one statement at a time starting from the first statement at the top and proceeding toward the bottom. This scheme, without any additional flow logic, will execute each statement precisely once. However, if a programming language is to allow you to write programs to solve real-life problems, it must recognize the conditional logic that is at work in real life. For example, if it is Sunday and sunny, you will go to the beach, if it is a weekday, you will go to work, there are a few things in life that you will do over and over again, and so on. Java, like most other languages, offers conditional flow logic for the program execution. A set of statements may be executed once, more than once, or skipped altogether, and the decision may be made at runtime (that is, at the time of program execution). This makes programming more dynamic, efficient, and powerful.

We will explore three kinds of execution flow control offered by Java: to skip a block of statements, to execute a block of statements more than once, and to stop execution iteration at any point in the block. The comparison operators discussed in Chapter 2 are used to define conditions for the flow control.

Using Selection Statements

A selection statement allows the conditional execution of a block of statements. If a condition is true, a block of statements will be executed once, else it will be skipped. The selection statements, also called the decision statements, are of two types: if and switch.

The if Statements

The if statements can handle a range of conditions starting from very simple to quite sophisticated. Accordingly, they come in four different constructs: if, if-else, if-else if, and if-else if-else.

The if Construct

The if construct allows the execution of a single statement or a block of statements enclosed within curly braces. The syntax of the if construct is shown here:

```
if( <expression> ) {
    // if <expression> returns true, the statements in this
    // blocks are executed.
}
```

If there is only one statement in the block, the curly braces are not mandatory, but it is a good programming practice to use the curly braces regardless of whether there is one or more statements to execute. Following is an example of an if statement:

```
if ( x > 0 ) {
    System.out.println("x is greater than zero.");
}
```

In this code, assume that x is an integer variable already declared. If the value of x is greater than zero, the following statement will be sent to the standard output (e.g. displayed on the screen):

```
x is greater than zero.
```

If x is not greater than zero, then the print statement in the block will not be executed; the whole if block will be skipped.

Now consider the case in which we don't use the curly braces:

```
1. if ( x > 0 )
2.       System.out.println("x is greater than zero.");
3.       System.out.println("Who cares what x is.");
```

Line 2 will be executed only if x is greater than 0, whereas line 3 will always be executed independent of the value of x.

Remember that the <expression> in the parentheses of if() must evaluate to a boolean value: true or false. Also remember that = is an assignment operator and not the comparison operator. For example, if(x=y) is illegal whereas the legal form is if(x==y). However, if x and y are boolean, then if(x=y) will compile but will give the wrong results. As an illustration, consider Listing 6-1.

Listing 6-1. *IfTest.java*

```
1. class IfTest {
2. public static void main(String[] args)
3. {
4.     boolean b1 = false;
5.     boolean b2 = true;
6.     if(b1=b2){
7.        System.out.println("The value of b1: " + b1);
8.     }
9. }
10.}
```

Line 6 will compile, but it will change the value of b1 from false to true because it assigns the value of b2 to b1, and now, because b1 is true, the test will pass, and the body of the if block will be executed. The output from Listing 6-1 follows:

```
The value of b1: true
```

■**Note** The legal argument type of an if() statement is a boolean. That means the expression in the parentheses of the if() statement must result in a boolean value.

The if construct handles a very simple situation and takes an action only if the condition is true. A bit more sophisticated case will do something if a condition is true, else do something else.

The if-else Construct

You can handle two blocks of code with the if-else construct. If a condition is true, the first block of code will be executed, otherwise the second block of code will be executed. The syntax for the if-else construct follows:

```
if( <expression> ) {
    // if <expression> returns true,  statements in this block are executed.
}
else {
  // if <expression> is false, then statements in this block will be executed.
}
```

For example, consider the following code fragment:

```
if ( x > 0 ) {
    System.out.println("x is greater than zero.");
}
else {
    System.out.println("x is not greater than zero.");
}
```

If the value of x is greater than zero, the output of this code is

```
x is greater than zero.
```

Otherwise the output is

```
x is not greater than zero.
```

The if and if-else constructs can test only one expression, which may contain one or more conditions. However, you may encounter situations in which multiple conditional expressions exist and you want to test one after the other. You handle this type of situation with the if-else if construct.

The if-else if Construct

With the if-else if construct you can handle multiple blocks of code, and only one of those blocks will be executed at most. The syntax for the if-else construct follows:

```
if( <expression1> ) {
    // if <expression1> returns true,  statements in this block are executed.
}
else if ( <expression2>) {
  // if <expression1> is false and <expression2>  is true,
     then statements in this block will be executed.
}
```

```
    else if (<expression3>) {
        // if <expression1> is false, and <expression2> is false, and <expression3> is
            true, then statements in this block    will be executed.
    }
```

Note that in an `if-else if` construct, the expressions will be tested one by one starting from the top. If an expression returns `true`, the block following the expression will be executed and all the following `else if` blocks will be skipped. Also note that it is possible that no block will be executed, a possibility that does not exist with the `if-else` construct. However, Java does offer a construct that enables you to handle multiple blocks of code and ensure that one of them will certainly be executed, discussed next.

The if-else if-else Construct

The syntax for the `if-else if-else` construct follows:

```
if( <expression1> ) {
    // if <expression1> returns true, statements in this block are executed.
}
else if (<expression2>) {
    // if <expression1> is false and <expression2>  is true,
        then statements in this block will be executed.
}
else if (<expression3>) {
    // if <expression1> is false and <expression2>  is false, and
        <expression3> is true, then statements in this block
        will be executed.
}
else {
    // if the expression in the if statement and the expressions
        in all the else if statements were false, then the statements
        in this block will be executed.
}
```

Keep in mind that the condition in the `if` or `else if` statement can be a compound condition, such as:

```
if(i > 2 && j < 100)
```

However, the condition should always evaluate to a `boolean`.

Summary of the if Constructs

The following list summarizes the `if` family of constructs:

- There are two constructs for a single expression: `if` where it is possible that no block will be executed, and `if-else` where one block will certainly be executed.

- There are also two constructs corresponding to multiple expressions: `if-else if` where it is possible that no block will be executed, and `if-else if-else` where one block will certainly be executed.

- The first construct is always `if`.

- Any of these constructs may be nested inside any other construct. The condition for the inner construct will be tested only if the condition for the outer construct was tested and was true.

Again, consider the if-else if construct, and assume that it finds the expression in an else if statement to be true. In this case, the code block related to that else if statement will be executed and all the other following blocks will be ignored. What if you want all or some of the following blocks executed as well after a block with a true expression is found? You can handle this situation with another selection statement, the switch statement.

The switch Statement

The switch statement is used to make the choices for multiple blocks with the possibility of executing more than one of them. Let's start with an example:

```
switch (x){
        case 5:
                System.out.println("The value of x is 5." );
                break;
        case 4:
            System.out.println("The value of x is 4." );
        case 7:
                System.out.println("The value of x is 7." );
        case 2:
                System.out.println("The value of x is 7." );
        case 1:
                System.out.println("The value of x is 1." );
        default:
                System.out.println("The value of x is default.");
}
```

In this code, x is an integral variable (any integral variable except long) with a certain value assigned to it. If the value of x is 5, the print statement under case 5 is executed. Following this, the break statement is executed. Execution of the break statement moves the execution control to the first line after the switch block. If the value of x is not 5, the next case is tested; that is, it would be checked if the value of x is equal to 4. If it is, the print statement under case 4 is executed. Because there is no break statement after this, all the following statements under all case labels, including the default label, would be executed. This is called a *fall through*. If the value of x is not equal to any value following any case label, the statement(s) under label default are executed.

For example, for x=1, the preceding code will generate the following output:

```
The value of x is 1.
The value of x is default.
```

The default label could go anywhere in the switch block; it does not have to be put at the end. In this case, it was executed because there was no break statement in the previous block executed before it.

■**Caution** In the switch statement, the default case does not have to appear at the end. It can appear anywhere in the switch block.

If the default case is not at the end, and is executed, the execution can fall through in this case as well if there is no break statement in it. For example, the following is a perfectly valid code fragment:

```
    int x=3
switch (x) {
        case 1:
                System.out.println("The value of x is 1." );
                break;
        case 2:
            System.out.println("The value of x is 2." );
        default:
                System.out.println("The value of x is default.");

        case 4:
                System.out.println("The value of x is 4." );
}
```

It will generate the following output:

```
The value of x is default.
The value of x is 4.
```

Remember the following about the default block:

- The default does not have to be at the end of the switch.

- When the execution control faces a default block, it executes it.

- If there is no break statement in the default block, there will be fall through just like in any other block.

The comparison of values following the case labels with the value of the argument of switch determines the execution path. Once the execution path of a particular case is chosen, the execution falls through until it runs into a break statement.

Note the following:

- The argument of switch() must be one of the following types: byte, short, char, int, or enum.

- The argument of case must be a literal integral type number, such as 2, or a literal number expression that could be evaluated at compile time, such as 2+3.

- There should be no duplicate case labels; that is, the same value cannot be used twice.

- The variable x in switch(x) cannot be declared inside the parentheses.

To illustrate the last point, the following statement is illegal:

```
switch ( int x=2;)
```

However, a simple mathematical expression inside the parentheses is fine, such as the following:

```
switch ( x+ y )
```

or

```
switch(x++)
```

where x and y are already declared variables of the correct type.

So, the legal argument type of a switch statement is int, or any other type that can be promoted to int: byte, short, or char. If you use some other type, such as long, float, or double, you will receive a compiler error. Also be careful about the implications of this. For example, the following code fragment is illegal because one of the case labels is too big to be a byte:

```
byte x=5;
switch(x){
  case 5 : System.out.println("five");
  case 130 : System.out.println("one thirty"); // compiler error
}
```

This generates a compiler error because the compiler will look at 130 as an int, which can't fit into a byte.

Also note that an enum, the new kid on the block, can also be used as a legal argument for a switch statement.

Note The legal argument types of a switch statement are byte, short, char, int, and enum. You will receive a compiler error if you use any other type.

To summarize, starting from the top of the switch block, each non-default case is tested. If a case turns out to be true, the statements in that case and all the following cases are executed until a break statement is encountered. If none of the non-default cases is true, and the execution control faces the default case, then the statements in the default case and all the following cases are executed until a break statement is encountered. The default statement can be anywhere in the switch block.

To illustrate this, Listing 6-2 presents a complete runnable example of a switch statement that uses an enum as an argument.

Listing 6-2. *SwitchTest.java*

```
1.  class SwitchTest {
2.  public static void main(String[] args)
3.  {
4.      Signal sig = Enum.valueOf(Signal.class, args[0].toUpperCase());
5.      switch(sig){
6.        case RED:
7.            sig.redSays();
8.            break;
9.        case YELLOW:
10.           sig.yellowSays();
11.        case bGREEN:
12.            sig.greenSays();
13.      }
14.  }
15. }

16.  enum Signal {RED, YELLOW, GREEN;
17.    public void redSays(){
18.        System.out.println("STOP");
19.    }
20.    public void yellowSays(){
21.        System.out.println("STOP if it is safe to do so.");
22.        System.out.println("Otherwise");
23.    }
24.    public void greenSays(){
25.        System.out.println("Keep going.");
26.    }
27. }
```

As an example, you can execute this code with the following command:

```
java SwitchTest yellow
```

The output follows:

```
STOP if it is safe to do so.
Otherwise
Keep going.
```

You have learned how the selection statements determine if a block of statements will be executed at all. But, what if you want a block of statements executed more than once? This is accomplished with the iteration statements, which we explore next.

Iteration Statements

There will be situations in programming in which you will want to have a block of statements executed over and over again as long as a certain condition is true. This is accomplished by using the iteration statements. In order to facilitate iterative execution, Java offers four iteration constructs: while, do-while, for, and for-each.

The while Loop Construct

The while loop construct handles the situation in which a block is executed for the first time only when a condition is true. After execution the condition is checked again, and as long as the condition stays true, the block is executed repeatedly.

The syntax for the while loop construct follows:

```
while ( <expression> ) {
// if the <expression> is true, execute the statements in this block.
// After the execution,  go back to check the condition again.
}
```

The <expression> in the parentheses of while is a boolean condition that returns true or false. If the expression is true, the statements in the while block are executed. After executing the block, the execution control goes back to the while statement to check if the expression is still true. If it is, the while block is executed again, and so on. When the expression returns false, the execution control falls to the first statement immediately after the while block. For example, consider the following code fragment:

```
int i=0;
while ( i < 3 ) {
   System.out.println("Round and round we go." + i);
     i++;
}
```

The output is the following:

```
Round and round we go. 0
Round and round we go. 1
Round and round we go. 2
```

For the first time, the value of i is 0, so the condition i<3 returns true. Therefore the while block is executed. In the second iteration, the value of i is incremented to 1, and the condition is checked again, which returns true. The block execution produces the output again. The value of i is incremented to 2, and so on. When the print line is printed the third time, the value of i is incremented to 3, and the condition is checked; it returns false. At this point, the control falls to the first statement after the while block. Therefore, the preceding piece of code will print the line Round and round we go. three times to the standard output (for example, to the monitor).

Note that the code block in the while loop may not be executed at all. How do you handle the situation in which you want to make sure that a block is executed once even before checking the condition? Well, the do-while loop construct comes to your rescue here.

The do-while Loop Construct

The do-while loop construct says: go ahead and execute the block for the first time, and then start checking the condition. The syntax for the do-while construct follows:

```
do {
        // Execute the statements in this block.
} while ( <expression> );
```

Again, the <expression> is a boolean condition that returns true or false. When the execution control arrives at do, it enters the do block. After executing the statements in the do block, the expression specified by <expression> is executed. If it returns true, the control goes back to the do statement and the do block is executed again. Following that, the expression is executed again, and so on. When the expression returns false, the control goes to the first statement immediately after the while statement. Note that the do-while loop will be executed at least once, whereas if the expression is initially false, the while loop will not be executed at all.

■**Caution** The do-while loop will be executed at least once, whereas, depending upon the expression, the while loop may not be executed at all.

Sophisticated alternatives to the while constructs are the for constructs, discussed next.

The for Loop Construct

The for loop is the most sophisticated of all the loop constructs and provides a richer functionality as a result. This section discusses the syntax for the for loop construct and some rules for its arguments.

The for Construct Syntax

The syntax for the for loop construct is shown here:

```
for ( <statement>; <test>; <expression>) {
   // if the <test> is true, execute the block.
}
```

The following list explains the arguments (the three elements appearing in the parentheses) of the for construct:

- `<statement>`: Often used to initialize the iteration variable that will monitor the iteration (e.g. i=0). The variable may also be declared and initialized (e.g. int i = 0). The `<statement>` is executed only once, when the control comes to the for loop for the first time.

- `<test>`: A boolean condition that returns either true or false. The for block is executed repeatedly until the `<test>` returns false. Depending upon the test, and the value of the iteration variable, the for block may never be executed.

- `<expression>`: Executed immediately after the execution of the for block, each time the for block is executed. Generally, it is used to change the value of the iteration variable, also called the loop counter.

If the `<test>` returns true, the for block will be executed. Immediately after the block execution, `<expression>` will be executed. Then the `<test>` will be executed again. If it returns true, the block will be executed again. Following this, `<expression>` will be executed again, and so on. When `<test>` returns false, the execution control jumps to the first statement immediately after the for block.

For example, consider the following code fragment:

```
int i;
for ( i=0; i < 3;  i++) {
   System.out.println("The value of i: " + i );
}
```

This code fragment will generate the following output:

```
The value of i: 0
The value of i: 1
The value of i: 2
```

■**Caution** Note that the expression in the parentheses of for() that involves the loop counter is executed after an iteration and not before.

There is more to the elements in the parentheses of the for() construct than what meets the eye.

More About Arguments of the for() Construct: Beware!

You must remember some rules for the elements in the parentheses of the for() construct.

To start, the `<statement>` in for() has to be a code statement. For example, if i is already declared and initialized, the following code line will generate a compiler error:

```
for (i; i<5;  i++)
```

However, the following code line will work:

```
for (i=i+1; i<5;  i++)
```

The `<statement>` may have two non-declarative expressions, separated by a comma. For example, the following is a valid code line:

```
for( i++,  j++ ;  i+j < 5 ; i++)
```

However, the `<statement>` cannot have multiple declarations or a mix of a declarative and non-declarative statement. For example, both of the following lines of code are illegal and will generate compiler errors:

```
for ( int i = 0, int j = 0;  i+j < 5;  i++)

for (int i = 0; i = i + 1; i + j < 5;  i++ )
```

Any of the three components in the parentheses of for() may be omitted, but the semicolons cannot be. For example, the following is a legal code fragment that generates an infinite loop:

```
for(; ;) {
    System.out.println ("Round and round we go for ever.");

}
```

However, the following code fragment will generate a compiler error:

```
for() {
    System.out.println ("Round and round we go for ever.");

}
```

Overwhelmed? Well, you were warned that the for() construct is the most sophisticated of all.

Another thing to note is that a variable declared inside a for loop will not exist (and hence cannot be used) outside the for loop. If a variable is declared before the for loop, even though initialized in the for() statement, it will exist (and hence can be used) even after the for loop.

■**Caution** A variable declared inside a for loop cannot be accessed from outside the for loop, whereas a variable only initialized inside a for loop, and declared before it, can also be accessed after the for loop is executed.

A programmer often iterates over the elements of a list, array, or any other collection. Previously, there was not an automated way to do it in Java, and hence such looping was prone to errors. J2SE 5.0 has introduced a solution to this problem in the form of the for-each loop construct.

The for-each Loop Construct

The for-each loop construct, introduced in J2SE 5.0, makes it easier and less error prone to iterate through the elements of an array and any other collection. (Collections are discussed in Chapter 10.) The syntax for this construct is shown here:

```
for (<variable> : <collection>) {
  // the block code
}
```

It sets the <variable> to the first element of the collection during the first iteration, to the second element during the second iteration, and so on. Iterations are performed automatically for all the elements of the collection. Consider Listing 6-3.

Listing 6-3. *ForEachTest.java*

```
1.   class ForEachTest {
2.     public static void main(String[] args) {
3.       int[] myArray = new int[3];
4.       myArray[0]= 10;
5.       myArray[1] = 20;
6.       myArray[2] = 30;
7.       for(int i : myArray) {
8.          System.out.println (i);
9.       }
10.   }
11. }
```

The output of Listing 6-3 follows:

```
10
20
30
```

Note that the keyword for the for-each loop is for, not for each. It is called *for-each* because the statement means "for each element in this collection."

There will be situations in which you will want the execution to get out of the block without completing it. This is accomplished through the block breaker statements.

Block Breaker Statements

There will be situations in a program when you want to quit either the current iteration of a loop or the entire loop altogether. To handle such situations, Java offers two block breaker statements: continue and break. Both of these statements add more sophistication to the execution control flow. These statements result in breaking (stopping) the current iteration of the block execution. To which point the control jumps depends upon the particular statement, and how it's used, as you will see in this section.

The continue Statement

The continue statement, in its simplest form, has the following syntax:

```
continue;
```

When this statement is executed, the current iteration of the block execution is terminated, and the control jumps to the next iteration of the block according to the following rules:

- If the continue statement is in the while, or do-while, block, control jumps to the boolean condition in the parentheses of while.

- If the continue statement is in the for block, control jumps to the <expression> in the for (<statement>; <test>; <expression>) statement.

For example, consider the following code fragment:

```
for ( int i = 0; i < 5;  i++ ) {
    if ( i == 3 ) continue;
    System.println ( "The value of i is " + i );
}
```

This generates the following output:

```
The value of i is 0
The value of i is 1
The value of i is 2
The value of i is 4
```

The line The value of i is 3 is missing from the output due to the continue statement.

In case of nested loops, you might need to specify from which loop you need to continue the next iteration. This is accomplished by using the labeled continue statement, which has the following syntax:

```
continue <indentifier>;
```

The `<identifier>` in this statement specifies the label. You use this form of the `continue` statement, for example, when there are nested blocks and you want the execution control to jump from an inner block to an outer block. The beginning of the outer block will be labeled. For example, consider the following code fragment:

```
OuterLoop: for ( int i = 3; i >0;  i-- ) {
    for (int j = 0; j<4; j = j + 1) {
        System.out.println ( "i=" + i + " and j=" + j);
        if ( i == j ) continue OuterLoop;
    }
}
```

This will generate the following output:

```
i=3 and j=0
i=3 and j=1
i=3 and j=2
i=3 and j=3
i=2 and j=0
i=2 and j=1
i=2 and j=2
i=1 and j=0
i=1 and j=1
```

If you comment out the line with the `continue` statement, the output will go up to j=3 for each value of i. Note that the `continue` statement can be used only inside a loop: `while`, `do-while`, `for`, or `for-each`.

■**Caution** The `continue` statement is only valid inside a loop. If you write it outside the loop, your program will generate a compiler error.

The `continue` statement stops only the current iteration. To stop the block execution (loop), you need the `break` statement.

The break Statement

Whereas the `continue` statement breaks the execution control out of the current block iteration to the next iteration, the `break` statement throws the execution control out of the block altogether. However, note that a `break` statement may be used either in a loop or in a `switch` block. You have already seen an example of `break` during the discussion of the `switch` statement. The `break` statement may also be used in the nested blocks. The `break` statement, in its simplest form, has the following syntax:

```
break;
```

For example, consider the following code fragment:

```
for ( int i = 3; i >0;  i-- ) {
    for (int j = 0; j<4;  j++) {
        System.out.println ( "i=" + i + " and j=" + j);
        if ( i == j ) break;
    }
}
```

This will generate the following output:

```
i=3 and j=0
i=3 and j=1
i=3 and j=2
i=3 and j=3
i=2 and j=0
i=2 and j=1
i=2 and j=2
i=1 and j=0
i=1 and j=1
```

In case of nested loops, you might need to tell from which loop you want to break. This is accomplished by using the labeled break statement, which has the following syntax (where <identifier> is the label):

```
break    <identifier>;
```

You use this form of break statement when there are nested blocks and you want the execution control to break out of not just the current block but also an outer block. The beginning of the outer block will be labeled. For example, consider the following piece of code:

```
OuterLoop: for ( int i = 3; i >0;  i-- ) {
    for (int j = 0; j<4; j = j + 1) {
        System.out.println ( "i=" + i + " and j=" + j);
        if ( i == j ) break OuterLoop;
    }
}
```

This will generate the following output:

```
i=3 and j=0
i=3 and j=1
i=3 and j=2
i=3 and j=3
```

In this case, consider the following statement:

```
break OuterLoop;
```

When this statement is executed, the control breaks out of the inner block in which the break statement exists, and also out of the block labeled by OuterLoop.

■**Caution** The continue statement can only be used in a loop block, whereas a break statement can be used in a loop or in a switch statement. Violation of these rules will generate a compiler error. The labeled break statement must be inside a loop. The label in the labeled statement must match the loop label.

Codewalk Quicklet

The code for the codewalk quicklet exercise in this chapter is presented in Listing 6-4.

Listing 6-4. *CodeWalkFive.java*

```
1.  class CodeWalkFive {
2.      public static void main(String [] args) {
3.          boolean x = true;
4.          boolean y = false;
5.          int i = 1;
6.          int j = 1;
7.          if((i++ == 1) && (y = true))i++;
8.          if((++j == 1) && (x = false))j++;
9.          if((x = false) || (++i == 4))i++;
10.        if((y = true) || (++j == 4))j++;
11.          System.out.print("i=" + i);
12.          System.out.print(" j=" + j);
13.         System.out.print(" x=" + x);
14.         System.out.print(" y=" + y);
15.       }
16.  }
```

To get you started on this exercise, following are some hints:

- *Input*: Lines 3 through 6.

- *Operations*: Lines 7 through 10.

- *Output*: Lines 11 through 14.

- *Rules*: How do the increment operators and the if constructs work?

Looking at the code from this angle, see if you can handle the last question in the "Review Questions" section based on this code.

The most important takeaway from this chapter is that Java offers three kinds of tools for execution flow control:

- The constructs to dynamically decide whether a block of statements should be executed: if and switch

- The constructs to dynamically decide if a block of statements should be executed repeatedly: while, do-while, for, and for-each

- The statements to stop the execution of a block in the middle: break and continue

Summary

Java allows a program to dynamically make three kinds of decisions about the execution control: if a block of statements will be skipped, if a block of statements will be executed repetitively, and if the current iteration of a block of statements will be terminated. The decision about skipping a block of statements is made by using an if or a switch statement. If the condition in the argument of an if statement is true, then the related block of statements is executed, otherwise it is skipped. In case of a switch construct, each non-default case starting from the top is tested. If a case turns out to be true, the statements in that case and all the following case blocks are executed until a break statement is encountered. If none of the non-default cases is true, then the statements in the default block and all the blocks are executed until a break statement is encountered. The default case can be anywhere in the switch block, not necessarily at the end.

The decision to execute a block of statements repetitively is made by using one of the loop statements: while, do-while, for, or for-each. Both the for and for-each constructs use the keyword for but use different elements in the parentheses. The break statement can be used in a loop to break out of the loop or in a switch block, whereas the continue statement is only used to stop an iteration in a loop.

By now, you may have encountered errors at compile time and exceptions thrown during runtime. You may just be ready to dive into this topic: where do these errors and exceptions come from and how should I deal with them? This is the subject of the next chapter.

EXAM'S EYE VIEW

Comprehend

- The legal argument type for an if statement and for a while statement must be boolean.

- The legal argument types of a switch statement are byte, short, char, int, and enum. You will receive a compiler error if you use any other type.

- In case of nested constructs, the condition for an inner construct will be tested only if the condition for the outer construct was tested and was true.

- The default case can appear anywhere in the switch block.

Look Out

- A do-while loop is executed at least once, whereas a while loop may never be executed if the condition is never true.

- A variable declared in the for loop cannot be used outside of the for loop.

- The = operator does not compare the values of the two operands, it assigns the value of the right operand to the left operand. For comparison, use the == operator.

- A variable declared inside a for loop cannot be accessed from outside the for loop, whereas a variable only initialized inside a for loop and declared before it can also be accessed after the for loop is executed.

Memorize

- A continue statement can be used only inside a loop, whereas a break statement can be used inside either a loop or a switch statement.

- Any two cases in a switch statement cannot have the same value. Duplicate case values will generate a compiler error.

- The keyword for the for-each loop construct is for and not for each.

Review Questions

1. Consider the following code fragment:

```
1   int i = 0;
2   do
3   {
4     System.out.println ( " I am in the do block.");
5   } while( i > 0)
```

What would be the output of this code fragment? (Choose all that apply.)

A. I am in the do block.

B. A compiler error occurs at line 5.

C. A runtime error occurs.

D. It compiles and runs but produces no output.

2. Consider the following code fragment:

```
1   for (int  i = 0; i  < 2;  i++) {
2       for ( int j = 1; j < 4; j++) {
3           if ( i == j ) {
4               continue;
5           }
6               System.out.println ( " i = " + i + " j = " + j );
7       }
8   }
```

Which of the following lines would be part of the output? (Choose all that apply.)

A. i = 0 j = 1

B. i = 0 j = 2

C. i = 0 j = 3

D. i = 1 j = 1

E. i = 1 j = 2

F. i = 1 j = 3

3. Consider the following piece of code:

```
1 OuterLoop:  for (int  i = 0; i  < 2;  i++) {
2       for ( int j = 1; j < 4; j++) {
3           if ( i == j ) {
4               continue OuterLoop;
5           }
6               System.out.println ( " i = " + i + " j = " + j );
7       }
8   }
```

Which of the following lines would be part of the output? (Choose all that apply.)

A. i = 0   j = 1

B. i = 0   j = 2

C. i = 0   j = 3

D. i = 1   j = 1

E. i = 1   j = 2

F. i = 1   j = 3

4. Consider the following piece of code:

```
1    long i = 2;
2    switch (i) {
3        case 1:
4              System.out.println ("Case 1");
5        case 2:
6              System.out.println ("Case 2");
7          case 3:
8              System.out.println ("Case 3");
9        default:
10              System.out.println ("Default");
11   }
```

Which of the following lines will be included in the output? (Choose all that apply.)

A. Case 1

B. Case 2

C. Case 3

D. Default

E. There will be a compiler error due to line 1.

5. Consider the following code fragment:

```
1    int i = 0;
2    do
3    {
4      System.out.println ( " I am in the do block.");
5    } while( i > 0);
```

What would be the output from this code fragment?

A. I am in the do block.

B. A compiler error occurs at line 5.

C. A runtime error occurs.

D. It compiles and runs but produces no output.

6. Consider the following code fragment:

```
1    int i = 0;
2    while( i > 0)
3    {
4      System.out.println ( " I am in the do block.");
5    }
```

What would be the output from this code fragment?

A. I am in the do block.

B. A compiler error occurs at line 2.

C. A runtime error.

D. It compiles and runs but produces no output.

7. Consider the following piece of code:

```
1     int  i = 1, j=1;
2     switch (i + j) {
3       case 1:
4               System.out.println ("Case 1");
5       case 2:
6               System.out.println ("Case 2");
7         case 3:
8                 System.out.println ("Case 3");
9         default:
10                System.out.println ("Default");
11      }
```

Which of the following statements is true about this piece of code?

A. The code will not compile due to line 2.

B. The output would be Case 2.

C. The output would be Case 2 followed by Case 3.

D. The output would be Case 2 followed by Case 3 followed by Default.

E. There will be a compiler error due to line 1.

8. Consider the following code:

```
1. class ContinueTest {
2.  public static void main(String[] arg)
3.  {
4.      int i = 2;
5.      Outer:
6.        if ( i < 5 ) {
7.              System.out.println("I: " + i);
8.              i++;
9.              continue Outer;
10.        }
11.  }
12. }
```

What is the result?

A. A compiler error occurs at line 9.

B. I: 2
   I: 3
   I: 4

C. I: 2

D. The program compiles but throws an exception when executed.

9. Consider the following code fragment:

```
1. class RevQOne{
2.   public static void main(String [] args) {
3.     boolean i = true;
4.     boolean j = false;
5.     short k = 10;
6.     if((k == 10) && (j = true))k--;
7.     if((i = false) || ( k == 9))
8.         k--;
9.         k--;
10.    System.out.println("k=" + k);
11.   }
12. }
```

What is the result?

A. Compilation fails.

B. K=7

C. K=8

D. k=9

E. k=10

F. An exception is thrown at runtime.

10. Consider the following code:

```
1. class RevQTwo{
2.   static int[] myArray = new int[3];
3.   public static void main(String [] args) {
4.     myArray[0]=1; myArray[1]=2; myArray[2]=3;
5.
6.         System.out.print(i);
7.   }
8. }
```

Which of the following inserted in line 5 will generate the output 123?

A. for(int[] i : myArray)

B. for(int i : myArray)

C. for(myArray : int i)

D. for(int I : myArray.iterator())

11. Consider the code in Listing 6-4. What is the result?

A. i=5 j=3 x=true y=false

B. i=6 j=4 x=false y=true

C. i=5 j=3 x=false y=true

D. Compilation fails at lines 9 and 10.

PART 3

■ ■ ■

Advanced Java Programming

To program a sophisticated, robust application, you'll typically require more than just the basic features discussed in Part 2. For example, even the most carefully written computer application may experience problems when the application is running due to reasons that are internal or external to the application. Java offers a comprehensive mechanism called exceptions to deal with such problems, or errors. Furthermore, an application usually takes some input and produces some output. Java offers support for the applications to interact with I/O devices such as files. This support is offered by some built-in classes that you can use. There are additional built-in classes in the utility and language packages of Java to provide support for text processing, Strings, and treating primitive data types as objects.

In solving a real-world problem, you often have to deal with a group of related data items. Java offers special data types called collections to deal with such situations effectively. Another advanced feature that Java offers is the multithreaded programming environment, which allows an application to perform multiple tasks concurrently. So, in this part, we will explore some advanced topics in Java programming, including exceptions, I/O, classes in the utility and language packages, collections, and multithreaded programming.

CHAPTER 7

Exceptions and Assertions

Exam Objectives

2.3 Develop code that makes use of assertions, and distinguish appropriate from inappropriate uses of assertions.

2.4 Develop code that makes use of exceptions and exception handling clauses (try, catch, finally), and declares methods and overriding methods that throw exceptions.

2.5 Recognize the effect of an exception arising at a specified point in a code fragment. Note that the exception may be a runtime exception, a checked exception, or an error.

2.6 Recognize situations that will result in any of the following being thrown: ArrayIndexOutOfBoundsException, ClassCastException, IllegalArgumentException, IllegalStateException, NullPointerException, NumberFormatException, AssertionError, ExceptionInInitializerError, StackOverflowError, or NoClassDefFoundError. Understand which of these are thrown by the virtual machine and recognize situations in which others should be thrown programatically.

Errors do happen in a computer program. Generally speaking, there are two kinds of possible errors in a program. One kind happens due to problems originating from the execution environment, such as running out of memory, and is represented in Java by the class Error and its subclasses. The second kind of error, called an *exception*, happens due to problems originating inside the application itself, and is represented by the class Exception and its subclasses. When an exception happens, either there is code to handle it or it is ignored. If it is ignored, the program terminates. However, Java offers an extensive mechanism to handle exceptions. When an exception happens, the exception propagates, changing the normal execution control flow of the application. In other words, exceptions are the messengers that carry the bad news inside the world of an application. Programmers may use the exception-handling mechanism of Java to write well-behaved, robust Java applications.

Testing is an important stage in the process of developing solid applications and minimizing the possibilities for exceptions to occur. You can use Java's assertion facility for testing to uncover internal programming errors.

So, the core issue in this chapter is how exceptions and assertions work in Java. To understand that, you will explore three avenues: checked and unchecked exceptions, the execution control flow after an exception is thrown, and the rules that must be followed in declaring exceptions.

Understanding Exceptions in Java

An exception is an error that happens when an application is running. When an exception condition happens, the exception is said to be *thrown*, and it changes the normal execution control flow of the program. Java offers a very comprehensive and flexible system for exception handling. The main benefit of such a system is that it largely automates the process of error handling, which otherwise would need to be coded into each application: what a waste of resources that would be. All exceptions are represented by classes organized into a hierarchy tree. Let's take a look at that tree…well, a part of it.

The Exception Tree in Java

As they say, everything in Java is a class (or object), and the exceptions are no exception. They are organized into a hierarchy of classes, a part of which is shown in Figure 7-1.

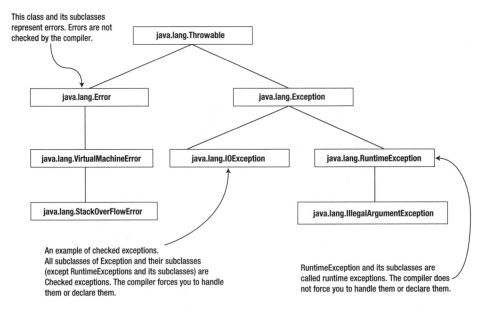

Figure 7-1. *A part of the hierarchy tree of classes representing exceptions in Java, the root of which is the Throwable class*

The Throwable class, which is the root of the exceptions tree, is the base class of all the exceptions in Java. The two subclasses of Throwable, directly derived from Throwable, are Error and Exception.

Errors (represented by subclasses of Error) occur in the Java virtual machine (JVM) and not in the application itself. An error generally represents an unusual problem from which it is difficult to recover. These problems generally originate from the execution environment of the application (for example, running out of memory). Because it is impossible (or difficult at best) to recover from errors during runtime, you, the programmer, are not required to handle them.

The exceptions (represented by subclasses of Exception), on the other hand, generally originate from within the application. They may also be related to the way in which the program is interacting with the environment (for example, referring to a nonexistent remote machine). The exceptions, if handled, should generally be handled in the program, but you are not required to handle all of them. Some examples of exceptions are division by zero, out of boundary arrays, and file input/output problems. The Exception class has a multitude of subclasses, which can be grouped into two main categories: checked exceptions and runtime exceptions.

Checked Exceptions and Runtime Exceptions

When in a program, if you perform an operation that causes an exception—that is, an exception is thrown—you can always catch the exception (you will see how later in the chapter) and deal with it in the code. This is called *handling the exception*. Based on whether or not you are required to handle them, the exceptions in Java are classified into two categories: checked exceptions and runtime exceptions.

Checked Exceptions

This is the category of exceptions for which the compiler checks (hence the name *checked exceptions*) to ensure that your code is prepared for them: prepare for unwelcome but expected guests. These exceptions are the instances of the Exception class or one of its subclasses, excluding the RuntimeException subtree. Checked exceptions are generally related to how the program interacts with its environment; for example, URISyntaxException and ClassNotFoundException are checked exceptions.

The conditions that generate checked exceptions are generally outside the control of your program, and hence they can occur in a correct program. However, you can anticipate (expect) them, and thus you must write the code to deal with them. The rule is: when a checked exception is expected, either declare it in the throws clause of your method or catch it in the body of your method, or do both; i.e. you can just throw it without catching it, you can catch it and recover from it, or you can catch it and rethrow it after doing something with it. Just throwing it without catching it is also called *ducking* it. You will get more comfortable with the throw and catch terminology by the end of this chapter.

■**Note** The programmer is required to write code to deal with checked exceptions. The compiler checks that such code exists. Dealing with (or handling) an exception means either declaring it in the throws clause of your method or catching it inside the method, or both.

As opposed to the checked exceptions, the runtime exceptions are not checked by the compiler.

Runtime Exceptions

The exceptions of type RuntimeException occur due to program bugs. The programmer is not required to provide code for these exceptions because if the programming were done correctly in the first place, these exceptions wouldn't occur, anyway. Because a runtime exception occurs as a result of incorrect code, catching the exception at runtime is not going to help, although doing so is not illegal. However, you would rather write the correct code to avoid the runtime exceptions than write the code to catch them. An exception represented by the ArithmeticException class is an example of runtime exceptions. Again, you do not need to declare or catch these exceptions.

Runtime exceptions (exceptions of type RuntimeException or its subclasses) and errors (of type Error or its subclasses) combined are also called *unchecked exceptions* and they are mostly thrown by the JVM, whereas the checked exceptions are mostly thrown programmatically. However, there is no rigid rule.

■**Note** Runtime exceptions are not checked by the compiler, and you are not required to deal with them, but it is not illegal to catch them.

Before we get into the details of how you duck an exception, or catch and rethrow, let's take a look at some of the standard exceptions in Java.

Standard Exceptions

As examples, Table 7-1 lists a number of unchecked exceptions along with the conditions that cause them.

Table 7-1. *Some Examples of Unchecked Exceptions in Java*

Exception	Subclass Of	Caused By	Typically Thrown
ArrayIndexOutOf ➥ BoundsException	RuntimeException	Illegal array index, negative index, or index greater than or equal to the array size	By the JVM
AssertionError	Error	Failure of an assertion	Programmatically
ClassCastException	RuntimeException	Attempt to cast an object to a subclass of which the object is not an instance	By the JVM
ExceptionIn ➥ InitializerError	Error	Problem with the initializer for a static variable	By the JVM
IllegalArgument ➥ Exception	RuntimeException	An illegal or inappropriate argument passed to a method	Programmatically
IllegalStateException	RuntimeException	A method invocation at an illegal or inappropriate time	Programmatically
NullPointerException	RuntimeException	An attempt to use null instead of an object	By the JVM
NumberFormatException	RuntimeException	Attempt to convert a string to a numeric type when the string is not in an appropriate format	Programmatically
StackOverflowError	Error	Stack overflow	By the JVM
NoClassDefFoundError	Error	Attempt to load in the definition of a class that cannot be found	By the JVM

These are the unchecked exceptions, which are typically thrown by the JVM or programmatically, as shown in the table. Remember, it is not illegal to write code for handling unchecked exceptions, but it will not be of much use. However, you are required to write code for handling checked exceptions. The basics of exception handling are covered in the next section.

Basics of Exception Handling

You are required to handle the checked exceptions in your code, because otherwise the compiler will generate errors. The Java exception-handling mechanism contains five keywords: try, catch, throw, throws, and finally. In this section, you explore how to use them to handle exceptions.

You are not required to handle the unchecked exceptions, because you cannot recover from them. However, you can use the Java exception-handling mechanism on them, if you wish to for whatever purpose. Just for sake of convenience, this section uses runtime exceptions such as

ArithmeticException to demonstrate the use of this mechanism. For example, consider the following code fragment:

```
1.      int x = 15;
2.      int y = 0;
3.      System.out.println ("x/y: " + x/y);
4.      System.out.println("x*y: " + x*y);
5.      System.out.println("x-y: "   + (x-y));
```

Notice the problem in line 3: the division by zero. This problem will cause an exception of type ArithmeticException. But because this is a runtime exception, the code will compile without any error from the compiler. However, at runtime, the exception would be thrown and the program would terminate at line 3; lines 4 and 5 would never be executed.

Although catching this runtime exception is not required, we will do so just to demonstrate how the catch block works.

Using the try and catch Blocks

When your program performs an operation that causes an exception, an exception will be thrown. You can catch that exception and handle it by using the try and catch blocks. As an example, Listing 7-1 presents a very simple but complete program.

Listing 7-1. *ExceptionHandle1.java*

```
1.  public class ExceptionHandle1{
2.    public static void main(String[] args) {
3.      int x = 15;
4.      int y = 0;
5.        try{
6.        System.out.println ("x/y: " + x/y);
7.        System.out.println("x*y: " + x*y);
8.        }
9.       catch (ArithmeticException ae) {
10.         System.out.println("An exception occurred: " + ae);
11.       }
12.         System.out.println("x-y: "   + (x-y));
13.   }
14. }
```

The suspected code is embraced in the try block, followed by the catch block in which the code to handle the exception is written. You can actually type this code into a file named ExceptionHandle1.java, compile it, and execute it. An exception of type ArithmeticException would be thrown due to line 6 (division by zero), and this exception would be caught at line 9. The variable ae is an object reference to the instance of ArithmeticException, and contains the message regarding the exception. The message is printed by line 10, where the programmer could also add to the message. In the catch block, the programmer can also write the code to recover from the exception. Note that the execution control jumps from line 6 directly to line 9. The execution continues after the last catch block as if nothing happened. Therefore, the output of Listing 7-1 will be as follows:

```
An exception occurred:java.lang.ArithmeticException / by zero
x-y: 15
```

If an exception is thrown from the try block and an appropriate catch block (to catch the exception) did not exist, the method would be terminated without executing any other line from the method. For example, replace line 9 (with catch) in Listing 7-1 with the following line:

```
catch (ArrayIndexOutOfBoundsException oe) {
```

If you compile and execute your program now, line 6 will cause an `ArithmeticException`. But there is no appropriate `catch` block to catch this exception. As a result, the execution will terminate at line 6.

■**Caution** A `catch` block is executed only if it catches the exception coming from within the corresponding `try` block.

It is possible to have multiple `catch` blocks, in which case the execution control will jump to the first line immediately following the last `catch` block, after executing the right (matching) `catch` block. The point is: the only `catch` block that catches the exception is executed, while all other are skipped. That means if no exception arises from within the `try` block, all the `catch` blocks are skipped.

If there is no matching `catch` block for the checked exception and the method does not throw the exception by using the `throws` clause, the code will not compile. If there is no matching `catch` block for an unchecked exception, the execution will leave the method. What if you want to do something in the method before the execution leaves it even if there is no matching `catch` block for the exception that occurred? For example, suppose you want to do some cleaning up, and maybe release some resources. The `finally` block offers the solution to this problem.

Using the finally Block

If an exception is caused inside a `try` block, and there is no matching `catch` block, the method terminates without further executing any line of code from that method. If you want some lines of code to be executed regardless of whether or not there is a matching `catch` block, you can put those lines inside the `finally` block, which should follow the last `catch` block. You may need a `finally` block, for example, to write the cleanup code. As an example, consider the complete runnable program in Listing 7-2.

Listing 7-2. *ExceptionHandle2.java*

```
1. public class ExceptionHandle2{
2.        public static void main(String[] args) {
3.        int x = 15;
4.        int y = 0;
5.          try{
6.        System.out.println ("x/y: " + x/y);
7.         System.out.println("x*y: " + x*y);
8.           } catch  (ArrayIndexOutOfBoundsException oe) {
9.            System.out.println("An exception occurred: " + oe);
10.        }
11.         finally {
12.             System.out.println("finally block must be executed!");
13.         }
14.              System.out.println("x-y: "  + (x-y));
15.     }
16.    }
```

An `ArithmeticException` is caused by line 6, and there is no matching `catch` block. Therefore, the execution control jumps to the `finally` block. After executing the `finally` block, the execution leaves the method. Accordingly, the output of Listing 7-2 will be as follows:

```
finally block must be executed!
java.lang.ArithmeticException: / by zero...// The output truncated here.
```

However, note that line 14 was not executed. So, the finally block is almost always executed. Following are some circumstances that could prevent the execution of the finally block:

- An exception arises inside the finally block, or a return statement exists in the finally block.

- The System.exit() method is called before the execution of the finally block.

Note Once execution enters a try block and an exception happens, the finally block, if one exists, is always executed regardless of whether or not the exception is caught, unless under extreme circumstances such as the execution of System.exit().

Note that a try block without a catch block is legal if it has a finally block, but a catch block or a finally block without a try block is not legal; the compiler will generate an error. However, this should be common sense, because if an exception has been thrown by a try block, it has to be dealt with somewhere either in the catch block, or in the finally block, or in both. If, on the other hand, no exception is to be thrown, then what is the use of the catch or the finally block? Multiple catch blocks with a try block are also legal.

You may be asking yourself a question: If there are multiple catch blocks, which one will be executed, and in which order should they be placed? In other words, how do you determine the matching catch block for an exception thrown from within a try block? Let's explore this next.

Using Multiple catch Blocks

A catch block catches exceptions of a specific category. This category includes the class specified in the parentheses of catch(...), and its subclasses. In other words, a catch block catches exceptions only from a subtree of the exceptions hierarchy tree. The higher you are in the exceptions tree in determining what to put in the parentheses of catch(...), the better the possibility of catching the exception, but it would be more generic. So, you need to strike a balance between two opposing requirements: the certainty for catching, and pinpointing where specifically the exception is coming from. The trade-off is to use multiple catch blocks following a single try block, followed by a single finally block.

To elaborate on this, recall that the class Throwable makes the root of the exception hierarchy tree; that is, the class Throwable represents the most general exception. The farther down in the hierarchy tree an exception is from Throwable, the more specific it gets: a subclass is more specific than its parent class. If multiple catch blocks follow the same try block, it is possible that exception classes in these catch blocks may be at different levels of the hierarchy; e.g. one catch block handles an exception, which is a subclass of an exception handled by another catch block. If the catch block that handles the subclass exception did not exist, then the subclass exception would be handled by the catch block with the parent class exception. Therefore, now that both catch blocks with parent and subclass exceptions are present, the question arises: Which of these two catch blocks will handle the subclass exception? To answer this question, there are two rules:

- Only one relevant catch block, encountered first by the execution control, will be executed for a given exception.

- The more specific catch block must precede the less specific catch block. Violation of this rule will generate a compiler error.

■**Note** An exception can be caught only by a matching catch block, which is a block with a catch statement that has in its parentheses either the same class as the exception itself or its parent class (i.e. one of the classes higher up in the hierarchy).

As an example, consider the complete runnable program in Listing 7-3.

Listing 7-3. *MultipleExceptions.java*

```
1. public class MultipleExceptions{
2.         public static void main(String[] args) {
3.         int[] x = {0, 1, 2, 3, 4};
4.           try{
5.            System.out.println ("x[6]: " + x[6]);
6.            System.out.println("x[3]: " + x[3]);
7.            }
8.            catch (ArithmeticException ae) {
9.            System.out.println("An arithmetic exception occurred: " + ae);
10.        }
11.        catch (ArrayIndexOutOfBoundsException oe) {
12.            System.out.println("Array index out of bound! ");
13.        }
14.        catch  (IndexOutOfBoundsException ie) {
15.            System.out.println("Some kind of index out of bound! ");
16.        }
17.        finally {
18.                System.out.println("finally block must be executed!");
19.        }
20.                System.out.println("x[0]: "  + x[0]);
21.        }
22.    }
```

The output of Listing 7-3 follows:

```
Array index out of bound!
finally block must be executed!
x[0]: 0
```

Note that the execution skipped the first catch block (lines 8–10) and the third catch block (lines 14–16) because it entered the first available catch block that matched the array out of bound exception (line 11). But it did execute the finally block, and because the exception was caught, the execution continued after the try-catch-finally blocks.

■**Note** The catch block with a more specific exception must appear before the catch block with a less specific exception. If more than one matching catch blocks exist, the first one encountered would be executed, and it would be the most specific one.

To sum up the rules for execution flow in try-catch-finally blocks in case the exception happens:

- If an exception is not caught by any catch block, one of the following happens:
  - If there is no finally block, the execution stops right at the point of exception and returns to the calling method.
  - If there is a finally block, the execution jumps from the point of exception to the finally block, and returns to the calling method after the finally block.
- If the exception is caught by a catch block, one of the following happens:
  - If there is a finally block, the execution jumps after executing the catch block to the finally block, and continues until the end of the method.
  - If there is no finally block, the execution jumps after executing the catch block to the first statement immediately after the last catch block and continues to the end of the method.

■**Note** The try block must be followed by either a catch block or a finally block, or both. The try block by itself is not legal. Any catch block must immediately follow a try block, and any finally block must immediately follow the last catch block, or the try block if there is no catch block.

So, now you know how an exception is caught and handled. You must be wondering: How is an exception thrown in the first place?

Throwing Exceptions

In the preceding examples, the try blocks have been trapping the exceptions thrown by the JVM. The programmer may also throw exceptions using the keyword throw. You can either throw a caught exception that originated somewhere else or originate an exception. For example, in case of numbers of type double, division by zero does not throw an ArithmeticException. Suppose you do want to throw (originate) an ArithmeticException in this case. Listing 7-4 does exactly that.

Listing 7-4. *ThrowExample.java*

```
1. public class ThrowExample{
2.      public static void main(String[] args) {
3.      double x = 15.0;
4.      double y = 0.0;
5.        try{
6.            ThrowExample te = new ThrowExample();
7.            double z = te.doubleDivide(x, y);
8.            System.out.println ("x/y: " + x/y);
9.        }
10.        catch  (ArithmeticException ae) {
11.        System.out.println("An exception occurred: " + ae);
12.      }
13.            System.out.println("x-y: "  + (x-y));
14.    }
```

```
15.     double doubleDivide(double x, double y) {
16.         if(y==0.0) {
17.             throw new ArithmeticException("Integer or not,
                    please do not divide by zero!");
18.         } else {
19.             return x/y;
20.         }
21.     }
22. }
```

Consider line 17 from Listing 7-4:

```
throw new ArithmeticException("Integer or not, please do not divide by zero!");
```

This specifies the syntax for creating and throwing an exception. The message in the parentheses will be caught with the exception. Also note that in this example, the `ArithmeticException` is instantiated and thrown in the same statement. You could replace line 17 with two lines: the first one to instantiate the exception and the second one to throw it. But this is not recommended, because the exception builds information at the point it was instantiated, and that information is shown in the stack trace when the exception is reported. It would be more consistent if the point at which the exception is created and the point from which the exception is thrown were the same. Therefore, combining the instantiation of the exception and throwing the exception in one statement has become a norm. The output Listing 7-4 follows:

```
An exception occurred: java.lang.ArithmeticException: Integer or not,
please do not divide by zero!
x-y: 15
```

So, an exception is created by instantiating the corresponding exception class and is thrown by using the keyword `throw`. When an exception is thrown, it changes the normal flow of the execution control.

Control Flow in Exception Condition

It is important to understand the flow of execution control after an exception is thrown. You were introduced briefly to this issue earlier in the chapter during the discussion of multiple `catch` blocks. This section presents the full picture by listing the rules that govern this flow:

- If a line of code in a try block causes the exception and there is no matching `catch` block, the exception is said to be *uncaught*. This happens when there is no `catch` block whose parentheses contain either the same exception class that has been thrown or its parent class. For a checked exception, the code will not even compile if the method does not throw the exception by using the `throws` clause. In the case of unchecked exceptions, one of the following would happen:
  - If the `finally` block does not exist, the execution control jumps from the line in the `try` block that caused the exception to the calling method.
  - If the `finally` block exists, the execution control jumps from the exception point in the try block to the `finally` block. Immediately after executing the `finally` block, the control is returned to the calling method.
  - The calling method would either handle the exception or throw it back to its own calling method, and so on until either the exception is handled or the control reaches the top of the execution process, and the process then dies.

- If a line of code outside the try block causes an exception, the method is terminated right away at that line, and the control is returned to the calling method. This is equivalent to an uncaught exception, discussed at the beginning of this list.

- If a line of code in the try block causes an exception and there is a matching catch block—that is, a catch block whose parentheses contain either the same exception class that is thrown or its parent class—the matching catch block will be executed. Following this catch block, execution control has two options:

  - If the finally block exists, it will be executed right after the execution of the matching catch block. After the execution of the finally block, the control would jump to the first line immediately after the finally block and the execution would continue as normal.

  - If the finally block does not exist, the matching catch block will be executed, after which the control will jump to the first line immediately after the last catch block and the execution will continue as normal from there on.

- At most, only one catch block is executed.

- If there is a System.exit() statement anywhere in the method, once that statement is encountered, the control will leave the method without even executing any following finally block.

■**Caution** If an exception is not caught by a catch block, the execution control jumps to the calling method right after the finally block. If the exception is caught in a catch block, the execution control resumes to normal right after the finally block as if there were no exception.

All these rules for control flow in case of an exception are summarized in Table 7-2.

Table 7-2. *Execution Control Flow, Assuming No System.exit() Statement Exists in the Code*

Exception Thrown?	try Exists?	Matching catch Found?	Execution Control Flow Behavior
No	N/A	N/A	Normal control flow.
Yes	No	N/A	Method terminates.
Yes	Yes	No	Method terminates If a finally block exists, it would be executed after the try block, and before the method terminates.
Yes	Yes	Yes	Execution jumps from the exception point in the try block to the matching catch block. The catch block is executed and control jumps to the first line after the last catch block. Normal control flow continues from there on.

By now, you know how to trap an exception by using the try block and how the exception propagates from try to catch to finally and then out of the method to the calling method. If the method handles the exception in a catch block (and does not throw it from the catch block), normal execution resumes. However, if a method throws an exception, it must be declared in the method definition.

Declaring Exceptions

Let's start with a question: From where does your method receive an exception? Well, you can create it in your method, or you can receive it from a method that your method called. How do you know that a called method may throw an exception? Well, each method that may throw a checked exception has to declare it. In this section, we explore the rules of how to do this.

Checked Exception: Duck It or Catch It

Every checked exception that a method may throw must be declared with the throws keyword, as shown here:

```
public void test() throws <testException1>, <testException2> {
// code goes here
}
```

Note that in the examples in the previous sections, we did not declare the exceptions in the throws clause, because we were using the unchecked exceptions just for demonstration purposes. However, note that if you declare an exception in a method, it does not mean that you have to throw the exception from that method; you are not bound to. But if you want to throw it, you have to declare it.

If your method calls another method that throws a checked exception, then your method must either duck it or catch it. *Ducking it* simply means to declare it with the throws clause in the method declaration and to have no try-catch blocks in the method body. *Catching it* means having try-catch blocks in the method body for that exception. When you catch an exception, you can either recover from it or throw it from inside the catch block. If you do throw it from the catch block (or from anywhere in your method), you must have declared it by using the throws keyword in the method declaration. For example, consider the following code:

```
1.    void callingMethod() {
2.      calledMethod();
3.    }
4.    void calledMethod() throws IOexception {
5.      throw new IOException();
6.    }
```

This code will generate a compiler error because the callingMethod() method neither declares IOException nor catches it, but it calls the calledMethod() method, which throws IOException. One fix to this problem with the code is to replace line 1 with the following:

```
void callingMethod() throws IOException {
```

In this case, the calling method will simply pass on the IOException to the method that called the callingMethod() method, an example of ducking the exception.

Note Every checked exception that a method may throw must be declared with the throws keyword. If your method calls a method that throws an exception, then your method must either catch the exception or throw it, or both.

The calling method may also declare other exceptions (if it wants to throw them) in addition to the exceptions thrown by the called methods that it must declare. However, there is a restriction on what exceptions your method can declare if your method is overriding another method.

Declaring Exceptions when Overriding

Recall that a class can override the methods that it inherited from its parent class. Overriding imposes some restrictions on throwing exceptions. If in a subclass you override a method of the parent class, the exception thrown by the overriding method must be the same as, or a subclass of, the exception thrown by the overridden method. In other words, the overriding method cannot throw any exception that is not the same as, or a subclass of, the exception class thrown by the overridden method. This also implies that the overriding method does not *have* to throw an exception, even if the overridden method is throwing some exceptions. The compiler checks on this rule, and gives the compiler error if the rule is violated.

For example, consider Listing 7-5.

Listing 7-5. *OverrideException.java*

```
1.   import java.io.*;
2.   public class OverrideException{
3.     public void someMethod() throws IOException {
4.     }
5.   }
6.   class SubClassLegalOne extends OverrideException {
7.     public void someMethod() throws IOException {
8.     }
9.   }
10.   class SubClassLegalTwo extends OverrideException {
11.       public void someMethod()  {
12.       }
13.   }
14.   class SubClassLegalThree extends OverrideException {
15.     public void someMethod() throws EOFException, FileNotFoundException {
16.     }
17.   }
18.   class SubClassIllegalOne extends OverrideException {
19.     public void someMethod() throws ClassNotFoundException {
20.     }
21.   }
22.   class SubClassIllegalTwo extends OverrideException  {
23.     public void someMethod() throws Exception {
24.     }
25.   }
26.   class SubClassIllegalThree extends OverrideException  {
27.     public void someMethod() throws IOException, ClassNotFoundException {
28.      }
29.   }
```

The method someMethod() (line 3) in the class OverrideException throws IOException. The following classes are all subclasses of OverrideException, and they override the method someMethod(). Therefore, they must follow the restrictions in throwing exceptions. Line 7 is legal because the overriding method throws the same exception as the overridden method, IOException. Line 11 is legal because the overriding method throws no exception—that is, it does not throw any exception that is not the same as, or a subclass of, IOException. Line 15 is legal because the overriding method throws EOFException and FileNotFoundException, both of which are subclasses of IOException. Line 19 is illegal because ClassNotFoundException is not a subclass of IOException. For the same reason, lines 23 and 27 are illegal. Note that in line 27, IOException is legal, but ClassNotFoundException makes this line illegal. Therefore, the compiler would generate errors on lines 19, 23, and 27.

So, the exception thrown by the overriding method must be the same as, or a subclass of, the exception thrown by the overridden method. In other words, the overriding method cannot throw any exception class that is not the same as, or a subclass of, the exception class thrown by the overridden method. It has the following implications:

- If the overridden method does not throw any exception, the overriding method cannot throw any checked exception, but it can still throw a runtime exception.

- If the overridden method throws an exception, it's legal for the overriding method to throw no exception.

As you know, an exception is a condition that you don't want to see happen, but there can be some conditions in a program that you will always want to be true. For example, a method may expect that a certain argument should always be an integer. Such conditions are very helpful in testing and debugging a program.

Assertions

Sometimes in programming, there are some assumptions that must be true; for example, if you are going to calculate the square root of a number, the number must be positive. To facilitate the test of such assumptions, Java offers the assertion facility, which refers to the verification of a condition that is expected to be true during the execution of a program. It is implemented using the keyword assert, introduced to the Java language in Java 2, version 1.4. The assertion facility can be enabled or disabled during compilation and runtime. This feature is mostly used during development for testing and debugging, and is disabled before the product distribution.

The syntax for using assertions follows:

```
assert <condition>;
```

or

```
assert <condition>:<expression>;
```

The <condition> must evaluate to a boolean. The <expression> is used to send the error message. If assertions are enabled during compilation and runtime, the condition is evaluated. If the condition is true, no further action is taken; if the condition is false, an AssertionError is thrown. If <expression> is specified, it is passed into the constructor of the AssertionError, where it is used as an error message.

As a demonstration of the assertion facility, consider Listing 7-6.

Listing 7-6. *OverrideExample.java*

```
1. public class AssertionExample{
2.     public static void main(String[] args) {
3.         int x = 15;
4.         DataAccess da = new DataAccess();
5.         assert da.dataIsAccesible():"Data is not acceptable";
6.         System.out.println("Value of x: " + x);
7.     }
8.  }
9.  class DataAccess {
10.    public boolean dataIsAccesible(){
11.       return false;
12.    }
13. }
```

Assertions are disabled by default. To enable assertions, compile and execute Listing 7-6 with the following commands:

```
javac -source 1.4 AssertionExample.java
java -ea AssertionExample
```

If you compile and execute the code with these options, the output of Listing 7-6 would be the AssertionError with the following message:

```
Data is not acceptable
```

Line 6 will not be executed. If you run the program with the command

```
java AssertionExample
```

the assertion code would be ignored, and the output would be

```
Value of x: 15
```

■**Caution** The compiler flag –source 1.4 is not necessary in version 5.0; it was required in version 1.4. However, assertions are turned off by default during execution of the program.

The support for assertions is enabled by default when compiling code in J2SE 5.0. However, assertions are turned off by default during execution of the program. If you want to turn them on, you need to use the –ea (enableassertions) flag. You can also use this flag to turn assertions on only for specific classes in your application, as shown here:

```
java –ea:<myClass1>  -ea:<myClass2>  <myApp>
```

Similarly, you can turn assertions off in specified classes and packages by using the flag –da, or disableassertions as in the command line here:

```
java    -disableassertions  <myApp>
```

Note that you do not need to recompile your program to turn the assertions on or off during the execution. This is a function of the class loader. Also note that when the assertions are disabled during execution for a class, the class loader strips off the assertion code, and it does speed up the execution. In other words, by enabling assertions, you do pay the performance price.

Remember that assertion failures are unrecoverable errors, and you only use the assertion mechanism to uncover programming errors during testing of the applications. So, do not handle the assertion errors in the program; you detect them and fix them in the code.

There are certain situations in which you should not use assertions. Following are some examples:

- Do not use assertions to check the arguments passed to a `public` method. There are two reasons for not doing that:
  - If argument checking is needed, it must be part of the method specifications and must become part of the permanent method behavior. Remember that assertions are not always enabled during execution.
  - Erroneous argument passing should result in a more specific and appropriate runtime exception such as `IllegalArgumentException`, `IndexOutOfBoundsException`, or `NullPointerException`.

    This also implies that you should not use assertions to check the command-line arguments.

- Do not use assertions to enforce the correct operation required by your application because, again, assertions may not be enabled during the application execution. You do not want to count on assertions to check the correct behavior of your running application. For example, you want to make sure that a list `myList` does not have any `null` elements in it. Doing the following is an inappropriate use of assertions:

  ```
  assert    myList.remove(null);
  ```

  This removal will not happen if the assertion is not enabled.

- The expression in an `assert` statement must not produce any side effects such as modifying the variable values.

The key factor to remember for the appropriate use of assertions is that assertions are typically used to test and debug an application before its deployment and are not guaranteed to be enabled when the application is running.

Codewalk Quicklet

The code for the codewalk quicklet exercise in this chapter is presented in Listing 7-7.

Listing 7-7. *CodeWalkSix.java*

```
1. class CodeWalkSix {
2.     public static void main(String [] args) {
3.             String stri = "inner";
4.             String stro = "outer";
5.       try {
6.             throw new Exception();
7.       } catch (Exception eo) {
8.               try {
9.                   throw new Exception();
10.              } catch (Exception ei) {
11.                  System.out.print(stri);
12.              } finally {
13.                  System.out.print(" finally ");
14.       }
15.             System.exit(1);
16.     }finally {
17.             System.out.print(stro);
18.     }
19.             System.out.print(stro);
20.   }
21. }
```

To get you started on this exercise, following are some hints:

- *Input*: Lines 3 and 4
- *Operations and output*: Lines 11, 13, 17, and 19
- *Rules*: The execution control flow when an exception is thrown

Looking at the code from this angle, see if you can handle the last question in the "Review Questions" section based on this code.

The three most important takeaways from this chapter are as follows:

- You must prepare your code for the checked exceptions: duck them or catch them. You can catch the unchecked exceptions but you don't have to.

- If you catch an exception and recover from it (that is, don't rethrow it), the execution will resume as normal. If you throw (or rethrow) an exception from a method, you must declare it using the throws keyword in the method declaration.

- Assertions are typically used to test and debug an application before its deployment and are not guaranteed to be enabled when the application is running.

Summary

Exceptions and assertions are two of the three mechanisms, logging being the third, that Java offers to deal with application failures. An exception is an error condition that happens while the application is running. Java has a comprehensive exception-handling mechanism. Checked exceptions are the exceptions for which you must write code to handle (duck or catch) them, otherwise the compiler will generate errors. Unchecked exceptions, which include runtime exceptions, are the exceptions for which you are not required to write code.

The exceptions are handled inside a method with the try-catch-finally blocks. The finally block is optional, but if it exists and an exception happens, it will be executed before execution control leaves the method. To trap an exception, the code line that causes it must be inside a try block. When a code line inside a try block causes an exception, execution control returns to the calling method if there is no matching catch block. A matching catch block is a catch block with a catch statement that has in its parentheses either the same class as the exception itself or its parent class (i.e. one of the classes higher up in the hierarchy). If there is a matching catch block, execution control jumps to that block; after executing the catch block, execution control jumps to the finally block; and after executing the finally block, execution control continues immediately after the finally block as if no exception happened. If there was no finally block, execution control will jump after executing the matching catch block to the first line after the last catch block, and execution will continue as if no exception happened.

There are some conditions that must be true in a program. You can check (assert) this by using the assertion facility in Java.

While an application is executing, it may need to read input data from a file or write the output data to a file. Java offers classes in the java.io package to facilitate these input/output (I/O) operations. You will learn how to use these classes in the next chapter.

EXAM'S EYE VIEW

Comprehend

- At most only one `catch` block is executed corresponding to a `try` block.

- If there is no matching `catch` block corresponding to a `try` block, method execution stops at the line that caused the exception and the control returns to the calling method. If there is a `finally` block, that will be executed before returning the control to the calling method.

- If there is a matching `catch` block, execution jumps from the line that caused the exception to the matching `catch` block; after executing the `catch` block, execution jumps to the `finally` block, if it exists; and after executing the `finally` block (or the last `catch` block if the `finally` block does not exist), execution continues as if no exception happened.

Look Out

- The `try` block must be followed by either a `catch` block or a `finally` block, or both. The `try` block by itself is not legal. Any `catch` block must immediately follow a `try` block, and any `finally` block must immediately follow the last `catch` block, or the `try` block if there is no `catch` block.

- The `finally` block will not be executed if a `System.exit()` statement is executed before the `finally` block, or an uncaught exception is raised inside the `catch` block that is executed before the `finally` block. The execution of the `finally` block will be incomplete if an exception arises inside the `finally` block.

- The condition in the `assert` statement must evaluate to a `boolean` value.

- If you declare an exception in a method using the `throws` clause, it does not mean that you actually have to throw the exception from that method.

Memorize

- If your method calls another method that throws a checked exception, your method must do one or both of the following:
  - Declare the exception in the `throws` clause of your method.
  - Catch the exception in the body of your method.

- The overriding method cannot throw any exception class that is not the same as, or a subclass of, the exception class thrown by the overridden method. It has the following implications:
  - If the overridden method does not throw any exception, the overriding method cannot throw any checked exception, but it can still throw a runtime exception.
  - If the overridden method throws an exception, it's legal for the overriding method to throw no exception.

- Once execution enters a `try` block and an exception happens, the `finally` block, if it exists, is always executed regardless of whether or not the exception is caught, unless under extreme circumstances such as execution of `System.exit()`.

- A `catch` block can catch an exception that is either the same class as specified in the parentheses of `catch` or a subclass of it.

- Following a `try` block, the `catch` block with a more specific exception must appear before the `catch` block with a less specific exception.

Review Questions

1. Consider the following code fragment:

```
1.  public class ExceptionHandleNot2{
2.    public static void main(String[] args) {
3.     String[] week_days = {"Monday", "Tuesday", "Wednesday",
          "Thursday", "Friday", "Saturday", "Sunday"};
4.      for (int i=1; i<=7; i++) {
5.        System.out.println("The day of the week: " + week_days[i]);
6.      }
7.   }
8.  }
```

What is the output of this code?

A. Line 5 prints out the names of all the days of the week.

B. A compiler error occurs.

C. A runtime error occurs and nothing is printed out.

D. A runtime error occurs after printing out some days of the week.

2. Which one of the following code fragments presents the most appropriate way of throwing exceptions? Assume that the variable i is already properly defined elsewhere, is in scope, and has an appropriate value.

A. ```
if (i > 10) {
throws new IndexOutOfBoundsException("Index is out of bound!");
}
```

B. ```
if ( i > 10) {
throw new IndexOutOfBoundsException("The value of index i=" +
   i + " is out of bound!" );
}
```

C. ```
IndexOutOfBoundsException iob = new IndexOutOfBoundsException
     ("Index out of bound!");
if (i > 10) {
throw iob;
}
```

D. ```
if ( i > 10) {
throw "Index is out of bound!";
}
```

3. Consider the following code fragment:

```
public class ExceptionHandleTest{
     public static void main(String[] args) {
     int x = 15;
     int y = 1;
      try{
     System.out.println ("x/y: " + x/y);
      System.out.println("x*y: " + x*y);
       } catch  (ArithmeticException ae) {
        System.out.println("An exception occurred: " + ae);
       }
```

```
            catch  (ArrayIndexOutOfBoundsException oe) {
            System.out.println("An exception occurred: " + oe);
        }
        finally {
            System.out.println("finally block must be executed!");
        }
            System.out.println("x-y: "  + (x-y));
    }
    }
```

Which of the following lines would be part of the output? (Choose all that apply.)

A. x/y: 15

B. x*y: 15

C. finally block must be executed!

D. x-y: 14

4. Consider the following code fragment:

```
    public class Question4{
        public static void main(String[] args) {
        int[] x = {0, 1, 2, 3, 4};
        try{
          System.out.println ("x[6]: " + x[6]);
          System.out.println("x[3]: " + x[3]);
          } catch  (IndexOutOfBoundsException  ie) {
          System.out.println("Some kind of index out of bound! ");
        }
        catch  (ArrayIndexOutOfBoundsException oe) {
          System.out.println("Array index out of bound! " );
        }
        finally {
            System.out.println("finally block must be executed!");
        }
                System.out.println("x[0]: "  + x[0]);
    }
    }
```

What is the output of this code?

A. Array index out of bound!

   finally block must be executed!

B. Some kind of index out of bound!

   finally block must be executed!

C. Some kind of index out of bound!

   Array index out of bound!

   finally block must be executed!

D. A compiler error occurs.

5. Consider the following code fragment:

```
public class AssertionExample2 {
 public static void main(String[]  args) {
     System.out.println(args.length);
     assert args.length != 0;
 }
}
```

Which of the following must be done in order for the code to throw an `AssertionError`? (Choose all that apply.)

A. The code must be compiled with the -`source 1.4` option if you are using JDK 5.0.

B. The program must be executed with the -`ea` option.

C. At least one argument must be given in the execution command.

D. No argument should be given in the execution command.

6. Which of the following is true about assertions in Java? (Choose all that apply.)

A. You use assertions to report errors to the users of an application.

B. Assertions are mostly used during testing to uncover internal program errors.

C. Assertions are used to report recoverable problems from one part of an application to another part.

D. An assertion error is thrown if the condition specified by <condition> in assert: <condition> is true.

E. An assertion error is thrown if the condition specified by <condition> in assert: <condition> is false.

7. Consider the following code fragment:

```
1. public class TryFinallyTest{
2.  public static void main(String[] args) {
3.    try{
4.        System.out.println ("I was in try");
5.    }
6.    finally {
7.      System.out.println("I was in finally");
8.    }
9.  }
10. }
```

What is the result of executing this code?

A. I was in try
   I was in finally

B. I was in try

C. I was in finally

D. A compiler error occurs at line 6.

E. The program compiles but throws an exception during execution.

8. Consider the following code fragment:

```
1. public class TryFinallyTest{
2.  public static void main(String[] args) {
3.    try{
4.        System.out.println ("I was in try");
5.    }
9.  }
10. }
```

What is the result of executing this code?

A. `I was in try`

B. A compiler error occurs.

C. The program runs but produces no output.

D. The program compiles but throws an exception during execution.

9. Consider the code in Listing 7-7. What is the result?

A. inner finally

B. inner finally outer outer

C. inner finally outer

D. Compilation fails.

E. No output.

CHAPTER 8

■■■

Input and Output in Java

Exam Objectives

3.2 Given a scenario involving navigating file systems, reading from files, or writing to files, develop the correct solution using the following classes (sometimes in combination), from java.io: BufferedReader, BufferedWriter, File, FileReader, FileWriter, and PrintWriter.

3.3 Develop code that serializes and/or de-serializes objects using the following APIs from java.io: DataInputStream, DataOutputStream, FileInputStream, FileOutputStream, ObjectInputStream, ObjectOutputStream, and Serializable.

You already know that data and operations on data are important parts of a computer program. Sometimes your application will need to read input data from a file or write the output data to a file. Java offers classes in the java.io package to facilitate these input/output (I/O) operations. Data can be of various types, ranging from raw bytes to characters, to primitive data types, and to objects. Java treats I/O in a standard, uniform way in the form of streams. Conceptually, a stream on one end is connected to an I/O device (e.g. a file or a socket), to another stream (or a program), and ultimately to a program on the other end. The data flows between a program and the I/O device through these streams.

Only a low-level stream capable of reading bytes or characters can be directly connected to an I/O device, while a computer program can be connected to a low-level or a high-level stream. A high-level stream does some kind of data processing; it converts the low-level data (e.g. bytes and characters) into high-level data (e.g. primitive data types). Because in the I/O devices (such as a file) the data always lives in the form of bytes or characters, you cannot directly connect a high-level stream to an I/O device. Instead, a high-level stream is connected to a low-level stream, which in turn is connected to an I/O device. From the perspective of a Java application, the data falls into three categories: raw bytes and characters, primitive data types, and objects.

So, the focus of this chapter is to understand how to perform I/O in a Java program by using streams. To accomplish that, we explore three avenues: how to read and write data in binary format (including bytes and data types), how to read and write data in text format, and how to read and write objects.

Handling Files in Java

By using streams, Java offers a standard way to perform I/O operations on any I/O device, such as a file or a socket. However, in this book, we only deal with files. Before you can read from a file or write to a file, you must have a way to represent a file in your program, and to navigate the file system. This is done by using the File class from the java.io package.

Understanding the File Class

The java.io package offers the File class to enable you to work with the file system on your machine. You can use this class (actually, an object of this class) to represent a file or a directory in the file system, navigate the file system, and perform several operations on the files in the file system. You will see how in this section.

The Path Name

While dealing with the files, a source of confusion for a beginner in Java programming is the path name. For example, consider the following path name on a Unix/Linux machine:

```
/java/scjp/temp
```

The first forward slash represents the root directory. This path name in Windows machines may be written as

```
C:\java\scjp\temp
```

The symbol C:\ represents the hard disk drive. The point here is that the path names are system dependent whereas Java is supposed to be system independent. Java accomplishes that by providing a system-independent way of dealing with the path names, by introducing the concept of abstract path names. You can enter a string for the path name in a system-independent way, and Java converts that string to an abstract path name that has the following two components:

- A system-dependent prefix string, such as a disk-drive specifier, say C:\ for Windows, or a forward slash (/) for the Unix/Linux root directory.

- A sequence of zero or more string names, each representing a directory except the last one, which may represent a directory or a file name. Each name is separated from the next name by a system-dependent separator (\ for Windows, / for Unix/Linux).

You need the path name to use the File class. As with any other class, you need to know the constructors of the File class before you can use it effectively.

File Path Names and File Constructors

The *path name* is an address of a file in the file system, and thereby uniquely identifies a file. The File constructors provide ways for you to enter the path name. You can enter a path name by using a string or an object of the File class that already represents the path. Different ways of passing in the path names and the corresponding File constructors are summarized in Table 8-1.

Table 8-1. *Constructors for the File Class*

Constructor	Description
File(String pathname)	Creates an instance of the File class by converting the path name String to an abstract path name.
File(String parent, String child)	Creates an instance of the File class by concatenating the child String to the parent String, and converting the combined String to an abstract path name.
File(File parent, String child)	Creates an instance of the File class by constructing an abstract path name from the abstract path name of the parent File, and the String path name of child.

■**Caution** An instance of the `File` class is immutable. This means that once you have created a `File` object by providing a path name, the abstract path name represented by this object will never change.

Listing 8-1 presents an example to demonstrate how to use these constructors in your program.

Listing 8-1. *TestFileConstructors.java*

```
1.  import java.io.*;
2.  class TestFileConstructors {
3.   public static void main (String[] args){
4.     try{
5.        File f1 = new File("java/scjp");
6.        File f2 = new File("java/scjp", "temp/myProg.java");
7.        File f3 = new File(f1, "temp/myProg.java");

8.        System.out.println("path for f1: " + f1.getCanonicalPath());
9.        System.out.println("path for f2: " + f2.getCanonicalPath());
10.       System.out.println("path for f3: " + f3.getCanonicalPath());
11.    }catch (IOException ioe){
12.        ioe.printStackTrace();
13.    }
14.  }
15. }
```

The `getCanonicalPath()` method of the `File` class (lines 8 to 10) returns the system-dependent abstract path name. Note that the forward slash is used as a separator in the path name string (lines 5 through 7) . This program was executed in the `C:\temp` directory on a Windows machine and the output was as follows:

```
path for f1: C:\temp\java\scjp
path for f2: C:\temp\java\scjp\temp\myProg.java
path for f3: C:\temp\java\scjp\temp\myProg.java
```

Note the following in constructing the abstract path name:

- We did not care what system it was while entering the path name (we used the Unix convention on a Windows machine). When entering the path name, the platform isn't relevant.

- Abstract path names returned by the `getCanonicalPath()` method are system dependent.

- The parent and child paths (lines 6 and 7) have been combined.

- The system-dependent disk-drive symbol (`C:\` in this case) has been prefixed to the path.

■**Note** If you do need to find out the system-dependent file separator, you can obtain it by using the following line of code:

```
String fs = System.getProperty("file.separator");
```

And if you do (for some reason) want to use the Windows-based file separator, you should use double backslash (`\\`) as a separator, such as `C:\\temp\\test.txt`.

Finally, note that no real file has been created on the system disk as a result of execution of Listing 8-1. In other words, when you create an instance of the class `File`, it does not create a file in the file system. You can create the file by invoking an appropriate method (as discussed in the next section) on the object of the `File` class.

■**Caution** When you create an instance of the `File` class, no real file is created in the file system.

After you have created a `File` instance, you can use it to interact with the file system.

Navigating the File System

After you've created an instance of the `File` class, it is your handle to the file system. You can use it to navigate the file system, create a file, and perform several operations on the files in the file system. You perform these tasks by invoking the appropriate methods on the `File` object—that is, the instance of the `File` class that you created. Some commonly used methods of the `File` class are described here:

- `boolean canRead()`: Returns `true` if the file (or directory) represented by the `File` instance can be read by the program.

- `boolean canWrite()`: Returns `true` if the file (or directory) represented by the `File` instance can be modified by the program.

- `boolean createNewFile()`: Creates a new file by using the abstract name associated with the `File` instance, if and only if the file with this path name does not exist already.

- `boolean delete()`: Deletes the file or directory represented by this `File` instance—that is, denoted by the abstract path name associated with this `File` instance.

- `boolean exists()`: Returns `true` if the file (or directory) denoted by the path name associated with this `File` instance exists.

- `String getAbsolutePath()`: Returns the absolute (as opposed to relative) path, also called full path, of the file (or directory) represented by this `File` instance.

- `String getCanonicalPath()`: Same as `getAbsolutePath()`, but the separators in the path name are system-dependent separators (such as / or \).

- `String getName()`: Returns the name of the file (or directory) represented by this `File` instance.

- `String getParent()`: Returns the name of the file (or directory) that contains the file (directory) represented by this `File` instance.

- `boolean isAbsolute()`: Returns `true` if the path name associated with this `File` instance is an absolute path name (as opposed to a relative path name).

- `boolean isDirectory()`: Returns `true` if this `File` instance represents a directory (as opposed to a normal file).

- `boolean isFile()`: Returns `true` if this `File` instance represents a normal file (as opposed to a directory).

- `String[] list()`: Returns an array that contains the names of files and directories contained in the directory represented by this `File` instance. Obviously, this method should only be invoked on a `File` instance that represents a directory.

- `String[] listFiles()`: Returns an array that contains the names of files only (and not directories) contained in the directory represented by this `File` instance. Obviously, this method should only be invoked on a `File` instance that represents a directory.

- `boolean mkDir()`: Creates a directory by using the abstract path name associated with this `File` instance.

- `boolean mkDirs()`: Creates a directory by using the abstract path name associated with this `File` instance. This also creates any nonexistent parent directory that appears in the path name.

- `boolean renameTo(File <newName>)`: Renames the file (or directory) represented by this `File` instance to the new name specified by `<newName>`.

Listing 8-2 shows how to use some of these methods in navigating the file system. You can modify this program to try other methods as well. This program will navigate the subtree of directories recursively and list the names of all the directories and their content. The default root (the beginning point) of the subtree is the current directory in which the program is started, but you can change it by passing in, as a command argument, the full path to the directory from where you want to start navigating. However, take extra precautions, because you can lose files on your system. The best policy is to create a separate directory such as `C:\temp` and a subtree of files and directories underneath it on your system, and practice the I/O programs in there. Make sure you do not put any file in there that you cannot afford to lose.

Listing 8-2. *FileNavigator.java*

```
1.  import java.io.*;
2.  class FileNavigator {
3.   public static void main (String[] args){
4.     String treeRoot = "."; //default root
5.     if (args.length >=1)treeRoot=args[0];
6.     File rootDir = new File(treeRoot);
7.     System.out.println("Root of navigation:" + rootDir.getAbsolutePath());
8.     // check if the root exists as a directory.
9.     if(!(rootDir.isDirectory())){
10.      System.out.println("The root of the naviagtion subtree does not exist
             as a directory!");
11.      System.exit(0);
12.     }
13.      FileNavigator fn = new FileNavigator();
14.      fn.navigate(rootDir);
15.    }

16.   public void navigate(File dir){
17.       System.out.println(" ");
18.       System.out.println("Directory " + dir + ":");
19.       String[] dirContent = dir.list();
20.       for (int i=0; i<dirContent.length; i++){
21.        System.out.print(" " + dirContent[i]);
22.        File child = new File(dir, dirContent[i]);
23.        if(child.isDirectory())navigate(child);
24.       }
25.   }
26. }
```

So, you can use the `File` class to represent a file in your Java program. Now, how do you read from this file and write into this file from your program? You do it by using streams.

Understanding Streams

Java deals with I/O in a very general way: whether the source (from which the data is being read) or destination (to which the data is being written) is a file or a socket, data always moves into a stream (i.e. the sequence of data items such as bytes). Figure 8-1 shows the relationship between a source from which the data is read, such as a file, a data stream, a Java program, and a destination to which the data is written, such as a file.

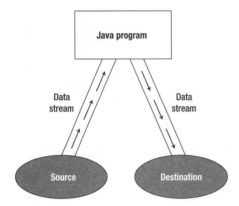

Figure 8-1. *Data flows in a stream from the source to the Java program in case of a read and from the Java program to the destination in case of a write. A source or a destination may be any I/O device, such as a file or a socket.*

Whether the source or destination is a file or a socket, any read or write is performed in three simple steps:

1. Open the stream.

2. Until there is more data, keep reading in a read, or writing in a write.

3. Close the stream.

There are low-level streams, which read and write data in bytes or characters, and high-level streams, which read data in bytes from a low-level stream and return formatted data to the caller (and vice versa).

In this section, we explore the low-level and high-level streams that you can use when the data needs to be written to an output device or read from an input device in units of 8-bit bytes.

The Low-Level Streams

A low-level input stream reads data and returns it in bytes, and a low-level output stream accepts data as bytes and writes the output in bytes. Two examples of low-level streams are represented by the classes `FileInputStream` and `FileOutputStream`, which are subclasses of `InputStream` and `OutputStream`, respectively.

The FileInputStream Class

The `FileInputStream` class is designed for reading image files as it reads a stream of raw bytes. When you instantiate the `FileInputStream` class, an opaque connection is created to the specified file, and this connection is represented by an object of the FileDescriptor class. You can specify the file with which you want to connect your program in one of the following three ways:

- Specify a File object that represents an actual file in the file system.

- Specify a path (in String format) to an actual file in the file system.

- Specify a FileDescriptor object that represents a connection to an actual file in the file system.

The constructors of the FileInputStream class corresponding to these three options are described in Table 8-2.

Table 8-2. *Constructors for the FileInputStream Class*

Constructor	Description
FileInputStream(FileDescriptor fdObj)	Used to create a FileInputStream object by using an existing FileDescriptor object specified by fdObj, which represents an existing connection to an actual file in the file system.
FileInputStream(File file)	Used to create a FileInputStream object by opening a connection to an actual file, specified by file, in the file system. A new FileDescriptor object is created to represent this file connection.
FileInputStream (String name)	Used to create a FileInputStream object by opening a connection to an actual file, specified by the path name, name, in the file system. A new FileDescriptor object is created to represent this file connection. .

■Note An object of the FileDescriptor class serves as an opaque handle to the underlying machine-specific structure that represents a source or sink of bytes, such as an open file, or an open socket. The main practical use for a file descriptor is to facilitate a connection to a file for FileInputStream or FileOutputStream.

Note that you can create a stream connection only with a regular file, and not with a directory. This makes sense, because you can only write bytes or characters to a file and not to a directory. If the specified file is a directory rather than a regular file, or it does not exist, or it cannot be read for some reason, a FileNotFoundException is thrown.

The following are the signatures of the FileInputStream constructors with the File or String parameter:

```
public FileInputStream(…) throws FileNotFoundException;
```

After you create an instance of the FileInputStream class, you can use it to perform operations such as reading a single byte, an array of bytes, or a part of an array of bytes by invoking the following methods:

- int read() throws IOException: Returns the next byte of data, or -1 if the end of the file is reached

- int read(byte[] bytes) throws IOException: Reads bytes.length number of bytes from the stream into an array, and returns the number of bytes read, or -1 if the end of the file is reached

- `int read(byte[] bytes, int offset, int len) throws IOException`: Reads up to a total of `len` bytes (starting from `offset`) into an array, and returns the number of bytes read, or –1 if the end of the file is reached

- `void close()`: Closes the input stream and releases any system resources assigned to the stream

All of these read methods block until an input is available. :

So, the `FileInputStream` reads 8-bit bytes. The counterpart of `FileInputStream` to write the bytes is `FileOutputStream`.

The FileOutputStream Class

The `FileOutputStream` class is meant for writing streams of raw bytes into files, such as image files. When you instantiate the `FileOutputStream` class, an opaque connection is created to the specified file, and this connection is represented by an object of the `FileDescriptor` class. Just as with `FileInputStream`, you can specify the file with which you want to create a connection either by specifying the file directly or by specifying the `FileDescriptor` object. The corresponding commonly used constructors for `FileOutputStream` are described in Table 8-3.

Table 8-3. *Constructors for the FileOutputStream Class*

Constructor	Description
`FileOutputStream` `(FileDescriptor fdObj)`	Used to create a `FileOutputStream` object by using an existing `FileDescriptor` object, `fdObj`, which represents an existing connection to an actual file in the file system.
`FileOutputStream` `(File file)`	Used to create a `FileOutputStream` object by opening a connection to an actual file, specified by the `File` object, `file`, in the file system. A new `FileDescriptor` object is created to represent this file connection.
`FileOutputStream` `(String name)`	Used to create a `FileOutputStream` object by opening a connection to an actual file, specified by the path name, `name`, in the file system. A new `FileDescriptor` object is created to represent this file connection.

.Note that you can create a stream connection only with a regular file, and not with a directory. A `FileNotFoundException` is thrown if the specified file is a directory rather than a regular file, if it does not exist and cannot be created, or if it cannot be accessed to write to for some reason. The signatures of the `FileOutputStream` constructors with the `File` or `String` parameter are shown here:

```
public FileOutputStream(…) throws FileNotFoundException;
```

After you create an instance of the `FileOutputStream` class, you can use it to perform operations such as writing a single byte, an array of bytes, or a part of an array of bytes by invoking the following methods:

- `void write(int b) throws IOException`: Writes the passed-in byte to the stream

- `void write(byte[] bytes) throws IOException`: Writes `bytes.length` number of bytes from the passed-in array to the stream

- `void write(byte[] bytes, int offset, int len) throws IOException`: Writes up to a total of `len` bytes (starting from `offset`) from the passed-in array to the stream

- `void close()`: Closes the output stream and releases any system resources assigned to the stream

■**Caution** Note that the constructors of both `FileInputStream` and `FileOutputStream` throw `FileNotFoundException` (a subclass of `IOException`), and the read/write methods of these classes throw `IOException`. Therefore, when you call these constructors or methods from your method, you must catch the exception in the body of your method, or declare the exception in the `throws` clause of your method, or both. In other words, your method code must be prepared to deal with these exceptions.

As an example, Listing 8-3 shows how to use the `FileInputStream` and `FileOutputStream` classes to read and write files. It copies a file `scjp.txt` (which must exist in the directory where you execute this program) to another file named `scjpcopy.txt`, which is created if it does not exist.

Listing 8-3. *FileByteCopier.java*

```
1.   import java.io.*;
2. public class FileByteCopier {
3.  public static void main(String[] args) throws IOException {
4.        File inputFile = new File("scjp.txt");
5.        File outputFile = new File("scjpcopy.txt");
6.   FileInputStream in = new FileInputStream(inputFile);
7.   FileOutputStream out = new FileOutputStream(outputFile);
8.    int c;
9.    while ((c = in.read()) != -1)out.write(c);
10.   in.close();
11.   out.close();
12. }
13.}
```

This example demonstrates that although `FileInputStream` and `FileOutputStream` are more suitable to read image files, it is legal to use them for text files too. However, the `FileReader` and `FileWriter` classes (which you will explore later in this chapter) are more suitable to read and write streams of characters (from text files).

When byte is the unit of information that you are interested in, such as image files, you can work directly with the low-level streams such as `FileInputStream` or `FileOutputStream`, and these are the low-level streams that are actually attached to the input and output devices, such as files or sockets. However, if you are only interested in high-level data types such as an `int`, a `float`, or a `String` (of course, composed of bytes) and don't want to deal directly with bytes, then you can work with high-level streams offered by Java.

The High-Level Streams

When the unit of information you are interested in is a high-level data type such as a `float`, an `int`, or a `String`, and you don't want to deal with bytes directly, you can work with high-level streams. However, these streams do not directly read from or write to an I/O device; rather, they are attached to low-level streams, which in turn are attached to the I/O device. In other words, data is always read from an input device or written to an output device by a low-level stream.

Two examples of high-level streams are `DataInputStream` and `DataOutputStream`, discussed next.

The DataInputStream Class

Java offers the `DataInputStream` class to enable an application to read primitive data types from an underlying input stream in a machine-independent way. However, as Figure 8-2 shows, it does not read directly from an input device such as a file, but rather is attached to a low-level stream that reads bytes from the input device and processes the bytes into values of desired high-level data types.

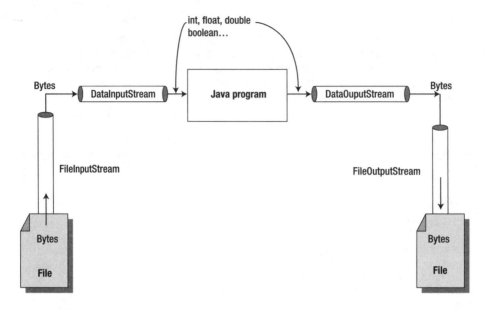

Figure 8-2. *The DataInputStream is attached to the FileInputStream, which in turn is attached to the file.*

The constructor for the DataInputStream class is

```
public DataInputStream(InputStream in)
```

Note that because the FileInputStream class extends InputStream, you can also invoke the constructor by passing in an instance of FileInputStream rather than InputStream. This is how you attach a low-level stream with a high-level stream. You can use DataInputStream to read any primitive data type by invoking the corresponding method from the following list:

- boolean readBoolean() throws IOException
- byte readByte() throws IOException
- char readChar()throws IOException
- double readDouble() throws IOException
- float readFloat() throws IOException
- int readInt() throws IOException
- long readLong() throws IOException
- short readShort() throws IOException

The counterpart of DataInputStream is DataOutputStream, which you can use in your program to write primitive data types to a file.

The DataOutputStream Class

Java offers the DataOutputStream class to enable an application to write primitive data types to an underlying output stream in a machine-independent way. However, it does not write directly to an output device such as file, but rather is attached to a low-level stream that writes bytes to the output device.

The constructor for the DataOutputStream class is

```
public DataOutputStream(OutputStream out)
```

Note that the FileOutputStream class extends OutputStream. Therefore, you can also invoke the constructor by passing in an instance of FileOutputStream rather than OutputStream. You can use DataOutputStream to write any primitive data type by invoking the corresponding method from the following list:

- void writeBoolean(boolean b) throws IOException
- void writeByte(byte b) throws IOException
- void writeBytes(String s) throws IOException
- void writeChar(int c) throws IOException
- void writeChars(String s) throws IOException
- void writeDouble(double d) throws IOException
- void writeFloat(float f) throws IOException
- void writeInt(int i) throws IOException
- void writeLong(long l) throws IOException
- void writeShort(short s) throws IOException

The writeBytes(…) and writeChars(…) methods write out strings as sequences of bytes and chars, respectively, to the underlying output streams.

As an example, Listing 8-4 shows how to use the DataInputStream and DataOutputStream classes to read and write files. To begin with, the data is stored in arrays of int, double, and String types (lines 6 through 8). First, the data is written out to a file named orders.txt (lines 10 through 18), and then it is read back into the program and printed to the screen (lines 20 through 42). Note how you connect an output file with the FileOutputStream and the DataOutputStream with the FileOutputStream in line 5, and also how in a similar way you connect an input file with the FileInputStream, and the DataInputStream with the FileInputStream in line 20.

Listing 8-4. *ReadWriteDataTest.java*

```
1.    import java.io.*;
2. public class ReadWriteDataTest {
3.  public static void main(String[] args) throws IOException {
4.    String dataFile = "orders.txt";
5.    DataOutputStream out = new DataOutputStream(new
          FileOutputStream(dataFile));
6.    double[] priceList = { 19.99, 29.99, 39.99};
7.    int[] copies = { 100000, 50000,70000};
8.    String[] titleList = { "SCJP Study Guide",
        "SCBCD Study Guide" , "SCSA Study Guide"};
9. // Write out into the file.
10.   for (int i = 0; i < priceList.length; i++) {
11.     out.writeDouble(priceList[i]);
12.     out.writeChar('\t');
13.     out.writeInt(copies[i]);
14.     out.writeChar('\t');
15.     out.writeChars(titleList[i]);
16.     out.writeChar('\n');
17.   }
```

```
18.    out.close();
19. // read back in again
20.    DataInputStream in = new DataInputStream(new
            FileInputStream(dataFile));
21.    double price;
22.    int copy;
23.    StringBuffer title;
24.    double grandTotal = 0.0;
25.    try {
26.      while (true) {
27.        price = in.readDouble();
28.        in.readChar(); //throws away the tab
29.        copy = in.readInt();
30.        in.readChar(); //throw away the tab
31.        char ch;
32.        title = new StringBuffer(25);
33.        char lineSep = System.getProperty("line.separator").charAt(1);
34.        while ((ch = in.readChar()) != lineSep)title.append(ch);
35.        System.out.println("Your order: " + copy + " copies of " + title +
            " at $" + price);
36.        grandTotal = grandTotal + copy * price;
37.      }
38.    } catch (EOFException e) {
39.      System.out.println("End of File!");
40.    }
41.      System.out.println("Grand Total: $" + grandTotal);
42.      in.close();
43.    }
44. }
```

The output of this code follows:

```
Your order: 100000 copies of SCJP Study Guide at $19.99
Your order: 50000 copies of SCBCD Study Guide at $29.99
Your order: 70000 copies of SCSA Study Guide at $39.99
End of File!
Grand Total: $6297800.0
```

All the streams discussed in this section are collectively called *byte streams* because, regardless of which stream you are using, the data is always being written to the output device and being read from an input device in units of bytes. These streams are better suited to read binary files such as image files and primitive data types. You can also read text files (characters) in their 8-bit byte representation. Java offers another type of streams called character streams, which are used to read from the input device and write to the output device in units of 16-bit (Unicode) characters. These streams are also called readers and writers.

Readers and Writers

To read and write data in binary format, you have FileInputStream/FileOutputStream (low-level streams) and DataInputStream/DataOutputStream (high-level streams). To read data in text format, Java offers so-called reader and writer streams. Note that some authors do not refer to readers and writers as streams. All the classes corresponding to reader and writer streams are subclasses of the Reader and Writer classes and are used to read character streams. Subclasses of Reader and Writer implement specialized streams and are divided into two categories: those that read characters from or write characters to data devices directly (low-level streams) and those that are attached to the low-level streams and perform some kind of processing on the data (high-level streams).

Low-Level Readers and Writers

The low-level reader streams read data and return it in characters, and low-level output streams accept data as characters and write the output in characters. Two examples of low-level reader and writer streams are FileReader and FileWriter.

The FileReader Class

The FileReader class is meant for reading text files, because it reads a stream of characters. When you instantiate the FileReader class, an opaque connection is created to the specified file, and this connection is represented by an object of the FileDescriptor class. You can specify the file to which you want to create the connection either by specifying the file directly or by specifying the FileDescriptor object. The corresponding commonly used constructors for the FileReader class are described in Table 8-4.

Table 8-4. *Constructors for the FileReader Class*

Constructor	Description
FileReader(FileDescriptor fdObj)	Used to create a FileReader object by using an existing FileDescriptor object specified by fdObj, which represents an existing connection to an actual file in the file system.
FileReader(File file)	Used to create a FileReader object by opening a connection to an actual file, specified by the File object, file, in the file system. A new FileDescriptor object is created to represent this file connection.
FileReader(String name)	Used to create a FileReader object by opening a connection to an actual file, specified by the path name, name, in the file system. A new FileDescriptor object is created to represent this file connection.

You can create a stream connection only with a regular file, and not with a directory. An IOException is thrown if the specified file is a directory rather than a regular file, if it does not exist and cannot be created, or if it cannot be accessed for some reason. The signature of the FileReader constructors with the File or String parameter follows:

```
public FileReader(…) throws IOException;
```

After you create an instance of the FileReader class, you can use it to perform operations such as reading a single character, an array of characters, or a part of an array of characters by invoking the following methods:

- int read() throws IOException: Returns the next character of data, or -1 if the end of the file is reached

- int read(char[] cbuf) throws IOException: Reads characters from the stream into the array cbuf, and returns the number of characters read, or -1 if the end of the file is reached

- int read(char[] cbuf, int offset, int len) throws IOException: Reads up to a total of len characters (starting from offset) into the array cbuf, and returns the number of chars read, or –1 if the end of file is reached

- void close(): Closes the input stream and releases any system resources assigned to the stream

All the read methods block until an input is available.

So, the FileReader reads 16-bit characters. The counterpart of FileReader to write the characters is FileWriter.

The FileWriter Class

The FileWriter class is meant for writing streams of characters into files. When you instantiate the FileWriter class, an opaque connection is created to the specified file, and this connection is represented by an object of the FileDescriptor class. Just as with FileReader, you can specify the file to which you want to create a connection either by specifying the file directly or by specifying the FileDescriptor object. The corresponding commonly used constructors for the FileWriter class are described in Table 8-5.

Table 8-5. *Constructors for the FileWriter Class*

Constructor	Description
FileWriter(FileDescriptor fdObj)	Used to create a FileWriter object by using an existing FileDescriptor object, fdObj, which represents an existing connection to an actual file in the file system.
FileWriter(File file)	Used to create a FileWriter object by opening a connection to an actual file, specified by the File object, file, in the file system. A new FileDescriptor object is created to represent this file connection.
FileWriter (String name)	Used to create a FileWriter object by opening a connection to an actual file, specified by the path name, name, in the file system. A new FileDescriptor object is created to represent this file connection.

Note that you can create a stream connection only with a regular file, and not with a directory. An IOException is thrown if the specified file is a directory rather than a regular file, if it does not exist and cannot be created, or if it cannot be accessed to write for some reason. The signature of the FileWriter class constructors with the File or String parameter follows:

```
public FileWriter(…) throws IOException;
```

After you create an instance of the FileWriter class, you can use it to perform operations such as writing a single character, an array of characters, or a part of an array of characters by invoking the following methods:

- void write(int c) throws IOException: Writes the passed-in single character to the stream

- void write(char[] ch) throws IOException: Writes ch.length number of characters from the passed-in array to the stream

- void write(String str) throws IOException: Writes the passed-in string to the stream

- void write(char[] cbuf, int offset, int len) throws IOException: Writes up to a total of len characters (starting from offset) from the passed in array to the stream

- void write(String str, int offset, int len) throws IOException: Writes up to a total of len characters (starting from offset) from the passed-in string to the stream

- void flush() throws IOException: Flushes the stream, which means the remaining (buffered) data that you have written to the stream is sent out to the file before closing

- void close(): Closes the output stream and releases any system resources assigned to the stream

As an example, Listing 8-5 shows how to use the FileReader and FileWriter classes to read and write files. It copies a file named scjp.txt (which must exist in the directory where you execute this program) to another file named scjpcopy.txt, which is created if it does not exist.

Listing 8-5. *FileCharCopier.java*

```
1.   import java.io.*;
2. public class FileByteCopier {
3.   public static void main(String[] args) throws IOException {
4.     File inputFile = new File("scjp.txt");
5.     File outputFile = new File("scjpcopy.txt");
6.     FileReader in = new FileReader(inputFile);
7.     FileWriter out = new FileWriter(outputFile);
8.     int c;
9.     while ((c = in.read()) != -1)out.write(c);
10.    in.close();
11.    out.flush();
12.    out.close();
13. }
14.}
```

In your program, you may not like to deal with characters. You may prefer to deal with chunks (blocks) of data. You can do that, because just like FileInputStream and FileOutputStream classes, FileReader and FileWriter also have corresponding high-level streams to which they can be chained.

High-Level Readers and Writers

As you know, you can use DataInputStream and DataOutputStream to read and write the primitive types in binary format. Similarly, you can read and write characters in character streams in big chunks (buffers) and in text format by using the BufferedReader and BufferedWriter classes, respectively.

The BufferedReader and BufferedWriter Classes

From your program, you can read and write primitive data types (rather than bytes) by using DataInputStream and DataOutputStream. Now you can get a bit more ambitious and say: Can I read and write data in blocks to minimize I/O overhead? The answer is: yes, you can do it by using the BufferedReader and BufferedWriter classes. These classes are chained to low-level streams such as FileReader and FileWriter.

The BufferedReader class has the following constructors:

```
BufferedReader(Reader in);
BufferedReader(Reader in, int size);
```

The size specifies the buffer size. If the buffer size is not specified, a default value is used. Similarly, the following are the constructors for the BufferedWriter class:

```
BufferedReader(Writer out);
BufferedReader(Writer out, int size);
```

Note that theses constructors do not throw any exception. Because FileReader and FileWriter are subclasses of Reader and Writer, respectively, their objects can also be passed in to the BufferedReader and BufferedWriter constructors. As an example, consider Listing 8-6.

Listing 8-6. *FileBufferCopier.java*

```
1. import java.io.*;
2. public class FileBufferCopier {
3.  public static void main(String[] args) throws IOException {
4.    File inputFile = new File("scjp.txt");
5.    File outputFile = new File("scjpcopy.txt");
6.    BufferedReader in = new BufferedReader(new FileReader(inputFile));
7.    BufferedWriter out = new BufferedWriter(new FileWriter(outputFile));
8.    String line;
9.    while ((line = in.readLine()) != null){
10.   out.write(line);
11.   out.newLine();
12.   }
13.   in.close();
14.   out.close();
15. }
16.}
```

Note that the readLine()method (line 9) of the BufferedReader class is used to read the next line in the input, and the write(...) method (line 10) of the BufferedWriter class is used to write a string. The newLine() method (line 11) is used to start a new line in the file to which the data is being written. The BufferedReader class also has the following method to read a single character:

```
int read();
```

So far, you have studied two types of streams: one that reads and writes the data in binary format, and the other that reads and writes the data in text format. How about building a bridge between the two? For example, there will be situations in which you have binary data, say in various data types, and you want to write them in text format. Java offers the PrintWriter class to let you do that.

The PrintWriter Class

The PrintWriter class, a subclass of the Writer class, has the capability of writing various data types as text strings. Because objects are also data types, PrintWriter can be used to print formatted representations of objects to a text-output stream. Note that methods in this class never throw I/O exceptions, but some of its constructors may.

Just like high-level I/O streams, when you construct a high-level reader or writer, you pass in the next lower-level stream object. For example, following is a constructor for the PrintWriter class:

```
PrintWriter (Writer out)
```

The most commonly used methods of the PrintWriter class are

```
public void print(...)
```

and

```
public void println(...)
```

Both methods are overloaded and accept one argument of any of the following types: boolean, char, int, long, float, double, array of chars, String, or Object. The only difference between println(...) and print(...) is that println(...) terminates the current line by writing the line-separator string, which is defined by the system property line.separator, and therefore is not necessarily a single newline character ('\n').The value of the line separator can be obtained with the following line of code:

```
System.getProperty("line.separator")"
```

When you are using the methods of the various stream classes (including readers and writers) to perform I/O operations, you should be aware of the exceptions that they can throw.

Exceptions During I/O Operations

You learned about exceptions in Chapter 7. Table 8-6 presents a summary of the exceptions thrown by the methods of the various stream classes discussed in the preceding sections.

Table 8-6. *Exceptions Thrown by Various Stream Class Methods*

Stream Class	Constructors	Read/Write Methods
FileInputStream FileOutputStream	FileNotFoundException	IOException
DataInputStream DataOutputStream	None	IOException
FileReader FileWriter	FileNotFoundException	FileNotFoundException
BufferedReader BufferedWriter	None	IOException
PrintWriter	FileNotFoundException	None

You have learned that low-level streams such as FileInputStream and FileOutputStream read and write the bytes, and that high-level streams such as DataInputStream and DataOutputStream, when chained to the low-level streams, enable the programs to read and write primitive data types: byte, char, short, int, long, float, double, and boolean. Java enables you to go beyond primitive data types and write your own data types: the classes. So, a natural question to ask is: Can I have a stream to read and write objects? The answer is yes.

Object Streams and Serialization

Java offers high-level streams DataInputStream and DataOutputStream to read and write primitive data types. Similarly, Java offers high-level streams ObjectInputStream and ObjectOutputStream, which, when chained to low-level streams such as FileInputStream and FileOutputStream, can be used by programs to read and write objects. The process of writing an object to somewhere is called *object serialization*, and the process of reading a serialized object back into the program is called *deserialization*.

The goal here is to save the state of an object. Even without serialization, you could use the I/O classes to save the object state and restore it at a later time. However, all programmers would need to do it in their own way, and the process would be prone to errors. Serialization standardizes and automates the process of saving the state of an object, and hence makes it robust. Simply put, through serialization, Java allows you to say: save this object along with its instance variables, except this variable and that variable. For example, if you declare a variable transient, it will not be saved in serialization.

To make the objects of a class serializable, the class must implement the interface Serializable:

```
class  MySerialClass implements Serializable {
// body of the class
}
```

The Serializable interface is an empty interface (i.e. no methods are declared inside it) and is used to just tag a class for possible serialization. To make your class serializable in this way is the necessary condition to enable the objects of the class to be serialized. Obviously, you need to do more work to actually serialize the objects.

Writing with ObjectOutputStream

To write an object to a file, you use the ObjectOutputStream to write it to a low-level stream, which in turn will write it to the file. For example, consider the following code fragment:

```
FileOutputStream out = new FileOutputStream("objectStore.ser");
ObjectOutputStream os = new ObjectOutputStream(out);
os.writeObject("serialOut");
os.writeObject(new MySerialClass());
os.writeObject("End of storage!");
os.flush();
```

Note that ObjectOutputStream must be chained to another stream because it cannot write directly to a device (file or socket). In the preceding example, we chain an ObjectOutputStream to a FileOutputStream, which can write it to a file. Also note that a string and two objects are written to the stream by invoking the writeObject(…) method. If you pass in an object that is not serializable, the writeObject method will throw a NotSerializableException.

Only the data of the object (along with the class name) is saved, and not the class definition. The static and transient variables are not saved. To be specific, the following are saved in serialization:

- The values of the instance variables of the serialized object.

- The class description of the object, which includes the class name, the serial version unique ID, a set of flags describing the serialization method, and a description of the data fields.

- All the objects that a serialized object refers to through object reference variables. That means those objects must be serializable; otherwise, you will get a compiler error.

The objects can be read back in the same order in which they were stored.

Reading with ObjectInputStream

Once you've written objects and primitive data types to a stream, you'll likely want to read them again and reconstruct the objects. This is also straightforward. Here is a code fragment that reads in the String and the Date objects that were written to the file named objectStore.ser in the previous example:

```
FileInputStream in = new FileInputStream("objectStore.ser");
ObjectInputStream is = new ObjectInputStream(in);
String note = (String)is.readObject();
MySerialClass serialIn1 = (MyClassSerial)is.readObject();
MySerialClass serialIn2 = (MyClassSerial)is.readObject();
```

Just like ObjectOutputStream, ObjectInputStream must be chained to another stream because it cannot read directly from the device (file or socket). In the preceding example, our code chains an ObjectInputStream to a FileInputStream, and uses the ObjectInputStream's readObject() method to read the two objects and a string that we stored earlier in a file. Note that the objects must be read in the same order in which they were written. Further note that the object returned by the readObject() method is cast to a proper type before assigning it to a declared object reference.

Caution A class can be serialized only if it is serializable. That means either the class itself or its superclass must implement the `Serializable` interface.

Note the following points about serialization:

- If a class is serializable, then all the subclasses of this superclass are implicitly serializable even if they don't explicitly implement the `Serializable` interface.

- If you want to serialize an array (or some other collection), each of its elements must be serializable.

- Static variables are not saved as part of serialization. Recall that the purpose of serialization is to save the state of an object, and a static variable belongs to the class and not to an object of the class.

Codewalk Quicklet

The code for the codewalk quicklet exercise in this chapter is presented in Listing 8-7.

Listing 8-7. *CodeWalkSeven.java*

```
1. import java.io.*;
2. class CodeWalkSeven{
3. public static void main(String [] args) {
4.   Car c = new Car("Nissan", 1500, "blue");
5.   System.out.println("before: " + c.make + " "
       + c.weight);
6.   try {
7.     FileOutputStream fs = new FileOutputStream("Car.ser");
8.     ObjectOutputStream os = new ObjectOutputStream(fs);
9.     os.writeObject(c);
10.    os.close();
11.  }catch (Exception e) { e.printStackTrace(); }
12.  try {
13.    FileInputStream fis = new FileInputStream("Car.ser");
14.    ObjectInputStream ois = new ObjectInputStream(fis);
15.    c = (Car) ois.readObject();
16.    ois.close();
17.  }catch (Exception e) { e.printStackTrace(); }
18.    System.out.println("after: " + c.make + " "
  .      + c.weight);
19.  }
20. }
21. class NonLiving {}
22. class Vehicle extends NonLiving {
23.   String make = "Lexus";
24.   String color = "Brown";
25. }
```

```
26. class Car extends Vehicle implements Serializable {
27.   protected int weight = 1000;
28.   Car(String n, int w, String c) {
29.     color = c;
30.     make = n;
31.     weight = w;
32.   }
33. }
```

To get you started on this exercise, following are some hints:

- *Input*: Lines 4, 23, and 24.

- *Operations*: Lines 9 and 15.

- *Output*: Lines 5 and 18.

- *Rule*: Only the serializable objects will be written to a file.

Looking at the code from this angle, see if you can handle the last question in the "Review Questions" section based on this code.

The three most important takeaways from this chapter are as follows:

- The low-level `FileInputStream`/`FileOutputStream` and the high-level `DataInputStream`/`DataOutputStream` are used to read and write data in binary format.

- The low-level `FileReader`/`FileWriter` and the high-level `BufferedReader`/`BufferedWriter` are used to read and write data in text format.

- `ObjectInputStream` and `ObjectOutputStream` can be used to read and write objects by chaining these high-level streams to low-level streams such as `FileInputStream` and `FileOutputStream`.

Summary

Java offers classes in the `java.io` package to perform input/output (I/O) operations in a program.

Java treats I/O in a standard, uniform way in the form of streams. Conceptually, a stream on one end is connected to an I/O device (e.g. a file or a socket), to another stream (or a program), and ultimately to a program on the other end. The data flows between a program and the I/O device through these streams. A file in a file system is represented in your program by an instance of the `File` class. Just creating an instance of the `File` class does not create a file in the file system. However, you can invoke methods on a `File` instance to create a file or a directory, navigate the file system, and perform operations on a file (such as rename a file, find out if a file is a directory or a normal file, and list the content of a directory).

While the `File` class is used to interact with the file system and to represent a file on the system, the stream classes are used to perform read/write operations on the file. You can perform read/write operations on binary files such as an image file by using the low-level streams `FileInputStream` and `FileOutputStream`, which read and write in units of bytes. You can read and write data in units of primitive data types by using the high-level streams `DataInputStream` and `DataOutputStream`, which are chained to `FileInputStream` and `FileOutputStream`, which in turn are connected to files. These I/O streams are used to read and write data in binary format. The analog for reading and writing data in text format are the reader and writer streams. The low-level streams `FileReader` and `FileWriter` read and write 16-bit Unicode characters, while the high-level streams `BufferedReader` and `BufferedWriter` can be chained to `FileReader` and `FileWriter` to read and write text data in blocks. The `PrintWriter` stream is used to write primitive data types and objects as text strings.

The process of writing an object to a file is called object serialization. You can read and write objects in your program by using the high-level streams ObjectInputStream and ObjectOutputStream chained to low-level streams such as FileInputStream and FileOutputStream.

Between reading the input data from one device, such as a file, and writing the output data to an output device, an application processes the data, which may include parsing and formatting the data. You will learn how to do it in the next chapter.

EXAM'S EYE VIEW

Comprehend

- You can use the low-level classes such as FileInputStream and FileOutputStream to perform read/write operations on binary files such as image files, because these streams work at byte level.

- It is always the low-level classes, such as FileInputStream/FileOutputStream or FileReader/FileWriter, that can directly perform read/write operations on the files. If you want to use the high-level streams in your program to perform read/write operations, they must be chained to low-level streams.

Look Out

- Creating an instance of the File class does not create a real file in the file system.

- ObjectInputStream and ObjectOutputStream cannot read from or write to a file directly; they must be chained to low-level streams such as FileInputStream and FileOutputStream.

- The PrintWriter stream has a built-in capability to write primitive data types and objects as text strings.

Memorize

- By invoking methods on a File instance, you can create and delete files and directories in a file system.

- Constructors of both the FileInputStream and FileOutputStream classes throw FileNotFoundException, and the read/write methods of these classes throw IOException. Constructors of DataInputStream and DataOutputStream do not throw any exception, but the methods of these classes do throw IOException.

- FileReader and FileWriter read and write 16-bit characters, while FileInputStream and FileOutputStream read and write 8-bit bytes.

- FileReader and FileWriter are more suitable to read and write text files, while FileInputStream and FileOutputStream are designed to read and write image files.

- An object can only be stored if the corresponding class implements the Serializable interface.

Review Questions

1. While navigating the file system by using the methods of the `File` class, which of the following operations can you perform?

    A. Change the current working directory.

    B. Delete a file.

    C. Create a file.

    D. Change the security on the file.

2. When you instantiate the `File` class, a file is created on the file system.

    A. True

    B. False

3. Which of the following streams will enable you to read the primitive data types from a file into your Java program?

    A. `DataInputStream` and `FileInputStream`

    B. `DataInputStream`

    C. `FileInputStream`

    D. `FileReader`

4. Which of the following statements are true? (Choose all that apply.)

    A. Readers and writers are used for I/O on 16-bit Unicode characters.

    B. `FileInputStream` and `FileOutputStream` can be used to handle I/O on 16-bit Unicode characters.

    C. `FileInputStream` and `FileOutputStream` can be used to read image files.

    D. `FileInputStream` and `FileOutputStream` can be used to read text files.

5. Which of the following streams enables you to write an object to a file?

    A. `ObjectOutputStream` and `FileOutputStream`

    B. `FileOutputStream`

    C. `ObjectOutputStream`

    D. `ObjectInputStream`

6. Consider the following code:

    ```
    1. FileOutputStream out=new FileOutputStream("objectStore.ser");
    2. ObjectOutputStream os = new ObjectOutputStream(out);
    3. os.writeObject("Object on the fly!");
    ```

    What is the result of this code?

    A. The string `"Object on the fly!"` is written into the file `objectStore.ser`.

    B. Line 3 causes a compiler error.

    C. The code compiles fine but an exception is thrown at line 3 when the code is executed.

    D. An exception occurs at line 2.

    E. A compiler error occurs at line 2.

7. Consider the following code:

```
FileOutputStream fo = FileOutputStream("myFile.txt");
DataOutputStream do = DataOutputStream(fo);
do.writeByte(9);
do.writeFloat(4.20f);
do.close();
```

How many 8-bit bytes does the code write into the file?

A. 2

B. 5

C. 3

D. 10

8. Consider the following code:

```
1. import java.io.*;
2. public class QuestionEight {
3. public static void main(String[] args) throws IOException {
4.   File inputFile = new File("scjp.txt");
5.   File outputFile = new File("scjpcopy.txt");
6.   BufferedReader in = new BufferedReader(inputFile);
7.   BufferedWriter out = new BufferedWriter(new
        FileWriter(outputFile));
8.   String line;
9.   while ((line = in.readLine()) != null){
10.    out.write(line);
11.    out.newLine();
12.   }
13.    in.close();
14.    out.close();
15.  }
16.}
```

What is the output of this code?

A. A compiler error occurs at line 3.

B. A compiler error occurs at line 6.

C. The code compiles fine but throws an exception during execution at line 6.

D. A compiler error occurs at line 7.

E. The code compiles and executes without any error or exception.

9. Which of the following statements are true? (Choose all that apply.)

A. When an object is serialized, the whole class definition is saved.

B. When an object is serialized, the whole object state (all the data variables with their values) are saved.

C. FileInputStream cannot read text files; you can only use it to read image files.

D. You cannot read a file directly from FileReader.

E. None of the above.

10. Consider the code in Listing 8-7. What is the result?

A. `before: Nissan 1500 after: Lexus 1000`

B. `before: Nissan 1500 after: Lexus 1500`

C. `before: Nissan: 1000 after: Lexus 1000`

D. `before: Nissan: 1000 after: Lexus 1500`

E. Compilation fails.

■ ■ ■

CHAPTER 9

Strings, Formatters, and Wrappers

Exam Objectives

3.1 Develop code that uses the primitive wrapper classes (such as Boolean, Character, Double, Integer, etc.), and/or autoboxing & unboxing. Discuss the differences between the String, StringBuilder, and StringBuffer classes.

3.4 Use standard J2SE APIs in the java.text package to correctly format or parse dates, numbers, and currency values for a specific locale; and, given a scenario, determine the appropriate methods to use if you want to use the default locale or a specific locale. Describe the purpose and use of the java.util.Locale class.

3.5 Write code that uses standard J2SE APIs in the java.util and java.util.regex packages to format or parse strings or streams. For strings, write code that uses the Pattern and Matcher classes and the String.split method. Recognize and use regular expression patterns for matching (limited to: . (dot), * (star), + (plus), ?, \d, \s, \w, [], ()). The use of *, +, and ? will be limited to greedy quantifiers, and the parenthesis operator will only be used as a grouping mechanism, not for capturing content during matching. For streams, write code using the Formatter and Scanner classes and the PrintWriter.format/printf methods. Recognize and use formatting parameters (limited to: %b, %c, %d, %f, %s) in format strings.

It is hard to imagine an application without data. An application typically receives data from an I/O device (for example, a file or a socket), processes (or produces) data, and sends it to another I/O device, and the data travels between the I/O device and the application in the form of streams. The processing of data includes parsing (splitting apart) the incoming data and formatting (putting together) the outgoing data. Both parsing and formatting can be done at data item levels (for example, strings, numbers, and dates) and at data stream levels. For example, you format the data items, and then format the stream of the data items, and send the stream. On the receiving end, you parse the stream to get hold of some data items, and then you can do parsing at data item levels to examine the item further. In data processing, handling strings (chains of characters) is a very important task for any programming language. In Java, `String` is an object, while primitive data types are not. Java offers a so-called wrapper class for each primitive data type so that the primitives can participate in object-like activities.

So, the focus of this chapter is to understand some aspects of data processing and manipulation in an application. To help you get your arms around this issue, we explore three avenues: different ways of constructing and manipulating strings and wrappers, formatting and parsing data at data item levels, and formatting and scanning data at data stream levels.

Using the String Class

As you already know, the primitive data type char represents a character. A chain of characters is called a string, and the capability to handle strings is an important feature of any programming language. Java offers a final class java.lang.String, which handles strings by treating characters in 16-bit *Unicode* in order to accommodate characters from a wide spectrum of languages. In this section we explore how to use the String class offered by Java to handle strings.

Constructing Strings with the String Class

There are several ways to construct a string, an object of String. To start with, let's assume you want to chain together three characters, I, 4, and U. You can do it by using an array of characters, as shown here:

```
char chara[] = {'I', '4', 'U'};
```

But this is an array, and although each character in the array is related to other characters, each character is a separate data element. You can convert this array of characters into one data item of type String by passing the char array as an argument to the String constructor:

```
String str = new String(chara);
```

Equivalently, you could have passed in a literal value for the string:

```
String str = new String("I4U");
```

You can also create a string without the new operator:

```
String str = "I4U";
```

Finally, you can also create a string by adding two (or more) literals together:

```
String str = "I4U" + "U4I";
```

or equivalently:

```
String str = new String("I4U" + "U4I");
```

In both cases the string I4UU4I will be created and assigned to the variable str. You can see that the + operator is overloaded here. Java does not allow operator overloading. However, it provides special support for this string concatenation operator (+), and for conversion of other variables to strings. For example, the following is a valid code fragment:

```
double d = 12.34;
String str = "I4U"+d;
```

The value of d is transparently converted to a string and concatenated to the literal string I4U. The variable str now refers to the string I4U12.34. Note that when the compiler sees a literal string, it creates and puts it into the pool, and if it sees the same literal string again, it uses the one already in the pool (which is not a thread-safe thing to do, because more than two reference variables can refer to the same string). However, if the same literal string appears in a new statement, that string will be created again at runtime and hence a duplicate of the same string will exist.

All these different methods for constructing strings are used in Listing 9-1.

Listing 9-1. *StringGenerator.java*

```
1.  public class StringGenerator{
2.    public static void main(String[] args){
3.      char[] chara = {'I','4','U'};
```

```
4.    String s1 = new String(chara);
5.    String s2 = new String("I4U");
6.    String s3 = "I4U";
7.    String s4 = "I4U";
8.    String s23 = new String("I4U" + "U4I");
9.    String s32 = "I4U" + "U4I";
10.    double d = 12.34;
11.    String s123 = "I4U" + d;

12.    System.out.println("s1:" + s1 + " s2:" + s2 + "s3:" + s3);
13.    System.out.println("s23:" + s23 + " s32:" + s32);
14.    System.out.println("s123:" + s123);
15. }
16. }
```

The output from Listing 9-1 follows:

```
s1: I4U s2:I4U s3:I4U
s23:I4UU4I s32:I4UU4I
s123: I4U12.34
```

Note the overloaded operator + in action in lines 12, 13, and 14 as well. You should understand how the compiler treats String literals such as those used in lines 5 and 6, as explained here:

- When the compiler encounters a string literal, it adds an appropriate string to the pool.

- If the same literal string appears again in the class, the compiler does not create the duplicate. The one already in the pool would be used.

- If a string literal appears in an expression after the keyword new (such as new ("abc")), the string is created at runtime even if it already exists in the pool.

This means (from lines 5 and 6) that s2 and s3 refer to the different strings: s3 refers to the one in the pool, and s2 refers to the one created at runtime. Although both strings are identical, they are not the same, whereas s3 and s4 (lines 6 and 7) refer to the same string.

Once you have a string, you can manipulate it by using the methods offered by the String class.

Methods of the String Class

The String class offers a wide spectrum of methods to handle strings in an application. You can use these methods to perform operations on a string, including the following:

- Concatenate a string to another string

- Examine individual characters of the string

- Compare strings

- Search for a character or substrings in a string

- Extract a substring from a string

- Create a copy of a string with all characters uppercased

- Create a copy of a string with all characters lowercased

Some of these methods are shown in Table 9-1.

Table 9-1. *Methods of the Class String (All Methods Are Public)*

Method	Description
`char charAt(int index)`	Returns the character at position denoted by the integer `index`. The first character of the string is at `index=0`.
`String concat(String str)`	Returns the new string, which is the old string followed by `str`.
`int compareTo(String str)`	Makes a lexical comparison. Returns a negative integer if the current string is less than `str`, 0 if the two strings are identical, and an integer greater than zero if the current string is greater than `str`.
`Boolean endsWith(String suffix)`	Returns `true` if the current string ends with `suffix`, else returns `false`.
`Boolean equals(Object obj)`	Returns `true` if the string that `obj` refers to matches the string that the calling object refers to.
`Boolean equalsIgnoreCase(String s)`	Compares the two strings by ignoring case.
`int indexOf(int ch)`	Returns the index within the string of the first appearance of `ch`.
`int lastIndexOf(int ch)`	Returns the index within the string of the last appearance of `ch`.
`int length()`	Returns the total number of characters in the calling string.
`String replace(char oldchar, char newchar)`	Returns the new string generated by replacing every occurrence of `oldchar` in this string with `newchar`.
`boolean startsWith(String prefix)`	Returns `true` if this string starts with the specified `prefix`.
`String substring(int beginIndex)`	Returns a new string that is a substring of this string starting from the index `beginIndex`, and extending to the end of this string.
`String toLowerCase()`	Returns the string that is generated by converting all the characters of the current string to lowercase.
`String toString()`	Returns the calling object itself.
`String toUpperCase()`	Returns the string that is generated by converting all the characters of the current string to uppercase.
`String trim()`	Returns the string generated from the current string after omitting the leading and trailing white spaces.

The `equals(…)` method in the `String` class is inherited from the `Object` class and is overridden to perform the *deep* comparison—that is, it compares the characters of the two strings. It returns true if the two strings contain an identical chain of characters. The *shallow* comparison, which is done in the `Object` class version of the `equals(…)` method, simply uses the `==` operator. It returns true if the two object references are equal—that is, they refer to the same `String` object.

Listing 9-2 illustrates some of these points.

Listing 9-2. *StringEqual.java*

```
1. public class StringEqual {
2.    public static void main(String[] args) {
3.       String str1 = "Hello Dear!";
4.       String str2 = "Hello Dear!";
5.       String str3 = new String ("Hello Dear!");
```

```
6.     if (str1.equals(str2)) {
7.       System.out.println("str1 and str2 refer to identical strings.");
8.     } else {
9.       System.out.println("str1 and str2 refer to non-identical strings.");
10.    }
11.    if (str1 == str2) {
12.      System.out.println("str1 and str2 refer to the same string.");
13.    } else {
14.      System.out.println("str1 and str2 refer to different strings.");
15.    }

16.    if (str1.equals(str3)) {
17.        System.out.println("str1 and str3 refer to identical strings.");
18.    } else {
19.      System.out.println("str1 and str3 refer to non-identical strings.");
20.    }
21.    if (str1 == str3) {
22.      System.out.println("str1 and str3 refer to the same string.");
23.    } else {
24.      System.out.println("str1 and str3 refer to different strings.");
25.    }
26.  }
27. }
```

The output from Listing 9-2 follows:

```
str1 and str2 refer to identical strings.
str1 and str2 refer to the same string.
str1 and str3 refer to identical strings.
str1 and str3 refer to different strings.
```

When the compiler encounters line 3, it adds the string Hello Dear! to the pool. When it encounters line 4, it knows it already has this string, so it does not create a new string. As a result, str1 and str2 point to the same string. The string str3 (line 5) is created at runtime, so str3 refers to a different string, which is identical to what str1 and str2 refer to. Obviously, to create strings by using the new operator is a waste of memory if you are creating the same literal string several times.

■**Note** A String literal is created at compile time and the compiler never creates a duplicate String literal. However, a string with the new operator is created at runtime and it always creates a new string even if it is identical to an already existing string.

So, a String literal is created at compile time and the compiler never creates a duplicate String literal. However, a string with the new operator is created at runtime and always creates a new string even if it is identical to an already existing string. Furthermore, when the methods of the String class modify a string, a new string is generated and returned. The original string is not changed. I repeat: the original string is not changed. In other words, the strings created by the String class are immutable.

The Immutability of Strings

To understand the String behavior, you must understand that the strings created by using the String class are immutable. That means, once you create a string, you cannot change it. However, you can change the reference variable that refers to a string, which means you can make it refer to another string. When you use a method that apparently changes a string and returns the changed string, it is actually a new string that is created and returned; the old string still exists in its unchanged form. So, it appears to you that the string has been changed.

■**Caution** While the value of a string (the String object) cannot be changed, the value of a string reference can be changed; that is, you can assign another string to it.

To understand these concepts, consider the following code fragment:

```
1. String s = "I4U";
2. String s1 = s.concat( " and U4I");
3. s1.toUpperCase();
```

Figure 9-1 shows what happens when each of these code lines is executed. Note that the execution of line 2 creates a new string and a new reference, s1, that refers to it. The string reference s still refers to the old string. The execution of line 3 creates a new string but no reference variable that would refer to it.

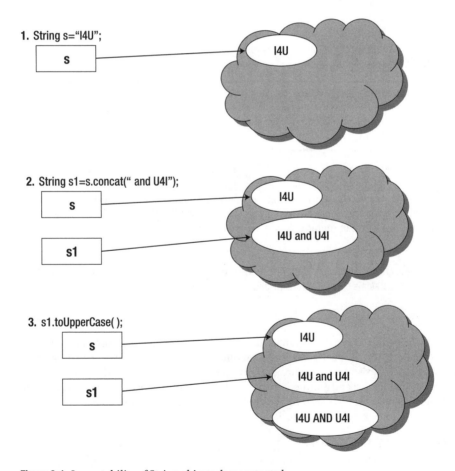

Figure 9-1. *Immutability of String objects demonstrated*

Note the following two facts:

- The compiler does not create a duplicate string literal.
- The modifying methods return a new string.

These two facts are connected to each other in the following way. The fact that the compiler does not create duplicates implies there may be more than one string reference referring to one string in the pool. Now, if you were to actually modify this original string by invoking a method on one reference, the other references to this string would suddenly be referring to the modified string without being aware of the modification. That could create a disaster in the application. So, after we have said that the compiler does not create duplicate literal strings, the immutability of strings becomes a requirement to maintain consistency.

Now, consider a programming situation in which you need to make lots of manipulations to strings. Because the String objects are immutable, lots of new strings will be created and a lot of abandoned strings will still be using the memory. A solution to this problem is the StringBuffer class.

The StringBuffer Class

The instances of the String class represent a string that cannot be modified. If you do want to create modifiable strings because you are going to do lots of string manipulation, you should use the StringBuffer class. You can create a string by passing the string value as an argument of the StringBuffer class constructor, as shown here:

```
StringBuffer sb = new StringBuffer("Hello Dear!");
```

You can also pass in a String reference as a variable:

```
String str = "Hello Dear!";
StringBuffer sb = new StringBuffer(str);
```

You can also create an empty string and assign it a value later by modifying it:

```
StringBuffer sb = new StringBuffer();
```

Some methods of the StringBuffer class are presented in Table 9-2. They return the original string after modifying it.

Table 9-2. *Some Methods of the StringBuffer Class (All Methods Are Public)*

Method	Description
StringBuffer append(String str)	Appends str to the current string buffer.
StringBuffer insert(int offset, ➡ String str)	Inserts str into the current string buffer at the position specified by offset.
StringBuffer reverse()	Reverses the characters in the current string buffer.
StringBuffer setCharAt(int ➡ offset, char ch)	Replaces the character at position offset in the current buffer string with the new character specified by ch.
StringBuffer setLength(int ➡ nlength)	Sets the new length of the current string buffer to nlength. If nlength is smaller than the length of the current string buffer, it is truncated. If nlength is greater than the current length, the null characters are added to the end of the string buffer.
String toString()	Returns the String object that contains the sequence of characters contained by the StringBuffer on which the method is invoked. A new String object is created in this case.

The effects of some of these methods are shown in the following code fragment:

```
1. StringBuffer  sb =  new  StringBuffer("Hello");
2. sb.reverse();                  // olleH
3. sb.insert(1, "My");            // oMylleH
4. sb.append("ello");             // oMylleHello
```

Listing 9-3 demonstrates that when you append a string to an original string by calling a method, a new string is created and the original string remains unchanged if it was created using the String class (lines 3, 4, 6, and 7). However, the original string is modified if it was created using the StringBuffer class (lines 5, 8). This is demonstrated by the values of the references s1, sn, and sb in the output, keeping in mind that the references still refer to the original strings because no assignments have been changed.

Listing 9-3. *StringAndBuffer.java*

```
1.  public class StringAndBuffer{
2.   public static void main(String[] args) {
3.      String sl = "String literal!";
4.      String sn = new String("String new");
5.      StringBuffer sb = new StringBuffer ("String buffer");
6.      sl.concat(" Ya!");
7.      sn.concat(" Ya!");
8.      sb.append(" Ya!");

9.      System.out.println("sl after concat(): " + sl);
10.     System.out.println("sn after concat(): " + sn);
11.     System.out.println("sb after append(): " + sb);
12.   }
13. }
```

The output from Listing 9-3 follows:

```
sl after concat(): String literal!
sn after concat(): String new
sb after append(): String buffer Ya!
```

The output demonstrates that only sb refers to the concatenated string, while s1 and sn keep referring to the old strings. That means the concat operation on s1 and sn created new concatenated strings, whereas the append operation on sb modified the old string itself.

Unlike the String class, the StringBuffer class does not override the equals(...) method of the Object class. Thus, it would return true only if the two object references are referring to the same string buffer object.

Note A string created with the String class cannot be modified, whereas a string created with the StringBuffer class can be modified. The equals(...) method in the String class returns true if both strings are identical, while the equals(...) method in the StringBuffer class returns true only if both string references refer to the same string.

Because the StringBuffer class, unlike the String class, is designed to be thread safe (i.e. multiple threads can use a StringBuffer string in a synchronized way), you pay some price in terms of performance. If you know that your application is only a single-threaded application, you can use the StringBuilder class (which has the same functionality as the StringBuffer class), which will somewhat improve the performance but will not guarantee synchronization. You will learn more about multithreaded programming in Chapter 11.

The second level of string manipulation comes into play when applications process data, especially the text data that needs to be formatted or parsed. In simple words, *formatting* means putting the data items together in a certain fashion, and *parsing* means taking those data items apart to manipulate them at individual levels.

Formatting and Parsing for the World

While writing applications in the Internet age, it is impossible to ignore the aspect of internationalization. Because formatting and parsing deal with the end user (accepting data or presenting data), you have to deal with the internationalization issue while working with formatting and parsing.

Definitions of Internationalization and Localization

If you have no experience with internationalization and localization in programming, these terms may sound a bit challenging. However, this section will help you break the ice with this very important subject. The issues of internationalization and localization arise because we live on a planet that has a wide spectrum of diversity in language, culture, and conventions for doing things. And you don't have to look to the other side of the planet to find an example; I confuse my friends across the border (in Canada) by writing a date such as 7/4, which is July 4 to me here in United States but 7 April to them in Canada. So, when you write a Java application, there may be some location-sensitive information that the application will display, such as a number, date, and currency, and you don't want to write different versions of your application for each location. Internationalization is the process of designing and writing an application so that it can be used in an environment that supports various languages and regions without engineering changes.

This is how it is accomplished:

1. You program your application using the international standards set by the International Organization for Standardization (ISO) so that your application can execute worldwide.

2. Your application delivers the data using local standards that are not hard-coded in the application but are supported by the Java language environment outside the source code.

Internationalization has an essential component called localization, which is the process of enabling an application for a specific region or language by providing support for locale-specific formats and conventions. So, internationalization and localization are two sides of the same coin. In this section, you will learn how to format information such as numbers, currencies, and dates with the following requirements:

- Keep your application code independent of any locale.

- Format data elements in a locale-sensitive fashion.

- Avoid the need to write formatting code for specific locales.

You accomplish this by creating a `Locale` object whose locality may be specified at runtime. So, you program by assuming the standard codes defined by ISO without hard-coding the locale, and then you use the locale object to present the locale-sensitive information to a user in an appropriate format. The locale object is created by using the `java.util.Locale` class.

Understanding the Locale Class

An object of the `java.util.Locale` class, which we will refer to by locale, lets you present locale-sensitive information to a user in a locale-specific way. As you will see, you do not need to hard-code the locality, because you may provide it at runtime. You create a locale object by using the `Locale` class, which offers the following constructors:

```
Locale(String language)
Locale(String language, String country)
```

The language parameter specifies the language code defined by ISO-639, and the country parameter specifies the country code defined by ISO-3166. Partial lists of these codes are presented in Tables 9-3 and 9-4, respectively. You don't need to memorize all of these codes; they are presented here just to demonstrate how it works in an application.

There is a way to create Locale objects without using the constructors in your code explicitly. The Locale class offers a number of constants that you can conveniently use to create Locale objects for commonly used locales. For example, the following line of code creates a Locale object, america, for the United States:

```
Locale america = Locale.US
```

Table 9-3. *Partial List of ISO-639 Codes for Languages*

Language Name	ISO-639 Code
Afrikaans	af
Arabic	ar
Chinese	zh
English	en
French	fr
German	de
Greek	el
Hindi	hi
Irish	ga
Italian	it
Japanese	ja
Panjabi (also spelled Punjabi)	pa
Russian	ru

Table 9-4. *Partial List of ISO-3166 Codes for Countries*

Country Name	ISO-3166 Code
Australia	AU
Bahamas	BS
Brazil	BR
Canada	CA
China	CN
Egypt	EG
France	FR
Germany	DE
Greece	GR
India	IN
United States	US

By using the language code, the country code, or both, you create an object for a specific locale (at runtime). Then, in your code, you can manipulate that object to get the locale-specific information by using the methods of the Locale class. The commonly used methods are described in Table 9-5. The Locale class also offers static methods that you can invoke on the Locale class directly to get some standard information. For example, the following line of code will return an array of ISO-639 codes for all the supported languages:

```
Locale.getISOLanguages();
```

Table 9-5. *Methods of the Locale Class*

Method	Description
boolean equals(Object obj)	Returns true if the locale on which this method is invoked is equal to obj
static Locale[] getAvailableLocale()	Returns an array of all installed locales
String getCountry()	Returns the ISO-3166 two-letter code (uppercase) for the country/region corresponding to the locale on which the method is invoked
static Locale getDefault()	Returns the default locale for this Java virtual machine
String getDisplayCountry() String getDisplayCountry(Locale in)	Returns the name for the country corresponding to the locale that is appropriate for display to the user
String getDisplayLanguage() String getDisplayLanguage(Locale in)	Returns the name for the language corresponding to the locale that is appropriate for display to the user
String getDisplayName() String getDisplayName(Locale in)	Returns the name for the locale that is appropriate for display to the user
static String[] getISOCountries()	Returns an array of two-letter codes for all countries defined by ISO-3166
static String[] getISOLanguages()	Returns a list of two-letter codes for all languages defined by ISO-639
String getLanguage()	Returns the ISO-639 lower case code for the language corresponding to this locale

You can use the getCountry() method to get the ISO country code and use the getLanguage() method to get the ISO language code for a given locale. You can invoke the getDisplayCountry() method to get the name of the country suitable for displaying to a user, while you can invoke the getDisplayLanguage() method to get the name of the language suitable for displaying to the user. Note that the getDisplay<XXX> methods are locale sensitive and have two versions: one with no arguments that uses the default locale, and the other that uses the specified locale as an argument.

To understand how to apply the Locale concepts discussed so far, consider Listing 9-4.

Listing 9-4. *LocalityTest.java*

```
1. import java.util.*;
2. class LocalityTest {
3.  public static void main(String[] args){
4.      Locale india= new Locale("pa", "IN");
5.      Locale unitedStates = new Locale("en", "US");
6.      Locale america = Locale.US;
7.      Locale english = new Locale("en");
```

```
8.    if(unitedStates.equals(america)){
9.        System.out.println("For some folks, America means United States!");
10.  }
11.    if(unitedStates.equals(india)){
12.        System.out.println("There is some bug in the code!");
13.    }else {
14.        System.out.println("The fact that Columbus stumbled into America
            when he was looking for India does not make America and India
            the same!");
15.  }
16.        System.out.println("The default Locale of this JVM is: "+
                Locale.getDefault());
17.        System.out.println("The default language for this instance of India
                is: "+ india.getLanguage());
18.        System.out.println("The display language for this instance of India
                is: "+ india.getDisplayLanguage());
19.        System.out.println("The display name for this instance of US: "+
                america.getDisplayName());
20.    }
21. }
```

The output from Listing 9-4 follows:

```
For some folks, America means United States!
The fact that Columbus stumbled into America when he was looking
for India does not make America and India the same!
The default Locale of this JVM is: en_US
The default language for this instance of India is: pa
The display language for this instance of India is: Panjabi
The display name for this instance of US: English (United States)
```

A part of this output will differ if the language setting of your OS is not en_US. Also note that in the real application, you will not hard-code locales such as IN and US, but you will work with the variables instead, and your application will pick up the values either from the command line or from a configuration file.

So, the Locale class provides a mechanism for specifying (at runtime) the kind of information object that you would like to get. For example, it enables you to say: give me the currency object that I could present to a German user. Java offers a number of classes that use the locale objects to perform locale-sensitive operations. For example, you can use the NumberFormat class to format numbers, currency, or percentages in a locale-sensitive fashion. Let's explore this topic.

Formatting Numbers and Currencies

The java.text.NumberFormat class helps you to format and parse numbers for any locale, and yet your code can be completely independent of the locale conventions. It offers a number of convenient methods for creating an object of its own type corresponding to either a default locale or a specific locale. For example, you can use any of the following three static methods to create a default NumberFormat object corresponding to the desired task:

```
NumberFormat.getInstance();
NumberFormat.getCurrencyInstance();
NumberFormat.getPercentInstance();
```

You can use these methods when you want to do the formatting for the locale that is the default for your machine. When you want to do the formatting for a specific locale, you can use the following static methods:

```
NumberFormat.getInstance(myLocale);
NumberFormat.getCurrencyInstance(myLocale);
NumberFormat.getPercentInstance(myLocale);
```

These and some other methods are described in Table 9-6.

Table 9-6. *Some Methods of the NumberFormat Class*

Method	Description
String format(double number)	Formats the number and returns it as a String
String format (long number)	Formats the number and returns it as a String
Currency getCurrency()	Returns the currency object used by this number format to format the currency values
static NumberFormat getCurrencyInstance()	Returns a currency format object for the current default locale
static NumberFormat getCurrencyInstance(Locale in)	Returns the currency format object for the locale passed in as an argument
static NumberFormat getNumberInstance()	Returns a general-purpose number format object for the default local
static NumberFormat getNumberInstance(Locale in)	Returns a general-purpose number format object for the locale specified in the argument
static NumberFormat getPercentInstance()	Returns a percentage format object for the default locale
static NumberFormat getPercentInstance(Locale in)	Returns a percentage format object for the locale specified in the argument
Number parse(String str)	Parses the passed-in string to produce a number and returns it as a Number object
void setMaximumFractionDigits(int n) void setMinimumFraction Digits(int n)	Sets maximum/minimum number of digits allowed in the fraction part of a number
void setMaximumIntegerDigits(int n) void setMinimumInteger Digits(int n)	Sets maximum/minimum number of digits allowed in the integer part of a number

Here are the steps you follow to specify formatting in your code:

1. Create a locale.

2. Create an appropriate NumberFormat object by using the locale from step 1 as an argument.

3. Use the NumberFormat object to format a number by invoking the format(...) method on the NumberFormat object and by passing the number (to be formatted) as an argument.

The code example in Listing 9-5 demonstrates this process.

Listing 9-5. *NumberFormatter.java*

```
1. import java.util.*;
2. import java.text.*;
3. class NumberFormatter{
4. public static void main(String[] args){
```

```
5.    double amount = 1276789.34;
6.    double percent = 0.95;
7.    Locale india= new Locale("en", "IN");
8.    Locale america = new Locale("en", "US");
9.      Locale germany = new Locale("de", "DE");

10.   NumberFormat nfIndia = NumberFormat.getNumberInstance(india);
11.   NumberFormat nfAmerica = NumberFormat.getNumberInstance(america);
12.   NumberFormat nfGermany = NumberFormat.getNumberInstance(germany);
13.   System.out.println(nfIndia.format(amount));
14.   System.out.println(nfAmerica.format(amount));
15.   System.out.println(nfGermany.format(amount));

16.   nfIndia = NumberFormat.getCurrencyInstance(india);
17.   nfAmerica = NumberFormat.getCurrencyInstance(america);
18.   nfGermany = NumberFormat.getCurrencyInstance(germany);
19.   System.out.println(nfIndia.format(amount));
20.   System.out.println(nfAmerica.format(amount));
21.   System.out.println(nfGermany.format(amount));

22.   nfIndia = NumberFormat.getPercentInstance(india);
23.   nfAmerica = NumberFormat.getPercentInstance(america);
24.   nfGermany = NumberFormat.getPercentInstance(germany);
25.   System.out.println(nfIndia.format(percent));
26.   System.out.println(nfAmerica.format(percent));
27.   System.out.println(nfGermany.format(percent));
28.   }
29. }
```

The output from Listing 9-5 follows:

```
1,276,789.34
1,276,789.34
1.276.789,34
Rs.1,276,789.34
$1,276,789.34
1.276.789,34 Ç
95%
95%
95%
```

You can also chain the method calls as shown here:

```
String formattedNumber = NumberFormat.getInstance(myLocale).format(myNumber);
```

You may see this kind of chaining methods in the exam. Read it like this: the leftmost method is executed first, the second-to-leftmost method is invoked on the return of the first method execution, and so on. Also remember that the NumberFormat class itself is an abstract class, so you cannot instantiate it directly. For example, the following code is invalid:

```
NumberFormat nf = new NumberFormat();
```

So, you can format the numbers and the currencies using the NumberFormat class for a specific locale. Similarly, you can use the DateFormat class to format the date for a specific locale.

Formatting Dates

Different localities use different formats to represent dates. The `java.text.DateFormat` class provides several methods for formatting the date/time for a default or a specific location, and yet you can keep your code completely independent of the locale conventions for months, days of the week, days of the months, and so on. Some of the methods offered by the `DateFormat` class are presented in Table 9-7.

Table 9-7. *Methods of the DateFormat Class*

Method	Description
`String format(Date date)`	Formats the date passed in as an argument, and returns it in the form of a `String`.
`static DateFormat getDateInstance()` `static DateFormat getDateInstance ➡` `(int style)` `static DateFormat getDateInstance ➡` `(int style, Locale in)`	Return the `DateFormat` object for formatting the date. You can specify a style for a default locale or a specific locale, or specify nothing. Unspecified style or locale will assume the default value.
`static DateFormat getDateTimeInstance()` `static DateFormat getDateTimeInstance ➡` `(int dateStyle, int timeStyle)` `static DateFormat getDateTimeInstance ➡` `(int dateStyle, int timeStyle, Locale in)`	Return the `DateFormat` object for formatting the date/time. You can specify a date style and time style for a default or a specified locale, or specify nothing. Unspecified style or locale will assume the default value.
`Date parse(String date)`	Parses the passed-in string to produce a date and returns the date as a `Date` object.

As Listing 9-6 shows, the process is very similar to using the `NumberFormat` class.

Listing 9-6. *DateFormatter.java*

```
1. import java.util.*;
2. import java.text.*;
3. class DateFormatter{
4.   public static void main(String[] args){
5.     Date today = new Date();
6.     Locale india= new Locale("en", "IN");
7.     Locale america = new Locale("en", "US");
8.     Locale germany = new Locale("de", "DE");
9.     DateFormat nfIndia = DateFormat.getDateInstance(DateFormat.DEFAULT, india);
10.    DateFormat nfAmerica = DateFormat.getDateInstance(DateFormat.DEFAULT, america);
11.    DateFormat nfGermany = DateFormat.getDateInstance(DateFormat.DEFAULT, germany);
12.    System.out.println(nfIndia.format(today));
13.     System.out.println(nfAmerica.format(today));
14.     System.out.println(nfGermany.format(today));
15.   }
16. }
```

The output from Listing 9-6 follows:

```
17 May, 2005
May 17, 2005
17.05.2005
```

Note the difference in formats for different locales. Again, a reminder: although in this example we have hard-coded the locale information, in the real application it will come from the command line (to run the application) or from a configuration file; so it can be determined at runtime.

The concept of data formatting is very close to data processing, for example text processing. You may need text processing to check if the data is in the correct format, for example. Applications often require text processing to perform certain tasks such as validating the format of an email address or credit card, searching for specific words in files, and so on.

Text Processing with Regular Expressions

A string can be formatted or parsed based on a specified pattern that will be searched in the string. In order to format or parse data (text or data types), you want to be able to say: pick up that thing (data item) from there and do this to it. How do you say which thing to pick up and from where? You do it through a search based on pattern matching. The search pattern is described by what is called a regular expression (*regex* for short). In other words, regular expressions can be used to process text. A piece of text (sequence of characters) that is found to correspond to the search pattern is called a *match*. For example, you may want to say: find a dot (.) in a string and split the string around each dot you find. That means if there are two dots in a string, the string will be split into three pieces.

Java provides support for regular expressions (to define search patterns) and for matching the patterns (to the text in the string) by providing the following elements:

- The java.util.regex.Pattern class
- The java.util.regex.Matcher class
- The regular expression constructs

The simplest form of a regular expression is a literal string such as Kant, for example, if you want to find out if there is a word Kant in the input text. However, you can build very sophisticated expressions using what are called regular expression constructs. Consider the following expression:

```
[A-Za-z0-9]
```

Any character in the range of A through Z, a through z, or 0 through 9 (any letter or digit) will match this pattern. Any other character will match the pattern described by the following expression:

```
[^A-Za-z0-9]
```

Yes, you are right, the character ^ negates.

The important points about the constructs are summarized here:

- Use backslash (\) as an escape character. For example, \. matches a period, whereas \\ matches a backslash.

- Use | for logical OR, ^ to match the beginning of a line, and $ to match the end of a line. Remember that ^ inside [ ] means negation.

- A character class is a set of character alternatives enclosed in brackets; for example, [abc] means a, b, or c. The character – denotes a range, and the character ^ inside [ ] denotes a negation (that is, all the characters except those specified here). For example, the character class [^a-zA-Z] means all the characters that are not included in the range a through z and A through Z. The character classes are listed in Table 9-8. There are several character classes that are already defined for you, such as \d means all digits. The predefined character classes are presented in Table 9-9.

- If you are looking for a regular expression, say X, to repeat itself a number of times, you can say it in the pattern by using a quantifier immediately following X. For example, X+ means one or more X. The quantifiers are listed in Table 9-10, and some other useful constructs are listed in Table 9-11.

Table 9-8. *Character Classes (Brackets Used as Grouping Mechanism)*

Construct	Description
[ABC…]	Any of the characters represented by A, B, C, etc.
[^ABC…]	Any character except A, B, C, etc. (negation)
[a-zA-Z]	a through z or A through Z (range)
[...&&...]	Intersection of two sets (AND)

Table 9-9. *Predefined Character Classes*

Construct	Description
. (dot)	Any character if the DOTALL flag is set, else any character except the line terminators
\d	A digit: [0-9]
\D	A non-digit: [^0-9]
\s	A whitespace character: [\f\n\r\t\x0B]
\S	A non whitespace character: [^\s]
\w	A word character: [a-zA-Z0-9]
\W	A non-word character: [^\w]

Table 9-10. *Greedy Quantifiers (X Represents Regular Expression)*

Construct	Description
X?	X, zero or one time
X*	X, zero or more times
X+	X, one or more times
X{n}	X, exactly n times

Table 9-11. *Some Other Constructs*

Construct	Description
^	The beginning of a line
XY	Y following X
X|Y	Either X or Y
(?:X)	X, as a noncapturing group
(?idmsux-idmsux)	Turns match flag on or off
(?idmsux-idmsux:X)	X, as a noncapturing group with a given flag on or off

The following is the typical process for pattern matching:

1. Compile the regular expression specified as a string into an instance of the Pattern class, for example, with a statement like the following:

```
Pattern p = Pattern.compile("[^a-zA-Z0-9]");
```

2. Create a `Matcher` object that will contain the specified pattern and the input text to which the pattern will be matched:

```
Matcher m = p.matches("thinker@thinkingman.com")
```

3. Invoke the `matches(…)` method or the `find()` method on the `Matcher` object to find if a match is found:

```
boolean b = m.find();
```

This process is demonstrated in Listing 9-7, which checks the format of an email address.

Listing 9-7. *EmailValidator.java*

```
1. import java.util.regex.*;
2. public class EmailValidator {
3. public static void main(String[] args)  {
4. String email="";
5. if(args.length < 1){
6.   System.out.println("Command syntax: java EmailValidator <emailAddress>");
7.   System.exit(0);
8.   }else {
9.     email = args[0];
10. }

//Look for for email addresses starting with
//invalid symbols: dots or @ signs.
11.     Pattern p = Pattern.compile("^\\.+|^\\@+");
12.     Matcher m = p.matcher(email);
13.     if (m.find()) {
14.       System.err.println("Invalid email address: starts with a dot or an @ sign.");
15.       System.exit(0);
16.     }
//Look for email addresses that start with www.
17. p = Pattern.compile("^www\\.");
18. m = p.matcher(email);
19.     if (m.find()) {
20.       System.out.println("Invalid email address: starts with www.");
21.       System.exit(0);
22.     }
23.     p = Pattern.compile("[^A-Za-z0-9\\@\\.\\_]");
24.     m = p.matcher(email);

25.   if(m.find()) {
26.       System.out.println("Invalid email address: contains invalid characters");

27.     } else{
28.       System.out.println(args[0] + " is a valid email address.");
29.     }

30.   }
31. }
```

To execute the code in Listing 9-7, you need to give a string as a command-line argument, for example:

```
java EmailValidator  www.paulsanghera.com@aol.com
```

This will produce the following output:

```
Invalid email address: starts with www.
```

■**Note** A single backslash (\) means escape sequence. The first backslash in a double backslash, such as \\., tells the compiler that what follows should be taken literally and not as an escape sequence.

Some useful methods in pattern matching are listed in Table 9-12. A CharSequence is passed in as an argument in the same way as a String.

Table 9-12. *Some Useful Methods for Pattern Matching*

Method	Class	Description
static Pattern compile (String regex)	Pattern	Compiles the input regular expression passed in as a string into a pattern
boolean find()	Matcher	Scans the input sequence only to find the next sub-sequence that matches the pattern
Matcher matcher (CharSequence input)	Pattern	Creates a Matcher object with the input that will be used to match against a pattern
static boolean matches ➥ (String regex, CharSequence input)	Pattern	Attempts to match the entire input sequence against the pattern
boolean matches()	Matcher	Attempts to match the entire input sequence against the pattern
String[ ] split (CharSequence input)	Pattern	Splits the given input sequence around matches of this pattern and returns the pieces as an array of strings
String toString()	Pattern	Returns the pattern as a string

An important method listed in Table 9-12 but not covered in Listing 9-7 is the split(…) method. Its use is demonstrated in Listing 9-8.

Listing 9-8. *SplitTest.java*

```
1. import java.util.regex.*;
2. public class SplitTest {
3.   public static void main(String[] args)  {
4.       String input= "www.cs.cornell.edu";
5.        Pattern p = Pattern.compile("\\.");
6.      String pieces[] = p.split(input);
7.      for (int i=0; i<pieces.length; i++){
8.         System.out.println(pieces[i]);
9.            }
10.   }
11. }
```

The output of Listing 9-8 follows:

```
www
cs
cornell
edu
```

This output is produced by splitting (line 6) the string www.cs.cornell.edu (line 4), around the pattern "." (line 5).

In applications, rarely, there will be one string to format or parse. Usually there is a stream of data that you deal with. The streams may be connected to sockets, files, or any other I/O devices. You learned about streams in Chapter 8, and now it's time to explore how to format and parse them.

Formatting and Parsing Streams

Formatting and parsing are two sides of the same coin. For example, on the sending end, an application formats the data into a certain format, and on the receiving end, it breaks (parses) the data into useful pieces.

Formatting Streams

You can format the numerics and strings by using the format(…) method in the Formatter, PrintWriter, and String classes. As you'll see, the method works pretty much the same way in all three classes. After you have formatted the input by using the format(…) method, you can stream the formatted output into an I/O device such as a file by using the Formatter class or the PrintWriter class.

Chapter 8 already discussed the java.io.PrintWriter class, which represents objects to a text output stream in the print format. The java.util.Formatter class, more detailed and intensive in formatting, provides support for numeric, string, common data types, date/time data, and, above all, locale-specific output. Some commonly used constructors and the methods for the Formatter class are described in Table 9-13.

Table 9-13. *Some Constructors and Methods of the Formatter Class*

Method/Constructor	Description
Formatter(), Formatter(File file), Formatter(OutputStream os) Formatter(PrintStream ps)	Some constructors of the Format class
void close()	Closes this formatter
void flush()	Flushes this formatter
Formatter format(String format, Object… args)	The format method with a format string and one or more arguments that will be formatted following the instructions in the format string
String toString()	Returns the content of the Formatter in the String format

The format(…) method has the following form:

```
format(<format specifier>, <argument>);
```

The <argument> specifies the data to be formatted, and the <format specifier> provides instructions for formatting. The <format specifiers> has the following syntax:

```
%[<argumentIndex>$][<flags>][<width>][.<precision>] <type>
```

Different elements of this syntax are described here:

- <argumentIndex>: Specifies the position of the argument in the argument list in case there is more than one argument. If there is only one argument, you don't need to specify this element.

- <flags>: Its value is a set of characters that further specify the output format. For example, a comma (,) means format an integer number by using commas. The flags can be omitted if no further specification is required.

- <width>: Specifies the minimum number of characters to be written to the output. Remember that it is the minimum number. For example, if a number is seven characters wide and <width> has the value 5, the whole number still will be written.

- <precision>: Specifies the precision in number of decimal places. For example, a float value 23.4321 will be converted to 23.43 by the <precision> value of 2.

- <type>: Specifies the format type related to the data type, such as int, double, and float. These types are listed in Table 9-14. Note that a format type is related to the argument type.

The format specifier is illustrated in Figure 9-2 with an example.

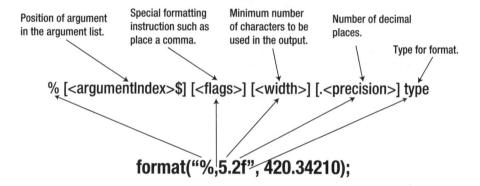

Figure 9-2. *The format specifier used in the format(...) method*

Table 9-14. *Partial List of Format Types*

Parameter	Type	Description
%b	Boolean	If the argument is null, the result is false. If the argument is boolean or Boolean, the result is String.valueOf(), else the result is true.
%c	Character	The result is a Unicode character. The argument must be a byte, short, char, or int (either primitives or wrappers). Wrappers are discussed later in this chapter.
%d	Decimal	The result is formatted as a decimal integer. The argument must be compatible with an int; that is, it must be byte, short, char, or int (either primitives or wrappers).
%f	Floating point	The result is formatted as a decimal number. The argument must be a float or a double (primitive or wrapper).
%s	String	If the argument is null, the result is null. The result is obtained by invoking arg.toString().

■**Caution** The format types and the argument types are related to each other. For example, if the format type is float (%f), the argument can only be float or double (primitive or wrapper).

A simple code example for the use of Formatter is presented in Listing 9-9.

Listing 9-9. *FormatterTest.java*

```
1.   import java.util.*;
2.   public class FormatterTest {
3.   public static void main(String[] args)  {
4.     Formatter formatter = new Formatter();
5.     System.out.println(formatter.format("%c", 33).toString());
6.     System.out.println(formatter.format("%8.2f", 420.23).toString());
7.     System.out.println(formatter.format("%8.2f", new
Double(4234.23)).toString());
8.     System.out.println(formatter.format("%5b", " ").toString());
9.     System.out.println(formatter.format("%20d", 42042042).toString());
10.     System.out.println(formatter.format("%,20d", 42042042).toString());
11.     System.out.println(formatter.toString());
12.   }
13. }
```

The output from Listing 9-9 follows:

```
!
!  420.23
!  420.23 4234.23
!  420.23 4234.23 true
!  420.23 4234.23 true            42042042
!  420.23 4234.23 true            42042042            42,042,042
!  420.23 4234.23 true            42042042            42,042,042
```

Note how the Formatter object is accumulating the input. Also note that this example demonstrates how the primitive data types are being formatted using Formatter. The strings may also be formatted using the static method String.format(). The String version of Listing 9-9 is presented in Listing 9-10.

Listing 9-10. *StringFormatTest.java*

```
1. public class StringFormatTest {
2.   public static void main(String[] args)  {
3.       System.out.println(String.format("%c", 33));
4.       System.out.println(String.format("%8.2f", 420.23));
5.       System.out.println(String.format("%8.2f", new Double(4234.23)));
6.       System.out.println(String.format("%5b", " "));
7.       System.out.println(String.format("%20d", 42042042));
8.       System.out.println(String.format("%,20d", 42042042));
9.   }
10. }
```

The output from Listing 9-10 follows:

```
 !
   420.23
 4234.23
 true
   42042042
 42,042,042
```

Note that unlike `Formatter`, there is no accumulation of the input. The `format(…)` method is also available in the `PrintWriter` class. You can format the input using the `format(…)` method in the `Formatter` class or in the `PrintWriter` class and then stream the formatted output into an appropriate I/O device such as a file. Both versions, using `Formatter` and `PrintWriter` classes, are demonstrated in Listings 9-11 and 9-12, respectively.

Listing 9-11. *FormatterStreamTest.java*

```
1.  import java.util.*;
2.  import java.io.*;
3.  public class FormatterStreamTest {
4.    public static void main(String[] args) throws IOException {
5.        Formatter formatter = new Formatter("c:\\tmp\\formatterTest.txt");
              //The path to the file must exist before the code is executed.
6.        formatter.format("%c", 33);
7.        formatter.format("%8.2f", 420.23);
8.        formatter.format("%8.2f", new Double(4234.23));
9.        formatter.format("%5b", " ");
10.       formatter.format("%20d", 42042042);
11.       formatter.format("%,20d", 42042042);
12.       formatter.flush();
13.   }
14. }
```

Listing 9-12. *PrintFormatTest.java*

```
1.  import java.io.*;
2.  public class PrintFormatTest {
3.    public static void main(String[] args) throws IOException {
4.      PrintWriter pw = new PrintWriter("C:\\tmp\\writerTest.txt");
            //The path to the file must exist before executing this code.
5.      pw.format("%c", 33);
6.      pw.format("%8.2f", 420.23);
7.      pw.format("%8.2f", new Double(4234.23));
8.      pw.format("%5b", " ");
9.      pw.format("%20d", 42042042);
10.     pw.format("%,20d", 42042042);
11.     pw.flush();
12.   }
13. }
```

The formatted output from both Listings 9-11 and 9-12 will go to the files specified in lines 5 (Listing 9-11) and 4 (Listing 9-12). Open the files to see the output.

If you are a veteran C programmer, you may prefer to use the `printf(…)` method (*déjà vu*) instead of the `format(…)` method. These two methods exhibit the exact same behavior. We will us the `printf(…)` method in the "Codewalk Quicklet" section of this chapter.

Now that you know how to format streams, let's take a look at the flip side: how to parse them.

Parsing Streams

In a previous section, "Text Processing with Regular Expressions," you learned how to use the regular expressions for text processing, such as validating the format of an email address. You can also use regular expressions to process (parse) streams. A regular expression defines a pattern that acts as a delimiter to break the input into pieces, and each piece is called a *token*. By default, the white space acts as a delimiter pattern. You can use the Scanner class as a simple text scanner to parse primitive types and strings using regular expressions.

The input text that needs to be parsed can be passed to the Scanner constructor as a String, File, or an InputStream. The individual tokens can be converted into values of different types by using a suitable next method. Some constructors and methods of the Scanner class are described in Table 9-15.

Table 9-15. *Some Constructors and Methods of the Scanner Class*

Methods/Constructors	Description
Scanner(File source) Scanner(InputStream source) Scanner(String source)	Constructors
void close()	Closes the scanner
boolean hasNext()	Returns true if this scanner has another token in its input
boolean hasNext(String pattern)	Returns true if the next token matches the pattern passed in as a string argument
boolean hasNextBoolean() boolean hasNextByte() boolean hasNextDouble() boolean hasNextFloat() boolean hasNextInt() boolean hasNextLong() boolean hasNextShort()	Returns true if the next token in the input of this scanner can be interpreted as the type spelled by the last word of the method name; for example, byte for hasNextByte()
boolean hasNextLine()	Returns true if there is another line in the input of this scanner
boolean nextBoolean() byte nextByte() double nextDouble() float nextFloat() int nextInt() long nextLong() short nextShort()	Returns the next token as a data type specified by the last word of the name (and the return type) of the method
String next()	Returns the next complete token from the scanner's input, in String format
String nextLine()	Returns the current line from the scanner's input and advances the scanner to the next line in String format
String toString()	Returns the scanner content in String format
Scanner useDelimiter(String regex)	Sets the passed-in regular expression as a pattern delimiter to parse (break) the scanner's input

Listing 9-13 demonstrates the use of some of these methods. In this example, a string is passed to the scanner (lines 5 and 19). If you could pass in a File or an InputStream, the rest of the code would work just fine as it is.

Listing 9-13. *ScannerTest.java*

```
1. import java.util.*;
2.    public class ScannerTest {
3.    public static void main(String[] args)  {
4.        String input = "cheque from publisher um 2000 dollars um buy
                diet pepsi um and peanuts";
5.        Scanner sc = new Scanner(input);
6.        System.out.println("Parsing round 1:");
7.        System.out.println(sc.next());
8.        System.out.println(sc.next());
9.         System.out.println(sc.next());
10.        System.out.println(sc.next());
11.        int salary = sc.nextInt();
12.        System.out.println("Advance:" + salary);
13.        sc.useDelimiter("um");
14.        System.out.println(sc.next());
15.        System.out.println(sc.next());
16.        System.out.println(sc.next());
17.        sc.close();
18.        System.out.println("Parsing round 2:");
19.        sc = new Scanner(input).useDelimiter("um");
20.         while(sc.hasNext()){
21.            System.out.println(sc.next());
22.         }
23.     }
24. }
```

The output from Listing 9-13 follows:

```
Parsing round 1:
cheque
from
publisher
um
Advance:2000
dollars
buy diet pepsi
and peanuts
Parsing round 2:
cheque from publisher
2000 dollars
buy diet pepsi
and peanuts
```

In parsing round 1 (lines 6 to 17), we first parse without specifying a delimiter, so the white space is assumed to be the delimiter. After parsing a few fields, we specify the delimiter um (line 13), and keep parsing. Note that at this time, the input has already been processed up to the int 2000; therefore, the string starting with the word dollars remains unprocessed and becomes the first parsed field with the um delimiter. In parsing round 2 (lines 18 to 21), the parsing is performed with um as delimiter (line 19).

Java is an object-oriented language, and yet we have been talking about formatting primitive data types, which cannot participate in the object-like activities. To create a connection between the primitive world and the object world, Java offers the so-called wrapper classes.

Wrapping the Primitives

Java is an object-oriented language, and as they say, everything in Java is an object. But, how about primitives? Primitives are sort of left out in the world of objects; that is, they cannot participate in the object activities, such as being returned from a method as an object, and being added to a Collection of objects (a Collection is a group of data items, discussed further in Chapter 10). As a solution to this problem, Java allows you to include the primitives in the family of objects by using what are called wrapper classes.

Creating Objects of Wrapper Classes

Corresponding to each primitive data type in Java is a class called a *wrapper class*. This class encapsulates a single value for the primitive data type. For example, the Integer class would hold an integer value. The wrapper object of a wrapper class can be created in one of two ways: by instantiating the wrapper class with the new operator or by invoking a static method on the wrapper class. We explore this next.

Creating Wrapper Objects with the new Operator

Before you can instantiate a wrapper class, you need to know its name and the arguments its constructor accepts. The name of the wrapper class corresponding to each primitive data type, along with the arguments its constructor accepts, is listed in Table 9-16. Note that unlike the primitive names, the data types in the wrapper class names are fully spelled out.

Table 9-16. *Primitive Data Types and Corresponding Wrapper Classes*

Primitive Data Type	Wrapper Class	Constructor Arguments
boolean	Boolean	boolean or String
byte	Byte	byte or String
char	Character	char
short	Short	short or String
int	Integer	int or String
long	Long	long or String
float	Float	double, float, or String
double	Double	double or String

Take notice of three important points in Table 9-16:

- Obviously, you can always pass the corresponding primitive data type as an argument to a wrapper class constructor: a no-brainer choice.

- You can also pass a String as an argument to any wrapper class constructor except Character.

- The Character constructor only takes the obvious argument: char.

- You can pass double as an argument to the Float constructor but not vice versa.

All the wrapper classes except Boolean and Character are subclasses of an abstract class called Number, whereas Boolean and Character are derived directly from the Object class.

■**Caution** All the wrapper classes are declared `final`. That means you cannot derive a subclass from any of them.

An instance of a wrapper class may be created by calling the corresponding constructor and by passing an appropriate argument. Here are some examples:

```
Boolean wboo = new Boolean("false");
Byte wbyte = new Byte("2");
Short wshort = new Short("4");
Integer wint = new Integer("16");
Long wlong = new Long("123");
Float wfloat = new Float("12.34f");
Double wdouble = new Double("12.56d");
```

The value may also be passed as a variable, as shown in the following example:

```
boolean boo = false;
Boolean wboo = new Boolean(boo);

byte b = 2;
Byte wbyte = new Byte(b);

short s = 4;
Short wshort = new Short(s);

int i = 16;
Integer wint = new Integer(i);

long l = 123;
Long wlong = new Long(l);

float f = 12.34f;
Float wfloat = new Float(f);

double d = 12.56d;
Double wdouble = new Double(d)
```

Note that there is no way to modify a wrapped value—that is, the wrapped values are immutable.

■**Caution** The wrapped value in a wrapper class cannot be modified. To wrap another value, you need to create another object.

So, if you want to wrap a value of a primitive data type in an object, pass it as an argument to the constructor of the corresponding wrapper class while instantiating it with the new operator. There will be situations in your program when you really don't need a new instance of the wrapper class, but you still want to wrap a primitive. In this case, pass the primitive type as an argument to the static method `valueOf()` of the corresponding wrapper class.

Wrapping Primitives Using a static Method

You can create a wrapper object by using the static `valueOf()` method that all the wrapper classes offer. Because it's a static method, it can be invoked directly on the class (without instantiating it), and will return the corresponding object that is wrapping what you passed in as an argument. The valid method arguments are shown in Table 9-17.

Table 9-17. *Methods to Create Wrapper Objects*

Wrapper class	Method Signature	Method Arguments
Boolean	static Boolean valueOf(…)	boolean or String
Character	static Character valueOf(…)	char
Byte	static Byte valueOf(…)	byte, String, or String and radix
Short	static Short valueOf(…)	short, String, or String and radix
Integer	static Integer valueOf(…)	int, String, or String and radix
Long	static Long valueOf(…)	long, String, or String and radix
Float	static Float valueOf(…)	float or String
Double	static Double valueOf(…)	double or String

Note the following about the arguments allowed in the valueOf(…) method calls:

- The valueOf(…) method in the Character class accepts only char as an argument, while any other wrapper class will accept either the corresponding primitive type or String as an argument.

- The valueOf(…) method in the integer number wrapper classes (Byte, Short, Integer, and Long) also accepts two arguments together: a String and a radix, where radix is the base; for example, a decimal is radix 10 and a binary is radix 2.

For example, consider the following statement:

```
Integer wint1 = Integer.valueOf("10111", 2);
Integer  wint2 = Intger.valueOf("10111", 10);
```

Now wint1 is a wrapper object that contains the value 23, and wint2 is a wrapper object that contains the value 10111.

Now that you know how to wrap a primitive in a wrapper class, a natural question to ask is: How can I get my primitive back? Yes, you are right; there are some methods you can use to retrieve the primitive values from the wrapper objects.

Methods to Extract the Wrapped Values

A storage capability without the corresponding retrieval capability is not of much use. Once you store a primitive in a wrapper object, often you will want to retrieve the stored primitive at a later time. The methods to extract the values from the wrapper classes are listed in Table 9-18.

Table 9-18. *Methods to Retrieve Primitives from Wrapper Classes (All Methods Are No-Argument Methods)*

Method	Class
public boolean booleanValue()	Boolean
public char charValue()	Character
public byte byteValue()	Byte, Short, Integer, Long, Float, Double
public short shortValue()	Byte, Short, Integer, Long, Float, Double
public int intValue()	Byte, Short, Integer, Long, Float, Double
public long longValue()	Byte, Short, Integer, Long, Float, Double
public float floatValue()	Byte, Short, Integer, Long, Float, Double
public double doubleValue()	Byte, Short, Integer, Long, Float, Double

Look carefully at Table 9-18: Did you notice something powerful? All the number wrapper classes (Byte, Short, Integer, Long, Float, and Double) have the <xxx>Value methods, where <xxx> can specify byte, short, int, long, float, or double. This is because all of these classes are subclasses of the Number class, which originally has these methods. It means you can store one primitive type in a wrapper and retrieve another one. For example, you can store a double value in a Double wrapper and retrieve an integer value by invoking the intValue() method on it. In other words, there is a type conversion going on, so you can use the wrappers as a conversion machine. Consider Listing 9-14.

Listing 9-14. *ConversionMachine.java*

```
1.  public class ConversionMachine{
2.    public static void main(String[] args){
3.      Byte b = 4;
4.      Byte wbyte = new Byte(b);
5.      double d = 354.56d;
6.      Double wdouble = new Double(d);
7.      System.out.println("wrapped Inside Byte: " + b);
8.      System.out.println("double value extracted from Byte: " +
            wbyte.doubleValue());
9.      System.out.println("Wrapped Inside Double: " + d);
10.   System.out.println("byte value extracted from Double: " +
            wdouble.byteValue());
11. }
12.}
```

The output from Listing 9-14 follows:

```
wrapped Inside Byte: 4
double value extracted from Byte: 4.0
Wrapped Inside Double: 354.56
byte value extracted from Double: 98
```

Note that the double value 354.56 has been converted to a byte value, 98. You learned this lesson in Chapter 5: if you convert a value into a narrower type, you run the risk of losing accuracy. So use these conversions with caution.

So, the extraction methods point to the fact that you can use the wrapper classes not only for storing the primitive values, but also for other instant usages such as type conversion.

The Instant Use of Wrapper Classes

If you do not need to store a value in a wrapper but just want to perform a quick operation on it, such as converting the type, you can do it by using an appropriate static method of the appropriate wrapper class. For example, all the wrapper classes except Character offer a static method that has the following signature:

```
static <type> parse<Type>(String s)
```

The <type> may be any of the primitive types except char (byte, short, int, long, float, double, or boolean), and the <Type> is the same as <type> with the first letter uppercased; for example:

```
static int parseInt (String s)
```

Each of these methods parses the string passed in as a parameter and returns the corresponding primitive type. For example, consider the following code:

```
String s = "123";
int i = Integer.parseInt(s);
```

The second line will assign an int value of 123 to the int variable i. A complete list of these methods is provided in Table 9-19.

Table 9-19. *Methods to Convert Strings to Primitive Types*

Wrapper Class	Method Signature	Method Arguments
Boolean	static boolean parseBoolean(…)	String
Character	Not available	
Byte	static byte parseByte(…)	String, or String and radix
Short	static short parseShort(…)	String, or String and radix
Integer	static int parseInt(…)	String, or String and radix
Long	static long parseLong(…)	String, or String and radix
Float	static float parseFloat(…)	String
Double	static double parseDouble(…)	double or String

You have learned that the wrapper classes are used for two main purposes: to store a primitive type in an object so that it can participate in object-like operations, and to convert one primitive type into another. However, as you have seen, you do this conversion between primitives and objects manually in the code. You can be more ambitious and ask the question: If Java is a truly object-oriented language, why do I have to manually wrap the primitives into objects, why is the process not made transparent by automating wrapping? Well, that is exactly what *autoboxing* offers, which is introduced in J2SE 5.0 and discussed in Chapter 10.

For the exam, you should remember which package contains a specific class discussed in this chapter. Table 9-20 shows which package to import to include a specific class in your program.

Table 9-20. *Java Packages that Contain Classes Discussed in This Chapter*

Java Package	Classes
java.io.*	I/O classes such as FileInputStream and FileOutputStream
java.lang.*	Wrapper classes, and string-related classes such as String, StringBuffer, and StringBuilder
java.text.*	Classes related to formatting such as NumberFormat and DateFomat
java.util.*	Currency, Date, Locale, and Scanner

Codewalk Quicklet

The code for the codewalk quicklet exercise in this chapter is presented in Listing 9-15.

Listing 9-15. *CodeWalkEight.java*

```
1. import java.io.PrintWriter;
2. class CodeWalkEight{
3.    public static void main(String [] args) {
4.      TheBooleanGame bg = new TheBooleanGame();
5.    bg.printBoolean();
6.  }
7. }
8. class TheBooleanGame {
9.    public void printBoolean(){
10.      String s1 = "1";
11.      String s2 = "0";
12.      String s3 = "null";
13.      String s4 = "True";
14.      String s5 = null;
15.      Boolean b = new Boolean("True");
16.      boolean b2 = false;
17.      System.out.printf("%b %b %b %b %b %b %b", s1, s2, s3,s4, s5, b, b2);
18.    }
19. }
```

To get you started on this exercise, following are some hints:

- *Input*: Lines 10 through 16

- *Operations*: Line 15

- *Output*: Line 17

- *Rule*: Formatting, wrappers, and autoboxing

Looking at the code from this angle, see if you can handle the last question in the "Review Questions" section based on this code.

The three most important takeaways from this chapter are the following:

- A string created with the String class cannot be modified, while a string created with the StringBuffer class can be modified. When a method apparently modifies a String object, it actually creates a new object, and the original object stays unchanged. A string in Java is an object, whereas primitive data types are not objects. Java offers a wrapper class corresponding to each primitive type to enable them to participate in object-like activities.

- You can use the Locale, NumberFormat, and DateFormat classes to format the numbers, currencies, and dates for the end user in a locale-sensitive fashion and without changing the code in the application. You can also use regular expressions, the Pattern class, and the Matcher class to do some parsing for examining some data items such as validating the format of an email address.

- Data flows between an I/O device (such as a file or a socket) and a program in a stream. You can use the Formatter class to format an outgoing stream, and the Scanner class to parse an incoming stream.

Summary

Constructing and handling strings (chain of characters) is an important feature of any programming language. For this purpose, Java offers several string classes such as String, StringBuilder, and StringBuffer to meet varying requirements of applications. You can save memory by creating String literals with the String class, because when a compiler creates a string literal, it puts it into the pool, and when it sees any other reference to an identical string literal, it does not create the duplicate string. Instead it points the new reference to the existing string. Therefore, more than one reference can point to the same string literal. Because more than one reference can point to an object of the String class, as per rule, the String methods are not allowed to modify the original string; instead, a modifying method creates and returns a new string without modifying the original string. If you are doing a lot of string manipulation in your program, then using String may result in lots of abandoned strings, and hence you should use StringBuffer, whose modifying methods do modify the original strings.

Data flow is at the core of any application. Conceptually, formatting and parsing makes the two ends of the data flow: on one end, you send the data in a certain format, and on the other end, you receive the data and parse it to make sense of it and manipulate it. Java offers the Locale, NumberFormat, and DateFormat classes to format the data in a locale-sensitive fashion. These classes enable you to write Java applications that will execute in an environment with diverse languages and conventions without changing the code. Whereas these classes let you format the numbers, dates, and currencies, the Formatter class enables you to form the streams, and the data flows in streams. Once you have formatted a stream, it may need to be parsed somewhere down the road. The Scanner class provides support for parsing by using regular expressions as delimiters. By using the Pattern and Matcher classes, you can examine further specific pieces of data, such as to validate the format of an email address.

Although Java is an object-oriented language, we are still talking about formatting the primitive data types, which are not objects and hence cannot participate in object-like activities. In order to allow primitives to behave like objects, Java offers a wrapper class corresponding to each primitive type.

In real-world applications, you will be dealing with not only individual data items but also with data structures such as a collection of related objects on which you could perform some operations. We will explore this topic in the next chapter.

EXAM'S EYE VIEW

Comprehend

- Corresponding to each primitive type there is a wrapper class that has a very similar name as the primitive, but it's fully spelled and the first letter is uppercased. For example, the wrapper class for char is Character.

- The String class overrides the equals(...) method of the Object class and performs a deep comparison: two string references are considered equal even if they refer to two separate but identical strings.

- The StringBuffer class does not override the equals(...) method of the Object class and hence performs a shallow comparison: two string references are considered equal only if they refer to the same string.

Look Out

- A string created with the String class cannot be modified, while a string created with the StringBuffer class can be modified. Therefore, the modifying methods in the String class actually create and return a new String object, and the original object remains unchanged.

- String literals are created at compile time, and the compiler does not create a duplicate String literal. The strings with the new operator are created at runtime, and a new string will be created even if there is an identical string already in the pool created at compile time.

- The wrapped value in a wrapper class cannot be modified.

Memorize

- A String literal (String object created without the new operator) is created at compile time and the compiler does not duplicate it. Therefore, more than two references may refer to the same String literal.

- In the format(...) method, the format type in the format specifier and the argument type should be compatible with each other.

Review Questions

1. Given the following:

```java
public class StringIndexMute{
  public static void main(String[] args){
    StringBuilder str = new StringBuilder("0123 456 ");
    if (str.length() == 9)
      str.insert(9, "abcde");
    str.delete(2,5);
    System.out.println(str.indexOf("d"));

  }
}
```

   What is the result?

   A. 9

   B. 8

   C. 7

   D. -1

   E. Compilation fails.

   F. An exception is thrown at runtime.

2. Consider the following code fragment:

```java
1. public class MyStringClass extends String {
2.  public static void main(String[] args) {
3.       String str= "I" + "We";
4.       System.out.println(str);
5.  }
6.}
```

   Which of the following is true about this code fragment?

   A. A compiler error occurs at line 3.

   B. A compiler error occurs at line 1.

   C. An exception is thrown at execution time.

   D. The code compiles and executes without any error, and generates the output IWe.

3. Consider the following line of code:

```java
String str = new String("Hello");
```

   Which of the following lines of code modify the string to which str refers? (Choose all that apply.)

   A. str.concat("dear");

   B. str.substring(2);

   C. str.replace('H', 'M');

   D. str.trim();

   E. None of the above

4. Consider the following code fragment:

```
1. String s1 = "Hello";
2. String  s2 =  new  String(s1);
3. if ( s1 == s2 ) {
4.      System.out.println("s1 and s2 point to the same  thing!");
5.    }else {
6.        System.out.println("s1 and s2 do not point to the same  thing!");
7.    }
```

What would be the output of this code fragment?

A. s1 and s2 point to the same thing!

B. s1 and s2 do not point to the same thing!

C. Compiler error at line 3

D. Error at execution time

5. Consider the following code fragment:

```
1. String s1 = "Hello";
2. String  s2 =  new  String(s1)
3. if ( s1.equals(s2) ) {
4.      System.out.println("s1 and s2 point to identical strings!");
5.    }else {
6.        System.out.println("s1 and s2 do not point to identical  thing!");
7.    }
8.    }
```

What would be the output of this code fragment?

A. s1 and s2 point to identical strings!

B. s1 and s2 do not point to identical strings!

C. Compiler error at line 3

D. Exception thrown at execution time

6. Consider the following code fragment:

```
1.   String str = new String("Hello");
2.   str.concat(" dear");
3.   System.out.println(str);
```

What would be the output of this code fragment?

A. Hello dear

B. Hello

C. Compiler error at line 1

D. Exception thrown at execution time

E. dear

7. Consider the following code fragment:

```
1. StringBuffer sbuf = new StringBuffer("Hello");
2.   sbuf.append(" dear");
3.   System.out.println(sbuf);
```

What would be the output of this code fragment?

A. `Hello dear`

B. `Hello`

C. Compiler error at line 1

D. Exception thrown at execution time

E. `dear`

8. Consider the following lines of code:

```
String s1 = "Whatever";
String s2 = new String("Whatever");
String s3 = new String ("Who");
```

Which of the following statements is true? (Choose all that apply.)

A. The compiler will create two strings `Whatever` and `Who` and put them in the pool, and there will be a string `Whatever` and `Who` created at runtime.

B. The compiler will create two strings `Whatever` and `Who` and put them in the pool, and there will be no string created at runtime.

C. The compiler will create two copies of `Whatever` and one copy of `Who` and put them in the pool, and there will be strings `Whatever` and `Who` created at runtime.

D. The compiler will create one copy of `Whatever` and put it in the pool, and there will be strings `Whatever` and `Who` created at runtime.

E. The compiler will create a string `Whatever` and put it in the pool, and there will be a string `Who` created at runtime.

9. Given the following:

```
class PrintWriterFormat{
  public static void main(String[] args){
    int x = 123456789;
    int y = 987654321;
    float z = 7;
     System.out.format("-%5d ", x);
     System.out.printf("-%5d- ", y);
     System.out.printf("-%4.1d- ", z);

  }
}
```

What is the result?

A. `-123456789 -987654321-`

B. `-12345 -98765-`

C. `-  123456789 -  987654321  -`

D. Compilation fails.

E. An exception is thrown at runtime.

10. Consider the code in Listing 9-15. What is the result?

    A. `true false true true false true false`

    B. `true false false true false true false`

    C. `true true true true false true false`

    D. Compilation fails.

    E. An exception is thrown at runtime.

CHAPTER 10

■■■

Collections and Generics

Exam Objectives

6.1 Given a design scenario, determine which collection classes and/or interfaces should be used to properly implement that design, including the use of the Comparable interface.

6.2 Distinguish between correct and incorrect overrides of corresponding hashCode and equals methods, and explain the difference between == and the equals method.

6.3 Write code that uses the generic versions of the Collections API, in particular, the Set, List, and Map interfaces and implementation classes. Recognize the limitations of the non-generic Collections API and how to refactor code to use the generic versions.

6.4 Develop code that makes proper use of type parameters in class/interface declarations, instance variables, method arguments, and return types; and write generic methods or methods that make use of wildcard types and understand the similarities and differences between these two approaches.

6.5 Use capabilities in the java.util package to write code to manipulate a list by sorting, performing a binary search, or converting the list to an array. Use capabilities in the java.util package to write code to manipulate an array by sorting, performing a binary search, or converting the array to a list. Use the java.util.Comparator and java.lang.Comparable interfaces to affect the sorting of lists and arrays. Furthermore, recognize the effect of the "natural ordering" of primitive wrapper classes and java.lang.String on sorting.

Everything in Java is an object. As you learned in Chapter 9, you can even make the primitive values act like objects by wrapping them in the wrapper classes. The wrapping and unwrapping of primitive values, which is also called boxing and unboxing, has been automated in J2SE 5.0 and is called *autoboxing*. So, you can assume that all the data types in Java can be treated like objects of classes. All the objects in Java share some methods, which they inherit from the Object class at the root of the Java class hierarchy—that is, it is a superclass of all classes in Java.

An application that is solving a real-world problem will generally deal with a group of data items that can be represented in Java by collections. The collections in Java are supported by two superinterfaces, Collection and Map, which have subinterfaces as well. Java also presents some implementations of the collections interfaces that can be used as data structures to store and manipulate groups of data items, that is, objects.

So, the focus of this chapter is to understand how you can use objects as data items in Java, starting from a primitive in a wrapper to a collection of objects. To accomplish that, we will explore three avenues: the Object class, the collections of objects, and autoboxing.

The Mother of All Classes: Object

Everything in Java, except primitives, is an object. As you know from Chapter 9, you can make even the primitives behave like objects by using wrappers. The Java language offers a class called Object from which all the other classes are explicitly or implicitly derived.

The Object Class

Java supports single inheritance; that is, a class cannot be a subclass of more than one class. That means the class hierarchy tree in Java must have a root represented by a single class. The Object class is that root from which all the other classes are derived directly or indirectly. As a result, the classes that Java offers, such as the classes in its various packages, and every class that you write automatically inherit the methods of the Object class even if you don't extend Object explicitly in your class declaration.

The Object class has a very simple constructor:

```
public Object()
```

Because all the classes in Java are subclasses of the Object class, it makes sense to define some general-purpose methods in the Object class. These methods of the Object class are described in Table 10-1.

Table 10-1. *Methods of the Object Class*

Method	Description
protected Object clone()	Creates and returns a copy of this object.
public boolean equals(Object obj)	Returns true if this object is equal to the object passed in as an argument. Equality here means both references refer to the same instance.
protected void finalize()	Invoked by the garbage collector when there are no references to the object.
public final Class<? extends Object> ➥ getClass()	Returns the runtime class of this object. You will learn about the generics syntax within <> later in this chapter.
public int hashcode()	Returns a hashcode value for this object. This method is offered to support the hashtables.
public String toString()	Returns this object in its string representation.
public final void notify() public final void notifyAll() public final void wait() public final void wait(...)	Methods to support threads.

Three of these methods, namely wait(), notify(), and notifyAll(), facilitate thread control and are discussed in Chapter 11. The hashcode() method is offered to support hashtables, a data structure, and is discussed later in this chapter when we explore some data structures implemented in Java.

When you write a class, even if you do not extend the Object class explicitly, it is automatically extended. That means your class inherits all the methods of the Object class, which implies that you can override a method from the Object class in your class. However, you must keep in mind the general rules of overriding, which include the following:

- You cannot override a `final` method.

- When you override a non-final method, you must obey the overriding rules, such as you cannot override a method to be less accessible, and a (checked) exception thrown by the overriding method must be the same as the exception thrown by the overridden method or a subclass of it.

■**Caution** When you write any class, your class automatically inherits the methods of the `Object` class. You can override any of the non-final methods, but you must follow the overriding rules, such as you cannot override a method to be less accessible. For example, if you override the `equals(…)` method (which is declared `public` in the `Object` class), you have to declare it `public` because otherwise you will be making it less accessible and the compiler will generate an error.

One of the general-purpose methods defined in the `Object` class is the `equals(…)` method, which allows you to compare any two objects with each other to check if they are equal.

The equals() Method

If everything in Java is an object, you should be able to identify if two objects are equal. The equality test is an important operation in programming. For example, some data structures do not allow duplicates to be stored. To facilitate the equality test, the `Object` class offers the `equals(…)` method, which has the following signatures:

```
public boolean equals(Object obj)
```

The implementation of the `equals(…)` method in the `Object` class is very shallow; it just uses the `==` operator for comparison. For example, consider the two object references x and y. The code `x.equals(y)` will return `true` only if x and y refer to the same object. However, you can override this method in the class that you write and give it a deeper meaning.

A valid implementation of the `equals(…)` method must honor the following contract:

- *The method is reflexive*: for any non-null reference x, `x.equals(x)` should return `true`.

- *The method is symmetric*: For any non-null references x and y, `x.equals(y)` should return `true` if and only if `y.equals(x)` returns `true`.

- *The method is transitive*: For any non-null references x, y, and z, if `x.equals(y)` returns `true` and `y.equals(z)` returns `true`, then `x.equals(z)` should return `true` as well.

- *The method is consistent*: for any non-null references x and y, multiple invocations of `x.equals(y)` consistently return `true` or consistently return `false`, provided no information used in the `equals` comparisons on the objects is modified.

- *It can check for the null references*. For any non-null reference x, `x.equals(null)` should always return `false`.

Well, with a little bit of understanding of logic, it's hard to imagine a more reasonable and obvious contract than this one.

Listing 10-1 demonstrates the use of the `equals(…)` method.

Listing 10-1. *ObjectTest.java*

```
1. public class ObjectTest {
2.   public static void main(String[] args) {
3.       ObjectOne obj1a = new ObjectOne(1,2);
4.       ObjectOne obj1b = new ObjectOne(1,2);
5.       ObjectTwo obj2 = new ObjectTwo();
6.       if  (obj1a.equals(obj1b)) {
7.               System.out.println("obj1a is equal to obj1b");
8.       }else {
9.         System.out.println("obj1a is not equal to obj1b");
10.       }

11.       if(obj2.equals(obj1a)){
12.         System.out.println("obj1a is equal to obj2");
13.       }else {
14.           System.out.println("obj1a is not equal to obj2");
15.       }
16.   }
17. }
18. class ObjectOne {
19.   private int   x = 0;
20.   private int   y = 0;
21.   ObjectOne(int x, int y) {
22.     this.x = x;
23.     this.y = y;
24.   }
25.   public int getX() {
26.     return x;
27.   }
28.   public int getY() {
29.     return y;
30.   }
31. }
32. class ObjectTwo {
33.   private int x  = 1;
34.   private int y  = 2;
35.     public boolean equals(Object object) {
36.         ObjectOne obj = (ObjectOne) object;
37.         if ((obj.getX() ==  x) && (obj.getY() == y)) {
38.                 return true;
39.         } else {
40.               return false;
41.         }
42.     }
43.   }
```

The output from Listing 10-1 follows:

```
obj1a is not equal to obj1b
obj1a is equal to obj2
```

Note that the class ObjectOne does not override the equals(…) method. Therefore, when an instance of class ObjectOne calls the equals(…) method (line 6), the equals(…) method of the Object class would be executed. The test in line 6 fails because obj2 and obj1a do not refer to the same object, even though they belong to the same class. The class ObjectTwo overrides the equals(…)

method of the Object class. It would return true if the calling object had the same values of x and y. This is the reason why the test in line 11 passes. You can also be sure that our simple implementation of the equals(…) method in ObjectTwo honors the equals(…) contract discussed earlier.

There may be situations in programming where you just want to know something about an object. It's like that most popular question that people on this planet ask each other: Where are you from? If you want to ask this question of an object or you want to make an object better equipped to answer this question, the method to use is toString().

The toString() Method

The implementation of the toString() method in the Object class is very minimal. This method invoked on an object returns a string representation of the object. Generally speaking, the toString() method should return a string that textually represents the object. The result is supposed to be a concise but informative representation of the object that is easy to read. The default implementation (in the Object class) returns the object's class name, followed by the at sign (@) character, followed by the hashcode of the object in hexadecimal representation. Following is an example of the output from invoking the toString() method on an object of class OurClass:

```
OurClass@18d107f
```

You will learn more about the hashcode later in this chapter. When the default implementation of this method is not useful, you can override it to your needs.

So, where are you from? I'm from OurClass. No, I mean where are you originally from? Oh, originally! Well, originally, I'm from where we are all from: the Object class. So, all the objects in Java are originally from the Object class. An object in Java is a data item. In the real-world applications, the isolated data items are rarely useful; the useful data items often come in groups—that is, in collections.

Understanding Collections

In writing an application, you usually deal with multiple data items related to each other, such as departments in a company, employees in a department, and so on. To deal with a group of data items, Java offers collections. A collection is an object that organizes multiple data items into a single group. As said earlier, in a real-world problem, the collections typically represent the data items that are related to each other. Collections are used to manipulate data (perform operations on it), store and retrieve data, and transfer data between methods.

There is another way of looking at collections. In computer science, we define an abstract data type (ADT) as a set of objects combined with a set of operations that can be performed on the objects. When it comes to implementation of an ADT, the set of related data items is organized into a data structure and the operations are implemented in the form of methods. Java presents a unified architecture called the *collections framework* that makes a collection as an implementation of an ADT. The collections framework consists of three elements:

- *Interfaces*: Pretty much like abstract data types, and allow you to manipulate collections independently of the implementation details.

- *Implementations*: The concrete implementations of the collections interfaces. You can look upon them as reusable data structures.

- *Algorithms*: The methods that perform operations such as search and sorting on the objects in the data structures. You can also look upon them as reusable functionality.

Let's begin by exploring the interfaces.

The Collections Interfaces

The root of the hierarchy of the collections interfaces is the Collection interface, also referred to as the superinterface of the collections. There is another kind of collections called maps, which are represented by the superinterface Map, which is not derived from the Collection interface. Both kinds of collections interfaces are shown in Figure 10-1.

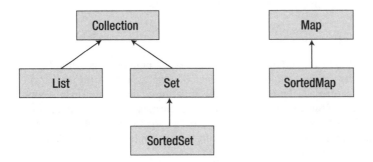

Figure 10-1. *The hierarchy of collection interfaces. Each child interface in this hierarchy extends the parent interface.*

The List and Set interfaces extend from the Collection interface, and there is no direct implementation of the Collection interface. The following list discusses some characteristics of the subinterfaces of Collection (that is, List and Set) and of Map:

- List: An ordered collection of data items; i.e. you know exactly where each item is in the list. A list can contain duplicate elements. ArrayList, LinkedList, and Vector are the classes that implement the List interface.

- Map: An object that maps keys to values: each key can map to at most one value. Maps cannot contain duplicate keys. HashMap and HashTable are examples of classes that implement the Map interface. No duplicate keys are allowed in maps; duplicate values are allowed.

- Set: A collection of unique items; i.e. there are no duplicates. HashSet and LinkedHashSet are examples of classes that implement the Set interface.

To avoid confusion in terminology, remember the following points:

- Collection (with uppercase *C*) is the java.util.Collection interface.

- A collection (with lowercase *c*) refers to any implementation (that is, data structure) of a Collection interface such as Set or List.

- Collections is the java.util.Collections class, which offers a number of static utility methods that can be invoked on collections.

- When the text uses the term List, Map, or Set, you need to figure out from the context if it is talking about the interface or the objects of the class that implement the interface.

■Note Both a Map object and a Set collection cannot contain duplicates data items, while a List collection can contain duplicates.

The List and the Set interfaces extend the Collection interface. Some methods in the Collection interface are shown in Table 10-2. The JDK does not provide any direct implementation of the Collection interface. However, it does provide implementations of its subinterfaces such as List and Set. The methods of this interface are typically used to pass collections around and manipulate them where generality is needed.

Table 10-2. *Some Methods in the Collection Interface*

Method	Description
boolean add(Object obj)	Adds obj (any object reference) to the collection and returns true if an equal object is already not in the collection, else returns false.
boolean addAll(Collection c)	Adds all the elements in the passed-in collection c to this collection. Returns true if the collection changed as a result of the method call.
void clear()	Remove all the elements from this collection.
boolean contains(Object obj)	Returns true if this collection contains the specified element obj.
boolean containsAll(Collection c)	Returns true if this collection contains all the elements of the collection specified in the argument.
boolean isEmpty()	Returns true if this collection has no element in it.
boolean equals(Object obj)	Returns true if the object specified in the argument is equal to this collection.
int hashcode()	Returns the hashcode for this collection as an int type.
boolean remove(Object obj)	Removes the element specified in the argument, and returns true if this collection changes as a result of this method invocation.
boolean removeAll(Collection c)	Removes from this collection all the elements in the collection specified in the method argument, and returns true if this collection changes as a result of this method invocation.
Iterator<E> iterator()	Returns an iterator over the elements (E) in this collection. You will learn more about the angle bracket (<>) notation later in this chapter.
<T> T[] toArray(T[] array)	Returns an array that contains all the elements in this collection. T represents the data type of array elements.

Some commonly used methods of the Map interface are shown in Table 10-3.

Table 10-3. *Methods of the Map Interface*

Method	Description
`void clear()`	Removes all key-value pairs in the map.
`booelan containsKey(Object key)`	Returns `true` if this map contains the key-value pair for the specified key.
`boolean containsValue(Object value)`	Returns `true` if this map contains one or more keys corresponding to the specified value.
`boolean equals(Object obj)`	Returns `true` if the specified object is equal to this map.
`Object get(Object key)`	Returns the value corresponding to the specified key.
`int hashcode()`	Returns the hashcode value for this map.
`Boolean isEmpty()`	Returns `true` if this map does not have any key-value pair in it.
`Object put(Object key, Object value)`	Stores the specified key-value pair. If the key already had a value in the map, it is overwritten with the new value.
`void putAll(map m)`	Stores all the key-value pairs from the specified map to this map.
`Object remove(Object key)`	Removes the key-value pair for this key if it is present. Returns the existing value (before the `remove` operation) corresponding to this key or `null` if there was no (or null) value.
`int size()`	Returns the number of key-value pairs in this map.
`Collection values()`	Returns the values in this map as a `Collection`.

In addition to offering collections interfaces, the JDK also provides some implementations of these interfaces that you can use in your applications.

Implementations of Collections Interfaces

Implementations of the collections interfaces are the classes that implement the interfaces and represent reusable data structures to hold the data items. As you know, the purpose of a collection is to represent a group of related objects, known as its elements. The related data items can be grouped together in various ways depending upon the application requirements. That is why we have several ADTs and corresponding data structures, and that is also why Java offers several collections interfaces and several implementations of a given interface.

Features of Implementations

To meet varied application requirements, some collections allow duplicate elements and others do not. Some are ordered and others are unordered. Some implementations have restrictions on the elements that they are allowed to contain, such as no `null` elements, and others may have restrictions on the types of their elements.

The JDK does not offer any direct implementations of the Collection interface. However, it does provide implementations of the subinterfaces such as Set and List. So, each implementation contains general features of the interface it implements and its own specific features. Which implementation you will like to use depends upon which of the following features is important for your application:

- *Performance*: Performance refers to the time taken by a specific operation on the data as a function of the number of data items in the structure, such as accessing a given data item (search) and inserting or deleting an item in the data structure. In some data structures, the search and insertion/deletion may have opposing performance requirements. That means if a data structure offers fast search, the insertion/deletion may be slow.

- *Ordered/sorted*: A data structure is said to be ordered if the data items are in some order. For example, an array is an ordered data structure because the data items are ordered by index; that is, we can refer to the data items by their index, such as *the fifth element*. A data structure is said to be sorted if the data items are ordered by their essence, such as in ascending order of their values. So, by definition, a sorted data structure is an ordered data structure, but the reverse is not necessarily true.

- *Uniqueness of items*: Your data requirements may be such that each data item in the structure must be uniquely identifiable, or on the contrary, you may want to allow duplicate items.

- *Synchronized*: Some implementations are synchronized, which means they offer support for thread safety (i.e. they can be run in a multithreaded environment). Other implementations are unsynchronized. However, this should not be a big factor in choosing an implementation, because even if the implementation you chose is unsynchronized, you can always use synchronization methods from the Collections class.

Figure 10-2 shows the hierarchy of collection and map implementations. A solid line indicates an interface extending another interface, and a broken line indicates a class implementing an interface.

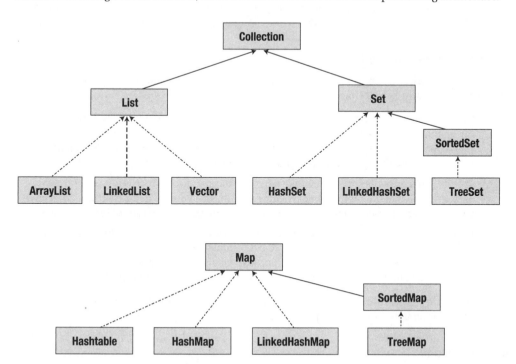

Figure 10-2. *The hierarchy of collection and map implementations*

Implementing the List Interface

You can use a list when duplication is acceptable and order is required. The following classes implement the List interface:

- ArrayList: Think of ArrayList as an array that can grow in number of elements. Just like an array, it provides constant-time access to a specific element in the list, but insertions and deletions are linear in time. If you need to do insertions and deletions frequently and random access of elements rarely, use LinkedList, instead. So, random access (or search) is fast in ArrayList, but insertions and deletions are not.

- LinkedList: A node in a LinkedList contains the data item and the pointer to the next node. So, a given element is searched by traveling from node to node. Therefore, random access in LinkedList is linear in time, but insertions and deletions are constant in time. So, insertions and deletions are fast in LinkedList, but random access (or search) is not.

- Vector: Vector is pretty much like ArrayList but it provides support for synchronization for thread safety. If you are not programming for a multithreaded environment (that is, you don't need thread safety), use ArrayList instead of Vectors, because otherwise you are impeding the performance for no gain. Even if you are programming for a multithreaded environment, you can still use ArrayList and use the synchronization methods provided by the Collections class.

So, ArrayList and LinkedList are two general-purpose implementations of the List interface. The most commonly used implementation is ArrayList because, unlike LinkedList, it provides fast search (random access) and has no overhead of maintaining nodes associated with each element.

Implementing the Set Interface

You use the Set classes when you don't want to allow duplicates in the data structure. The following classes implement the Set interface:

- HashSet: This provides the faster access to a data item as compared to TreeSet, but it offers no guarantee that the items will be ordered. Assume that it is unsorted and unordered. Note that it does not offer synchronization, so if you use it in a multithreaded environment, you may need to use the synchronization methods from the Collections class.

- TreeSet: This presents sorted data items, but the access performance is not as good as HashSet. Note that it does not offer synchronization, so if you use it in a multithreaded environment, you may need to use the synchronization methods from the Collections class.

- LinkedHashSet: A LinkedHashSet is like a HashSet that maintains a doubly linked list that runs through all the data items. It is an ordered collection, ordered by insertion, but not sorted. Note that it does not offer synchronization, so if you use it in a multithreaded environment, you may need to use the synchronization methods from the Collections class.

HashSet and TreeSet are two general-purpose implementations of the Set interface. You should use HashSet if order is not important, else TreeSet.

Implementing the Map Interface

Maps are a perfect data structure when the data is stored in key-value pairs and each key is unique (that is, there are no duplicate keys). The following classes implement the Map interface:

- HashTable: This implementation is based on the hashtable data structure, and it can use any non-null object as a key or a value. It offers no guarantee that the data items will stay ordered. The objects used as keys must implement the hashCode() method and the equals(…) method in order to successfully store and retrieve objects from a hashtable. This implementation is synchronized.

- HashMap: This implementation is also based on the hashtable data structure. It is like the HashTable implementation, but it allows null and is unsynchronized. It offers no guarantee that the data items will stay ordered.

- LinkedHashMap: This implementation is different from HashMap in that it maintains a doubly linked list that runs through all of its entries. Furthermore, it defines the iteration order, which is usually the order in which the keys are inserted into the map. Use this list if the unspecified ordering provided by Hashtable and HashMap is not suitable for your application.

- TreeMap: TreeMap implements the SortedMap interface. It guarantees that the map will be in the ascending key order (that is, sorted). This implementation is unsynchronized.

So, HashMap and TreeMap are general-purpose implementations of the Map class. If you need sorted data items, use TreeMap, else use HashMap.

The characteristics of different implementations of the collections interfaces are summarized in Table 10-4. Note that you can always use the synchronized methods from the Collections class even if you use an unsynchronized implementation. Also, remember that the Map implementations do not implement the Collection interface.

Table 10-4. *Some Implementations of Map and Collection Interfaces and Their Characteristics*

Class	Interface	Duplicates Allowed?	Ordered/Sorted	Synchronized
ArrayList	List	Yes	Ordered by index Not sorted	No
LinkedList	List	Yes	Ordered by index Not sorted	No
Vector	List	Yes	Ordered by index Not sorted	Yes
HashSet	Set	No	Not ordered Not sorted	No
LinkedHashSet	Set	No	Ordered by insertion Not sorted	No
TreeSet	Set	No	Sorted either by natural order or by your comparison rules	No
HashMap	Map	No	Not ordered Not sorted	No
LinkedHashMap	Map	No	Ordered	No
Hashtable	Map	No	Not ordered Not sorted	Yes
TreeMap	Map	No	Sorted either by natural order or by your comparison rules	No

> ■Caution The data items in a Map are in key-value pairs. A Map cannot have duplicate keys, but it can have duplicate values. Also remember that maps do not implement the Collection interface. This is why you may run into statements such as "maps are not true collections."

In case of a Map data structure, we need a mechanism to figure out where a data item will be stored, or where we can find a stored item. This is done through hash functions. You can pass in a key to a hash function, and the hash function will run an algorithm and return a value called *hashcode*, which is used to determine where to store the item (or retrieve it). Java provides the hash function, called hashCode(), in the Object class.

The hashCode Method

The hashcode is an integer value attached to an object that, on one hand, specifies the uniqueness of an object and, on the other hand, helps to store an object in a data structure and to retrieve it. To calculate the hashcode for an object, the Object class offers the hashCode() method, which has the following syntax:

```
public int hashCode()
```

The method calculates and returns a *hashcode* of type int for the object on which it is invoked. When you write a class that will be used in a Map, you can override the hashcode() method to implement the algorithm that you will use to calculate the hashcode, but you must follow the rules for returning the hashcode, called the *hashcode contract*. The rules of the hashcode contract are listed here:

- If the hashCode() method is invoked multiple times on the same object during the execution of an application, it must consistently return the same integer value each time. However, the returned integer value can change from one execution of an application to another execution of the same application.

- If two objects are equal according to the equals(…) method, then invoking the hashCode() method on each of the two objects must return the same integer value for the hashcode.

- If two objects are unequal according to the equals(…) method, it is not required that invoking the hashCode() method on each of these two objects must return unequal integer values as hashcodes. However, you should be aware that returning distinct integer values as hashcodes for unequal objects may improve the performance of hashtables.

To understand the contract in concrete terms, study Table 10-5 for two objects, obj1 and obj2.

Table 10-5. *Implications of the hashcode() Contract*

Condition	Requires	Not Required But Allowed
obj1,equals(obj2) == true	obj1.hashCode( ) == ➥ obj2.hashCode( )	
obj1.equals(obj2) == false	No hashCode() requirement	obj1.hashCode() != ➥ obj2.hashCode()
obj1.hashCode() == ➥ obj2.hashCode()	No equality requirement	obj1.equals(obj2) == true
obj1.hashCode() != ➥ obj2.hashCode()	obj1.equals(obj2) == false	

A trivial implementation of the hashCode() method that will honor the contract is one that returns a constant. Because the method returns the same constant number each time it is invoked, it will obviously return equal numbers for the equal objects. It will also return equal numbers for unequal objects, but that does not violate the hashcode contract. A little more sophisticated implementation of the hashCode() method follows:

```
return f(key)%mapSize;
```

The variable key is the key of the data item stored, f(key) is the function of the key returning an integer value, and mapSize is the size of the map that stores the key-value pairs. As an example, consider Listing 10-2.

Listing 10-2. *HashTest.java*

```
1.  public class HashTest{
2.    public static void main(String[] args) {
3.        HashStore hs1 = new HashStore(89, 101);
4.        HashStore hs2 = new HashStore(75, 101);
5.        HashStore hs3 = new HashStore(89, 101);

6.        System.out.println("Hashcode for hs1: " + hs1.hashCode());
7.        System.out.println("Hashcode for hs2: " + hs2.hashCode());
8.        System.out.println("Hashcode for hs3: " + hs3.hashCode());

9.      if(hs1.equals(hs2)) {
10.        System.out.println("hs1 is equal to hs2");
11.      }else {
12.        System.out.println("hs1 is not equal to hs2");
13.      }
14.      if(hs1.equals(hs3)) {
15.        System.out.println("hs1 is equal to hs3");
16.      }else {
17.        System.out.println("hs1 is not equal to hs3");
18.      }
19.    }
20.  }

21. class HashStore {
22.    private int key=0;
23.    private int value=0;
24.    private int storeSize = 10;
25.    HashStore(int key, int value){
26.        this.key=key;
27.        this.value=value;
28.    }
29.    public boolean equals(Object obj) {
30.      if (!(obj instanceof HashStore)) {
31.        return false;
32.      }
33.      HashStore hs = (HashStore) obj;
34.      return (key==hs.key && value==hs.value);
35.    }
36.    public int hashCode() {
37.        return key%storeSize;
38.    }
39. }
```

The following is the output from Listing 10-2:

```
Hashcode for hs1: 9
Hashcode for hs2: 5
Hashcode for hs3: 9
hs1 is not equal to hs2
hs1 is equal to hs3
```

The objects hs1 and hs2 are unequal and have unequal hashcodes. The objects hs1 and hs3 are equal and have the same hashcode: 9. This is in accordance with the hashcode contract.

■**Note** Two objects that are equal, as determined by the equals(…) method, must return the same hashcode. The reverse is not required to be true; that is, the two objects that are not equal do not have to return unequal hashcodes.

During the data manipulation in collections, when the equality of two objects needs to be tested, the equals(…) method is used. It is very important to override the equals(…) method from the Object class. For example, if you do not override the equals(…) method that your class inherits from the Object class, you cannot use the objects of your class as keys in a map. This is because the equals(…) method in the Object class uses the == operator to test the equality, and two object references will be equal only if they refer to the same object. That means if you lose the reference to a key object after storing the key, you can never refer to that key object again. You can create an identical key, but it will not be equal to the key that is stored because it is not referring to the same object. For example, consider the following lines of code:

```
Integer wi1 = new Integer(1);
Integer wi2 = new Integer(1);
```

According to the equals(…) method in the Object class, wi1 and wi2 are not equal because they do not refer to the same object. However, we might like to see them as equal because we might have used wi1 as a key when we were storing a map, and now we should be able to use wi2 as the key when we want to retrieve it because we may not have the wi1 reference at the time of retrieval. For that to happen, you need to override the equals(…) method and define it accordingly.

In nutshell, you can pass in a key to a hash function, and the hash function will run an algorithm and return a value called *hashcode*, which specifies the uniqueness of a data item in a data structure.

If you know the identity of a data item, you can search for it in a data structure.

Performing a Search on Collections

Search is an important operation that can be performed on a data structure to look for a particular data item. The Arrays class and the Collections class present methods that can be used for this purpose.

You can search for a specified element in a collection or array by using the binarySearch() method, which will return the integer index of the searched element if the search is successful. The index of the first position is 0. If the search is not successful, a negative integer will be returned.

During the search, keep the following points in mind:

- You must sort the collection (or array) before conducting a search on it. If you do not, the accuracy of the results is not guaranteed.

- A collection sorted in natural order must be searched in natural order; that is, do not send a Comparator as an argument in the binarySearch(…) method.

- A collection sorted using a Comparator must be searched using the same Comparator. That means you must pass the Comparator as an argument in the binarySearch(…) method, otherwise the accuracy of the results is not guaranteed.

■Caution You cannot use a Comparator while searching an array of primitives.

Listing 10-3 demonstrates these points.

Listing 10-3. *SearchArrayTest.java*

```
1.  import java.util.*;
2. class SearchCollectionTest {
3.  public static void main(String[] args) {
4.    String [] str = {"Mark", "Ready", "Set", "Go"};
5.
6.    System.out.println("Unsorted:");
7.    for (String s : str) System.out.print(s + " ");
8.    System.out.println("\nGo = " + Arrays.binarySearch(str, "Go"));

9.    Arrays.sort(str);
10.   System.out.println("Sorted in natural order:");

11.   for (String s : str) System.out.print(s + " ");
12.   System.out.println("\nGo = " + Arrays.binarySearch(str, "Go"));
13.   System.out.println("Sorted in reverse order using a Comparator:");
14.   MyReverseSorter ms = new MyReverseSorter();
15.   Arrays.sort(str, ms);
16.   for (String s : str) System.out.print(s + " ");
17.   System.out.println("\nGo = " + Arrays.binarySearch(str, "Go"));
18.   System.out.println("Go = " + Arrays.binarySearch(str, "Go", ms));
19. }

20.}
21.class MyReverseSorter implements Comparator<String> {
22. public int compare(String s1, String s2) {
23.   return s2.compareTo(s1);
24. }
25.}
```

The output from Listing 10-3 follows:

```
1.  Unsorted:
2.  Mark Ready Set Go
3.  Go = -1
4.  Sorted in natural order:
5.  Go Mark Ready Set
```

```
6.  Go = 0
7.  Sorted in reverse order using a Comparator:
8.  Set Ready Mark Go
9.  Go = -1
10. Go = 3
```

Note that I have numbered the output so that I can refer to it by line number. The result in line 3 of the output is incorrect because we did not sort the array before searching it. The result in line 9 of the output is also incorrect because we did not tell the `binarySearch(...)` method (code line 17) which Comparator was used to search the array. Lines 5 and 6 in the output are a result of sorting and searching in a natural order.

In a nutshell, following are the important defining points about collections:

- Maps have unique keys that facilitate search for their content.

- Sets and maps do not allow duplicate entries.

- Lists maintain an order, and duplicate elements may exist.

- Map implementations do not implement the `Collection` interface.

Following are the important points from the perspective of storage:

- In hashing, search is particularly fast (due to unique keys), but indexed access is slow. Furthermore, hashtables support insertion, deletion, and growing the storage.

- `TreeSet` also supports insertion, deletion, and growing the storage. Indexed access is slow but search is fast.

- `LinkedList` also supports insertion, deletion, and growing the storage. Indexed access is slow. Search is slow, but insertion and deletion are fast as opposed to `ArrayList`, which provides fast access but slow insertion and deletion.

Storing an element in a collection is much easier than retrieving the element, because when you retrieve an element, you have to cast it to its correct type. The problem with this is that if you make a mistake in the type of cast, the compiler will not catch it, and that leaves room for a runtime error. If you have to have an error, you would rather have it at compile time and not when the application is running. So the question is, how do we help the compiler to check the type consistency of collections? The generic collections provide the answer.

Understanding Generics

Reusability of code is an important characteristic of any object-oriented language. For example, class inheritance provides reusability of a class. J2SE 5.0 takes reusability to the next level by introducing a very powerful feature called *generic programming*, which enables you to write code that can be reused for different types of objects. In this section, we explore generic programming from the perspective of collections.

Generic Collections

When you retrieve an element from a collection, you need to cast it to the right type. If you make a type mistake in casting, the compiler will not catch it, but you will get a runtime error. It is desired that the errors be caught during compilation and not when the application is running. The solution to this problem is provided by the generic collections introduced in J2SE 5.0, which provide a way for you to declare the type of a collection so that the compiler can check it. You can still use the non-generic collections and they will work. However, using generic collections is less error prone.

For example, consider the following code fragment:

```
1.  ArrayList myList = new ArrayList();
2.  String st = "Flemingo";
3.  myList.add(st);
4.  String st1 = (String) myList.get(0);
5.  System.out.println(st1);
```

This is perfectly fine code for nongeneric collections and will compile and run even in J2SE 5.0 and generate the following output:

```
Flemingo.
```

However, it will generate a compiler error if you replace line 4 with the following line:

```
String st1 = myList.get(0);
```

That means the compiler requires you to cast to a type. However, it has no way of ensuring that you are casting to a correct type, as long as you are casting to an object. For example, the code will compile without an error if you replace line 4 with the following line:

```
Integer st1 = (Integer) myList.get(0);
```

Of course, you will get an exception at runtime. We can rewrite the same code fragment in generic collections as shown here:

```
1. ArrayList<String>  myList = new ArrayList<String>();
2. String st = "Flemingo";
3.  myList.add(st);
4.  String st1 =  myList.get(0);
5.  System.out.println(st1);
```

Note that line 4 does not have any explicit casting. However, it will still accept the correct cast, but it's not required. Unlike the nongeneric collections, here the compiler will not let you cast incorrectly. For example, you will receive a compiler error if you replace line 4 with the following line:

```
Integer st1 = (Integer) myList.get(0);
```

This has become possible due to line 1, where you have declared the type of the myList collection elements as String. You could have declared any object reference type. It's important that you get used to the angle bracket notation: when you see something like <E>, read it as of type E. The overall result of using generics, especially in large applications, is improved readability, robustness, and reliability. Listing 10-4 presents a complete code example to demonstrate the use of generic collections using ArrayList. Of course, the same principles apply to any Collection implementation.

Listing 10-4. *GenericTest.java*

```
1. import java.util.*;
2. public class GenericTest{
3.  public static void main(String[] args) {
4.      ArrayList<String> myList = new ArrayList<String>();
5.      String st1 = "ready";
6.      String st2 = "set";
7.     String st3 = "go";
```

```
8.      myList.add(st1);
9.      myList.add(st2);
10.     myList.add(st3);
11.     String st;
12.     Iterator<String> itr = myList.iterator();
13.     while(itr.hasNext()){
14.         st = itr.next();
15.         System.out.println(st);
16.     }
17.   }
18. }
```

The output of Listing 10-4 follows:

```
ready
set
go
```

Note that the iterator in line 12 has been declared of type String. This is essential, because otherwise the compiler will generate an error.

Generic programming goes beyond just collections and has a more general dimension to it: instead of specifying a type in a class or in a method, you can just say some type in a generic way, and then specify it at a later time.

Generic Programming

You can ask the question: Why could I write ArrayList<String> in declaring a variable of this class? The answer is that the class ArrayList has been declared in the java.util package in such a way that you can mention a type with its name:

```
public class ArrayList<E>
```

Here <E> means any object reference type. To successfully use the generic collections, you need to get used to some of the concepts in generic programming, such as angle bracket notation, <E>, and the wildcard, such as ?. For example, consider the following declaration of the List interface in the java.util package:

```
public interface List<E> extends Collection<E>
```

It means that the interface List extends the interface Collection, and that the List is a generic collection; that is, it can be a list of <E>, where E can be used to specify any object type at a certain point in programming (we will explore this later in the chapter). Now, consider the following method in the Collection interface:

```
<T> T[] toArray(T[] a)
```

This returns an array containing all of the elements in this collection. The runtime type of the returned array is that of the specified array, and we don't know that type yet; it is generic. Now, consider an example of a rather sophisticated generic parameter type, again an example from the java.util package:

```
HashSet(Collection<? extends E> c)
```

This constructs a new set containing the elements in the specified collection. But what's the following parameter?

```
Collection<? extends E>
```

It means that the parameter must be a collection whose type is compatible with the generic type E. Here is a more specific example:

```
public    void setCatalogue(List<? extends Book>   books){
        //Code goes here.
}
```

It means that the method will take any collection as an argument that is a subtype of List and compatible with Book; that is, either of type Book or one of the subtypes of Book. However, there is a restriction: you cannot add anything to the passed-in collection. For example, the following code will generate a compiler error:

```
public    void setCatalogue(List<? extends Book>   books){
        books.add(new ScienceBook())  //Compiler error.
}
```

In this code you are saying that the method can accept any List that is of type Book or of a type that extends Book. What if you want to say, accept any type that implements an interface instead of extends a class? Here is a surprise for you: you still use the keyword extends and not implements. For example, the following is valid code:

```
public    void setCatalogue(List<? extends Serializable>   books){
        //Code goes here
}
```

It says to take any List as an argument that is of a type that implements the interface Serializable. If you use implements instead of extends, you will get an error.

You can ask another obvious question here: What if I want to say, accept any List that is of type Book or a superclass of it? This obvious question has the following obvious answer: Replace the keyword extends with its counterpart super. This time, you can even add some elements to the passed-in collection. The compiler will be happy with the following code:

```
public    void setCatalogue(List<? super ScienceBook>   books){
        books.add(new ScienceBook())
}
```

Also, you can define a class with one or more generic type variables:

```
public class myClass<P, S> {
// in the body you can use the P and S types, for example,  as method return types,
//   method parameter types, and class variable types.
}
```

Most of these concepts are put together into the example presented in Listing 10-5.

Listing 10-5. *FullGenericTest.java*

```
1.   import java.util.*;
2.   public class FullGenericTest{
3.   public static void main(String[] args) {
4.     ArrayList<MyClass> myList = new ArrayList<MyClass>();
5.       Integer I1 = new Integer(1);
6.       MyClass<String, Integer> mc1 = new MyClass("ready", I1 );
7.       MyClass<String, Integer> mc2 = new MyClass("set", new Integer("2"));
8.       MyClass<String, Integer> mc3 = new MyClass("go", new Integer("3"));
9.       myList.add(mc1);
10.    myList.add(mc2);
11.      myList.add(mc3);
12.      MyClass mc = new MyClass();
```

```
13.      Iterator<MyClass> itr = myList.iterator();
14.      while(itr.hasNext()){
15.        mc = itr.next();
16.        Integer I = (Integer)mc.getS();
17.        int i = I.intValue();
18.        System.out.println(mc.getP() + " " + i);
19.      }
20.  }
21. }
22. class MyClass<P, S>{
23.  private P pvar;
24.  private S svar;
25.  MyClass(){}
26.  MyClass(P pvar, S svar){
27.      this.pvar=pvar;
28.      this.svar=svar;
29.  }
30.   public P getP(){
31.        return pvar;
32.   }
33.   public S getS(){
34.        return svar;
35.   }
36. }
```

The following is the output from Listing 10-5:

```
ready 1
set 2
go 3
```

■Note You will receive the following warning message during compilation of Listing 10-5:

```
Note: FullGenericTest.java uses unchecked or unsafe operations.
Note: Recompile with -Xlint:unchecked for details.
```

You can ignore it and run the compiled code.

The generic types are declared in line 22 in defining a generic class, myClass, and then these variables are used in the body of the class (lines 22 to 36). These generic types are specified when the class is instantiated (lines 6 to 8). You can easily realize that generic programming helps you avoid writing multiple classes, or overloaded methods to handle related situations. You can write a generic class with some generic types in it, and use it to handle different situations. It enhances the reusability of the code, which is one of the important features of any object-oriented language. Generic programming is perhaps the most important addition to Java since version 1.0.

In most situations, ordering of data in a collection is an important feature. In this chapter, we have been referring to sorting by natural ordering or by comparison rules. Now, let's explore what we mean by that.

Object Ordering

It is often desired that the data is stored in an ordered fashion, so that when we need a specific data item from a collection, we know where to go to get it. So, ordering improves performance of retrieval operations such as searches.

Natural Ordering

As you know, a list is ordered by index, but not sorted by the element values. Some kind of sort algorithm is used to sort the elements of a list by values. You can sort a list by using the following `static` method of the `Collections` class:

```
Collections.sort(list);
```

If the list consists of `String` elements, they will be sorted in alphabetical order; if it consists of the `Date` elements, they will be ordered in chronological order. How does it happen? Well, the `String` and `Date` classes implement the `Comparable` interface, which has a single method:

```
int compareTo(T obj)
```

`T` specifies the type of the passed-in object. It returns a negative integer, zero, or a positive integer if the object on which this method is invoked is less than, equal to, or greater than the object passed in as an argument. The objects of classes such as `String` and `Date` that implement the `Comparable` interface are ordered automatically when the sort() method is invoked on the list that contains those objects. This ordering is called *natural ordering*. Table 10-6 summarizes some of the common Java classes that implement the `Comparable` interface and thereby support natural ordering.

Table 10-6. *Some Java Classes that Implement the Comparable Interface to Support Natural Ordering*

Class	Natural Ordering
Boolean	FALSE < TRUE
Byte	Signed numerical
Character	Unsigned numerical
Short	Signed numerical
Integer	Signed numerical
Long	Signed numerical
Float	Signed numerical
Double	Signed numerical
Date	Chronological
String	Lexicographic
File	Lexicographic on path name; system dependent

Objects that can be compared to one another are called *mutually comparable*, or just *comparables*. Generally speaking, objects of different types may be mutually comparable. However, note that none of the classes listed in Table 10-6 allows interclass comparison.

■**Caution** `Collections.sort(list)` will throw a `ClassCastException` if you try to sort a list whose elements do not implement the `Comparable` interface or if the elements cannot be compared to one another for some other reason.

There will be situations in which you will need to sort the list elements in an order other than their natural order. In this situation, the Comparator interface comes to your rescue.

Defining Ordering Using Comparator

Suppose a collection has objects that you want to sort in a certain order, but either the class of the objects does not implement the Comparable interface or the order in which you want to sort the objects is other than the natural order. In this case, you need to use the Comparator interface. In other words, you need to provide a Comparator, an object of a class that implements the Comparator interface. Of course, you will write this class and define what it means to be greater than, equal to, or smaller than. So, the Comparator that you will provide will encapsulate an ordering.

Like the Comparable interface, the Comparator interface consists of a single method:

```
int compare(T o1, T o2)
```

The compare(...) method compares the two objects passed in as arguments, and returns a negative integer, zero, or a positive integer if the first argument is less than, equal to, or greater than the second. The compare(...) method throws a ClassCastException if either of the arguments has an inappropriate type for the Comparator.

Listing 10-6 demonstrates how to write and use a Comparator. A Comparator is written in lines 3 to 8 and is used in line 16 in this example. The employee objects are created and added to the collection employeeList (lines 11 to 15) and the list is sorted by invoking the sort method on it (line 16).

Listing 10-6. *OrderingTest.java*

```
1. import java.util.*;
2. class OrderingTest {
3.   static final Comparator<Employee> EMPLOYEE_ID =
4.                         new Comparator<Employee>() {
5.       public int compare(Employee e1, Employee e2) {
6.           return e1.getID().compareTo(e2.getID());
7.       }
8. };
9.  public static void main(String[] args) {
10.      ArrayList<Employee> employeeList = new ArrayList<Employee>();
11.      employeeList.add(new Employee("Adam", 200));
12.      employeeList.add(new Employee("Brian", 2));
13.      employeeList.add(new Employee("Ginny", 1));
14.      employeeList.add(new Employee("Kulwinder", 10));
15.      employeeList.add(new Employee("Shindy", 15));
16.      Collections.sort(employeeList, EMPLOYEE_ID);
17.      for(Employee e:employeeList){
18.         System.out.println(e.getName() + " " + e.getID());
19.      }
20.   }
21. }
22. class Employee{
23.   int id;
24.   String name;
25.   Employee(String name, int id){
26.      this.id = id;
27.      this.name = name;
28.   }
```

```
29.  public Integer getID(){
30.     return id;
31.  }
32.  public String getName(){
33.     return name;
34.  }
35. }
```

The output from Listing 10-6 follows:

```
Ginny 1
Brian 2
Kulwinder 10
Shindy 15
Adam 200
```

Note that the output demonstrates that the list is sorted by the employee IDs, as you would expect from the implementation of the Comparator (lines 3 to 7). If lines 29 and 30 confuse you, note that it is an example of *autoboxing*, discussed in the next section.

As you know by now, collections can only hold object references and not primitive types. However, if you do want to store primitive types, you can wrap the primitive values into corresponding wrappers (called boxing) and then store the wrappers (which are objects) into the collections. To retrieve the primitive values, you retrieve the wrappers from the collections first, and then retrieve the primitive values by using the methods of the wrapper classes (unboxing). You learned about wrappers in Chapter 9. The good news from J2SE 5.0 is that boxing and unboxing has been automated and therefore is called autoboxing, which we explore next.

Understanding Autoboxing

Primitive data types cannot participate in object-like activities. You learned about a solution to this problem in Chapter 9: the wrapper classes. Each primitive type has a corresponding wrapper class that stores the values of that type, and they can act as objects. So, you wrap a primitive value into the corresponding wrapper object and then that value can act as an object type. This process is called *boxing*. When you need the primitive value back, you retrieve it from the wrapper by invoking an appropriate method on it. This is called *unboxing*. If there is a lot of boxing and unboxing going on, your program becomes cluttered and you are doing the same thing over and over again: boxing and unboxing. J2SE 5.0 presents a solution to this problem by automating boxing and unboxing, a feature known as *autoboxing*.

Autoboxing is the capability to assign a primitive value to a corresponding wrapper type; the conversion from primitive type to wrapper type is automated. Auto-unboxing is the reverse of autoboxing—that is, the capability to assign a wrapper type to the corresponding primitive type; the conversion from wrapper to primitive is automated. "Autoboxing" is also sometimes used, for short, to refer to both autoboxing and auto-unboxing.

Without autoboxing, you will need to do wrapping and un-wrapping manually. As an example, consider the following code fragment:

```
public Double areaOfASquare(Double side){
    double d = side.doubleValue();
    double a = d*d;
     return new Double(a);
}
```

In this code fragment, you unwrap the double value, calculate area, and then wrap the result again before returning it. You had to do this boxing and unboxing manually before J2SE 5. But now in J2SE 5, you can simply replace the preceding code fragment with the following:

```
public Double areaOfASquare(Double side){
        return side*side;
}
```

The boxing and unboxing is still done, but it's done automatically; it's hidden from you. Therefore, although it may seem as if you can treat wrappers just like primitives, you can make mistakes if you forget the fact that boxing and unboxing is still being done transparently. One implication of that is that you can only assign a primitive value to the corresponding wrapper (for example, int to Integer and not short to Integer). For example, consider the following code fragment:

```
1.   short s = 5;
2.   int i = s;
3.   Integer wi = s;
```

According to the primitive conversion rules discussed in Chapter 2, line 2 will compile even though the right side is a short and the left side is an int. However, line 3 will not compile. So, the conversion between wrappers and primitives is one to one: it is between int and Integer, double and Double, and so on. It is easy to remember: if you cannot box a primitive type into a wrapper, you cannot autobox it either.

■**Caution** Autoboxing (and unboxing) will work only between corresponding primitives and wrappers, such as int and Integer, double and Double, and float and Float. If you cannot box a primitive type into a wrapper, you cannot autobox it either.

That said, autoboxing works with arithmetic expressions as well. This is demonstrated in Listing 10-7.

Listing 10-7. *AutoboxingTest.java*

```
1. import java.util.*;
2. public class AutoboxingTest{
3.  public static void main(String[] args) {
4.   Integer wi1 = 1;
5.   wi1++;
6.   Integer  wi2 = 2;
7.   if(wi1==wi2){
8.    System.out.println("Area: " + areaOfASquare(4.0d));
9.   }
10. }
11.   public static Double areaOfASquare(Double side){
12.        return side*side;
13.   }
14.}
```

Note that in lines 4 and 6 the int values are directly assigned to Integer wrapper types wi1 and wi2, and then both wrapper types are involved in mathematical expressions (lines 5 and 7). In line 8, we pass in a double primitive type to the method while the method expects the Double wrapper type. The conversion will be done automatically. All this was not allowed before J2SE 5.0.

We started the discussion on autoboxing with the issue of how to put primitive values into the collections using wrappers. Listing 10-8 demonstrates the use of autoboxing with collections, and the for-each loop discussed in Chapter 6.

Listing 10-8. *AutoboxingCollection.java*

```
1.  import java.util.*;
2.  public class AutoboxingCollection{
3.     public static void main(String[] args) {
4.        HashMap<String, Integer> hm = new HashMap<String, Integer>();
5.        for (String word : args) {
6.           Integer freq = hm.get(word);
7.           hm.put(word, (freq == null ? 1 : freq + 1));
8.        }
9.           System.out.println(hm);
10.    }
11. }
```

A line of text is passed in as an argument in the command line. The program computes and prints the frequency of each word in the command-line argument. For example, issue the following command:

```
java AutoboxingCollection He could not axe the tree with an axe
  because the axe could not axe
```

This will generate the following output:

```
{the=2, because=1, an=1, tree=1, axe=4, could=2, with=1, not=2, He=1}
```

The program instantiates a HashMap, hm, with a String to Integer key-value mapping (line 4). Lines 5 to 8 make the for-each loop: for each word in the argument passed through the command line. The for-each loop iterates over each word in the command line, associating to it a value equal to the number of times the word appears in the line. For each word (as a key), the for-each loop gets its frequency value from the map (line 6), and then, if the word was already there in the map, it adds 1 to the frequency and stores it (line 7). Autoboxing is at play in the loop. For example, in line 7, you are adding 1 to freq, which is of type Integer. So, freq is first unboxed, int 1 is added to it, the result is boxed again, and the Integer result is put into the collection.

So, you can largely ignore boxing and unboxing while programming as long as you remember that it is being done for you transparently. That means you should use it only when it is necessary (for example, you want to put numerical values into a collection). Remember that you are still paying the price for boxing and unboxing in terms of performance, so do not use the wrapper type where you can use the primitive type. In other words, autoboxing automates the conversion between primitives and wrappers but it does not eliminate their differences.

Codewalk Quicklet

The code for the codewalk quicklet exercise in this chapter is presented in Listing 10-9.

Listing 10-9. *CodeWalkNine.java*

```
1. class CodeWalkNine{
2.  public static void main(String [] args) {
3.     NissanMaxima s1 = new NissanMaxima();   s1.color = "blue";
4.     NissanMaxima s2 = new NissanMaxima();   s2.color = "blue";
5.     System.out.print("Nissan Maxima: ");
6.     if (s1.equals(s2)) System.out.print("equals ");
7.     if (s1 == s2) System.out.print("== ");
8.        s1=s2;
9.     if (s1.equals(s2)) System.out.print("equals_now ");
10.       if (s1 == s2) System.out.println("==_now");
11.       Lexus x1 = new Lexus();  x1.color = "red";
12.       Lexus x2 = new Lexus();  x2.color = "red";
13.       System.out.print("Lexus: ");
14.       if (x1.equals(x2)) System.out.print("equals ");
15.    if (x1 == x2) System.out.print("== ");
16.       x1=x2;
17.    if (x1.equals(x2)) System.out.print("equals_now ");
18.    if (x1 == x2) System.out.print("==_now");
19. }
20. }

21. class NissanMaxima {
22.  String color;
23.  public String getColor() {
24.     return color;
25.  }
26. }
27. class Lexus {
28.  String color;
29.  public boolean equals(Object o) {
30.     return color.equals(((Lexus)o).color);
31.  }
32. }
```

To get you started on this exercise, following are some hints:

- *Input*: Lines 3, 4, 11, and 12
- *Operations*: Lines 29 through 31
- *Output*: Lines 6, 7, 9, and 10
- *Rule*: The relationship between the == operator and the equals(…) method

Looking at the code from this angle, see if you can handle the last question in the "Review Questions" section based on this code.

The three most important takeaways from this chapter are the following:

- The Object class represents the root of the class hierarchy in Java. Even if your class does not explicitly extend Object, Object is still a superclass of your class; that is, your class inherits the methods of the Object class such as equals(…) and hashCode(…).

- Autoboxing automates the wrapping and unwrapping (boxing and unboxing) of primitives.

- Collections are used to store, retrieve, and manipulate a group of related data items represented by objects.

Summary

The `Object` class represents the root of the class hierarchy in the Java language and presents some general-purpose methods. The `equals(…)` method in the `Object` class can be used to test the equality of two object references, and will return `true` if the two references refer to the same object. If you want the objects of your class to be used as keys in maps, you must override the `equals(…)` method of the `Object` class. The `toString(…)` method returns the textual representation of the object: the class name and the hashcode. You can override these methods in your class. The `hashCode(…)` method returns an integer value called hashcode, which specifies the uniqueness of an object and helps to store the object in, and retrieve it from, a data structure. The hashcode values for two equal objects (as determined by the `equals(…)` method) must be equal, but the hashcode values of two unequal objects don't have to be equal.

Collections are used to organize related data items into a group. To support collections, the JDK offers some interfaces such as `List` and `Set`, which are subinterfaces of the superinterface `Collection`, and subinterfaces such as `SortedMap` of the superinterface `Map`. The JDK also offers implementations of these interfaces that you can use in your applications. Maps store data in terms of key-value pairs where each key has to be unique. A map and a set cannot have duplicate elements, while a list can. When you want to retrieve an element from a collection, you need to cast it to the right type, and if you cast it to an incompatible type, the error will be caught only during runtime. The generic collections solve this problem by allowing you to specify the types of the elements to be stored in the collection when you declare the collection. Therefore, any error related to the incompatibility of the types will be caught during compilation.

Lists are ordered by index, and they can be sorted in two ways: natural ordering, by using the `Collections.sort()` method on the list whose elements implement the `Comparable` interface, or an ordering of your choice, by using the `Collections.sort()` method on the list that implemented the `Comparator` interface. J2SE 5.0 introduces autoboxing, which is automation of the conversion between primitive types and wrapper types—that is, automation of storing a primitive into a wrapper and retrieving it.

Some of the collection implementations, such as `ArrayList` and `TreeSet`, are not synchronized, which means they are not thread safe. A collection is considered not thread safe if there is no guarantee that the data will stay consistent if more than one method call is executed on it at the same time. More than one method call can execute concurrently on the same data structure in a multithreaded environment, which is the topic of the next chapter.

EXAM'S EYE VIEW

Comprehend

- Two objects that are equal, as determined by the `equals(...)` method, must return the same hashcode. The reverse is not required to be true; that is, two objects that are not equal do not have to return unequal hashcodes.

- Natural ordering is the order in which a list is sorted when you call the `Collections.sort(list)` method on it and the list elements implement the `Comparable` interface.

Look Out

- Sets and Maps do not allow duplicate entries. A `Map` can have duplicate values but not duplicate keys.

- The `equals(...)`, `hashCode()`, and `toString()` methods are declared `public` in the `Object` class, so they must be overridden to be `public`.

- Autoboxing (and unboxing) will work only between corresponding primitives and wrappers, such as `int` and `Integer`, `double` and `Double`, and `float` and `Float`. If you cannot box a primitive type into a wrapper, you cannot autobox it either.

Memorize

- The implementation of the `equals(...)` method in the `Object` class returns `true` only if both the object references refer to the same object.

- If you want to use the objects of your class as keys in a map, you must override the `equals(...)` method of the `Object` class.

- `java.util.Collection` is an interface, while `java.util.Collections` is a class.

- The `compare(...)` method of the `Comparator` interface throws a `ClassCastException` if either of the arguments has an inappropriate type for the Comparator.

- `Collections.sort(list)` will throw a `ClassCastException` if you try to sort a list whose elements do not implement the `Comparable` interface or if the elements cannot be compared to one another for some other reason.

Review Questions

1. Which of the following statements is true? (Choose all that apply.)

A. A Set is a collection that does not allow duplicates.

B. A Map can store duplicate values.

C. A List is a collection that is ordered by index.

D. A List is a collection that cannot have duplicates.

E. The JDK provides a direct implementation of the Collection interface.

2. Which of the following classes implements the java.util.List interface? (Choose all that apply.)

A. java.util.Vector

B. java.util.LinkedLIst

C. java.util.HashTable

D. java.util.OrderedList

3. Which of the following statements is not true about the hashcode? (Choose all that apply.)

A. The hashcode values of two equal objects must be equal.

B. The hashcode values of two unequal objects must be unequal.

C. If the hashcode values of two unequal objects are always unequal, it improves the performance.

D. A function that always return a constant is not a very efficient function.

4. Consider the following code fragment:

```
1. int i = 5;
2. printIt(i);
3. void printIt(Integer wi) {
4.     int j = wi;
5.     System.out.println("The value is: " + j);
6. }
```

What is the output of this code?

A. The value is: 5

B. Compiler error at line 3

C. Compiler error at line 2

D. Compiler error at line 4

E. Runtime error

5. Which of the following are illegal lines of code?

A. HashMap<Integer, String> hmap = new HashMap<Integer, String>();

B. ArrayList<int> list = new ArrayList<int>();

C. List<String> list2 = new ArrayList<String>();

D. HashSet<String> set = new HashSet<String>;

6. Consider the following code fragment:

```
Integer w1 = new Integer(2);
Integer w2 = new Integer(2);
if(w1 == w2){
    System.out.println("w1 is equal to w2!");
}else {
        System.out.println("w1 is not equal to w2!");
}
```

What is the output of this code?

A. Compiler error

B. Runtime error

C. w1 is equal to w2!

D. w1 is not equal to w2!

7. Consider the following code fragment:

```
1.  ArrayList<ObjectOne> list = new ArrayList<ObjectOne>();
2. list.add(new ObjectOne());
3. list.add(new ObjectOne());
4. list.add(new ObjectOne());
5. Collections.sort(list);
6. class ObjectOne  {
7.      private int  x = 0;
8.      private int  y = 0;
9. }
```

What is the output of this code fragment?

A. Compiler error at line 5

B. Runtime error at line 5

C. Compiler error at line 3

D. Runtime error at line 3

E. No errors

8. Consider the following code fragment:

```
1. ArrayList<Integer> list = new ArrayList<Integer>();
2. list.add(new Integer(1));
3. list.add(new Integer(2));
4. list.add(new Integer(3));
5. Iterator<Integer> itr = list.iterator();
6. for(Integer wij:list){
7.   System.out.println("number: " + wij);
8. }
```

What is the output from this code fragment?

A. number: 1
   number: 2
   number: 3

B. Compiler error at line 5

C. Compiler error at line 6

D. Compiler error at line 7

E. Runtime error

9. Which of the following collections can you use to store key-value pairs and is thread safe?

A. HashTable

B. HashMap

C. TreeMap

D. Vector

10. Consider the following code fragment:

```
1. import java.io.*;
2. class MyClass{
3.   public static void main(String[] args) throws IOException {
4.     NumberStore ns = new NumberStore();
5.     System.out.println("The number: " + ns.getInteger());
6.     ns.setInteger(10);
7.     System.out.println("The number: " + ns.getInteger());
8.   }
9. }
10. class NumberStore {
11.   int i =5;
12. public void setInteger(Integer x){
13.     System.out.println("The number passed in is: " + x);
14.     i = x;
15. }
16. public int getInteger( ){
17.   return i;
18. }
19.}
```

What is the output?

A. Compiler error at line 6

B. Execution error at line 13

C. Compiler error at line 3

D. The number: 5
   The number passed in is: 10
   The number: 10

11. Consider Listing 10-9. What is the output?

A. Nissan Maxima: equals ==_now
   Lexus: equals ==_now

B. Nissan Maxima: equals equals_now
   Lexus: equals equals_now ==_now

C. Nissan Maxima: equals_now ==_now
   Lexus: equals_now ==_now

D. Nissan Maxima: equals_now ==_now
   Lexus: equals equals_now ==_now

CHAPTER 11

■ ■ ■ ■

Threads in Java

Exam Objectives

4.1 Write code to define, instantiate, and start new threads using both java.lang.Thread and java.lang.Runnable.

4.2 Recognize the states in which a thread can exist, and identify ways in which a thread can transition from one state to another.

4.3 Given a scenario, write code that makes appropriate use of object locking to protect static or instance variables from concurrent access problems.

4.4 Given a scenario, write code that makes appropriate use of wait, notify, or notifyAll.

All of the modern operating systems support concurrent execution of multiple programs. In other words, they all create the impression that you can run more than one program (or application) on your computer simultaneously. For example, you can open a text editor and a web browser and work with both of them at the same time. This is made possible by CPU time sharing, whereby the OS runs one program for a short duration of time (e.g. a few milliseconds), and then switches to the other program, and then switches back to the first program. The operating system can run several programs concurrently by switching back and forth among them.

Threads extend the concept of switching among several different programs to switching among different processes in the same program. Each process performs a task in its own thread of execution control, and several processes may be running concurrently, each in its own thread of execution control. These threads may be sharing resources and therefore need to be managed by a scheduler. As a result, they go through different states in their lifecycles. So, the central issue in this chapter is: how multithreaded programming in Java works. To understand this, you will explore three avenues: the creation of a thread, the lifecycle of a thread, and transition between different thread states.

Multithreaded Programming in Java

A program performs several tasks such as doing a calculation, reading from a disk, writing to the disk, and so on. In the absence of multithreaded programming, the program runs in a single thread of execution and therefore performs these tasks sequentially. Thus, it is more efficient to execute multiple independent tasks in a program concurrently, and this can be achieved by having multiple threads in the program. Let's explore what the threads are and how to create them.

Understanding Threads

An application program has an execution control that executes one instruction at a time from the application, top down sequentially. This flow of execution control is called an *execution thread*. So, every application has at least one thread of execution. In a multithreaded environment, you can create more than one thread inside an application. This is equivalent to spawning multiple processes, each process with its own execution thread, which allows more than one task to be performed concurrently within the same application program, as shown in Figure 11-1.

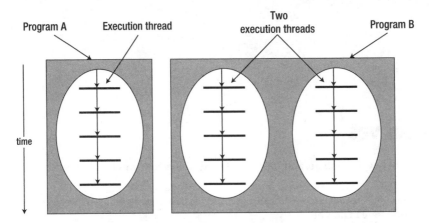

Figure 11-1. *Program A has only one thread, whereas program B has two threads executing concurrently.*

In order to avoid confusion, you must understand that there are two facets to the term thread: a process and an object. The process performs a task, and the task is coded in an object. So, a thread has an execution control that executes an object instantiated from a class that is written following some rules. It will be easy to tell from the context which of these two (the process or the object) I mean when I use the term thread.

In Java, the support for threads is provided by two classes and one interface:

- The java.lang.Thread class
- The java.lang.Object class
- The java.lang.Runnable interface

Even a non-multithreaded program has one thread of execution, called the *main thread*. In a multithreaded program, you can spawn other threads in addition to the main thread. You can write a thread class in one of two ways:

- Extend the java.lang.Thread class
- Implement the Runnable interface

The Object class contains some methods that are used to manage the lifecycle of a thread. You will meet these methods in this chapter. But, first, let's take a look at how a thread is created (defined, instantiated, and started) using the Thread class.

Creating a Thread Using the Thread Class

The execution control in a thread executes the code in an object, which is instantiated from a class written according to some rules. By creating a thread, we mean defining a thread class, instantiating it, and starting the execution. Accomplishing this by using the java.lang.Thread class involves the following three steps:

1. Define the thread by writing your class that extends the Thread class, and by overriding its run() method in your class.

2. Instantiate the thread by instantiating your class, for example, inside a method of another class.

3. Start the thread by executing the start() method that your class inherited from the Thread class.

Listing 11-1 presents a simple but complete example of how to define, instantiate, and start a thread by using the Thread class.

Listing 11-1. *ThreadTest.java*

```
1. public class ThreadTest {
2.   public static void main(String[] args) {
3.         Counter ct = new Counter();
4.         ct.start();
5.         System.out.println("The thread has been started");
6.     }
7. }
8. class Counter extends Thread {
9.   public void run() {
10.     for ( int i=1; i<=5; i++) {
11.         System.out.println("Count: " + i);
12.     }
13.   }
14. }
```

Lines 8 to 14 define a thread in the class Counter, which extends the Thread class. Line 3 instantiates the thread:

```
Counter ct  = new Counter();
```

Line 4 starts the thread:

```
ct.start();
```

Also note that the method run() of the class Thread is overridden in lines 9 through 12. This is where the task to be performed by the thread is coded. Understand that calling the method start() does not immediately execute the thread. It makes the thread a candidate for running, and the thread has to contend for the CPU time (remember, the whole idea of multithreading is to have more threads in one application, and hence they have to share the CPU). Eventually the scheduler will start running the thread by starting the execution of the method run().

■**Caution** Invoking the start() method does not immediately start the thread execution. The scheduler has to schedule the execution of the run() method as a result of the call to the start() method.

So, in Listing 11-1, the main execution thread creates and starts another thread in lines 3 and 4. Without waiting for the control to return back from the method start(), it continues to execute the next line, as both threads are executing concurrently. Therefore, it is possible that when you run this program, the output from line 5 will appear before the output of line 4 (the print statement in line 11), as shown here:

```
The thread has been started
Count: 1
Count: 2
Count: 3
Count: 4
Count: 5
```

Suppose you replace line 4 in Listing 11-1 with the following line:

```
ct.run();
```

In this case, no new thread would be started. The method `run()` will be executed in the main thread. That means the output of line 11 would certainly appear before the output of line 5, because line 5 will be executed only after control is returned from the method `run()` called by line 4. So, the output in this case will certainly be the following:

```
Count: 1
Count: 2
Count: 3
Count: 4
Count: 5
The thread has been started
```

In summary, you put the thread code in the `run()` method and the thread performs the task by executing this method. However, remember two things about the `run()` method:

- If you want the `run()` method to be executed in a separate thread, do not invoke it directly; invoke it by calling the `start()` method.

- For Java, the `run()` method is just another method; so, you can execute it directly, in which case it will be executed in the calling thread and not in its own thread.

As you already know, Java only supports single inheritance. That means if you are subclassing from `Thread`, you cannot subclass from any other class. What if the class that you want to write as type `Thread` also needs to be subclassed from a class other than `Thread`? In that case, we cannot subclass from `Thread` (due to the single inheritance rule). But you can still use the `Thread` facility by implementing the interface `Runnable`.

Creating a Thread Using the Runnable Interface

You have seen in the previous section how to write a thread class by subclassing the `java.lang.Thread` class. But if your thread class already extends another class, it cannot extend the `Thread` class because Java supports only single inheritance. In this case, your thread class can implement the `Runnable` interface. Defining, instantiating, and starting a thread using the `Runnable` interface involves the following four steps:

1. Write your class that implements the `Runnable` interface, and implement the `run()` method of the `Runnable` interface in your class.

2. Instantiate your class, for example, inside a method of another class.

3. Make an object of the `Thread` class by passing your class instance in the argument of the `Thread` constructor. This object is your thread object.

4. Start the thread by invoking the `start()` method on your `Thread` object.

Note that you still use the Thread class in addition to using the Runnable interface, but you use it in a different way. Listing 11-2 presents a simple but complete example of how to define, instantiate, and start a thread by using the Runnable interface.

Listing 11-2. *RunnableTest.java*

```
1. public class RunnableTest {
2.   public static void main(String[] args) {
3.        RunCounter rct = new RunCounter();
4.        Thread th = new Thread(rct);
5.        th.start();
6.        System.out.println("The thread has been started");
7.   }
8. }
9. class RunCounter extends Nothing implements Runnable {
10.   public void run() {
11.     for ( int i=1; i<=5; i++) {
12.     System.out.println("Count: " + i);
13.     }
14. }
15.}
15. class Nothing {
16. }
```

The Runnable interface has just one method, run(),which you implement in your class RunCounter (lines 9 to 15). You actually instantiate the class Thread and pass an instance of your class as an argument (lines 3 and 4) of the constructor, and then call the start() method on the instance of the class Thread. As a result, the run() method that you implemented is executed.

■Note The Runnable interface has only one method: void run(). You must implement this method in your class that implements the Runnable interface.

The output from Listing 11-2 is, for example:

```
The thread has been started
Count: 1
Count: 2
Count: 3
Count: 4
Count: 5
```

This is the same output as you received from Listing 11-1. So, you can accomplish the same task either by writing your thread class by extending the Thread class or by implementing the Runnable interface.

Note that, in Listing 11-2, we instantiated the Thread class by using the constructor Thread(Runnable r) in line 4, one of several constructors of the Thread class. The following is a complete list of the constructors of the Thread class:

- Thread()

- Thread(Runnable target)

- Thread(String name)

- Thread(Runnable target, String name)

- Thread(ThreadGroup group, String name)

- Thread(ThreadGroup group, Runnable target)

- Thread(ThreadGroup group, Runnable target, String name)

- Thread(ThreadGroup group, Runnable target, String name, long stackSize)

A ThreadGroup is a group of threads organized in a tree hierarchy. The details are out of the scope of this book.

■**Caution** When you are using the Runnable interface to create a thread, you start the thread by invoking the start() method on a Thread instance, and not on a Runnable instance.

Now you know how to define, instantiate, and start a thread. But the whole idea of threading is to create multiple threads, which we explore next.

Spawning Multiple Threads

You may need multiple threads to do the same task repeatedly or to do multiple tasks simultaneously. Let's first consider the case in which you want to do the same task again. First note that once the run() method returns, the corresponding thread is considered dead. It cannot be started again. However, you can still call its methods directly (not the start() method); it will run in the thread from which it is called, and not in a new thread. If you want to run the thread again, you have to create a new instance and invoke the start() method on it. In case of Runnable, you can create more than one instances of the class Thread by passing the same instance of your class (that implements Runnable) as an argument to the constructors of the Thread class. As an example, consider Listing 11-3.

Listing 11-3. *MultipleThreads.java*

```
1. public class MultipleThreads {
2.   public static void main(String[] args) {
3.       System.out.println("The main thread of execution started");
4.       RunCounter rct1 = new RunCounter("First Thread");
5.       RunCounter rct2 = new RunCounter("Second Thread");
6.       RunCounter rct3 = new RunCounter("Third Thread");
7.   }
8. }
9. class RunCounter implements Runnable {
10.      Thread myThread;
11.   RunCounter(String name) {
12.      myThread = new Thread(this, name);
13.      myThread.start();
14.   }
15.   public void run() {
16.     for ( int i=1; i<=5; i++) {
17.       System.out.println("Thread: " + myThread.getName() + " Count: " + i);
18.       }
19.   }
20. }
```

Compile and execute this code, and observe in which order the threads execute line 17. Execute the example several times and you will realize that the order is random. This is another demo of the fact that the threads have to go through the scheduler for their execution. Here is a sample output:

```
The main thread of execution started
Thread: First Thread Count: 1
Thread: First Thread Count: 2
Thread: First Thread Count: 3
Thread: First Thread Count: 4
Thread: First Thread Count: 5
Thread: Second Thread Count: 1
Thread: Second Thread Count: 2
Thread: Second Thread Count: 3
Thread: Second Thread Count: 4
Thread: Second Thread Count: 5
Thread: Third Thread Count: 1
Thread: Third Thread Count: 2
Thread: Third Thread Count: 3
Thread: Third Thread Count: 4
Thread: Third Thread Count: 5
```

During its lifetime, a thread goes through several states.

Lifecycle of a Thread: An Overview

A thread's life starts when the method start() is invoked on it. Subsequently, it goes through various states before it finishes its task and is considered dead. Upon calling the start() method, the thread does not start running immediately. The start() method puts it into the runnable state, also called the ready state. It stays in the runnable state until the scheduler puts it into the running state. When the thread goes into the running state, the method run() is called.

■**Caution** When the method start() is invoked on it, a thread does not start running immediately; it has to go through a scheduler.

Even during the execution of the run() method, the thread may temporarily stop executing and go into one of the nonrunning states, and eventually come back to the running state. The various states of a thread are listed here:

- *New*: This is the state of a thread when it has been instantiated but not yet started.

- *Ready/runnable*: A thread enters the runnable state for the first time when the start() method is invoked on the thread instance. Later, the thread can come back to this state from one of the nonrunnable states. In the runnable state, the thread is ready to run and waiting to be selected by the scheduler for running.

- *Running*: This is the state in which the thread is executing.

- *Nonrunnable states*: A thread in the running state may go into one of the three nonrunnable states when it is still alive but not eligible to run. These three states are listed here:
  - *Blocked*: A thread goes into this state when it's waiting for a resource such as I/O or an object's lock. The availability of the resource will send it back to the runnable state. You will learn about the object's lock later in this chapter.
  - *Sleeping*: This state is one of the timed waiting states because the thread stays in this state for a specific time. A thread goes into this state when its code tells it to sleep for a specific period of time by calling the `sleep(…)` method. Expiration of the sleep time sends it back to the runnable state.
  - *Waiting*: The thread goes into the waiting state when the object on which it's running invokes the `wait()` method. A call to `notify()` or `notifyAll()` (by another thread) will bring it back to the runnable state.
- *Dead*: A thread is considered dead after the execution of its `run()` method is complete. A dead thread can never be run as a separate thread again—that is, if you call its `start()` method, you will receive a runtime exception. However, it is still an object, and you can still call its methods (other than the `start()` method), but they will be executed in the caller's thread.

Figure 11-2 shows the relationship among all these states of a thread. A running thread may go into blocked or sleeping state and wait there for an event to happen. When the right event happens, the thread goes to the ready state and eventually is put into the running state again by the scheduler.

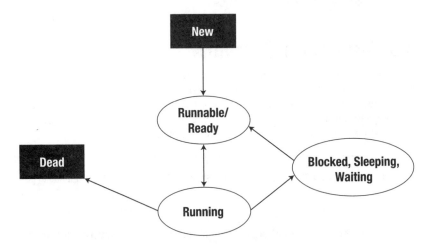

Figure 11-2. *Relationship between different states of a thread*

Now that you have a high-level view of a thread's lifecycle, you need to understand some details of the transition between different lifecycle states.

Understanding Transition Between Thread States

During its lifecycle, a thread goes from state to state. In this section, we examine these transitions. Let's start with the transition between two states: runnable and running.

Transition Between Running and Runnable States

When the start() method is called, it puts the thread into the runnable state. You have seen how to use the start() method in the code listings presented in the previous sections. The scheduler eventually transitions the thread from the runnable state into the running state. A call to the yield() method in the thread code puts the thread back into the runnable state. The yield() method is a static method of the class Thread. Therefore, it must be called as in the following example:

```
Thread.yield();
```

Yielding is important in prioritizing the threads, and especially in a time-consuming thread in order to allow other threads to share the CPU time. Upon a call to the yield() method, a thread goes into the runnable state. After that, one of the following happens:

- If no other threads are waiting for the CPU, the scheduler puts the thread back into the running state immediately.

- If there are other threads waiting for the CPU, then this thread may have to wait for its turn before it cam be put back into the running state.

Although a yield() call is designed to let the other threads with the same priority take their turn, it's not guaranteed that it will happen.

A thread can hop between the runnable and several nonrunnable states.

Transition Between Runnable and Nonrunnable States

There are three nonrunnable states of a thread: sleeping, waiting, and blocked. These states may come in the middle of the runnable and running state.

Sleeping State

A thread is put into the sleeping state by a call to the sleep(…) method in the thread code. The sleep(…) method, like the yield() method, is a static method of the Thread class. After the sleep time expires, the thread goes into the runnable state, and eventually is put back into the running state by the scheduler. The sleep time is passed in as an argument during the method call. The time could be passed in with a precision of milliseconds or nanoseconds. Accordingly, the method sleep(…) is overloaded, and the overloaded version of the method to support the precision of milliseconds is shown here:

```
public static void sleep(long milliseconds) throws InterruptedException { }
```

The method signature for the overloaded version to support the precision of nanoseconds is shown in the following:

```
public static void sleep(long milliseconds, int nanoseconds) throws
        InterruptedException { }
```

■**Caution** When its sleep time expires, a thread does not go directly into the running state. Instead it goes into the runnable state, and the scheduler will eventually put it into the running state. This means that the sleep time passed in during the sleep(…) method call is the minimum time the thread will take to start running again.

You call the method sleep(…) in your code to put the thread to sleep. Why would you do that? One ideal situation to do this would be when the task that the thread is performing is a loop. For example, consider a thread checking the available disk space repeatedly after a specified interval. That interval will be the sleep time.

There are various places in the code that will cause the thread to go to the blocked state by itself.

Blocked State

Sometimes a method has to wait for some event to happen before it can finish. This wait state is called blocking. For example, consider the following code fragment:

```
1. Socket clientSock = new Socket(195.45.3.4,  11000);
2. InputStream in = clientSock.getInputStream();
3. int len = 0;
4. BufferedOutputStream outFile = new BufferedOutputStream(new
        FileOutputStream("response.txt"));
5. byte buf[] = new byte[256];
6.  while ((len = in.read(buf)) != -1)
7.  {
8.      outFile.write(buf, 0, len);
9.  }
```

In this code fragment, we create a client socket and connect it to an application running on port 11000 on the machine with IP address 195.45.3.4 (lines 1 to 5). In line 6, the thread reads from the response of the application (i.e. from the input stream) by using the read(…) method. While this line is being executed, the application may have written nothing into the stream for the client to read. In that case the thread is blocked on method read(…) until there is something in the stream to read. When the blocking condition changes, the thread goes into the ready state and eventually is put into the running state again by the scheduler.

Following are the situations in which a thread may be blocked:

- In Java, all input/output methods are automatically blocked in certain situations.

- A thread is blocked if it fails to acquire the lock for a synchronized piece of code. You will learn about locks later in this chapter, in the section "Synchronization and Locks in Concurrent Access."

Note The sleep(…) and yield() methods are the static methods of the Thread class with return type void.

When a thread is running on an object, that object can put the thread into the waiting state by yelling: wait().

Waiting State

Several threads executing concurrently may share a piece of code. To synchronize a few things, you may put a thread into the waiting state by making a call to the wait() method in the shared code. A thread in the wait state is brought out of this state by a call to the notify() method or the notifyAll() method. The methods wait(), notify(), and notifyAll() are implemented in the Object class, and not in the Thread class. They can only be called in a synchronized piece of code.

Sometimes, you will need a thread to keep waiting until another thread has completed. For example, a thread that will read the data must wait until completion of another thread that copies the data to the place from where it will be read. This is accomplished by using the following over-loaded method of the thread class:

```
void  join();
void join(long millisec);
void join (long millisec, int nanosec);
```

Consider the following code:

```
        Thread  myThread =  new Thread();
myThread.start();
try{
 myThread.join();
}catch (Exception ex){}
```

This code blocks the current thread from becoming runnable until the thread to which myThread refers completes. In other words, the join method joins the current thread to the end of the thread to which myThread refers. The versions of the join method that takes the arguments put the limit on the maximum time the thread has to wait for this thread to complete.

To summarize, remember the following things about the three nonrunnable states:

- You call the sleep(…) method in your code to put the thread to sleep for a specified interval, after which it will automatically get into the runnable state.

- A thread automatically enters a blocked state when it cannot get something immediately that it needs to proceed, e.g. I/O or an object lock.

- You can put a thread into the waiting state by calling the wait() method from a synchronized piece of code.

Because the wait() method is called to maintain synchronization, before you can understand the details of the waiting state, you need to explore the concepts of synchronization and locks.

Synchronization and Locks in Concurrent Access

Because we have multiple threads running within the same program, they have access to the shared resources. For example, consider that one thread is writing into a file, and the other thread is reading from the same file. Multiple threads can access shared resources concurrently because they are running concurrently. This section introduces the concurrent access problem and explores the solution of using *synchronization* implemented by *locks*.

Understanding the Concurrent Access Problem

Because multiple threads can be executed concurrently, two threads may execute the same piece of code concurrently. When that happens, inconsistencies may arise depending upon the nature of the code. For example, consider the following code fragment:

```
1. public class Tracker {
2. private int counter=0;
3. public int nextCounter() {
4.     return counter++;
5. }
6.}
```

Assume that two threads start executing the method nextCounter() of the same object of the class Tracker concurrently. Because they are sharing the CPU time, the order in which they would execute the statements is random. Note that the method nextCounter() is not an atomic action. It involves three steps:

1. Read the instance variable `counter`.

2. Return `counter`.

3. Increment `counter` by one.

Now, consider the following scenario in which two threads, `thread1` and `thread2`, try to execute this method concurrently:

1. `thread1` reads `counter` = 0.

2. `thread2` reads `counter` = 0.

3. `thread1` adds one to the counter and sets `counter` = 1.

4. `thread2` adds one to the counter and sets `counter` = 1.

The final result is

```
counter = 1
```

The correct result should be

```
counter = 2
```

The solution to this problem is that when one thread is executing line 4, any other thread must be prevented from doing so until the first thread has finished. This is called *synchronizing* the access and it can be achieved by using locks on the code that should not be executed concurrently. There are two kinds of locks that can be used to synchronize the access: object locks and class locks.

Object Locks

Java includes the concept of the *monitor*. As the name suggests, the monitor controls access to a Java object. Access to portions of the object code may be made mutually exclusive by using the keyword `synchronized`. When a thread seeks access to a `synchronized` piece of code in a Java object, the monitor provides the access by providing a lock. That object holds the lock until it has finished executing the `synchronized` piece of code. No other thread may acquire the lock before the first thread releases the lock after it is done with the `synchronized` piece of code. The synchronization may be implemented on the code or on the whole method. For example, the code fragment shown previously may be rewritten as follows:

```
1. public class Tracker {
2. private int counter=0;
3. public synchronized int nextCounter() {
4.     return counter++;
5. }
6.}
```

Note the keyword `synchronized` in line 3, which will control access to the method `nextCounter()`. Alternatively, the code fragment may be rewritten as follows:

```
1. public class Tracker {
2. private int counter=0;
3. public int nextCounter() {
4     synchronized(this) {
5.     return counter++;
6.   }
7. }
8.}
```

Note that now the synchronized keyword is inside the method, which would control access to line 5. The expression synchronized(this) (line 4) means the access to this block requires the lock of this object (in this case it refers to the object of the class Tracker). So, the following is the syntax for synchronizing a block of code inside a method:

```
synchronized (<object>) {
// code goes here.
}
```

The <object> specifies the name of the object whose lock is needed for accessing this code. Most commonly, it is the object of the class in which this method exists. However, it is possible to require an object lock of an external class—that is, the class other than the class in which this synchronized block exists.

Note the following about the object locks:

- Every instance of a class (that is, object) has its own lock, called object lock.

- Every object has one and only one object lock.

- When a thread of execution wants to enter a synchronized piece of code in the object, it must acquire the object lock.

- When a thread has acquired an object lock, no other thread can acquire it until the previous thread releases the lock.

When a thread is seeking a lock and the lock is already held by another thread, the seeking thread waits until the lock becomes available. The programmer does not need to do programming for this. This is already built into Java. You, the programmer, just need to declare which piece of code is synchronized by using the synchronized keyword.

As you have seen in this section, you can protect the instance variables by using the object locks. To protect the static variables whose scope is the whole class, you need the class locks.

Class Locks

It makes sense for every object of a class to have its own lock, because the data of one object belongs to only that object and not to any other object of the same class. However, this is not true for the static data. If you change the value of a static variable in one object, the change will be visible to all other objects as well. Therefore, the object lock will not do the job for static variables. For this reason, every class has a class lock that controls access to the synchronized static code of the class. For example, consider the following code fragment:

```
class GlobalTracker {
    static count = 0;
     public static synchronized  int counter() {
            return count++;
        }
}
```

Suppose we call the counter() method from two different objects of the GlobalTracker class. They cannot acquire the lock at the same time because they are competing for the class lock and there is only one class lock. And that makes sense, because the static variable, which in this case is protected by the class lock, belongs to the class, and not any one object.

For example, if there is one class and five instances of the class, there will be one class lock and five object locks. That means at most there might be one thread that can have the class lock and five threads that can have the object locks (one each) at the same time.

Instead of synchronizing the whole method, you can also synchronize just a code block in the method. For example the counter() method in the preceding example can be replaced with the following:

```
public static synchronized  int counter() {
  // code
        synchronized(GlobalTracker.class) {
          return count++;
        }
  // Some more code
  }
```

Note the expression GlobalTracker.class in this code. Java offers a java.lang.Class class whose instances represent classes in a running application. The expression GlobalTracker.class means get an instance of the class Class that represent the GlobalTracker class. It is this instance of the Class class whose lock is used to synchronize the static method or a code block in the method.

While a thread is executing a synchronized piece of code, it may encounter the wait() method, which will put it into the wait state.

Monitoring the Wait State

As discussed previously, multiple threads in a program can have synchronized access to a shared piece of code in an object by using the object lock. The shared object may put a thread into the *wait* state by making a call to the wait() method. A thread in the wait state is brought out of this state by a call to the notify() method, or the notifyAll() method. Note the following about the methods wait(), notify(), and notifyAll():

- They are implemented in the Object class, and not in the Thread class.

- They can only be called in a synchronized piece of code.

■**Caution** The methods wait(), notify(), and notifyAll() are implemented in the Object class, and not in the Thread class. They can only be called from inside a synchronized piece of code.

When a thread encounters a wait() call in an object, the following happens:

- The thread gives up the CPU.

- The thread gives up the lock on the object.

- The thread goes into the object's waiting pool.

When a notify() call is made from inside the same object, the following happens:

- One arbitrarily chosen thread out of the waiting pool is put into the seeking lock state.

- After it obtains the lock, the thread is put into the runnable state.

When a notifyAll() call is made, all threads in the waiting pool of the object are put into the seeking lock state. As an example, consider Listing 11-4.

Listing 11-4. *TestCouponMachine.java*

```
1. public class TestCouponMachine {
2.  public static void main(String[] args) {
3.   //create the coupon machine.
4.     CouponMachine cm = new CouponMachine();
5.     Consumer[] con = new Consumer[5];
6.     for (int i=0; i<5; i++) {
7.         con[i] = new Consumer(cm);
8.         con[i].start();
9.  }
10.        Producer prod = new Producer(cm);
11.        prod.start();
12.           System.out.println("The main thread: All threads have been launched!");
13.  }
14. }
15.
16. class Producer extends Thread {
17.    int count =0;
18.    CouponMachine cpm;
19.    Producer(CouponMachine cpm) {
20.      this.cpm = cpm;
21.    }
22. public void run() {
23.    for (int i=0; i<5; i++){
24.    cpm.createCoupon(++count);
25.    System.out.println("Coupon produced: " + count);
26.  }
27. }
28.}
29.
30. class Consumer extends Thread {
31.    int count;
32.    CouponMachine cpm;
33.    Consumer (CouponMachine cpm) {
34.      this.cpm = cpm;
35.    }
36. public void run() {
37.    count=cpm.consumeCoupon();
38.    System.out.println("Coupon consumed: " + count);
39. }
40. }
41.
42. class CouponMachine {
43. private int couponID;
44. private boolean  couponExists =  false;
45.
46. public synchronized void createCoupon(int coup) {
47.   while(couponExists) {
48.   try {
49.        wait ();
50.   } catch (Exception e) {
51.       System.out.println("Exception: " + e);
52.   }
53.   }
```

```
54.        this.couponID =  coup;
55.        couponExists = true;
56.        notify();
57. }
58.
59. public synchronized int consumeCoupon() {
60.   while(!couponExists) {
61.     try {
62.          wait();
63.     } catch (Exception e) {
64.         System.out.println("Exception: " + e);
65.     }
66.   }
67.        couponExists = false;
68.        notify();
69.        return couponID;
70.  }
71.}
```

This is a rather involved example, but it clarifies a number of thread-related concepts. The class CouponMachine (lines 42 to 71) may have at maximum one coupon, represented by couponID, at a time. When the class is instantiated, there is no coupon in it—that is, the boolean variable couponExists is set to false. A consumer thread may call the consumeCoupon() (line 59) method at any time. If the coupon does not exist, the thread will be put into the waiting state. A producer thread may call the method createCoupon() (line 46) at any time. If the coupon does not exist, the producer thread creates the coupon, and makes a notify() call (lines 24 and 56). This call puts one of the waiting consumer threads (if any) out of the waiting state. The consumer thread will consume the coupon, set the boolean variable couponExists to false, and make the notify() call. The notify() call will bring the waiting producer thread (if any) out of the waiting state.

This ensures that, in our example, the coupons are produced and consumed with coupon ID in ascending order. It should not matter if we start the producer thread first or the consumer thread first. In this example, we start five consumer threads (lines 5 through 9) first. Then we start a producer thread (line 10 and 11). The producer thread (represented by the class Producer) makes five calls to the method createCoupon() of the class CouponMachine, and therefore is launched to create five coupons. There are five consumer threads (represented by the class Consumer) that would consume the coupons.

An example of the output of Listing 11-4 follows:

```
The main thread: All threads have been launched!
Coupon produced: 1
Coupon consumed: 1
Coupon produced: 2
Coupon consumed: 2
Coupon produced: 3
Coupon consumed: 3
Coupon produced: 4
Coupon consumed: 4
Coupon produced: 5
Coupon consumed: 5
```

Remember that the output depends upon in which order the threads get the CPU time to run. Getting out of the waiting state does not make the thread start running immediately, as you already know. It has to seek the lock on the object and then seek the CPU time (that is, the running state). For this reason, you may also occasionally see output like the following:

```
Coupon produced: 1
Coupon produced: 2
Coupon consumed: 1
Coupon consumed: 2
```

■**Caution** You cannot invoke the notify() method on a specific thread. A call to notify() will put one thread out of the waiting state, but you cannot specify which one if more than one thread is in the waiting pool.

Table 11-1 lists the methods discussed in this section along with the methods discussed in other sections of this chapter that play important roles in the lifecycle of a thread.

Table 11-1. *Important Methods that Play a Role in the Lifecycle of a Thread*

Method	Lives in the Class	Called
void start()	Thread	In the code that launches the thread
static void sleep(long millisec) static void sleep(long millisec, int nanosec)	Thread	In this thread's code
static void yield()	Thread	In this thread's code
wait()	Object	In the code of the object shared by threads, and on which this thread is running
notify()	Object	By another thread
notifyAll()	Object	By another thread

You can use all of these methods to control the lifecycle of a thread. However, you need to realize that there is one very important player of this game out of your direct control, and that is called the scheduler.

Scheduling Threads

You can use methods to help a thread get into the runnable state, but you cannot directly put the thread into the running state. A thread in the runnable state is eventually put into the running state by the scheduler. The scheduler follows some kind of algorithm to determine which thread should go into the running state (i.e. how multiple threads should share the CPU time). Generally speaking, there are two main categories of scheduling algorithms:

- *Preemptive scheduling:* A thread is put into the running state according to the priority. While a thread is running, it can be moved out of the running state only by one of the following conditions:

  - It calls one of the blocking I/O methods.
  - A higher-priority thread gets into the runnable state.

- *Time sharing:* A thread is allowed to execute only for a limited amount of time. After the time expires, it's put back into the runnable state, and another thread seeking its turn is put into the running state. Time sharing provides protection against a higher-priority thread using the whole CPU time and keeping all other threads from running.

Remember that the implementation of the scheduling algorithm in Java is platform dependent. Scheduling is performed to share a resource (the CPU) among multiple threads. Other resources in an application, such as a file, are shared properly by synchronizing the access, as you have already seen. However, sharing the same resource makes threads dependent upon each other, and that dependency may give rise to a deadlock.

Understanding the Deadlocks

A *deadlock* is a situation in which two or more processes are waiting indefinitely for an event to happen, and that event can only be caused by one of these waiting processes, but none of these processes can cause that event because they are in a wait state. In a multithreaded environment, because multiple threads are running concurrently, the deadlock is possible. Several situations can give rise to a deadlock. This section discusses a very simple situation, coded in Listing 11-5, in which two threads, t1 and t2, are sharing the resources resourceA and resourceB. These threads access these resources in reverse order (lines 5 and 6). Thread t1 seeks a lock on obj1 and then on obj2, while thread t2 seeks a lock on obj2 and then on obj1 (lines 5, 6, and 20 through 28). Although the lock access code that is executed for each thread is the same (lines 20 through 28), resourceA means obj1 for thread t1 and obj2 for thread t2, and resourceB means obj2 for thread t1 and obj1 for thread t2 due to lines 5, 6, 16, and 17.

Listing 11-5. *DeadLockTest.java*

```
1. public class DeadLockTest {
2.    public static void main(String[] args) {
3.      Object obj1 = "objectA";
4.      Object obj2 = "objectB";
5.      DeadLock t1 = new DeadLock(obj1, obj2);
6.      DeadLock t2 = new DeadLock(obj2, obj1);
7.      t1.start();
8.        t2.start();
9.        System.out.println("The threads have been started");
10.  }
11. }
12. class DeadLock extends Thread {
13.    private Object resourceA;
14.    private Object resourceB;
15.  public DeadLock(Object a, Object b){
16.    resourceA = a;
17.    resourceB = b;
18.  }
19.  public void run() {
20.    while (true) {
21.      System.out.println("The thread " + Thread.currentThread().getName()
                + " waiting for a lock on " + resourceA);
22.      synchronized (resourceA){
23.       System.out.println("The thread " + Thread.currentThread().getName()
                + " received a lock on " + resourceA);
24.       System.out.println("The thread " + Thread.currentThread().getName()
                + " waiting for a lock on " + resourceB);
25.        synchronized (resourceB){
26.          System.out.println("The thread " +
                Thread.currentThread().getName() + " received a lock on " +
                resourceB);
```

```
27.        try{
28.            Thread.sleep(500);
29.            }catch (Exception e){}
30..    }
31.    }
32.    }
33.  }
34. }
```

When you execute this code, the output is not deterministic. However, it is easy to see from lines 20 through 30 that eventually a deadlock will happen because t1 will not release a lock on obj1 until it receives a lock on obj2, whereas t2 will not release a lock on obj2 until it receives a lock on obj1. Following is one of the outputs that you may receive:

```
The threads have been started
The thread Thread-0 waiting for a lock on objectA
The thread Thread-0 received a lock on objectA
The thread Thread-1 waiting for a lock on objectB
The thread Thread-0 waiting for a lock on objectB
The thread Thread-1 received a lock on objectB
The thread Thread-1 waiting for a lock on objectA
```

This output indicates that t1 (Thread-0) has a lock on obj1 (ObjectA), and is waiting for a lock on obj2 (objectB), while t2 (Thread-1) has a lock on obj2 and is waiting for a lock on obj1. Therefore we have a deadlock situation. For the exam, you must be able to detect a situation in the code that can give rise to a deadlock. There are several design techniques that you can use to help avoid deadlocks in your code, but they are beyond the scope of this book.

Codewalk Quicklet

The code for the codewalk quicklet exercise in this chapter is presented in Listing 11-6.

Listing 11-6. *CodeWalkTen.java*

```
1. class CodeWalkTen {
2.  public static void main(String [] args) {
3.    Thread myThread = new Thread(new
            MyThreadClass(Thread.currentThread()));
4.    myThread.start();
5.    System.out.print("after_start ");
6.    myThread.run();
7.    System.out.print("Dead_thread ");
8.  }
9. }

10. class MyThreadClass implements Runnable {
11.    Thread mine;
12.    MyThreadClass(Thread mine) { this.mine = mine; }
13.    public void run() {
14.        System.out.print("In_run ");
15.    }
16. }
```

To get you started on this exercise, following are some hints:

- *Input*: Lines 3 and 11.
- *Operations*: Line 4.
- *Output*: Lines 5, 7, and 14.
- *Rule*: Creating a thread using the Runnable interface. Can you run the same thread twice?

Looking at the code from this angle, see if you can handle the last question in the "Review Questions" section based on this code.

The three most important takeaways from this chapter are the following:

- Creating a thread involves writing a class that either extends the Thread class or implements the Runnable interface.
- During its lifecycle, a thread goes through various states such as waiting, blocked, sleep, runnable, and running. You can use some methods to control the lifecycle, such as sleep(…), wait(), and notify().
- Before transitioning to the running state, a thread has to go through the scheduler, over which you have no control.

Summary

A Java thread is an object that runs in its own thread of execution, and an application may have multiple threads running concurrently. A thread may be defined, instantiated, and executed in one of two ways: extending the Thread class or implementing the Runnable interface. In both cases, your thread is an instance of the Thread class. You start the thread by invoking the start() method, which will put the thread into the runnable state, and the scheduler will move the thread from the runnable state to the running state, in which it will execute the run() method. The run() method contains the code for the task that the thread will perform. While running, the thread can come back to the runnable state by executing the yield() method.

A running thread can also go into various nonrunnable states: sleeping, waiting, and blocked. It will go into the sleeping state by executing the sleep(…) method in its code, and go back to the runnable state after the sleep time expires. It goes into the waiting state when an object on which it is running invokes the wait() method, and it comes out of the waiting state into the runnable state by a notify() or notifyAll() call from the object. You cannot specify which of the waiting methods a notify() call will wake up. The notifyAll() call will wake up all the methods in the waiting pool of the object that makes the call. The methods start(), run(), sleep(…), and yield() belong to the Thread class, while the methods wait(), notify(), and notifyAll() belong to the Object class.

A thread needs a lock to execute the synchronized code. Each object of a class has one and only one object lock that is used to protect the instance variables. Each class has a class lock that is used to protect the class variables. Only one thread can have a given lock at a given time; no other thread can get this lock before the thread that has it releases it.

EXAM'S EYE VIEW

Comprehend

- When the sleep(…) method is invoked, the sleep time passed in as an argument in the method call is the minimum time the thread will take to start running again, because the thread will have to go through scheduling.

- The methods wait(), notify(), and notifyAll() are implemented in the Object class, and not in the Thread class. They can only be called from inside a synchronized piece of code.

- You cannot invoke the notify() method on a specific thread. A call to notify() will put one thread out of the wait state, but you cannot specify which one if more than one thread is in the waiting pool.

Look Out

- When you are using the Runnable interface to create a thread, you start the thread by invoking the start() method on a Thread instance, and not on a Runnable instance.

- You call the method sleep(…) or yield() in the thread code, but you do not call methods such as wait(), notify(), or notifyAll() in the thread code.

- A yield() call is intended to give another thread with the same priority a chance to run. But there is no guarantee that this will happen.

- Upon calling the start() method, a thread does not start running immediately; it has to go through a scheduler.

Memorize

- The Runnable interface has only one method: void run().

- All the constructors of the Thread class.

Review Questions

1. Which method is used to perform interthread communications? (Choose all that apply.)

A. `yield()`

B. `sleep(…)`

C. `notify()`

D. `wait()`

2. Which of the following are the methods of the `Object` class? (Choose all that apply.)

A. `yield()`

B. `sleep(…)`

C. `run()`

D. `wait()`

E. `notify()`

3. Consider the following code fragment:

```
1. public class ThreadTest {
2.   public static void main(String[] args) {
3.       Counter ct = new Counter();
4.       ct.start();
5.       System.out.println("The thread has been started");
6.   }
7. }
8. class Counter extends Thread {
9. protected void run() {
10.    System.out.println("Hello");
11.  }
12. }
```

What would be the output of this code fragment? (Choose all that apply.)

A. The thread has been started.
   Hello

B. Hello
   The thread has been started.

C. Either A or B

D. Compiler error on line 9

4. What is true about the `wait()` method? (Choose all that apply.)

A. A thread calls the `wait()` method to temporarily stop another thread from running.

B. When a thread executes a call to the `wait()` method, it itself stops executing temporarily.

C. A call to `wait()` stops the application from executing.

D. The `wait()` method belongs to the `Object` class.

E. The `wait()` method belongs to the `Thread` class.

5. Consider the following code:

```
1. public  class ThreadOrder {
2.     static int count=0;
3.   public static void main(String[] args) {
4.      Counter ct = new Counter();
5.      Tracker trk1 = new Tracker(ct, "thread one");
6.       Tracker trk2 = new Tracker(ct, "thread two");
7.        trk1.start();
8.        trk2.start();
9.  }
10.}

11. class Tracker extends Thread {
12.    Counter ct;
13.    String message;
14.    Tracker(Counter ct, String msg) {
15.       this.ct = ct;
16.       message = msg;
17.    }
18.   public void run() {
19.     System.out.println(message);
20.  }
21. }

22. class Counter {
23.   private int count=0;
24.   public  int nextCounter() {
25.        synchronized(this) {
26.           count++;
27.           return count;
28.        }
29.    }
30. }
```

What would be the output of this code fragment? (Choose all that apply.)

A. thread one
   thread two

B. thread two
   thread one

C. Sometimes A, sometimes B

D. Runtime exception on line 8

6. What would happen when a thread executes the following statement in its run() method? (Choose all that apply.)

```
sleep(500);
```

A. It is going to stop execution, and start executing exactly 500 milliseconds later.

B. It is going to stop execution, and start executing again not earlier than 500 milliseconds later.

C. It is going to result in a compiler error because you cannot call the sleep(…) method inside the run() method.

D. It is going to result in a compiler error because the sleep(…) method does not take any argument.

7. A thread thr is waiting along with some other threads in the waiting pool. How could the method notify() be used to put this thread out of the wait state?

    A. Execute thr.notify() from a synchronized piece of code.

    B. Execute notify(thr) from a synchronized piece of code.

    C. With notify(), you cannot specify which thread would be put out of the wait state.

8. Which of the following methods guarantee to put a thread out of the running state?

    A. wait()

    B. yield()

    C. sleep(500)

    D. kill()

    E. notify()

9. Which of the following are the valid Thread constructors?

    A. Thread()

    B. Thread(int millisec)

    C. Thread(Runnable r)

    D. Thread(Runnable r, String name)

    E. Thread(int priority)

10. Which of the following are the methods defined in the Thread class? (Choose all that apply.)

    A. yield()

    B. sleep(…)

    C. run()

    D. wait()

    E. notify()

11. Given the code in Listing 11-6, what is the result?

    A. after_start In_run Dead_thread

    B. after_start In_run Dead_thread In_run

    C. after_start In_run In_run

    D. Exception thrown at runtime

PART 4

■■■

Appendixes

APPENDIX A

■■■

Installing and Testing J2SE 5.0

The purpose of this appendix is to help you set up the J2SE 5.0 (Java 2 Standard Edition version 5) development environment that you will use to write, compile, and execute Java programs. This appendix shows you exactly what software you need to install, how to set up the development environment, and how to write, compile, and execute a simple Java program. J2SE 5.0 supports the following operating systems: Solaris, Linux, and Microsoft Windows. The example used in this appendix for setting up a development environment is for Windows XP, but the procedure on other platforms is very similar.

Installing the Required Java Software

From the Java Development Kit (JDK) versions listed in Table A-1 for different platforms, you need to obtain the appropriate version for your machine. You can download J2SE 5.0 from the Sun web site: `http://java.sun.com/j2se/1.5.0/download.jsp`.

Table A-1. *JDK Versions Available for Different Platforms*

Platform	32-Bit Installation	64-Bit Installation
Linux	JDK for Linux	JDK for Linux 64-bit
Microsoft Windows	JDK for Windows	JDK for Windows 64-bit
Solaris Operating System Solaris 8, Solaris 9, and Solaris 10	JDK for Solaris	JDK for Solaris 64-bit

This web page offers multiple download options such as the J2SE Runtime Environment (JRE) to execute existing Java applications, and *NetBeans*, which contains an integrated development environment. For this book, I recommend that you just download JDK 5.0.

After you download the executable file, double-click the file and specify the root directory for installation when the installer asks for it. As shown in Figure A-1 (obtained from installation on Windows XP), the installer will prepare the InstallShield Wizard to guide you through the installation process, which is actually pretty simple and automated.

When the InstallShield Wizard gives you the choice to change the installation directory, I recommend that you do change the directory, because the default installation directory path it presents contains spaces in the name, such as `Program Files`. I assume that the root directory for your installation is `C:\jdk5.0`.

By installing the JDK, you have already started to set up the development environment. The next task is to set up the development environment variables.

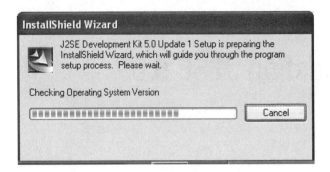

Figure A-1. *This screen is presented when you double-click the JDK executable that you downloaded.*

Setting Up the Development Environment Variables

To compile and execute Java programs successfully and conveniently on your computer, you need to understand two environment variables, PATH and CLASSPATH:

- PATH: When you issue a command on your machine, the operating system searches for the corresponding executable in directories listed in the value of the PATH variable. The executable files corresponding to the commands that you issue to compile a Java program (javac) and execute it (java) exist in the C:\jdk5.0\bin directory. So, this directory must be included in the value of the PATH variable, and you can do that by issuing the following command:

      set PATH=%PATH%;C:\jdk5.0\bin

  If you specify the full path of the commands javac and java, you will not need to set the PATH variable. However, it's a good idea to set it for convenience.

- CLASSPATH: This variable is used by the compiler and the java command to find class files. By default, the java command looks for the class file in the directory in which you are issuing the command. If the java command does not find the class file in the current directory, it searches directories listed in the value of the CLASSPATH variable. The syntax for setting the CLASSPATH variable is the same as for setting the PATH variable:

      set CLASSPATH=<Semicolon-separated list of directories>

  If you are issuing the java command from the directory where the class file that you want to execute exists, then you don't need to define the CLASSPATH variable. However, CLASSPATH and the package are related to each other, and their combined effect is discussed in Chapter 4.

Now that you have set up the environment variables PATH and, optionally, CLASSPATH, you are ready to develop, compile, and execute a simple Java program.

Writing, Compiling, and Executing a Java Program

This exercise walks you through the process of writing, compiling, and executing a simple Java program. It assumes that you copied the scjp folder (which you can downloaded from the Source Code area of the Apress website (www.apress.com)) to your C drive. There, you will find the SCJP.java file with the following path:

    C:\scjp\code\test\SCJP.java

This file has a very short program:

```
class SCJP {
  public static void main(String[] args){
          System.out.println("Here I come, SCJP!");
  }
}
```

You can write this file from scratch by following these simple steps:

1. Edit a new file with a text editor such as Notepad.

2. Type the preceding code into the file.

3. Save the file as SCJP.java, as shown in Figure A-2.

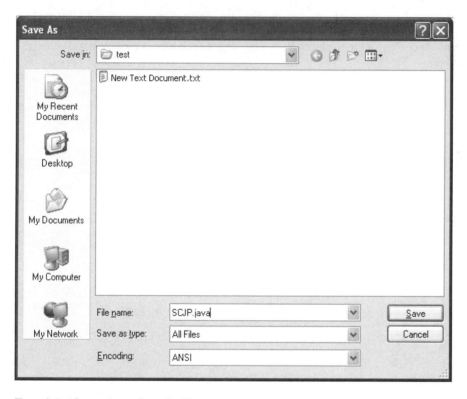

Figure A-2. *After typing code in the file, save it with the extension .java and choose All Files in the Save As Type drop-down list.*

The next step is to compile the java source file SCJP.java with the javac command:

```
javac  SCJP.java
```

This command generates the SCJP.class, which you can execute with the java command:

```
java SCJP
```

These commands and the output are shown in Figure A-3.

Figure A-3. *Compiling and executing the Java program that exists in the SCJP.java file*

Congratulations! You have set up the Java development environment and tested it. This environment is good enough to try the examples in the book and in the practice exam. You can download the source files for these examples from the Source Code area of the Apress website (www.apress.com).

■■■

SCJP 5.0 Upgrade Exam (CX-310-056)

The Sun Certified Programmer for the Java 2 Platform, Standard Edition 5.0 exam (CX-310-055), popularly known as the Sun Certified Java Programmer (SCJP) exam for Java 5, can be taken by candidates who do not have any Java certification as well as by those who already have passed the previous version of the SCJP exam. As an alternative, Sun offers the upgrade exam (CX-310-056) for those candidates who already have passed the previous version of the SCJP exam. This appendix presents information and analysis for those exam candidates who already have the SCJP certification for a previous version of the SCJP exam and are wondering whether they should take the SCJP exam for J2SE 5.0 or the upgrade exam. The purpose of this appendix is to help you decide which exam you want to take. To meet that end, this appendix performs the following three tasks:

- Present the information about the upgrade exam, CX-310-056
- Compare the upgrade exam with the regular exam, CX-310-055
- Link the upgrade exam objectives to the chapters in the book where they are covered

Essential Information About the Upgrade Exam

Following is the basic information about the upgrade exam:

- Delivered at: Authorized Worldwide Prometric Testing Centers
- Prerequisites: Successful completion of previous version of Sun Certified Programmer for Java 2 Platform exam
- Other exams/assignments required for this certification: None
- Exam type: Multiple choice and drag and drop
- Number of questions: 46
- Pass score: 58% (27 of 46 questions)
- Time limit: 105 minutes

Before you decide which exam to take (regular or upgrade), it's a good idea to compare the two.

Comparison Between the Regular and Upgrade Exams

Table B-1 presents a comparison between different features of the regular and upgrade exams.

Table B-1. *Comparison Between the Features of the Regular Exam and Upgrade Exam*

Item	Regular Exam	Upgrade Exam
Exam number	CX-310-055	CX-310-056
Prerequisite	None	Previous version of the exam (for example, SCJP for J2SE 1.4)
Price (in U.S. $)	$150.00	$100.00
Exam type	Multiple choice and drag and drop	Multiple choice and drag and drop
Number of questions	72	46
Number of questions required to be answered correctly to pass	43 of 72 (59.72%)	27 of 46 (58.70%)
Time limit (minutes)	175 (2.43 minutes per question)	105 (2.28 minutes per question)
Number of exam objectives	37	26

Note that there is a significant difference in the number of questions that you are asked: 46 in the upgrade exam compared to 72 in the regular exam. However, the time allowed per question and the percentage pass score are about the same for the two exams. Furthermore, you save $50 if you take the upgrade exam as opposed to the regular exam.

Common sense may demand that the upgrade exam should cover only the new features of the regular exam—that is, the topics that were not covered in the previous version of the exam but are covered in the new version of the regular exam. However, that is not the case, as the next section makes clear.

Upgrade Exam Objectives: Where Are They Covered?

The upgrade exam topics are listed in Table B-2, and the exam objectives for each topic are listed in Table B-3, which also links the exam objectives to the chapters in the book where they are covered. These tables can be helpful if you decide to take the upgrade exam.

Table B-2. *Upgrade Exam Topics*

Section	Topic
1	Declarations, Initialization and Scoping
2	Flow Control
3	API Contents
4	Concurrency
5	OO Concepts
6	Collections/Generics
7	Fundamentals

Table B-3. *Upgrade Exam Objectives and the Chapters in the Book Where They Are Covered*

Exam Objectives	Chapter Number
1.1 Develop code that declares classes (including abstract and all forms of nested classes), interfaces, and enums, and includes the appropriate use of package and import statements (including static imports).	2, 3
1.2 Develop code that declares, initializes, and uses primitives, arrays, enums, and objects as static, instance, and local variables. Also, use legal identifiers for variable names.	
1.3 Develop code that declares both static and non-static methods, and–if appropriate–use method names that adhere to the JavaBeans naming standards. Also develop code that declares and uses a variable-length argument list.	
1.4 Given a code example, determine if a method is correctly overriding or overloading another method, and identify legal return values (including covariant returns), for the method.	
1.5 Given a set of classes and superclasses, develop constructors for one or more of the classes. Given a class declaration, determine if a default constructor will be created, and if so, determine the behavior of that constructor. Given a nested or non-nested class listing, write code to instantiate the class.	
2.1 Develop code that implements an if or switch statement; and identify legal argument types for these statements.	6
2.2 Develop code that implements all forms of loops and iterators, including the use of for, the enhanced for loop (for-each), do, while, labels, break, and continue; and explain the values taken by loop counter variables during and after loop execution.	
2.3 Develop code that makes use of exceptions and exception handling clauses (try, catch, finally), and declares methods and overriding methods that throw exceptions.	7
2.4 Recognize situations that will result in any of the following being thrown: ArrayIndexOutOfBoundsException, ClassCastException, IllegalArgumentException, IllegalStateException, NullPointerException, NumberFormatException, AssertionError, ExceptionInInitializerError, StackOverflowError or NoClassDefFoundError. Understand which of these are thrown by the virtual machine and recognize situations in which others should be thrown programatically.	
3.1 Develop code that uses the primitive wrapper classes (such as Boolean, Character, Double, Integer, etc.), and/or autoboxing & unboxing. Discuss the differences between the String, StringBuilder, and StringBuffer classes.	9, 10 (for autoboxing)
3.2 Given a scenario involving navigating file systems, reading from files, or the correct solution using the following classes (sometimes in combination), from java.io: BufferedReader, BufferedWriter, File, FileReader, FileWriter and PrintWriter.	8
3.3 Develop code that serializes and/or de-serializes objects using the following APIs from java.io: DataInputStream, DataOutputStream, FileInputStream, FileOutputStream, ObjectInputStream, ObjectOutputStream and Serializable.	
3.4 Use standard J2SE APIs in the java.text package to correctly format or parse dates, numbers, and currency values for a specific locale; and, given a scenario, determine the appropriate methods to use if you want to use the default locale or a specific locale. Describe the purpose and use of the java.util.Locale class.	9
3.5 Write code that uses standard J2SE APIs in the java.util and java.util.regex packages to format or parse strings or streams. For strings, write code that uses the Pattern and Matcher classes and the String.split method. Recognize and use regular expression patterns for matching (limited to: . (dot), * (star), + (plus), ?, \d, \s, \w, [], ()). The use of *, +, and ? will be limited to greedy quantifiers, and the parenthesis operator will only be used as a grouping mechanism, not for capturing content during matching. For streams, write code using the Formatter and Scanner classes and the PrintWriter.format/printf methods. Recognize and use formatting parameters (limited to: %b, %c, %d, %f, %s) in format strings.	

continued

Table B-3. *Continued*

Exam Objectives	Chapter Number
4.1 Write code to define, instantiate, and start new threads using both java.lang.Thread and java.lang.Runnable.	11
4.2 Recognize the states in which a thread can exist, and identify ways in which a thread can transition from one state to another.	
5.1 Develop code that implements tight encapsulation, loose coupling, and high cohesion in classes, and describe the benefits.	5
5.2 Given a scenario, develop code that demonstrates the use of polymorphism. Further, determine when casting will be necessary and recognize compiler vs. runtime errors related to object reference casting.	
5.3 Explain the effect of modifiers on inheritance with respect to constructors, instance or static variables, and instance or static methods.	4
5.4 Given a scenario, develop code that declares and/or invokes overrideen or overloaded methods and code that declares and/or invokes superclass, overridden, or overloaded constructors.	5
6.1 Given a design scenario, determine which collection classes and/or interfaces should be used to properly implement that design, including the use of the Comparable interface.	10
6.2 Write code that uses the generic versions of the Collections API, in particular, the Set, List, and Map interfaces and implementation classes. Recognize the limitations of the non-generic Collections API and how to refactor code to use the generic versions.	
6.3 Develop code that makes proper use of type parameters in class/interface declarations, instance variables, method arguments, and return types; and write generic methods or methods that make use of wildcard types and understand the similarities and differences between these two approaches.	
6.4 Use capabilities in the java.util package to write code to manipulate a list by sorting, performing a binary search, or converting the list to an array. Use capabilities in the java.util package to write code to manipulate an array by sorting, performing a binary search, or converting the array to a list. Use the java.util.Comparator and java.lang.Comparable interfaces to affect the sorting of lists and arrays. Furthermore, recognize the effect of the "natural ordering" of primitive wrapper classes and java.lang.String on sorting.	
7.1 Given a code example and a scenario, write code that uses the appropriate access modifiers, package declarations, and import statements to interact with (through access or inheritance) the code in the example.	4
7.2 Given the fully-qualified name of a class that is deployed inside and/or outside a JAR file, construct the appropriate directory structure for that class. Given a code example and a classpath, determine whether the classpath will allow the code to compile successfully.	

As you can notice from Table B-2, the upgrade exam covers more than just the new features introduced in J2SE 5.0.

APPENDIX C

■■■

Answers to Chapter Review Questions

Chapter 2: Data Types and Operators

1. **Answer**: B and C

   B is invalid because it starts with a number, and C is invalid because it is a keyword and thus cannot be a variable name. The first character of an identifier must be a letter, a dollar sign ($), or an underscore (_).

2. **Answer**: E

   The data type short is signed and 16 bits in size.

3. **Answer**: A

   The data type char is unsigned and 16 bits in size.

4. **Answer**: C

   The data type byte is unsigned and 16 bits in size.

5. **Answer**: A and E

   B, C, and D will have compiler errors because a char literal is represented by a single character enclosed in single quotes unless it's being represented as a Unicode value.

6. **Answer**: B

   A boolean type is initialized to false by default.

7. **Answer**: C

   The value 1.25 is a double, and therefore cannot be assigned to a float variable.

8. **Answer**: A

   If the increment (or decrement) operator is followed by the operand (e.g. ++x), then it operates before the operand takes part in the rest of the expression. On the other hand, if the operand is followed by the operator (e.g. x++), then the operand takes part in the expression before the operator operates on it.

9. **Answer**: B

   If the increment (or decrement) operator is followed by the operand (e.g. ++x), then it operates before the operand takes part in the rest of the expression. On the other hand, if the operand is followed by the operator (e.g. x++), then the operand takes part in the expression before the operator operates on it.

10. **Answer**: B, C, and D

    The ! operator cannot be applied to an int, and the >> operator cannot be applied to a double. The operator ^ is not a unitary operator.

11. **Answer**: C

    By arithmetic promotion, the right side of line 4 would be an integer. An integer cannot be assigned to a byte without explicit conversion.

12. **Answer**: B

The result of a % operation gets the sign of the numerator.

13. **Answer**: A

```
    21 = 00010101
^  13 = 00001101
   --------------------
    00011000 = 24
```

The OR operation would produce 00011101 = 29.

14. **Answer**: B

In an OR (||) test, if the first condition is true, the second condition is not tested. In an AND (&&) test, if the first condition is true, the second condition will also be tested.

15. **Answer**: D

In an OR (||) test, if the first condition is true, the second condition is not tested. In an AND (&&) test, if the first condition is false, the second condition will not be tested.

16. **Answer**: E

E is the correct answer because the ternary test in line 4 fails, and as a result counts[1] is set equal to 99, which is printed in line 5.

Chapter 3: Classes, Methods, and Interfaces

1. **Answer**: C

The default constructor is provided by the compiler.

2. **Answer**: B

D is incorrect because MyNestedClass is static and cannot belong to a specific instance of the outer class.

3. **Answer**: C

The compiler would place a statement super() in the beginning of constructor B(). However, A() does not exist. The compiler will not provide it because class A already has a constructor.

4. **Answer**: D

A, B, C, and E are incorrect statements about an interface.

5. **Answer**: B

A static method cannot access non-static members of the class.

6. **Answer**: B and C

The constructor in B would be called from the first and third constructor SubClass(…) in the code, and the constructor in C would be called from the second constructor SubClass(…) in the code.

7. **Answer**: A

Because the MyClass class already has a constructor, the compiler would not provide a default constructor.

8. **Answer**: D

The super(j) statement should be the first line in the constructor SubClass(int j).

9. **Answer**: B and D

A class can inherit only from one class, but a class may inherit from more than one interface. A class inherits from an interface by using the keyword implements and it inherits from another class by using the keyword extends. An interface can inherit from more than one interface by using the keyword extends.

10. **Answer**: B and D

    The list of constants (names) of an enum must come first and must be terminated with a semi-colon (;). It's okay to have a constructor in an enum.

11. **Answer**: A

    A is the correct answer because the variables x and y declared in lines 2 and 3 are different from variables x and y declared in lines 5 and 6.

Chapter 4: Java Language Fundamentals

1. **Answer**: A, B, and C

    A class cannot be abstract and final at the same time, a variable cannot be declared abstract, and default is not a keyword (modifier) in Java.

2. **Answer**: A and B

    An abstract class does not have to have any abstract method and cannot have a finalize() method.

3. **Answer**: D

    A variable declared transient is not saved during serialization.

4. **Answer**: B

    A, C, and D are false statements about the static modifier.

5. **Answer**: C

    A method cannot be overridden to be less public.

6. **Answer**: A

    A call is being made to the message() method from the static method main(…). So, the message() method must be static.

7. **Answer**: C

    A, B, and D are false statements about the final modifier.

8. **Answer**: B

    The method variables cannot have access modifiers.

9. **Answer**: A

    There will be no compiler error at line 6 because a static method can access another static variable of the class. There will be no compiler error at line 7 either because the default constructor is provided by the compiler.

10. **Answer**: B

    RobotPlayer is in a different package from FunnyRobot and is not a subclass of FunnyRobot and thus has no access to protected members of FunnyRobot.

11. **Answer**: C

    C is the correct answer because the object references cw and cw2 point to different objects before the method call, and they point to the same object after the method call.

Chapter 5: Object-Oriented Programming

1. **Answer**: A

    A compiler error will occur because 9L is not an int literal. It is a long literal.

2. **Answer**: C

    A, B, and D are false statements about conversion.

3. Answer: C

No error would occur because the conversion rule is relaxed when an int literal value is assigned to a variable of type byte, short, or char, provided the value falls within the range of the target type.

4. Answer: A

The number 335 is not within the range of values that a byte can hold.

5. Answer: D

The result of the calculation on the right side of the assignment is an integer. An integer may be assigned to int, long, float, or double.

6. Answer: C

The short will be converted to int during the method call.

7. Answer: D

A, B, and C are false statements about object reference conversion.

8. Answer: D

Lines 9 and 11 will not produce errors because the conversion rules are being followed.

9. Answer: C

You cannot implicitly convert Facilities to Auditorium because Facilities is not a subinterface of Auditorium.

10. Answer: D

You cannot explicitly convert LectureHall into Auditorium because neither of these classes is a subclass of the other.

11. Answer: A, C, and D

A and C are properly overloaded. D is a different method. B has the same argument types in the same order, so it is not a valid overloading.

12. Answer: D and E

The Classroom class has a *has-a* relationship with the Student class and the Teacher class.

13. Answer: A and D

B, C, and E are incorrect statements about inheritance.

14. Answer: A and C

B and D are incorrect statements about the *is-a* relationship.

15. Answer: D

The no-argument constructor of the SuperClass class is called in the chain of constructor calls.

16. Answer: D

Due to the method call in line 4, the non-vararg version of the speedup(…) method of Lexus is called, whereas due to the call in line 6, the vararg version of the method is called.

Chapter 6: Execution Flow Control in Java

1. Answer: B

A colon (;) is required at the end of the while statement.

2. Answer: A, B, C, E, and F

The output in D will never be printed due to the continue statement.

3. Answer: A, B, and C

When the values of i and j are equal, the execution control jumps back to line 1.

4. **Answer**: E

   The argument of switch must be of type byte, short, char, or int. The compiler will give the error at line 2, which you can avoid by changing the type of the variable i in line 1.

5. **Answer**: A

   The do block will be executed at least once even if the condition is false.

6. **Answer**: D

   The condition in while() is false, so execution control will not enter the while block.

7. **Answer**: D

   There is no break statement, so a fall through will occur.

8. **Answer**: A

   The continue statement can only exist inside a loop.

9. **Answer**: B

   In line 6, the first condition is true, so the second condition is checked, which turns out to be true as well because j is set equal to true. So, k is decremented by 1. In line 7, i is set to false, so the first condition turns out to be false and the second condition is tested, which is true. Therefore, k is decremented again. Line 9 will always be executed because this is independent of the if statement.

10. **Answer**: B

    B is the correct answer because it is a for-each loop.

11. **Answer**: C

    In line 7, i is incremented after testing the condition, so y is set to true and i is incremented again. In line 8, j is incremented before testing the first condition. Because the first condition turns out to be false, the second condition is not even tested. In line 9, x is set to false, and because it is an OR, the second condition is evaluated.

Chapter 7: Exceptions and Assertions

1. **Answer**: D

   Line 5 will generate an ArrayIndexOutofBoundsException, which is an unchecked exception. So, it will be thrown only at runtime when i=7.

2. **Answer**: B

   B has the correct syntax, and you can use the keywords throw and new in the same statement. Note that the keyword to be used here is throw and not throws.

3. **Answer**: A, B, C, and D

   The finally block is always executed except under special circumstances.

4. **Answer**: D

   The following rule is violated: the more specific catch block should precede the less specific catch block.

5. **Answer**: B and D

   The support for assertions is enabled by default when compiling code in J2SE 5.0. The assert statement asserts that the number of command arguments is not equal to 0. Therefore, an AssertionError will be thrown if the number of arguments is 0.

6. **Answer**: B and E

   A, C, and D are false statements about assertions.

7. **Answer**: A

   The finally block can exist with the catch block, and the finally block is always executed instead under extreme circumstances such as a return or an exit statement.

8. Answer: B

The try block must be followed by either a catch block or a finally block.

9. Answer: A

The code is just fine. The execution will stop at the System.exit(1) statement.

Chapter 8: Input and Output in Java

1. Answer: B, C, and D

There is no method available to change the current working directory. You can create and delete a file by using the createNewFile() and delete() methods, respectively. You can also change the security on a file to read-only by invoking the method setReadOnly().

2. Answer: B

Creating an instance of the File class does not create a file on the system. However, you can invoke an appropriate method of the File instance to create the file if you want to.

3. Answer: A

You need DataInputStream chained to FileInputStream in order to read primitive data types from a file; just one of these streams will not do the job. FileInputStream reads bytes and passes them to DataInputStream, which converts them into data types. The FileReader class is used to read 16-bit characters, and not primitive data types.

4. Answer: A, C, and D

FileInputStream and FileOutputStream are limited to reading only 8-bit bytes; they cannot read 16-bit characters.

5. Answer: A

You need ObjectOutputStream chained to FileOutputStream in order to write an object from your program into a file; just one of these streams will not do the job.

6. Answer: A

The ObjectOutputStream can be used to write strings to a file.

7. Answer: B

The byte is 1 byte long and the float is 4 bytes long.

8. Answer: B

The high-level classes such as BufferedReader cannot be directly connected to I/O devices such as files.

9. Answer: E

When an object is serialized, the class name, non-static data, and non-transient data are saved. FileInputStream and FileReader are low-level streams and can be directly connected to a file. FileInputStream reads the data in binary format, but it can read the text files.

10. Answer: B

Only the Serializable objects are serialized. Although the class Car extends Vehicle, Vehicle is not Serializable. So, when the object of Car is retrieved, the constructor of Vehicle is executed and the make variable is reset to Lexus although it was stored as Nissan.

Chapter 9: Strings, Formatters, and Wrappers

1. Answer: A

Recall that the String indexing starts from 0 and spaces are counted.

2. Answer: B

You cannot extend the final class String.

3. **Answer**: E

Strings are immutable.

4. **Answer**: B

The statement with the new operator is executed at runtime, and a new string is created even if an identical string exists in the pool.

5. **Answer**: A

The equals(…) method in the String class performs a deep comparison; that is, even if two string references point to two different but identical strings, the comparison returns true.

6. **Answer**: B

The str still refers to the old string because it is not changed. The String objects are immutable.

7. **Answer**: A

The StringBuffer objects are changed; they are not immutable.

8. **Answer**: A

The compiler creates a string when it sees a string literal, but it does not create duplicates. The statement with the new operator will be executed at runtime, and the string will be created even if an identical string was created by the compiler.

9. **Answer**: E

An exception is thrown at runtime because d in the format string is used for integers and not for floats.

10. **Answer**: C

Any non-null string evaluates to true, and a null string evaluates to false. Also, note that line 15 involves wrappers.

Chapter 10: Collections and Generics

1. **Answer**: A, B, and C

A Set does not allow duplicate elements. In a Map, values can be duplicates but keys cannot be. A List is ordered by index and is allowed to have duplicates. JDK does not provide a direct implementation of the Collection interface, but it does provide implementations of its subinterfaces.

2. **Answer**: A and B

Vector and LinkedList both implement List, while HashTable implements Map. JDK does not offer the class java.util.OrderedList.

3. **Answer**: B

The hashcode values of two unequal objects don't have to be unequal, but a hash function that does provide unequal hashcode values for unequal objects does help improve performance.

4. **Answer**: A

The conversion between primitives and wrappers has been automated and is called autoboxing.

5. **Answer**: B and D

B is incorrect because collections contain only objects and not primitives. D is incorrect because the parentheses are required to specify the constructor HashSet<String>(). C is correct because this assignment conversion is possible as ArrayList implements List.

6. **Answer**: D

The object references w1 and w2 do not refer to the same object.

7. **Answer**: A

The ObjectOne class does not implement the Comparable interface, so you cannot ask for natural ordering.

8. **Answer**: A

   Line 5 defines a valid generic iterator, and line 6 is a for-each loop.

9. **Answer**: A

   HashTable, HashMap, and TreeMap are all implementations of the Map interface and hence let you store key-value pairs, but only HashTable is synchronized (that is, thread safe). Vector is thread safe, but it is an implementation of List and therefore does not allow you to store key-value pairs.

10. **Answer**: D

    The main(…) method can throw an exception. Lines 6 and 13 will not generate errors because autoboxing is in effect.

11. **Answer**: D

    To understand the answer, you need to recall the following facts:

    Lexus overrides the shallow equals(…) implementation in the Object class, whereas NissanMaxima does not.

    When two object references refer to the same object, they will pass the shallow equality test.

Chapter 11: Threads in Java

1. **Answer**: A

   A yield() call is designed to let the other threads with the same priority take their turn, although there is no guarantee that this will happen.

2. **Answer**: D and E

   The methods start(), run(), sleep(), and yield() belong to the Thread class, while the methods wait(), notify(), and notifyAll() belong to the Object class.

3. **Answer**: D

   The run() method in the class Thread is public. You cannot assign a weaker access privilege while overriding the method.

4. **Answer**: B and D

   A, C, and E are false statements about the wait() method.

5. **Answer**: C

   It is unpredictable in which order the threads will be executed.

6. **Answer**: B

   You cannot predict exactly when after 500 milliseconds the thread will be scheduled to run.

7. **Answer**: C

   You have no direct control over exactly which thread will be put out of the wait state as a result of the notify() method call.

8. **Answer**: A and C

   A call to yield() will only work if a thread of the same or higher priority is there. There is no method called kill().

9. **Answer**: A, C, and D

   The constructors specified in B and E do not exist in the Thread class.

10. **Answer**: A, B, and C

    The wait() and notify() methods belong to the Object class.

11. **Answer**: B

    B is a possible output because you can execute the run() method of a dead thread; it will execute in the caller's thread.

■ ■ ■

Practice Exam

Note: Although the answers to all the questions include an explanation, the best explanation that you can get is to run and experiment with the code yourself. You can download the code for the code-related questions in this practice exam by going to the Source Code area of the Apress website (www.apress.com) and selecting this book's title from the list.

Questions

1. Consider the following code fragment:

```
1. class Test {
2.     public static void main(String [] args) {
3.         Test t = new Test();
4.     }
5.     Test (){
6.       System.out.println("constructor");
7.     }
8.         static { System.out.println("static"); }
9. }
```

What is the result of this code?

A. constructor
   static

B. static
   constructor

C. The compiler generates an error.

D. static

E. An exception is thrown at runtime.

2. Consider the following code

```
1. class Test {
2.    public static void main(String [] args) {
3.        j=0;
4.     for(int i = 0; i < 5; ++i) {
5.             i = ++j;
6.     }
7.       System.out.println("i = " + i);
8.     }
9. }
```

What is the result of this code?

A. i = 4

B. i = 5

C. i = 0

D. Compilation error at line 7

E. Exception at runtime

3. Consider the following code fragment:

```
1. class ArrayTest {
2.   public static void main(String [] args) {
3.       char[] myArray = {'a','b','c','d'};
4.       System.out.println(myArray[1]+" " + myArray[2]);
5. // Insert here
6. }
7. }
```

Which two of the following inserted independently at line 5 will compile and execute ? (Choose two.)

A. `System.out.println(myArray.length());`

B. `int[] i;  System.out.println(i[0]);`

C. `char[] i = myArray;`

D. `char[] j = {myArray[2]};`

4. Consider the following code fragment:

```
1. class EnumTest{
2.     enum Size{small, medium, large, Xlarge};
3.     public static void main(String [] args) {
4.      for( Size s : Size.values()) {
5.        if (s == Size.small)
6.         System.out.print("small ");
7.        else if (Size.medium.equals(s))
8.          System.out.println("medium ");
9.        else if (s == Size.large)
10.          System.out.println("large ");
11.        else if (s.equals("Xlarge "))
12.          System.out.println("Xlarge ");
13.        else if ( s == "Xlarge ");
14.           System.out.println("Xlarge ");
15.     }
16.    }
17.  }
```

What is the result of this code?

A. `small medium large Xlarge Xlarge`

B. `small medium large Xlarge`

C. `small medium large`

D. Compiler error at line 11

E. Compiler error at line 13

F. Throws exception at runtime

5. Consider the following code:

```
1. class Foo {
2.    static boolean condition;
3.    public static void main(String [] args) {
4.     int i = 0;
5.     if((++i >= 1) || (condition == false))
6.       i++;
7.     if((i++ > 1) && (condition = true))
8.       i++;
9.     System.out.println(i);
10.  }
11. }
```

What is the result of this code?

A. 4

B. 3

C. 2

D. 1

E. Compiler error at line 7

F. Throws exception at runtime

6. Consider the following two Java source files:

```
1.  package com.myCompany;
2.  public class myClass {
3.    public static int counter = 0;
4.  }
```

and

```
5.  import static com.myCompany.myClass.*;
6.  public class Test {
7.    int i = counter;
8.    int j = myClass.counter;
9.    int k = myCompany.myClass.counter;
10.   int l = com.myCompany.myClass.counter;
11. }
```

Which of the following statements are true about this code?

A. Both source files compile and execute fine.

B. Both source files compile but the code in the second source file throws an exception at runtime.

C. The compiler generates an error at line 7.

D. The compiler generates an error at line 8.

E. The compiler generates an error at line 9.

F. The compiler generates an error at line 10.

7. Consider the following source file:

```
1. interface Animal {
2.   void saySomething();
3. }
4. class farm {
5.    void setName(String name){};
6. }
7. // insert code here
8. public class Cow implements Pasture  {
9.    public void graze() { }
10.   void saySomething(){}
11.}
```

Which of the following code lines inserted independently at line 7 will make this source file compile?

A. `interface Pasture {void graze();}`

B. `interface Pasture {void graze(){}}`

C. `interface Pasture extends Animal{void graze();}`

D. `interface Pasture extends Animal{void saySomething(){}}`

E. `interface Pasture implements Animal{void graze();}`

8. In the JavaBean naming standards, which of the following two are valid prefixes for a method name?

A. Get

B. get

C. set

D. put

E. retrieve

F. delete

9. Consider the following code:

```
1. public class Room{}
2. class Lab extends Room {
3. // Insert here
4. }
```

Which of the following code fragments inserted at line 3 will generate a compiler error?

A. `Lab(){}`

B.
```
Lab(){
   super();
}
```

C.
```
Lab(){}
Lab(int i){
   this();
}
```

D.
```
Lab(){}
Lab(int i){
   super();
   this();
}
```

E.
```
Lab(){
   System.out.println("Hello");
   super();
}
```

10. Consider the following code fragment:

```
1. class MusicGenre {
2.  MusicGenre() {
3.      System.out.print(" MusicGenre");
4.      }
5.  }
6.  public class EasyListening extends MusicGenre {
7.    public static void main(String [] args) {
8.        EasyListening el = new EasyListening("FleetwoodMac");
9.  }
10.   void EasyListening(String band) {
11.        super ();
12.        System.out.print(band);
13.   }
14.   public EasyListening() {
15.    System.out.print(" ManmohanWaris");
16.   }
17.  }
```

What is the result?

A. `MusicGenre FleetwoodMac ManmohanWaris`

B. `ManmohanWaris MusicGenre FleetwoodMac`

C. Compilation error at line 10

D. Compilation error at line 8

E. Compilation error at line 10

F. Compilation error at line 11

11. Consider the following code:

```
1. class ConventionCenter{
2.    class AudioSystem {
3.        public void test(String say){
4.            System.out.println(say);
5.        }
6.   }
7. }
8. public class JobFair{
9.  public static void main(String [] args) {
10.   String st = "Hello";
11. // Insert code here.
12.    as.test(st);
13.   }
14. }
```

Which of the following inserted independently at line 10 will generate the output `Hello`?

A. ConventionCenter.AudioSystem as = new ConventionCenter().new AudioSystem();

B. AudioSystem as = new ConventionCenter().new AudioSystem();

C. ConventionCenter.AudioSystem as = new AudioSystem();

D. ConventionCenter.AudioSystem as = new ConventionCenter().AudioSystem();

E. ConventionCenter cc = new ConventionCenter();
   ConventionCenter.AudioSystem as1 = cc.new AudioSystem();

12. Consider the following two source files:

```
1. package course;
2. public class TextBook {
3.    String textBook = "SCJP";
4.    public void printTextBook() {
5.        System.out.println(textBook);
6.    }
7. }
```

and

```
8. class CourseDetails {
9.    public static void main(String[] args) {
10.        //Insert code here
11.    }
12. }
```

Which of the following inserted at line 10 in the CourseDetails class will compile the class and generate the output SCJP?

A. course.TextBook tb = new course.TextBook();
   tb.printTextBook();

B. getTextBook;

C. new TextBook().getTextBook();

D. TextBook tb = new course.TextBook();
   tb.printTextBook();

13. Consider the following code:

```
1. class Animal {
2.    public static void saySomething() { System.out.print(" Gurrr!");
3.    }
4. }
5. class Cow extends Animal {
6.    public static void saySomething() {
7.     System.out.print(" Moo!");
8.    }
9.    public static void main(String [] args) {
10.        Animal [] animals = {new Animal(), new Cow()};
11.        for( Animal a : animals) {
12.          a.saySomething();
13.        }
14.        new Cow().saySomething();
15.    }
16. }
```

What is the output?

A. Compiler error at line 10

B. Compiler error at line 11

C. Gurrr! Moo! Moo!

D. Gurrr! Gurrr! Moo!

E. Gurrr! Gurrr! Gurrr!

F. Exception thrown at runtime

14. Consider the following code:

```
1. class Car extends Vehicle {
2.  public static void main(String [] args) {
3.    new Car().run();
4.  }
5.  private final void run() {
6.      System.out.println("Car");
7.  }
8. }
9. class Vehicle {
10.   private final void run() {
11.      System.out.println("Vehicle");
12.   }
13. }
```

What is the result?

A. Car

B. Vehicle

C. Compiler error at line 3

D. Compiler error at line 5

E. Exception thrown at runtime

15. Consider the following code:

```
1. class Animal {
2.    void saySomething() {
          System.out.print(" Gurrr!");
3.    }
4.  }
5.    class Cow extends Animal {
6.      protected void saySomething() {
7.        System.out.print(" Moo!");
8.      }
9.      public static void main(String [] args) {
10.       System.out.print(" MooYa!");
11.       Animal [] animals = {new Animal(), new Cow()};
12.       for( Animal a : animals) {
13.         a.saySomething();
14.       }
15.    }
16. }
```

What is the result?

A. Gurrr! Moo! MooYa!

B. Moo! MooYa! Gurrr!

C. MooYa Gurrr! Moo!

D. MooYa Gurrr! Gurrr!

E. Compiler error at line 6

F. Exception thrown at runtime

16. Consider the following code:

```
1. class MainArgTest {
2.    static int i=1;
3.    static public void main(String... args){
4.      System.out.println(i+1);
5.    }
6.      static { i = 10;}
7. }
```

If the code compiles, it is called by using the following command:

```
java MainArgTest
```

What is the result?

A. 2

B. 11

C. Compilation error at line 3

D. Compilation error at line 6

E. Exception thrown at runtime

17. Consider the following code:

```
1.  import java.util.*;
2.  class EqualTest {
3.  private static String[] partyTime = {"on", "off"};
4.    public static void main(String[] party){

5.       if(Arrays.equals(partyTime, party))
6.       System.out.println("Party is on!");

7.        if(party==partyTime)
8.        System.out.println(" Party is over!");
9.   }
10. }
```

If the code compiles, the following command is used:

```
java EqualTest on off
```

What is the result?

A. `Party is on!`
   `Party is over!`

B. `Party is on!`

C. The code compiles and runs fine but no output is produced.

D. Compilation fails.

E. An exception is thrown at runtime.

18. Consider the following code:

```
1.  class Cow{
2.     final static Cow cow = new Cow();
3.     public static void main(String [] args) {
4.       Cow cowOne = cow;
5.       Cow cowTwo = cow.dive(cow);
6.       Cow cowThree = cow;
7.       System.out.println(cowOne==cowTwo);
8.       System.out.println(cowOne==cowThree);
9.      }
10.    Cow dive(Cow c) {
11.       c = new Cow();
12.       return c;
13.    }
14. }
```

What is the result?

A. Compilation error at line 2

B. Compilation error at line 11

C. `true`
   `true`

D. `false`
   `true`

E. `false`
   `false`

F. `true`
   `false`

G. Exception thrown at runtime

19. Which of the following statements is true?

A. A Java application can never run out of memory due to the used-up objects, because the garbage collector frees up the memory from them.

B. The purpose of the garbage collector is to delete objects from the stack.

C. Executing System.gc() always guarantees that the garbage collector will delete all the eligible objects immediately.

D. You make an object eligible for garbage collection by calling system.gc().

E. A call to a garbage collector does not guarantee that the memory will be freed.

20. Consider the following two classes:

```
1. class Moo {
2.    private int count;
3.    int getCount(){
4.      return count;
5.    }
6.    void setCount(int c){
7.        count=c;
8.    }
9. }
10. class Baa {
11.    private int count;
12.     int getCount(){
13.      return count;
14.    }
15.    void setCount(int c){
16.        count=c;
17.        new Moo().setCount(count);
18.    }
19. }
```

Which of the following is true?

A. The two classes are tightly coupled.

B. The two classes are not coupled.

C. The two classes are loosely coupled.

D. These classes will not compile.

21. Consider the following class:

```
1. class Baa {
2.    int count;
3.    boolean speak;
4.    void setSpeak(boolean s){
5.      int i;
6.      speak=s;
7.    }
8.    void setCount(int c){
       int j;
9.        count=c;
10.        new Moo().setCount(count);
11.    }
12. }
```

At how many places do you need to add a modifier to make this class encapsulated?

A. 2

B. 3

C. 4

D. 0

E. 1

22. Consider the following code:

```
1. class AnimalCreator {
2. public static void main(String [] args) {
3.    Animal [] animals = {new Animal(), new Cow()};
4.    for (Animal a : animals){
5.       Animal x = a.getAnimal();
6.       System.out.println(x);
7.    }
8.  }
9.  }

10. class Animal {
11.  Animal getAnimal() {
12.    return new Animal();
13.  }
14. }

15. class Cow extends Animal {
16.  Cow getAnimal () {
17.    return new Cow();
18.  }
19. }
```

Which of the following is true?

A. A compilation error occurs at line 4.

B. A compilation error occurs at line 6.

C. A compilation error occurs at line 16.

D. An exception is thrown at runtime.

E. The code compiles and executes fine.

F. A compilation error occurs at line 5.

23. Consider the following code:

```
1. class MySuperClass {
2.    private int x;
3.    MySuperClass(int i){
4.       x=i;
5.       System.out.println("mySuperClass: "+ x);
6.    }
7. }

8. class MySubClass extends MySuperClass {
9.    public static void main(String[] args){
10.    new MySubClass();
11.    new MySubClass(3);
12.  }
13.  MySubClass(int i){
14.    super(i);
15.  }
16.  MySubClass() {
17.       System.out.println("Default");
18.  }
19. }
```

What is the result?

A. mySuperClass: 3
   Default

B. mySuperClass: 3

C. Default

D. An exception is thrown at runtime.

E. Compilation fails.

24. Consider the following code:

```
1. class MySuperClass {
2.    private int x;
3.    MySuperClass(int i){
4.       x=i;
5.       System.out.println("mySuperClass: "+ x);
6.    }
7.    // Insert code here.
8. }
9. class MySubClass extends MySuperClass {
10.    public static void main(String[] args){
11.          new MySubClass();
12.          new MySubClass(3);
13. }

14.    MySubClass(int i){
15.          super(i);
16.    }
17.    MySubClass() {
18. // Insert code here
19.    System.out.println("Default");
20.    }
21. }
```

Which of the following two actions will make this code compile and execute?

1. Insert MySuperClass(){} at line 7.

2. Insert this(5); at line 18.

  A. 1 only.

  B. 2 only.

  C. Either 1, or 2, or both.

  D. Only 1 and 2.

  E. Neither.

  F. Either 1 or 2 will make the code compile but it will throw an exception at runtime.

25. Consider the following code:

```
1. class OverTest extends MySuperClass{
2.    public static void main(String[] args){
3.          System.out.println("Hello");
4.    }
5.    // Insert code here
6. }

7. class MySuperClass {
8.    void mySuperMethod(boolean b){
9.      System.out.println("Super method!");
10. }
11.}
```

Which of the following can be placed independently at line 5 and the code will still compile and execute?

```
1. private void mySuperMethod(int i){
   System.out.println("Not really super!");
   }
2. void mySuperMethod(int i, int j){
   System.out.println("Not really super!");
   }
3. public void mySuperMethod(boolean i){
   System.out.println("Not really super!");
   }
4.  int mySuperMethod(double d){
   System.out.println("Not really super!");
   return 2;
   }
```

A. 4 only

B. 2, 3, or 4

C. 1, 2, or 3

D. 1, 2, 3, or 4

26. Which of the following statements are true?

A. Inheritance is used to establish an *is-a* relationship between two classes.

B. A class can have a *has-a* relationship only with one other class.

C. The *is-a* relationship must be cohesive.

D. A *has-a* relationship can make two classes tightly coupled.

E. If class A *is-a* class B, no other class can have an *is-a* relationship with class B.

F. A *has-a* relationship can be established by using object reference variables as local variables.

27. Consider the following code:

```
1.  class X extends Y implements I {
2.     public void goBear(){
3.        System.out.println("Go Bear go!");
4.     }
5.  }
6.  class Y {
7.     Z z=new Z();
8.  }
9.  interface I {
10.    public void goBear();
11. }
12. class Z { }
```

Which of the following statements are true?

A. X *is-a* Y.

B. X *is-an* I.

C. X *has-an* I.

D. Y *is-an* X.

E. Y *has-an* X.

F. Z *is-a* Y.

28. Consider the following code:

```
1.  class IfTest{
2.  public static void main(String [] args) {
3.     boolean b1 = true;
4.     boolean b2 = false;
5.     int i = 10;
6.     if((b1 == true) && (b2 = true))  i++;
7.     if((b2 == false) && (i++ == 12)){
8.          i++;
9.        }
10.    if((b2 == true) || (i++ == 11)){
11.         i++;
12.    }
13.        System.out.println("i = " + i);
14. }
15. }
```

What is the result?

A. i = 12

B. i = 13

C. i = 14

D. i = 11

E. Compilation error

F. Exception thrown at runtime

29. Consider the following code:

```
1. class IfTest2{
2.  public static void main(String [] args) {
3.    boolean b1 = true;
4.    boolean b2 = false;
5.    int i = 10;
6.    if((b1 == true) && (b2 == true))  i++;
7.    else {
8.        i--;
9.    }
10.   else {
11.      i++;
12.   }
13.       System.out.println("i = " + i);
14.   }
15. }
```

What is the result?

A. i = 11

B. i = 12

C. i = 13

D. Compilation error

E. Exception thrown at runtime

30. Consider the following code:

```
1. enum Colors {BLUE, GREEN, YELLOW, RED}
2. class Picture {
3.  public static void main(String [] args) {
4.    int x = 0;
5.    Colors c = Colors.GREEN;
6.      switch(c) {
7.      case BLUE:
8.        System.out.print(c);
9.      case GREEN:
10.       System.out.print(c);
11.     case YELLOW:
12.      System.out.print(c);
13.      default:
14.       System.out.print(" BlackWhite ");
15.       break;
16.     case RED:
17.         System.out.print(c);
18.     }
19.         System.out.println(" PicturePerfect");
20.     }
21. }
```

What is the result?

A. GREEN PicturePerfect

B. GREENGREEN PicturePerfect

C. GREENGREEN BlackWhite PicturePerfect

D. GREENYELLOW BlackWhite PicturePerfect

E. GREENGREEN BlackWhite Red PicturePerfect

F. Compilation fails at line 6.

G. Compilation fails at line 13.

31. Consider the following code:

```
1. enum Colors {BLUE, GREEN, RED}
2. class Picture {
3.  public static void main(String [] args) {
4.    int x = 0;
5.    Colors c = Colors.GREEN;
6.      switch(c) {
```

```
7.     case BLUE:
8.        System.out.print(c);
9.     case GREEN:
10.       System.out.print(c);
11.    case YELLOW:
12.       System.out.print(c);
13.    default:
14.       System.out.print(" BlackWhite ");
15.       break;
16.    case RED:
17.        System.out.print(c);
18.    }
19.        System.out.println(" PicturePerfect");
20.    }
21. }
```

What is the result?

A. GREEN PicturePerfect

B. GREENYELLOW PicturePerfect

C. GREENGREEN BlackWhite PicturePerfect

D. GREEN BlackWhite Red PicturePerfect

E. Compilation fails.

F. An exception is thrown at runtime.

32. Consider the following code:

```
1.   import java.util.*;
2.   class ForTest {
3.   static List list = new ArrayList();
4.   static List getList() { return list; }
5.     public static void main(String [] args) {
6.       list.add("Ready");
7.       list.add("Set");
8.       list.add("Go");
9. // insert code here
10.       System.out.print(obj);
11.   }
12.}
```

Which of the following placed independently at line 9 will generate the output ReadySetGo?

A. for (List obj:getList())

B. for (Object obj:getList();)

C. for (Object obj:getList())

D. for (Object obj:list.getList())

E. for (Object obj:obj.getList())

33. Consider the following code:

```
1. class MyClass {
2.  public static void main(String [] args){
3.  int i = 0;
4.  step1:
5.  for(; i < 10; i++) {
6.    if(i == 4) {
7.      i = 6;
8.      break step1;
9.    }
10.    else if(i == 2) {
11.      i++;
12.      continue;
13.    }
14.    System.out.print(i + " ");
15.  }
16. }
17.}
```

What is the result?

A. 0 1

B. 0 1 3

C. 0 1 6 7 8 9

D. Compilation error at line 4

E. Compilation error at line 5

34. Assume f is a reference to a valid File object, fr is a reference to a valid FileReader object, and br is a reference to a valid BufferedReader object. Consider the following code:

```
15.    String line = null;
16.    // insert code here
17.        System.out.println (line);
18.  }
```

Which of the following should be inserted at line 16, so that the loop will read the whole file line by line and print it out to the standard output device?

A. while ((line = br.readLine()) != null) {

B. while((line = fr.readLine()) != null) {

C. while((line = f.readLine()) != null) {

D. while((line = br.read()) != null) {

E. while((line = fr.read()) != null) {

F. while((line = fr.read()) != null) {

35. Consider the following code:

```
1. import java.io.*;
2. class Animal implements Serializable {}
3. class Cow extends Animal{
4.     Milk m = new Milk();
5. }
6. class Milk implements Serializable {
7.   SaturatedFat sf1 = new SaturatedFat();
8.   SaturatedFat sf2 = new SaturatedFat();
9.   SaturatedFat sf3 = new SaturatedFat();
10.}
11. class SaturatedFat implements Serializable { }
```

When you serialize an instance of Cow, how many objects will be serialized?

A. 0

B. 2

C. 3

D. 4

E. 5

F. 6

36. Which of the following are valid command-line invocations of a Java application, MyApp?

A. java -da   MyApp

B. java –assert MyApp

C. java -enableassertions MyApp

D. java –assertionOff   MyApp

E. jjavac -source 1.5 MyApp.java

37. Consider the following code:

```
1. class AssertionTest {
2.   public static void main(String [] args) {
3.       assert(false): "false ";
4.       System.out.print("assertion");
5.       assert(true): "true";
6.   }
7. }
```

By using J2SE 5.0, the code is compiled without using the -source flag. Which of the following will be the output of the following command?

```
java -ea AssertionTest
```

A. assertion true

B. false assertion

C. false assertion true

D. An AssertionError is thrown with the message false.

E. An AssertionError is thrown with the message true.

F. Compilation fails.

38. Consider the following code:

```
1.  import java.io.*;
2.  class MyCar extends Vehicle {
3.    int speed = 0;
4.    int year = 1960;
5.    int price =0;
6.    public static void main(String [] args) {
7.      System.out.println("There comes my car!");
8.    }
9.    int getPrice(int i){
10.            return price;
11.  }

12.  int getYear(int i)throws NullPointerException {
13.        return year;
14.  }
15.  int getSpeed (int i) throws IOException  {
16.      return speed;
17.  }
18. }

19.  class Vehicle {
20.    int getPrice(int i) throws IOException {
21.            return 50000;
22.    }
23.    int getYear(int i){
24.            return 1990;
25.    }
26.    int getSpeed(int i){
27.            return 60;
28.    }
29.  }
```

What is the result?

A. There comes my car!

B. Compilation fails at line 9.

C. Compilation fails at line 12.

D. Compilation fails at line 15.

E. An exception is thrown at runtime.

39. Consider the following code:

```
1. class AllMyExceptions {
2.  public static void main(String [] args) {
3.    try {
4.        System.out.println(Double.valueOf("420.00"));
5.    }catch (Exception e) {
6.      System.out.println("Some exception!");
7.    }catch (NumberFormatException ne) {
8.      System.out.println("Number format exception!");
9.    }
10.     System.out.println("All My Exceptions!");
11.  }
12. }
```

What is the result?

A. 420.0
   ```
   All My Exceptions!
   ```

B. ```
   Some exception!
   All my exceptions
   ```

C. ```
   Number format exception!
   All my exceptions
   ```

D. Compilation fails.

E. An exception is thrown at runtime.

40. Consider the following code:

```
1.  class MyTestClass{
2.    static Short s1,s2;
3.    public static void main(String [] args) {
4.     int i;
5.     s1 = 20;
6.     try{
7.       i = s1 + s2;
8. // insert here
9.            System.out.print("Ouch!");
10.        }
11.   }
12. }
```

Which of the following inserted independently at line 8 will generate the output Ouch!?

A. `}catch (NullPointerException ne){`

B. `}catch (ClassCastException ce){`

C. `}catch (RuntimeException re){`

D. `}catch (NumberFormatException ne){`

E. `}catch (StackOverflowError se){`

41. Which of the following methods exists in `java.lang.StringBuffer` but not in `java.lang.StringBuilder`?

A. `append(…)`

B. `delete(…)`

C. `insert(…)`

D. `length(…)`

E. `reverse(…)`

F. None of the above

42. Consider the following code:

```
1. class NumberMachine{
2.   public static void main(String [] args) {
3.     Integer wi1 = new Integer("420");
4.     int i = 101;
5.     Integer wi2 = i*420/101;
6.     if(wi1 == wi2) System.out.print(" ==");
7.     if(wi1.equals(wi2)) System.out.print(" equal");
8.     float f = 1.23f;
9.     new NumberMachine().printIt(f);
10.    }

11.    void printIt(Float f){
12.      System.out.println(" Float");
13.    }
14.    void printIt(double  d){
15.      System.out.println(" double");
16.    }
17. }
```

What is the result?

A. == equal Float

B. == equal double

C. equal Float

D. equal double

E. Compilation fails.

F. An exception is thrown at runtime.

43. Consider the following code:

```
1. import java.text.*;
2. class NumberMachine2{
3.  public static void main(String [] args) {
4.    NumberFormat nf = NumberFormat.getInstance();
5.    nf.setMaximumIntegerDigits(2);
6.        System.out.println((String) nf.format(420.101));
7.  }
8. }
```

What is the result?

A. 42.101

B. 20.101

C. 420.10

D. Compilation fails at line 4.

E. An exception is thrown at runtime.

44. Consider the following code:

```
1. import java.text.*;
2. class NumberMachine2{
3.  public static void main(String [] args) {
4.    NumberFormat nf = new NumberFormat();
5.    nf.setMaximumIntegerDigits(2);
6.        System.out.println((String) nf.format(420.101));
7.  }
8. }
```

What is the result?

A. 42.101

B. 20.101

C. 420.10

D. Compilation fails.

E. An exception is thrown at runtime.

45. Consider the following code:

```
1.  import java.util.*;
2.  class MyScanner{
3.    public static void main(String [] args) {
4.      String str = "a,b,cd,420";
5.      Scanner sc = new Scanner(str);
6.      while (sc.hasNext()) {
7.        System.out.print(sc.next());
8.      }
9.
10.   }
11. }
```

What is the result?

A. abcd420

B. a b cd 420

C. a,b,cd,420

D. Compilation error

E. Exception thrown at runtime

46. Consider the following code:

```
1.  import java.io.PrintWriter;
2.  class MyFormatter {
3.    public static void main(String [] args) {
4.      int i = 420;
5.      int j = 420101;
6.      float x = 1;
7.      System.out.format("*%4d* ", i);
8.      System.out.format("*%4d* ", j);
9.      System.out.format("*%4.1f* ", x);
10.   }
11. }
```

What is the result?

A. * 420* *420101* * 1.0*

B. *420* *420101* *1.0*

C. * 420* *42010* * 1.0*

D. Compilation fails.

E. An exception is thrown at runtime.

47. Consider the following code:

```
1. import java.util.*;
2. class MyDataStore {
3.   public static void main(String [] args) {
4. // Insert here
5.    structure.put("a", 420);
6.    System.out.println(structure.get("a"));
7.  }
8. }
```

Which of the following inserted at line 4 will make the code compile and execute?

A. Map structure = new HashMap();

B. HashMap structure = new LinkedHashSet();

C. HashMap structure = new TreeMap();

D. Map structure = new TreeMap();

E. Hashtable structure = new HashMap();

48. You want to create a collection to insert data in the form of key-value pairs to retrieve it at a later time. Which of the following classes can you use for that purpose?

A. SortedMap

B. SortedSet

C. Hashtable

D. LinkedHashMap

E. Vector

F. TreeMap

49. Consider the following code:

```
1.  class Car {
2.    String make;
3.    String model;
4. //Insert code here.
5.    public boolean equals(Object o) {
6.      Car c = (Car) o;
7.      return model.equals(c.model);
8.    }
9.  }
```

Which of the following inserted independently at line 4 will honor the hashCode contract?

A. `public int hashCode () {return (int) (Math.random()*101);}`

B. `public int hashCode () {return 420;}`

C. `public int hashCode () {return make.hashCode();}`

D. `public int hashCode () {return model.hashCode();}`

E. None of the above

50. Consider the following code:

```
1. import java.util.*;
2.  public class AnimalFarm {
3.    public static void main(String [] args) {
4.      // insert code here
5.        speak(a);
6.    }
7.    public static void speak(List<Cow> c) {
8.            System.out.println("Animal sound!");
9.    }
10. }

11.  class Animal { }
12.  class Cow extends Animal { }
13.  class Goat extends Animal{}
```

Which of the following inserted independently at line 4 will make the code compile and execute correctly?

A. `ArrayList a = new ArrayList();`

B. `ArrayList<Goat> a =  new ArrayList<Goat>();`

C. `ArrayList<Animal> a =  new ArrayList<Animal>();`

D. `ArrayList<Cow> a =  new ArrayList<Cow>();`

E. `HashSet<Cow> ag =  new HashSet<Cow>();`

51. Consider the following code:

```
1. import java.util.*;
2. public class StateFair {
3.    public static void main (String[] args) {
4.      Set<Animal> animals = new HashSet<Animal>();
5.      Set<Cow> calCow = new HashSet<Cow>();
6.      Set<Object> wisCow = new HashSet<Object>();
7.      talkingAnimals(animals);
8.      talkingAnimals(calCow);
9.      talkingAnimals(wisCow);
10.   }
11. //  insert code here
12.                   System.out.println("The animal talk!");
13.   }
14. }
15. class Animal { }
16. class Cow extends Animal{ }
```

Which of the following inserted independently at line 11 will make the code compile and execute correctly?

A. `public static void talkingAnimals(Set<Object> set) {`

B. `public static void talkingAnimals(Set<?> set) {`

C. `public static void talkingAnimals(Set<Cow> set) {`

D. `public static void talkingAnimals(Set<? extends Object> set) {`

E. `public static void talkingAnimals(Set<Animal> set) {`

52. Consider the following code:

```
1. import java.util.*;
2. class ThingsStore {
3.    public static void main(String [] args) {
4.      ArrayList<Things> al = new ArrayList<Things>();
5.      al.add(new Things(10));
6.      al.add(new Things(20));
```

```
7.      System.out.println(al.size());
8.  }
9. }
10. class Things implements Comparator{
11.   int i;
12.   Things(int s) { this.i = s; }
13.   public int compareTo(Object o) { return this.i - ((Things)o).i; }
14. }
```

What is the result?

A. 0

B. 1

C. 2

D. 10

E. Compilation fails.

F. An exception is thrown at runtime

53. Consider the following code:

```
1. public class MyThread {
2.   public static void main(String[] args) {
3.         Counter ct = new Counter();
4.         ct.run();
5.         ct.start();
6.         ct.run();
7.   }
8. }
9.  class Counter extends Thread {
10.  public void run() {
11.     System.out.print("Running");
12.  }
13. }
```

What is the output?

A. Running

B. Running Running

C. Running Running Running

D. Compilation fails.

E. An exception is thrown at runtime.

54. Consider the following code:

```
1. public class MyThreads {
2.   public static void main(String[] args) {
3.         Thread t1 = new Counter();
4.         Thread t2 = new Thread(t1);
5.         t1.start();
6.         t2.start();
7.   }
8. }
9. class Counter extends Thread implements Runnable {
10.  public void run() {
11.     System.out.println("Running");
12.  }
13. }
```

What is the output?

A. Running

B. Running
   Running

C. No output.

D. Compilation fails.

E. An exception is thrown at runtime.

55. Consider the following code:

```
1. class MySynchClass {
2.    synchronized int i;
3.    synchronized void saySomething() {
4.      MySynchClass ms = new MySynchClass();
5.      synchronized(this) { }
6.      synchronized(ms) { }
7.      synchronized() { }
8.    }
9. }
```

Which of the following statements are true about this code?

A. Compilation error at line 2
B. Compilation error at line 3
C. Compilation error at line 5
D. Compilation error at line 6
E. Compilation error at line 7
F. No compilation error

56. Which two of the following methods must be invoked from the synchronized code?

A. notify()
B. run()
C. sleep()
D. start()
E. wait()
F. yield()

57. Consider the following code:

```
1.   public class AllMyThreads {
2.     public static void main(String[] args) {
3.         Thread t = new Counter();
4.         t.start();
5.         System.out.print(" Started");
6.         try{
7.           t.join();
8.         } catch (Exception ex){}
9.          System.out.print(" Main");
10.
11.    }
12. }
13. class Counter extends Thread implements Runnable {
14.   public void run() {
15.      try{
16.           Thread.sleep(3000);
17.          }catch (Exception ex) {}
18.      System.out.print(" Running");
19.   }
20. }
```

Which of the following are possible outputs?

A. Started Main Running
B. Started Running Main
C. Running Started Main
D. Running Main Started
E. Started Running

58. Which of the following methods throw checked exceptions?

A. join()
B. run()
C. sleep()
D. start()
E. yield()

59. Which of the following are correct statements?

A. Inheritance represents an *is-a* relationship.

B. Inheritance represents a *have-a* relationship.

C. An instance represents an *is-a* relationship.

D. An instance represents a *have-a* relationship.

60. Consider the statement: A farmer has a friend who is a cow. Which of the following code fragments correctly represent the statement?

A.
```
class Farmer {
    BestFriend bf = new Cow();
}
class BestFriend {}
class Cow{}
```

B.
```
class Farmer {
    BestFriend  cow  = new BestFriend();
}
class BestFriend {}
```

C.
```
class Farmer {
    BestFriend bf = new BestFriend();
}
class BestFriend extends Cow {}
class Cow{}
```

D.
```
class BestFriend {
    Cow cow = new Cow();
}
class Farmer extends BestFriend {}
class Cow{}
```

E.
```
class BestFriend {
    Cow cow = new Cow();
}
class Farmer {
    BestFriend bf = new BestFriend();
}
class Cow{}
```

61. Consider the following code:

```
1. public class PrintMyStuff {
2.  public static void main(String[] args) {
3.      Thread t = new Counter();
4.      t.start();
5.      System.out.print(" Started");
6.      finally {
7.          System.out.print(" Finally");
8.      }
9.  }
10. }
11. class Counter extends Thread implements Runnable {
12.  public void run() {
13.      try{
14.          Thread.sleep(3000);
15.          }catch (Exception ex) {}
16.          System.out.print(" Running");
17.      }
18.  }
```

What is the result?

A. Started Finally Running

B. Started Running Main

C. Running Started Main

D. Running Finally Started

E. Started Running

F. Compilation fails.

62. Consider the following code:

```
1. public class MyCalculator {
2.    public static void main(String[] args) {
3.      // Insert here
4. }
5.}
```

Which of the following inserted at line 3 will print the number 3.1416?

A. `System.out.printf("%6.4f", Math.PI);`

B. `System.out.printf("%6d.4f", Math.PI);`

C. `new PrintWriter().format("%6.4f", Math.PI);`

D. `new Formatter().format("%6.4f", Math.PI);`

63. Consider the following code:

```
1. public class AssertionTest {
2.   public static void main(String[] args) {
3.   // insert here
4.        System.out.print(" After assert");
5.   }
6. }
```

Which of the following inserted at line 3 will generate the assertion error with the message Test?

A. `assert (true): Test;`

B. `assert (false): Test;`

C. `assert (true): "Test";`

D. `assert (false): "Test";`

E. `assert false: "Test";`

64. Consider the following code:

```
1. public class MyMainTest{
2.   public static void main(String[] args) throws Exception{
3.        assert (true): " Assert";
4.        System.out.print(" After ");
5.        Test().main("Hello");
6.   }
7. }
8. class Test {
9.   Test(){
10.      System.out.print(" Constructor");
11.   }
12.   public static void main(String[] args) {
13.        System.out.print(args[0]);
14.   }
15. }
```

What is the result?

A. `Assert After Constructor Hello`

B. `Assert After Hello`

C. `After Hello`

D. Compilation fails at line 2.

E. Compilation fails at line 5.

F. An exception is thrown at runtime.

65. Which of the following is not a valid Thread constructor?

A. `Thread()`

B. `Thread(Runnable target)`

C. `new Thread(String str)`

D. `Thread(Thread t)`

E. `Thread(String str, Integer i)`

66. Consider the following code:

```
1. public class MyVariables {
2.   public static void main(String[] args) {
3.         int $420 = 420;
4.         int _ohMy = 101;
5.         int %whatever = 30;
6.         Integer wi = 999;
7.   }
8. }
```

Which of the code lines are illegal?

A. 3, 4, 5, and 6

B. 6 only

C. 5 only

D. 3, 4, and 5 only

E. None

67. Consider the following code:

```
1. public class MyOutput {
2.   public static void main(String[] args) {
3.         int x = 10;
4.         int y = 20;
5.         int z = 30;
6.         System.out.println(x + y + z);
7.         System.out.println(" " + x + y + z);
8.         System.out.println(x + " " + y+z);
9.   }
10.}
```

What is the result?

A. 60
    102030
    10 2030

B. 60
    60
    10 50

C. 102030
    102030
    10 2030

D. 60
    60
    10 50

E. 60
    102030
    10 50

68. Consider the following code:

```
1. enum Villages {Pharwala, Gohawar, Phagwara, Goraya}
2. public class MyEnumTest {
3.   public static enum Colors{RED, BLUE, GREEN, YELLOW, ORANGE};
4.   private enum weekend { Saturday, Sunday};
5.   public static void main(String[] args) {
6.         enum Currency {Dollars, Rupees, Franc, Euro};
7.         System.out.println("Hello");
8.   }
9. }
```

What is the result?

A. Hello

B. Compilation fails at line 1.

C. Compilation fails at line 3.

D. Compilation fails at line 6.

E. An exception is thrown at runtime.

69. Consider the following code:

```
public class javac {

    public static void main(String[] args) {
        for (String str:args){
          System.out.println(str);
          }
    }
}
```

and the execution command:

```
java javac java java javac
```

What is the result?

A. java

B. java
   java
   javac

C. Compilation fails.

D. An exception is thrown at runtime.

70. Consider the following code:

```
1. import java.io.*;
2. public class AnimalFarm implements Serializable {
3.  public static void main(String[] args) {
4.     Cow cow = new Cow();
5.     Goat goat = new Goat();
6.     System.out.println("This farm can be serialized");
7.  }
8. }
9. class Cow implements Serializable {}
10. class Goat {}
```

What happens if you try to serialize an instance of AnimalFarm?

A. An object of AnimalFarm and an object of Cow are serialized.

B. An object of AnimalFarm, an object of Cow, and an object of Goat are serialized.

C. Compilation of this code fails.

D. An exception is thrown at runtime.

71. Which of the following classes support synchronization?

A. java.util.ArrayList

B. java.util.Hashtable

C. java.util.LinkedLIst

D. java.lang.StringBuffer

E. java.lang.StringBuilder

F. java.util.TreeSet

G. java.util.Vector

72. Consider the following code:

```
1. public class MyThreadTester {
2.  public static void main(String[] args) {
3.       Counter t1 = new Counter();
4.       Counter t2 = new Counter();
5.       t1.start();
6.       t2.start();
7.  }
8. }

9.  class Counter extends Thread {
10.     void run() {
11.       System.out.println("Running");
12.     }
13. }
```

What is the result?

A. Running
   Running

B. Running

C. It prints nothing.

D. Compilation fails.

E. An exception is thrown at runtime.

73. Consider the following code:

```
int i = aReader.read();
```

What is true of the type of variable aReader?

A. It has to be a BufferedReader.

B. It has to be a FileReader.

C. It can either be a FileReader or a BufferedReader.

D. It can be neither a FileReader nor a BufferedReader.

Answers and Explanations

1. Answer: B

The static block in a class is executed before the class initialization, that is, the constructor.

2. Answer: D

The scope of the variable i defined in the for(){} code block is within that block.

3. Answer: C and D

A is incorrect because there is no array function length(). To get the length of the myArray array, you will say myArray.length. B is incorrect because i is being used in the print statement without having initialized.

4. Answer: E

Line 13 will cause an incomparable types error because enums are not strings.

5. Answer: A

The variable i is incremented four times before printing. Because the default initial value of a boolean variable is false, the if statement in line 5 passes the test, and there is nothing wrong with line 7. It simply sets the value of the boolean variable condition to true and passes the test.

6. Answer: D and E

The class myClass from the package is already imported in line 5. So, you can just use the name of the class variable (line 7), or the entire import string with the name (line 10) but not in between these two choices (lines 8 and 9).

7. Answer: A and C

You cannot implement a method inside an interface. An interface can only extend another interface, and cannot implement another interface or a class.

8. Answer: B and C

get and set are the valid prefixes for a method name in the JavaBean naming standards.

9. Answer: D and E

You can make either a super() or a this() call in the beginning of the constructor body. Therefore, you cannot make both a super() and a this() call in the same constructor.

10. Answer: D and F

What is declared on line 10 is a method and not a constructor. You do not declare a return type, even if it is void, in a constructor. As a result, lines 8 and 11 will generate a compiler error because you can use the new operator only with a constructor, and not with a method, and you can make a super() call only from inside a constructor.

11. **Answer**: A and E

    This is the correct syntax for instantiating a nested class. D would be correct if AudioSystem were a static class.

12. **Answer**: A

    Because A specifies the fully qualified names, an import statement is not needed.

13. **Answer**: D

    If you expected Gurrr! Moo! Moo!, remember that polymorphism does not apply to static members.

14. **Answer**: A

    Although you cannot override a final method of the parent class in the subclass, you can always define another method with the same signature in the subclass.

15. **Answer**: C

    There is no compiler error at line 6 because the protected modifier makes a class member more accessible than the default.

16. **Answer**: B

    The main(…) method can take the variable arguments of type String, and you can specify the modifiers public and static in any order. The static code block is executed at class load time regardless of its location, and it sets the value of i to 4.

17. **Answer**: B

    The == operator presents a shallow equality test for objects. It passes the test if the object variables refer to the same object. So, two different array objects (even if they have the same content) can never pass the equality test when conducted with ==.

18. **Answer**: D

    Two object variables pass the equality test with == only if they refer to the same object. Also, only a copy of the reference is passed to the called method.

19. **Answer**: E

    The System.gc() call does not guarantee that the memory will be freed.

20. **Answer**: C

    The two classes are loosely coupled because Baa instantiates Moo, but Moo does not instantiate Baa.

21. **Answer**: A

    You need to declare the instance variables count and speak private.

22. **Answer**: E

    Line 16 is an example of a covariant return type, and line 5 is an example of polymorphism.

23. **Answer**: E

    Compilation fails at line 16 because the compiler wants to place a super() call right after this line but it cannot find the MySuperClass() constructor.

24. **Answer**: C

    The problem is that the compiler will place a call to super() immediately after line 17, and there is no MySuperClass() constructor.

    Action 1 will work because now we have a no-arg superclass constructor.

    Action 2 will work because the compiler will not place a call to super().

    Both 1 and 2 together will also work.

25. **Answer**: D

    1, 2, and 4 are valid overloads of the inherited method mySuperLoad(…), and 3 is a valid override.

26. **Answer**: A and D

    Although Java offers single inheritance, a class can have more than one subclass. For example, a cow is an animal, and an elephant is also an animal. Furthermore, you can instantiate more than one class in a class. Also, a class can "implement" one or more interfaces, and that is also an *is-a* relationship.

27. **Answer**: A and B

    Class X inherits Y and I. Z does not have an *is-a* relationship with Y, but Y *has-a* Z.

28. **Answer**: A

    In the second set of parentheses at line 6, b2 is set to true, so it is true. Hence, line 6 passes both tests and i is incremented to 11. In the second set of parentheses of line 7, the value of the variable i is not changed in the memory, even though the equality is tested between i+1 and 12. The same is true about line 10. The first test on line 7 fails, and hence it does not even test the second condition, and the body of the if statement is not executed. At line 10, the first test fails, and the second test passes, so the body is executed and i is incremented to 12.

29. **Answer**: D

    Compilation fails at line 10 because there is no if corresponding to this else.

30. **Answer**: C

    Compilation will not fail because enum is a valid type for a switch argument, and the default case can appear anywhere in switch. In the GREEN case block, there is no break statement, so the execution falls through, and RED is not printed because there is a break statement before it.

31. **Answer**: E

    Compilation fails at line 11 because YELLOW is not a value for the enum COLORS defined in line 1.

32. **Answer**: C

    A will generate the incompatible type compiler error. B, D, and E have the wrong syntax.

33. **Answer**: A

    The break statement at line 8 will not send the execution control back to line 4, instead it will go immediately after the for loop.

34. **Answer**: A

    The readline() method reads a line while the read() method reads a character, and only the BufferedReader class (out of the given classes) has the readline() method.

35. **Answer**: E

    If you serialize an object of Cow, the following five objects will be serialized: one object of Cow, one object of Milk, and three objects of SaturatedFat.

36. **Answer**: A, C, and E

    A will run MyApp without assertions on, and C will run MyApp with assertions on. You can use either enableasserions and disableasserions, or their shorts –ea and –da, to enable and disable assertions, respectively.

37. **Answer**: D

    The assertion facility asserts that the condition is true, and if it's not, it throws an exception.

38. **Answer**: D

    No compilation error occurs at line 9 because it's valid for the overriding method to not throw any exception when the overridden method throws one. Compilation does not fail at line 12, but it does at line 15 because even if the overridden method does not throw any exception, the overriding method can throw a runtime exception but not a checked exception.

39. **Answer**: D

    Compilation fails because the catch block for the broader exception Exception appears before the narrower exception NumberFormatException.

40. **Answer**: A and C

    A NullPointerException will be thrown due to line 7 because the variable s2 is being used without having it initialized first. A catch block catches exceptions of a specific category. This category includes the class specified in the parentheses of catch, and its subclasses.

41. **Answer**: F

    All these methods exist in both StringBuilder and StringBuffer. Both classes are designed to use the same API. The only difference is that StringBuffer supports synchronization while StringBuilder does not.

42. **Answer**: D

    Before J2SE 5.0, code such as in line 5 would generate a compiler error, but now it will compile fine due to autoboxing. Because wi1 and wi2 point to two different objects, the test at line 6 will fail. In the method call in line 9, f will be promoted (widened) to a double and hence the method at line 14 will be invoked.

43. **Answer**: B

    The answer is 20.101 and not 42.101 because only the farthest digits from the decimal point are removed.

44. **Answer**: D

    Compilation fails at line 4. NumberFormat is an abstract class, so you cannot instantiate it directly.

45. **Answer**: C

    Scanner considers a white space (and not a comma) as a separator by default.

46. **Answer**: A

    C is incorrect because the width element for the format method specifies the minimum (and not maximum) number of characters for the output.

47. **Answer**: A and D

    B is incorrect due to incompatible types: HashMap implements Map, while LinkedHashSet does not. C is incorrect because although both HashMap and TreeMap are maps, they are different implementations.

48. **Answers**: C, D, and F

    The classes that you can use must implement Map or SortedMap. A is incorrect because SortedMap is an interface and not a class.

49. **Answer**: B and D

    If two objects are verified to be equal by the equals() method, they must have the same hashcode returned by the hashCode method.

50. **Answers**: A and D

    Given the signatures of the speak(…) method (line 7), the method accepts only a List of Cows as argument.

51. **Answers**: B and D

    B and D have the correct syntax to handle the arguments being passed in by the method calls (lines 7 to 9).

52. **Answer**: E

    The Things class implements the Comparator interface, so it must implement the compare(…) method.

53. **Answer**: C

    You can call the run() method directly but it will not run in a new thread, but only on the thread of execution that invoked it.

54. **Answer**: B

    A class can extend Thread and implement Runnable, and hence both t1 and t2 are legal threads.

55. **Answer**: A and E

    Line 2 will generate a compilation error because you cannot synchronize a variable directly. Line 7 will generate a compiler error because you need to specify an object to synchronize a code block.

56. **Answer**: A and E

    The methods wait(), notify(), and notifyAll() can only be called in a synchronized piece of code.

57. **Answer**: B and C

    The join call on line 7 ensures that Main will be printed last. Started and Running can be printed in any order.

58. Answer: A and C

join() and sleep() both throw InterruptedException.

59. Answer: A and D

The *is-a* relationship is implemented by using inheritance and the *have-a* relationship is implemented by instantiating a class inside another class.

60. Answer: C

The *is-a* relationship is implemented by using inheritance and the *have-a* relationship is implemented by instantiating a class inside another class.

61. Answer: F

Compilation fails at line 6 due to the finally block without the try block.

62. Answer: A

C and D are incorrect uses of the classes PrintWriter and Formatter, respectively. The format specifier in B is incorrect.

63. Answer: D and E

A and B will not compile. An assertion error happens when the condition is false.

64. Answer: E

It's valid for the main() method to include the throws clause. However, a constructor cannot be invoked without the new operator (line 5).

65. Answer: E

The Thread constructor can be invoked with no argument or with an argument that is an instance of Runnable or Thread. E presents an invalid Thread constructor.

66. Answer: C

The special symbols $ and _ are allowed to be used as the first character in a variable name. Line 6 is legal due to autoboxing.

67. Answer: A

When there is at least one literal string, all the elements in the parentheses of System.out.print() are considered to be strings.

68. Answer: D

You cannot declare enum in a method, because it cannot be local. All other enum declarations in this code are valid.

69. Answer: B

It's a for-each loop.

70. Answer: D

An exception is thrown because AnimalFarm contains an instance of Goat, which is not serializable.

71. Answer: B, D, and G

Hashtable, StringBuffer, and Vector support synchronization.

72. Answer: D

Compilation fails at line 10 because the run() method must not be overridden to be less accessible. You must declare it public.

73. Answer: C

Both FileReader and BufferedReader have a method read() to read a character.

■■■

Exam Quick Prep

This appendix provides Quick Preparation Notes: a recap of all the important concepts that are covered in the exam objectives. Developed with a comprehensive coverage, these notes will help you brush through the key points in one go with ease and retain them until you take the exam, significantly increasing the probability of answering the questions correctly. You should go through this appendix one more time the night (or the hour) before you take the exam.

I have grouped the information according to the exam objectives provided by Sun. Therefore, the numbering of the objectives here (and in the chapters of the book) corresponds to the order in which they appear on Sun's website. Furthermore, the objectives are listed at the beginning of the chapters in which they are covered in the book. However, since the first chapter of the book is not focused on any specific exam objectives, the objectives in this appendix start at Chapter 2.

Chapter 2: Data Types and Operators (Exam Objectives 1.3, 7.6)

1.3 Develop code that declares, initializes, and uses primitives, arrays, enums, and objects as static, instance, and local variables. Also, use legal identifiers for variable names.

Important Concepts

- A data item in a computer program is held by a variable that refers to a piece of memory in the computer. A variable that holds a primitive data item is called a *primitive variable* and a variable that points to an object is called an *object reference*.
- To refer to a data item in your program, you use the corresponding variable name, called an *identifier*. The rules to name a variable are as follows:
    - The first character of an identifier must be a letter, a dollar sign ($), or an underscore (_).
    - Characters other than the first character in an identifier may be a letter, a dollar sign, an underscore, or a digit.
    - Any of the Java language keywords (or reserved words) cannot be used as identifiers.
- From their scope, the variables come in three categories:
    - *Local variable*: Declared inside a method. Its scope is the method itself; that is, it is destroyed when the metlhod completes. It lives on the *stack*.
    - *Instance variable*: Declared outside any method but inside a class. Its scope is within an instance of the class in which it is declared. It lives on the *heap*.
    - *Static variable*: An instance variable declared with the `static` modifier. It lives on the heap and is accessible to all the instances of the class (that is, its scope is the class).
- You can use the `enum` type to declare a variable that can hold only a predetermined set of values.
- You make operations on data in your program by using operators, which are represented by symbols such as = for an assignment operator.

Exam Tips

- true and false are the only valid values for a boolean variable.
- The default initial values for all instance and static variables of primitive types essentially correspond to zero. The local variables must be initialized explicitly in the code before they can be used.
- You can only use a given variable to hold a specific type of data. An array in Java is an object that can hold multiple items of the same type. These items may belong to a primitive or a nonprimitive type.
- It's illegal to include the size of an array in the array declaration. You can only specify the size when you create a declared array.
- Array indexing starts at 0, which means the first element of an array of five elements is [0] and the last element is [4], and the element [5] is out of range and an attempt to access it will give you a runtime error.

7.6 Write code that correctly applies the appropriate operators including assignment operators (limited to: =, +=, -=), arithmetic operators (limited to: +, -, *, /, %, ++, --), relational operators (limited to: <, <=, >, >=, ==, !=), the instanceof operator, logical operators (limited to: &, |, ^, !, &&, ||), and the conditional operator (? :), to produce a desired result. Write code that determines the equality of two objects or two primitives.

Important Concepts

- The unary operators ++ and -- increment and decrement the value of an operand by 1, respectively, while the unary operators + and - do not.
- The assignment operator is represented by the equal symbol, =, while the operator to test the equality is represented by the double equal symbol, ==.
- The instanceof operator tests whether its first operand is an instance of its second operand.
- Two primitive variables are equal when they hold the same value, and their equality can be tested with the == operator.
- If two reference variables are tested to be equal by the == operator, it means they point to the same object.
- For a deeper comparison of two objects, you can use the equals(...) method; for example, obj1.equals(obj2). The default implementation of the equals(...) method is the same as that of the == operator; that is, it will return true if two reference variables point to the same object. However, you can override the equals(...) method (of the Object class) to give it a deeper meaning.

Exam Tips

- If x is a boolean variable, then the following statement is not illegal:

      if (x=true)

  It simply sets x to be true and hence the condition in the if statement passes the test.
- The instanceof test will consider an object the instance of an interface if the object's class or any of its superclasses implements the interface. For example, if class A implements interface x, and class B extends A, then the (b instanceof x) condition is true where b is an object of class B.

Chapter 3: Classes, Methods, and Interfaces (Exam Objectives 1.1, 1.2, 1.4, 1.6)

1.1 Develop code that declares classes (including abstract and all forms of nested classes), interfaces, and enums, and includes the appropriate use of package and import statements (including static imports).

Important Concepts

- A *class* is a template to make objects and it can contain methods and variables. You can instantiate a class into multiple *objects*, which are also called *class instances*.
- A class is declared by using the keyword class, specifying the class name, and optionally specifying a modifier such as abstract to further define the class. For example, the following is a valid definition of a class named Test:

```
class Test { }
```

The code will go inside the curly braces.

- An object is created from a class by using the new operator. For example, the following code will create two objects, t1 and t2, of the already defined class Test:

```
Test t1 = new Test();
Test t2 = new Test();
```

Strictly speaking, t1 and t2 are object reference variables, each pointing to an object of the class Test.

- A normal class is called a *top-level* (or *outer*) *class* because you can also define a class inside a class, called a *nested class*. A non-static nested class is called an *inner class*.

- The instance variables, methods, and nested classes in a class are called the *class members*.

Exam Tips

- An instance of an inner class can only exist in an instance of the outer class, and has direct access to all the instance variables and methods of the outer instance.

- Just like static variables and methods of the outer class (also called class variables and methods), the scope of a static nested class is the outer class, as opposed to an instance of the outer class. Therefore, just like the static methods in the outer class, you cannot directly access the non-static variables or methods of the outer class from inside the static nested class.

- Because an inner class, being a non-static member, is associated only with an instance of its outer class, you cannot define a static member inside an inner class.

- Nested classes can be declared abstract or final, just like any other class with the same meaning.

- If you want to specify an access modifier for a top-level class, it can only be public; protected and private modifiers are not allowed for a top-level class.

1.2 Develop code that declares an interface. Develop code that implements or extends one or more interfaces. Develop code that declares an abstract class. Develop code that extends an abstract class.

Important Concepts

- An interface is declared just like a class but using the keyword interface instead of class.

- An interface can extend one or more interfaces, but it cannot extend a class, and it cannot implement another interface or a class.

- A class can extend one or more interfaces, even when it extends another class. A class can also implement one or more interfaces.

- All interface methods are inherently public and abstract. This means they must be implemented in the class that implements the interface and declared public in there. Because interface methods are inherently abstract, they cannot be declared final, native, strictfp, or synchronized.

- All interface variables are inherently public, static, and final.

Exam Tips

- Although interfaces are inherently abstract, it is perfectly legal to explicitly use the modifier abstract; for example:

```
public abstract  interface MyInterface { }
```

- Although interface methods are inherently public and abstract, you can explicitly declare them so. For example, all of the following declarations are valid and identical:

```
int  myMethod();
public int myMethod();
abstract int myMethod();
public abstract integer myMethod();
```

- Remember that because an interface variable is inherently final, it can never be assigned any value by the class that implements the interface, or by any other class for that matter.

- Because interface methods are inherently abstract, a class implementing an interface must provide implementation for all the methods in the interface unless the implementing class is abstract.

1.4 Develop code that declares both static and non-static methods, and – if appropriate – use method names that adhere to the JavaBeans naming standards. Also develop code that declares and uses a variable-length argument list.

Important Concepts

- When you declare a method, you must give it a return type and a name; the return type may be void, which means the method does not return anything.
- Like static variables, the static methods of a class are shared by all the instances of the class.
- A static method cannot access the non-static variables and methods of the class in which it is defined.
- Starting with J2SE 5.0, you can declare a parameter in a method in such a way that a variable number of arguments can be passed corresponding to this parameter in a method call. You define this parameter by appending three dots after the type, for example:

    ```
    void myMethod(int… values);
    ```

- There can be only one list of variable-length parameters in a method declaration and it must come at the end if there are some other parameters.

Exam Tips

- You cannot access a non-static instance variable of a class from the main(…) method because the main(…) method is static.
- It is valid in a method call not to pass any argument corresponding to the variable-length parameter.
- When there is a choice to be made between invoking a regular method or a var-arg method, the compiler will choose the regular method. For example, suppose you have the following two methods:

    ```
    public int methodA(int x, int y) {}
    public int methodA(int… i) { }
    ```

    The method call methodA(1,2) will invoke the first of the two methods listed.

1.6 Given a set of classes and superclasses, develop constructors for one or more of the classes. Given a class declaration, determine if a default constructor will be created, and if so, determine the behavior of that constructor. Given a nested or non-nested class listing, write code to instantiate the class.

Important Concepts

- Instantiating a class involves allocating memory for an object of the class by using the new operator, and initializing the memory by calling the class constructor. For example, the following statement instantiates (creates an object of) the class Student:

    ```
    Student st = new Student();
    The Student() is the class constructor.
    ```

- A class may have zero or more constructors. If you do not define any constructor for your class, then and only then the compiler will provide a default constructor (a constructor with no parameters).
- Outside of the class, a class constructor can be called only with the new operator, while inside the class in which the constructor is defined, a constructor can be called only from inside other constructors, and not from anywhere else.
- Unlike other methods, the constructors are not inherited. If the superclass has constructors, and the subclass does not, the compiler will assume that the subclass does not have any constructor and will create the default constructor.
- The keyword this is used to call another constructor in the same class, and the keyword super is used to call a constructor in the superclass.
- Before the variables of a class are initialized, the variables of its parent class must be initialized, and this is accomplished by a chain of constructor calls. You can explicitly call a constructor of the superclass by using the keyword super instead of the constructor name and by passing in the correct arguments.

Exam Tips

- If there is no super or this call in a constructor, then and only then the default super call is placed by the compiler (that is, a call to the default constructor of the superclass).
- The super or this call is always made in the beginning of the constructor body. That means a constructor can have either a super call or a this call but not both.
- If you define any constructor in a class, the no-argument default constructor will not be provided by the compiler. That means you will not be able to do something like new myClass() if you defined a constructor like myClass(String st){ } and did not define the no-argument constructor.

Chapter 4: Classes, Methods, and Interfaces (Exam Objectives 5.3, 7.1–7.5)

5.3 Explain the effect of modifiers on inheritance with respect to constructors, instance or static variables, and instance or static methods.

Important Concepts

- A private member of a class is accessible only from within the member's class. For example, you cannot access it from a subclass of the member's class.
- In a source code file, you can only declare one public class, and the name of the file must match the name of this class. For example, if the name of the public class is MyClass, the name of the source code file must be MyClass.java.
- A static method of a class cannot access the non-static members of the class.
- You cannot declare the following elements static: constructors, the top-level class interface, inner classes (the top-level nested class can be declared static), inner class methods and instance variables, and local variables.
- Here is what you can declare static: methods, variables, the top-level nested class, and a code block.
- A subclass does not inherit the constructors of its superclass.

Exam Tips

- The name of the parameters array in the main(String [] args) method does not have to be args, but its type must be an array of strings, that is, String [].
- The main(...) method must be declared public, static, and void.
- The source file does not have to have a public class, but if it does, only one class should be public.
- A constructor cannot have a return type (not even void), and it cannot be declared abstract, final, native, static, or synchronized.
- The static code block in a class is executed when the class is loaded (that is, before the class is instantiated or initialized).

7.1 Given a code example and a scenario, write code that uses the appropriate access modifiers, package declarations, and import statements to interact with (through access or inheritance) the code in the example.

Important Concepts

- When you make a package declaration in the beginning of a source file, all the classes in that file become parts of that package.
- An import statement can be one of two kinds: an explicit import that specifies the name of the class to be imported, and an implicit import that uses a wildcard (*) instead of a class name to mean any class in the package.
- Both the package declaration and the import statement should end with a semicolon (;).
- The compiler first resolves the explicit imports, then the classes from the current package, and then the implicit imports.

Exam Tips

- Make sure you understand how the classpath, package name, and the class name specified in the code combined make the full path that the compiler uses to look for the class in the directory structure.

- In an import statement, the wildcard (*) can only be used following a package name and not following a class name.

- If there is a package declaration and an import statement in a source file, they should appear before any class definition, and the package declaration should appear before the import statement. Furthermore, there can be only one package statement in a file, whereas there can be multiple import statements.

7.2 Given an example of a class and a command-line, determine the expected runtime behavior.

7.5 Given the fully-qualified name of a class that is deployed inside and/or outside a JAR file, construct the appropriate directory structure for that class. Given a code example and a classpath, determine whether the classpath will allow the code to compile successfully.

Important Concepts

- You execute a Java program by using the java command and the name of the class that contains the main(...) method followed by the arguments that you want to pass, such as:

    ```
    java myClass [arg1] [arg2] [arg3]
    ```

- The arguments that you pass by using the command line are stored in the array that you declared as a parameter of the main(...) method in the order you specify them in the command line. The argument specified first will be stored as the [0] element of the array, the argument specified second will be stored as the [1] element of the array, and so on.

- In the main(...) method, you can use the array variable length to find out how many arguments are being passed in. For example, args.length will give you the number of arguments being passed to the main(int [] args) method.

- A classpath is an environment variable whose value is a list of directories or JAR files in which the compiler and the interpreter search for the class files.

Exam Tips

- The name of the array parameter declared in the main(...) method does not have to be args; you can give it any name. However, it has to be an array.

- If param is the name of the parameter declared in the main(...) method, the first argument passed through the command line will be accessed by param[0], and not by param[1].

- The main(...) method can take the variable arguments of type String, such as main(String... args).

7.3 Determine the effect upon object references and primitive values when they are passed into methods that perform assignments or other modifying operations on the parameters.

Important Concepts

- The primitive variables are passed to a method by their values, while the object variables are passed by references. This should be obvious because a primitive variable holds the value itself, while an object variable only stores a reference to the object, and not the object itself.

- When a primitive variable is passed as an argument in a method call, only the copy of the original variable is passed. Therefore, any change to the passed variable in the called method will not affect the variable in the calling method.

- When you pass a reference variable to a method, you pass a copy of it and not the original reference variable. Because the copy of the reference variable points to the same object to which the original variable points, the called method can change the object properties by using the passed reference.

Exam Tip

- If the passed reference is changed in the called method (for example, set to null or reassigned to another object), it has no effect on the original variable in the calling method, because it is after all just a copy of the original variable.

7.4 Given a code example, recognize the point at which an object becomes eligible for garbage collection, and determine what is and is not guaranteed by the garbage collection system. Recognize the behaviors of System.gc and finalization.

Important Concepts

- The garbage collector frees up memory only from the eligible objects.
- An object is considered eligible for garbage collection when there is no reference pointing to it.
- You can make a request for garbage collection by making a system call to the garbage collector:

  ```
  System.gc();
  ```

Exam Tip

- You have no guarantee of when the memory will be freed up. Even running System.gc() does not necessarily mean the memory will be freed; in other words, you cannot force the garbage collector.

Chapter 5: Object-Oriented Programming (Exam Objectives 1.5, 5.1, 5.2, 5.4, 5.5)

1.5 Given a code example, determine if a method is correctly overriding or overloading another method, and identify legal return values (including covariant returns), for the method.

Important Concepts

- Method overriding allows you to declare a method in the subclass (the overriding method) that has the same signatures (method name and parameters) as a method in the superclass (the overridden method). Following are the rules for overriding a method:
  - You cannot override a method that has the final modifier.
  - You cannot override a static method to make it non-static, and vice versa.
  - The overriding method must have a return type that is compatible with the return type of the overridden method: identical with it or a subclass of it.
  - The number of parameters and their types in the overriding method must be the same as in the overridden method and the types must appear in the same order. However, the names of the parameters may be different.
  - You cannot override a method to make it less accessible. For example, to override a public method and declare it protected will generate a compiler error, while to override a protected method and declare it public will be fine.
  - If the overriding method has a throws clause in its declaration, then two conditions must be true: the overridden method must have a throws clause, and each exception included in the throws clause of the overriding method must be either one of the exceptions in the throws clause of the overridden method or a subclass of it.
  - If the overridden method has a throws clause, the overriding method does not have to.
- Method overloading allows you to define multiple methods with the same name in the same class. The key points about method overloading are listed here:
  - Two or more methods in the same class with the same name are called *overloaded* if they have either different sets of argument types or the same set of parameter types in different order.
  - The return type of two overloaded methods can be different or the same.
  - Overloaded methods are effectively independent of each other.
  - The compiler determines which of the overloaded methods to call by looking at the argument list of the method call.
  - Any of the methods inherited from the superclass can also be overloaded.
  - Overloaded versions of a method can have different or the same checked exceptions in the throws clause.
  - Overloaded versions of a method can have different modifiers.

Exam Tips

- Be careful in identifying whether a method is overloading or overriding. For example, if a method seems to be an invalid overriding, ask the following two questions:
  - Could it be a valid overloading?
  - Could it be just a brand new method? For example, you cannot override a `private` method of the superclass because it's not visible from the subclass. But it is perfectly legal to define a method in the subclass with the same signatures as the `private` method in the superclass.
- Keep in mind that an inherited method can also be overloaded.

5.1 Develop code that implements tight encapsulation, loose coupling, and high cohesion in classes, and describe the benefits.

5.5 Develop code that implements "is-a" and/or "has-a" relationships.

Important Concepts

- You can implement tight encapsulation by performing the following steps:
  - Declare the instance variables `private`.
  - Provide access to the instance variables only through the methods, which you can declare `public`.
  - You can use the JavaBean naming conventions (`set<property>` and `get<property>`) for the methods.
- Loose coupling refers to minimizing the dependence of an object on other objects. In other words, you can change the implementation of a class without affecting the other classes.
- Interfaces help to implement loose coupling.
- Cohesion refers to the well-structured classes. A cohesive class is a class that performs a set of closely related tasks.
- If class B extends class A, then class B *is-a* class A.
- If you instantiate class A inside class B, then class B *has-a* class A.

Exam Tip

- The exam expects you to understand *is-a* and *has-a* relationships in context of the real world. For example, be prepared to see statements such as a cow is an animal and has a tail, or a boombox is a stereo and has a CD player. Be able to interpret such statements in terms of inheritance and instantiation even if no code is given.

5.2 Given a scenario, develop code that demonstrates the use of polymorphism. Further, determine when casting will be necessary and recognize compiler vs. runtime errors related to object reference casting.

Important Concepts

- Polymorphism allows a variable of the superclass to refer to an object of the subclass.
- For primitive data types:
  - You can cast any non-boolean data type to any other non-boolean data types. The cast may be narrowing or widening.
  - You cannot cast a `boolean` type to a non-boolean type.
  - You cannot cast a non-boolean type to a `boolean` type.
  - In a narrowing conversion, the (explicit) casting is mandatory. In a widening conversion, the casting is not necessary, but it could be used to make the code more readable.
- For object references, the following rules apply at compile time:
  - When both source type and target type are classes, one class must be a subclass of the other.
  - When both source type and target type are arrays, the elements of both arrays must be object reference types and not primitive types. Also, the object reference type of the source array must be (implicitly) convertible to the object reference type of the target array.
  - Casting between an interface and an object that is not `final` is always allowed.

- For object references, if a casting passes compilation, then the following rules are enforced at runtime:
  - If the target type is a class, then the class of the expression being converted must be either the same as the target type or its subclass.
  - If the target type is an interface, then the class of the expression being converted must implement the target type.

Exam Tips

- Polymorphism does not apply to the `static` class members. For example, if you have a `static` method with identical signatures defined in the parent class and its subclass, and you assign an instance of the subclass to the reference variable of the parent class, and the variable invokes this `static` method, the parent version of the method will be executed.
- Generally speaking, implicit conversion to a narrower type is not allowed. However, a literal integer value can be assigned to variables of type `byte`, `short`, or `char` provided the value is within the legal range of the variable type.
- No conversion between `boolean` and non-boolean types is allowed.

5.4 Given a scenario, develop code that declares and/or invokes overridden or overloaded methods and code that declares and/or invokes superclass, overridden, or overloaded constructors.

Important Concepts

- To call the overridden version of the method from the subclass, you use the keyword `super`:

  ```
  super.[methodName]();
  ```

- A specific version of an overloaded method is invoked by passing in the right arguments corresponding to the parameters in the method's signature.
- A constructor of a superclass is invoked by using the `super` keyword. For example, if s is the `String` variable, the following line of code in the subclass constructor will invoke the superclass constructor with the `String` parameter:

  ```
  super(s);
  ```

- The overloaded versions of a constructor are invoked by using the following syntax:

  ```
  this([arguments]);
  ```

Exam Tip

- If you do not make a `super` call in the beginning of a constructor, the compiler will place a no-argument super call: `super()`. This will cause a problem if the superclass does not have a default constructor.

Chapter 6: Execution Flow Control in Java (Exam Objectives 2.1, 2.2)

2.1 Develop code that implements an if or switch statement; and identify legal argument types for these statements.

Important Concepts

- You can use the `if` construct by itself or in combination with `else if`, `else`, or both. If a combination is used, `if` must be in the beginning, and `else` should be at the end. The code following each of these constructs is placed in a block. For example:

  ```
  If (…) {
  // code goes here.
          }

  if (…) {
  // code goes here
          }
  ```

```
else if {
// code goes here.
}
else {
code goes here.
}
```

- If the if construct is by itself and there is only one line of code, you can omit the use of curly braces to mark the block.
- The legal argument type of an if statement is a boolean; that is, the expression in the parentheses of if() must evaluate to a boolean value.
- In an if-else if construct, the expressions will be tested one by one starting from the top. If an expression returns true, the block following the expression will be executed and all the following else if blocks will be skipped.
- The legal argument types for a switch statement are: byte, short, char, int, or enum constants.

Exam Tips

- For one if, there can be zero or more else if, and zero or one else.
- The default block does not have to be the last of the switch blocks.
- Look out for the assignment operator (=) and the equality operator (==) used in the parentheses of the if() statement; the two are not the same.
- If a block is being executed in a switch construct, and there is no break statement, the execution will fall through until a break statement is encountered.
- When the execution control encounters a default block in a switch construct, it executes it, because there is no condition to be tested.
- There should be no duplicate case labels in a switch construct.

2.2 Develop code that implements all forms of loops and iterators, including the use of for, the enhanced for loop (for-each), do, while, labels, break, and continue; and explain the values taken by loop counter variables during and after loop execution.

Important Concepts

- The body of a while loop can be executed zero or more times depending upon for how many iterations the condition stays true.
- The body of a for loop can be executed zero or more times depending upon for how many iterations the condition stays true.
- Note the semicolon in the syntax for the for loop:

```
for ( <statement>; <test>; <expression>) {
// if the <test> is true, execute the block.
}
```

- The for-each loop, also called the enhanced for loop, is used to iterate over the elements of a collection. For example, the following for-each loop will iterate over the elements of an array:

```
for(int i : myArray) {
System.out.println (i);
}
```

Note that in the for-each construct, you still use the keyword for and not for-each.

- Without labels, the continue statement breaks out of the current iteration of the loop, while the break statement breaks out of the current block (loop).
- A continue statement can be used only inside a loop; used otherwise, it will not compile. The break statement can be used either inside a loop or in a switch block.

Exam Tips

- Just like if, the expression in the while statement must evaluate to a boolean value. For example, the following will not compile:

    ```
    int  i =1;
    while (i) {}
    ```

- The body of a do-while loop will be executed at least once, because the while condition is tested after executing the body.

- If a variable is declared in the for loop, it cannot be used outside the for loop. If a variable is declared earlier but initialized in the for loop, it can be used after the for loop as well.

- The three elements of the for(...) statement are optional. For example, the following code will compile:

    ```
    for( ;  ; ) { }
    ```

Chapter 7: Exceptions and Assertions (Exam Objectives 2.3–2.6)

2.3 Develop code that makes use of assertions, and distinguish appropriate from inappropriate uses of assertions.

Important Concepts

- Assertions provide a mechanism to test the assumptions that you make during development—that is, to assert your assumptions. You always assert that something is true, and if it is not, then an AssertionError is thrown. For example, the following will throw an AssertionError if myNumber has a negative value:

    ```
    assert (myNumber>=0);
    ```

- In J2SE 1.4, assert was not a Java language keyword, so to enable assertions, you had to compile your code with the -source 1.4 flag. However, in J2SE 5.0, the -source flag is not necessary. In other words, the compiler support for assertions is enabled by default.

- Assertions are disabled by default during program execution. However, you can enable them when you run the program with the -ea flag.

- Following are some inappropriate uses of assertions:

    - Checking the arguments passed to a public method

    - Checking the command-line arguments

    - Modifying the variable values, such as removing null elements from a list

Exam Tips

- The expression of the assert statement must evaluate to a boolean value.

- Assertions are usually used to test and debug the code before deployment. So, you are not supposed to handle the AssertionError; you find out the problem and fix the code.

- You always assert that something is true: if the condition being tested is true, all is good; otherwise, an AssertionError is thrown.

2.4 Develop code that makes use of exceptions and exception handling clauses (try, catch, finally), and declares methods and overriding methods that throw exceptions.

2.5 Recognize the effect of an exception arising at a specified point in a code fragment. Note that the exception may be a runtime exception, a checked exception, or an error.

Important Concepts

- An exception is an object of the class Exception or one of its subclasses. Exceptions are of two kinds: checked and unchecked (runtime).

- If your method calls another method that throws a checked exception, your method must do one or both of the following:
  - Declare the exception in the throws clause of your method.
  - Catch the exception in the body of your method.

- You enclose the code that can cause exceptions in a try block. One or more catch blocks must immediately follow the try block to catch the exception. When an exception happens, the matching (at most one) catch block will be executed.

- An exception can be caught only by a matching catch block, which is a block with a catch statement that has in its parentheses either the same class as the exception itself or its parent class (that is, one of the classes higher up in the hierarchy).

- The finally code block is not required, but is usually used for cleanup that may be required by the code in the try block, and to release system resources. The finally block, if it exists, must appear immediately after the last catch block.

- The finally block is always executed after the try block if either no exception is thrown or an exception is thrown but is not caught by any catch block, or after the catch block is executed. The finally block will not be executed if a System.exit() statement is executed before the finally block or if an uncaught exception is raised inside the catch block, and it will not be completed if an exception arises inside the finally block.

- The overriding method cannot throw any exception that is not the same as, or a subclass of, the exception thrown by the overridden method. This also implies that the overriding method does not *have* to throw an exception, even if the overridden method is throwing some exceptions.

- If there is a matching catch block, execution jumps from the line that caused the exception to the matching catch block; after executing the catch block, execution jumps to the finally block, if it exists; and after executing the finally block (or the last catch block if the finally block does not exist), execution continues as if no exception happened.

Exam Tips

- A compiler error will occur if your method code calls a method that throws a checked exception and you neither put that call in a try block nor throw that exception or its parent class in your method declaration.

- The catch block with a more specific exception must appear before the catch block with a less specific exception. If more than one matching catch block exists, the first one encountered is executed, and it would be the most specific one.

- If there is no matching catch block, the method execution stops at the line that caused the exception and the control returns to the calling method. If there is a finally block, that will be executed before returning the control.

- The try clause must be followed immediately by the catch clause, the finally clause, or both. A catch (or finally) clause just by itself will generate a compiler error.

- The overriding method cannot throw any exception class that is not the same as, or a subclass of, the exception class thrown by the overridden method. This has the following implications:
  - If the overridden method does not throw any exception, the overriding method cannot throw any checked exception, but it can still throw a runtime exception.
  - If the overridden method throws an exception, it's legal for the overriding method to throw no exception.

2.6 Recognize situations that will result in any of the following being thrown: ArrayIndexOutOfBoundsException,ClassCastException, IllegalArgumentException, IllegalStateException, NullPointerException, NumberFormatException, AssertionError, ExceptionInInitializerError, StackOverflowError, or NoClassDefFoundError. Understand which of these are thrown by the virtual machine and recognize situations in which others should be thrown programmatically.

Important Concepts

- Remember the following runtime exceptions (subclasses of `RuntimeException`):
  - **ArrayIndexOutOfBoundsException**
  - **ClassCastException**
  - **IllegalArgumentException**
  - **IllegalStateException**
  - **NullPointerException**
  - **NumberFormatException**
- Remember the following errors (subclasses of `Error`):
  - **AssertionError**
  - **ExceptionInInitializerError**
  - **StackOverflowError**
  - **NoClassDefFoundError**

Exam Tips

- Runtime exceptions and errors combined are called unchecked exceptions.
- You are not required to catch unchecked exceptions, but your code will compile and execute even if you do so.

Chapter 8: Input and Output in Java (Exam Objectives 3.2, 3.3)

3.2 Given a scenario involving navigating file systems, reading from files, or writing to files, develop the correct solution using the following classes (sometimes in combination), from java.io: BufferedReader, BufferedWriter, File, FileReader, FileWriter, and PrintWriter.

3.3 Develop code that serializes and/or de-serializes objects using the following APIs from java.io: DataInputStream, DataOutputStream, FileInputStream, FileOutputStream, ObjectInputStream, ObjectOutputStream, and Serializable.

Important Concepts

- Both in read and write operations, Java treats data as a stream (i.e. a sequence of items such as bytes). A read or write operation consists of three steps:
  1. Open the data stream.
  2. Keep reading from the data stream in a read operation, or writing to it in a write operation, until there is more data to read/write.
  3. Close the stream.
- There are two kinds of data streams in Java:
  - *Low-level streams*: Low-level input streams read data and return it in bytes, and low-level output streams accept data as bytes and write the output in bytes. `FileInputStream` (a subclass of `InputStream`) and `FileOutputStream` (a subclass of `OutputStream`) are examples of low-level input and output streams, respectively.
  - *High-level streams*: High-level streams are used by Java programs to deal with data in terms of high-level data types such as integer and `String` rather than bytes. `DataInputStream` and `DataOutputStream` are high-level input and output streams, respectively.

- High-level I/O streams do not write directly to or read directly from the files; rather, they are connected to the low-level streams that read directly from or write directly to files.
- The text data is usually read and written by using the readers and writers:
  - The low-level reader streams read data and return it in characters, and low-level output streams accept data as characters and write the output in characters. Two examples of low-level reader and writer streams are `FileReader` and `FileWriter`.
  - You can also read and write characters in character streams in big chunks (buffers) and in text format by using `BufferedReader` and `BufferedWriter`, which are examples of the high-level readers and writers.
- Java objects are read and written by using the high-level streams `ObjectInputStream` and `ObjectOutputStream`, which can be chained to low-level streams such as `FileInputStream` and `FileOutputStream`, which in turn will directly read from the file or write to the file. The process of writing an object to a file is called *object serialization*.

Exam Tips

- An instance of the `File` class is immutable. This means that once you have created a `File` object by providing a path name, the abstract path name represented by this object will never change.
- When you create an instance of the `File` class, no real file is created in the file system.
- By invoking methods on a `File` instance, you can create and delete files and directories in a file system.
- You make read/write operations on data in binary format (such as image files) by using the low-level streams such as `FileInputStream` and `FileOutputStream`.
- You make read/write operations on data in text format by using the low-level readers and writers such as `FileReader` and `FileWriter`, which read and write characters, respectively.
- All the objects that the serialized object refers to (through instance variables) are also serialized when the object is serialized.
- An object can only be stored if the corresponding class implements the `Serializable` interface directly or indirectly (through inheritance).

Chapter 9: Strings, Formatters, and Wrappers (Exam Objectives 3.1, 3.4, 3.5)

3.1 Develop code that uses the primitive wrapper classes (such as Boolean, Character, Double, Integer, etc.), and/or autoboxing & unboxing. Discuss the differences between the String, StringBuilder, and StringBuffer classes.

Important Concepts

- There is a wrapper class corresponding to each primitive type in Java: `Boolean`, `Byte`, `Character`, `Short`, `Integer`, `Long`, `Float`, and `Double`.
- A wrapper object for a given wrapper type can be constructed from the corresponding primitive, such as:

  ```
  Integer wi1 = new Integer(420);
  ```

- A wrapper object for a given wrapper type, except char, can also be constructed from a string, such as:

  ```
  Integer wi2 = new Integer("420");
  ```

- The values wrapped inside wrappers can be tested for equality by using the `equals(...)` method on the wrapper objects; for example:

  ```
  Double d1 = new Double("3.0d");
  Double d2 = new Double("4.0d");
    if(d1.equals(d2))System.out.println("d1 is equal to d2");
  ```

- A value wrapped in a wrapper object can be extracted by using the corresponding `xxxValue()` method, where xxx can be `char`, `byte`, `short`, `int`, `long`, `float`, `boolean`, or `double`.

- Wrapper classes offer various utility methods, such as the following:
  - valueOf(...): Static method that takes a primitive as an argument and returns a wrapper object of the type that invoked the method. For example:

    ```
    Double d = Double.valueOf("4.20");
    ```

  - parseXXX(...): Static method that parses the string passed in as an argument and returns the corresponding primitive specified by XXX. For example:

    ```
    String s = "420";
    int i = Integer.parseInt(s);
    ```

- J2SE 5.0 automates wrapping and unwrapping by offering the following two features:
  - *Autoboxing*: The capability of assigning a primitive value to a corresponding wrapper type; the conversion from primitive type to wrapper type is automated. For example, the following code works:

    ```
    Integer wi = 420;
    ```

  - *Auto-unboxing*: The reverse of autoboxing—that is, the capability of assigning a wrapper type to the corresponding primitive type; the conversion from wrapper to primitive is automated. For example, the following code is valid:

    ```
    Integer wi = 420;
    int i = wi;
    ```

- A string created with the String class cannot be modified, while a string created with the String-Buffer class can be modified. Therefore, the modifying methods in the String class actually create and return a new String object, and the original object remains unchanged.

- The StringBuilder class offers the same functionality as the StringBuffer class but it does not guarantee synchronization.

Exam Tips

- The wrapper classes corresponding to primitive types char and int are Character and Integer and not Char and Int.

- All the wrapper classes are declared final. That means you cannot derive a subclass from any of them.

- The wrapped value in a wrapper class cannot be modified. To wrap another value, you need to create another object.

- There is no parseXxx(...) method corresponding to char.

- Because instances of StringBuilder are not safe for use by multiple threads, if such a synchronization is required, you should use StringBuffer instead.

3.4 Use standard J2SE APIs in the java.text package to correctly format or parse dates, numbers, and currency values for a specific locale; and, given a scenario, determine the appropriate methods to use if you want to use the default locale or a specific locale. Describe the purpose and use of the java.util.Locale class.

Important Concepts

- An object of the java.util.Locale class lets you present locale-sensitive information to a user in a locale-specific way, and yet you do not need to hard-code the locality; it may be provided at runtime.

- The java.text.NumberFormat class helps you to format and parse numbers for any locale, and yet your code can be completely independent of the locale conventions.

- Here are the steps you follow for formatting in your code:
  1. Create a locale using the Locale class.
  2. Create an appropriate NumberFormat object by using the locale from step 1 as an argument.
  3. Use the NumberFormat object to format a number by invoking the format(...) method on the NumberFormat object and by passing the number (to be formatted) as an argument.

- The java.text.DateFormat class provides several methods for formatting date/time for a default or a specific location, and yet you can keep your code completely independent of the locale conventions for months, days of the week, days of the months, and so on.

Exam Tips

- In the argument of the format(...) method, the format type and the type of the data to be formatted must be compatible with each other. For example, the format type is floating point (%f), the data to be formatted must be a float or a double (primitive or wrapper).

- The NumberFormat is an abstract class, so the following code will be invalid:

  ```
  NumberFormat nf = new NumberFormat();
  ```

  Instead, you should do something like this:

  ```
  NumberFormat nf = NumberFormat.getInstance();
  ```

3.5 Write code that uses standard J2SE APIs in the java.util and java.util.regex packages to format or parse strings or streams. For strings, write code that uses the Pattern and Matcher classes and the String.split method. Recognize and use regular expression patterns for matching (limited to: . (dot), * (star), + (plus), ?, \d, \s, \w, [], ()). The use of *, +, and ? will be limited to greedy quantifiers, and the parenthesis operator will only be used as a grouping mechanism, not for capturing content during matching. For streams, write code using the Formatter and Scanner classes and the PrintWriter.format/printf methods. Recognize and use formatting parameters (limited to: %b, %c, %d, %f, %s) in format strings.

Important Concepts

- The input text that needs to be parsed can be passed to the Scanner constructor as a String, File, or InputStream.

- The Scanner class provides support for parsing by using regular expressions as delimiters.

- By using the Pattern and Matcher classes, you can examine further specific pieces of data, such as validating the format of an email address.

Exam Tips

- The default separator for Scanner is a white space and not a comma.

- The width element in the parentheses of the format(...) method specifies the minimum (and not the maximum) number of characters to be written to the output.

Chapter 10: Collections and Generics (Exam Objectives 6.1–6.5)

6.1 Given a design scenario, determine which collection classes and/or interfaces should be used to properly implement that design, including the use of the Comparable interface.

Important Concepts

- Collections are used to deal with a group of data items. Generally speaking, you can perform the following operations on a collection:
  - Iterate through the collection.
  - Add objects (data items) to the collection and delete objects from the collection.
  - Search if an object is in the collection.
  - Retrieve an object from the collection without deleting it.
- List and Set are the interfaces that extend the Collection interface, while the SortedList interface extends the List interface.
- The SortedMap interface extends the Map interface.
- The ArrayList, LinkedList, and Vector classes implement the List interface.
- The HashSet and LinkedHashSet classes implement the Set interface, while the TreeSet class implements the SortedSet interface.
- The HashMap, HashTable, and TreeMap classes implement the Map interface, while TreeMap implements the SortedMap interface.

- Following are the important defining points about `Collections`:
  - Maps have unique keys that facilitate search for their content.
  - Sets and maps do not allow duplicate entries.
  - Lists maintain an order, and duplicate elements may exist.
  - Maps do not extend the `Collection` interface.
- Following are the important points from the perspective of storage:
  - In hashing, search is particularly fast (due to unique keys), but indexed access is slow. Furthermore, hashtables support insertion, deletion, and growing the storage.
  - `TreeSet` also supports insertion, deletion, and growing the storage. Indexed access is slow but search is fast.
  - `LinkedList` also supports insertion, deletion, and growing the storage. Indexed access is slow. Search is slow, but insertion and deletion are fast as opposed to `ArrayList`, which provides fast access but slow insertion and deletion.

Exam Tips

- `Collections` is a class, while `Collection` is an interface that declares methods common to most collections.
- The `Map` interface does not extend the `Collection` interface. That means `Map` implementations do not implement the `Collection` interface.
- The data items in a `Map` are in key-value pairs. A `Map` cannot have duplicate keys, but it can have duplicate values.
- Sets and maps do not allow duplicate entries.

6.2 Distinguish between correct and incorrect overrides of corresponding hashCode and equals methods, and explain the difference between == and the equals method.

Important Concepts

- The hashcode is an integer value attached to an object that, on one hand, specifies the uniqueness of an object and, on the other hand, helps to store an object in a data structure and to retrieve it. To calculate the hashcode for an object, the `Object` class offers the `hashCode()` method. If you override the `hashCode()` method, you must follow the rules for returning the hashcode, called the *hashcode contract*:
  - If the `hashCode()` method is invoked multiple times during an execution of an application on the same object, it must consistently return the same integer each time. However, the integer can change from one execution of an application to another execution of the same application.
  - If two objects are equal according to the `equals(…)` method, then invoking the `hashCode()` method on each of the two objects must return the same integer value for the hashcode.
  - If two objects are unequal according to the `equals(…)` method, it is not required that invoking the `hashCode()` method on each of theses two objects must return unequal integer values as hashcode. However, you should be aware that returning distinct integer values as hashcodes for unequal objects may improve the performance of hashtables.
- The implementation of the `equals(…)` method in the `Object` class is very shallow; it just uses the `==` operator for comparison. For example, consider the two object references x and y. The code `x.equals(y)` will return `true` only if x and y refer to the same object.
- You can override the `equals(…)` method in your class and give it a deeper meaning.

Exam Tips

- The implementation of the `equals(…)` method in the `Object` class returns `true` only if both the object references refer to the same object.
- The `equals(…)`, `hashCode()`, and `toString()` methods are declared `public` in the `Object` class, so they must be overridden to be `public`.
- Two objects that are equal, as determined by the `equals(…)` method, must return the same hashcode. The reverse is not required to be true; that is, the two objects that are not equal do not have to return unequal hashcodes.

6.3 Write code that uses the generic versions of the Collections API, in particular, the Set, List, and Map interfaces and implementation classes. Recognize the limitations of the non-generic Collections API and how to refactor code to use the generic versions.

6.4 Develop code that makes proper use of type parameters in class/interface declarations, instance variables, method arguments, and return types; and write generic methods or methods that make use of wildcard types and understand the similarities and differences between these two approaches.

Important Concepts

- The generic collections introduced in J2SE 5.0 provide a way to declare the type of a collection whose accuracy can be checked by the compiler.
- The following code involving nongeneric collections will not compile because it requires a cast in line 4:

  ```
  1. ArrayList myList = new ArrayList();
  2. String st = "Flemingo";
  3.  myList.add(st);
  4.  String st1 = myList.get(0);
  ```

- The following code will compile but will generate an exception at runtime because it has a wrong cast in line 4:

  ```
  1.  ArrayList myList = new ArrayList();
  2. String st = "Flemingo";
  3.  myList.add(st);
  4.  Integer wi = (Integer) myList.get(0);
  ```

- You can rewrite the same code fragment in generic collections as shown here:

  ```
  1. ArrayList<String>  myList = new ArrayList<String>();
  2. String st = "Flemingo";
  3.  myList.add(st);
  4.  Integer wi = (Integer) myList.get(0);
  ```

  Now the compiler will give you the error at line 4.

Exam Tips

- To use <?> instead of something like <T> in declaring generic classes or methods is illegal.
- The wildcard ? is legal in declaring a reference to a variable.

6.5 Use capabilities in the java.util package to write code to manipulate a list by sorting, performing a binary search, or converting the list to an array. Use capabilities in the java.util package to write code to manipulate an array by sorting, performing a binary search, or converting the array to a list. Use the java.util.Comparator and java.lang.Comparable interfaces to affect the sorting of lists and arrays. Furthermore, recognize the effect of the "natural ordering" of primitive wrapper classes and java.lang.String on sorting.

Important Concepts

- A data structure is said to be *ordered* if the data items are in some order. For example, an array is an ordered data structure because the data items are ordered by index.
- A data structure is said to be *sorted* if the data items are ordered by their essence, such as in ascending order of their values. So, by definition, a sorted data structure is an ordered data structure, but the reverse is not necessarily true.
- Random access (or search) is fast in ArrayList, but insertions and deletions are not, while insertions and deletions are fast in LinkedList, but random access is not.
- You use the Set classes when you don't want to allow duplicates in the data structure.
- HashSet provides faster access to a data item as compared to TreeSet, but it offers no guarantee that the items will be ordered, while TreeSet presents sorted data items, but the access performance is not as good as that of HashSet.
- Maps are a perfect data structure when the data is stored in key-value pairs and each key is unique (that is, there are no duplicate keys). If you need sorted data items, use TreeMap, else use HashMap.

Exam Tips

- The `compare(…)` method of the `Comparator` interface throws a `ClassCastException` if either of the arguments has an inappropriate type for the Comparator.
- **Collections.sort(list)** will throw a `ClassCastException` **if** you try to sort a list whose elements do not implement the **Comparable interface or if the** elements cannot be compared to one another for some other reasons.

Chapter 11: Threads in Java (Exam Objectives 4.1–4.4)

4.1 Write code to define, instantiate, and start new threads using both java.lang.Thread and java.lang.Runnable.

Important Concepts

- You can define and instantiate a thread in one of two ways:
  - Extend the `java.lang.Thread` class:
    1. Define the thread by writing your class that extends the `Thread` class, and by overriding its `run()` method in your class.
    2. Instantiate the thread by instantiating your class, for example, inside a method of another class.
    3. Start the thread by executing the `start()` method that your class inherited from the `Thread` class.
  - Implement the `java.lang.Runnable` interface. This is especially useful when your class already extends another class and hence cannot extend the `Thread` class.
    1. Write your class that implements the `Runnable` interface, and implement the `run()` method of the `Runnable` interface in your class.
    2. Instantiate your class, for example, inside a method of another class.
    3. Make an object of the `Thread` class by passing your class instance in the argument of the `Thread` constructor. This object is your thread object.
    4. Start the thread by executing the `start()` method of your `Thread` instance.
- The `java.lang.Object` class contains some methods that are used to manage the lifecycle of a thread.

Exam Tips

- A thread is started by executing the `start()` method, and not the `run()` method.
- When you are using the `Runnable` interface to create a thread, you start the thread by invoking the `start()` method on a `Thread` instance, and not on a `Runnable` instance.
- It is legal to call the `run()` method on a `Runnable` or `Thread` instance, but it will not start a separate thread. Instead, it will execute the `run()` method in the same execution thread in which it is invoked.
- The `Runnable` interface has only one method: `void run()`.

4.2 Recognize the states in which a thread can exist, and identify ways in which a thread can transition from one state to another.

Important Concepts

A thread can go through the following states during its lifecycle:

- *New*: This is the state of a thread when it has been instantiated but not yet started.
- *Ready/runnable*: A thread enters the runnable state for the first time when the `start()` method is invoked on the thread instance. Later, the thread can come back to this state from one of the non-runnable states. In the runnable state, the thread is ready to run and waiting to be selected by the scheduler for running.
- *Running*: This is the state in which the thread is executing.

- *Nonrunnable states*: A thread in the running state may go into one of the three nonrunnable states when it is still alive, but not eligible to run. These three states are listed here:
  - *Blocked*: A thread goes into this state when it's waiting for a resource such as I/O or an object's lock. The availability of the resource will send it back to the runnable state.
  - *Sleeping*: This state is one of the timed waiting states because the thread stays in this state for a specific time. A thread goes into this state when its code tells it to sleep for a specific period of time by calling the sleep() method. Expiration of the sleep time sends it back to the runnable state.
  - *Waiting*: The thread goes into the waiting state when the object on which it's running invokes the wait() method. A call to notify() or notifyAll() (by another thread) will bring it back to the runnable state.
- *Dead*: A thread is considered dead after the execution of its run() method is completed. A dead thread can never be run as a separate thread again; that is, if you call its start() method, you will receive a runtime exception. However, it is still an object, and you can still call its methods (other than the start() method), but they will be executed in the caller's thread.

Exam Tips

- Upon calling the start() method, a thread does not start running immediately, because it has to go through a scheduler.
- When the sleep() method is invoked, the sleep time passed in as an argument in the method call is the minimum time the thread will take to start running again, because the thread will have to go through scheduling.
- You call the method sleep() or yield() in the thread code, but you do not call methods such as wait(), notify(), or notifyAll() in the thread code.
- A yield() call is intended to give another thread with the same priority a chance to run. But there is no guarantee that this will happen.

4.3 Given a scenario, write code that makes appropriate use of object locking to protect static or instance variables from concurrent access problems.

Important Concepts

- Every instance of a class (that is, object) has its own lock, called *object lock*, and can be used to protect the instance variables from the concurrent access problems.
- Every object has one and only one object lock.
- When a thread of execution wants to enter a synchronized piece of code in the object, it must acquire the object lock.
- When a thread has acquired an object lock, no other thread can acquire it until the previous thread releases the lock.
- The static variables can be protected from concurrent access problems by using the class lock.

Exam Tips

- A class can have both synchronized and non-synchronized methods.
- Once a thread acquires an object lock, no other thread can enter any of the synchronized methods in that object.
- If a thread with a lock goes to sleep, it takes the lock with it.
- You synchronize a method or a piece of code in the method, and not the variables directly.
- A thread can acquire multiple locks.

4.4 Given a scenario, write code that makes appropriate use of wait, notify, or notifyAll.

Important Concepts

- You may put a thread into the waiting state by making a call to the wait() method in the shared code. When a thread encounters a wait() call in an object, the following happens:
  - The thread gives up the CPU.
  - The thread gives up the lock on the object.
  - The thread goes into the object's waiting pool.
- A thread in the wait state is brought out of this state by a notify() or notifyAll() call. When a notify() call is made from inside the same object, the following happens:
  - One arbitrarily chosen thread out of the waiting pool is put into the seeking lock state.
  - After it obtains the lock, the thread is put into the runnable state.
- When a notifyAll() call is made, all threads in the waiting pool of the object are put into the seeking lock state.

Exam Tips

- The methods wait(), notify(), and notifyAll() are implemented in the Object class, and not in the Thread class.
- The methods wait(), notify(), and notifyAll() can only be called in a synchronized piece of code.
- You cannot invoke the notify() method on a specific thread. A call to notify() will put one thread out of the wait state, but you cannot specify which one if there is more than one thread in the waiting pool.

Index

You Need the Companion eBook

Your purchase of this book entitles you to buy the companion PDF-version eBook for only $10. Take the weightless companion with you anywhere.

We believe this Apress title will prove so indispensable that you'll want to carry it with you everywhere, which is why we are offering the companion eBook (in PDF format) for $10 to customers who purchase this book now. Convenient and fully searchable, the PDF version of any content-rich, page-heavy Apress book makes a valuable addition to your programming library. You can easily find and copy code—or perform examples by quickly toggling between instructions and the application. Even simultaneously tackling a donut, diet soda, and complex code becomes simplified with hands-free eBooks!

Once you purchase your book, getting the $10 companion eBook is simple:

➊ Visit **www.apress.com/promo/tendollars/**.

➋ Complete a basic registration form to receive a randomly generated question about this title.

➌ Answer the question correctly in 60 seconds, and you will receive a promotional code to redeem for the $10.00 eBook.

2560 Ninth Street • Suite 219 • Berkeley, CA 94710

eBookshop